Assembly language subroutines for the 8086

L. A. LEVENTHAL
and
S. CORDES

McGRAW-HILL BOOK COMPANY

London · New York · St Louis · San Francisco · Auckland
Bogotá · Guatemala · Hamburg · Lisbon · Madrid · Mexico
Montreal · New Delhi · Panama · Paris · San Juan · São Paulo
Singapore · Sydney · Tokyo · Toronto

Published by
McGRAW-HILL Book Company (UK) Limited
MAIDENHEAD · BERKSHIRE · ENGLAND

British Library Cataloguing in Publication Data
Leventhal, Lance A, *1945–*
Assembly language subroutines for the 8086.
1. INTEL 8086 & 8088 microprocessor
systems. Assembly languages
I. Title II. Cordes, S.
005.2'65

ISBN 0-07-707151-4

Library of Congress Cataloguing-in-Publication Data
Leventhal, Lance A, 1945–
Assembly language subroutines for the 8086 / L. A. Leventhal and S. Cordes
p. cm.
Includes index.
ISBN 0-07-707151-4
1. Intel 8086 (Microprocessor) – Programming. 2. Intel 8088
(Microprocessor) – Programming. 3. Assembler language (Computer
program language) 4. Subroutines (Computer programs)
I. Cordes, S. II. Title.
QA76.8.I292L48 1989
005.265--dc 19 88-39562

First published in Japanese

1234CUP9089

Typeset by Ponting-Green Publishing Services, London,
and printed and bound in Great Britain at H Charlesworth & Co Ltd, Huddersfield

Contents

Preface

This book is intended as both a source and a reference for the 8086/8088 assembly language programmer. It contains a collection of useful subroutines described in a standard format and accompanied by extensive documentation. All subroutines employ standard parameter passing techniques and follow the rules from the most popular assembler. The documentation specifies the procedure, parameters, results, execution time, and memory usage; it also includes at least one example. The routines will also run on related microprocessors such as the 80188, 80186, 80286, 80376, 80386, and 80486.

The collection emphasizes common tasks that occur in many applications. These tasks include code conversion, array manipulation, arithmetic, bit manipulation, shifting functions, string manipulation, data structure management, sorting, and searching. We have also provided examples of input/output (I/O) routines, interrupt service routines, and initialization routines for common family chips such as parallel interfaces, serial interfaces, and timers. You should be able to use these programs as subroutines in actual applications and as starting points for more complex programs.

This book is intended for the person who wants to use assembly language immediately, rather than just learn about it. The reader could be

- An engineer, technician, or programmer who must write assembly language programs for a design project.
- A microcomputer or personal computer user who wants to write an

I/O driver, a diagnostic program, a utility, or a systems program in assembly language.

- An experienced assembly language programmer who needs a quick review of techniques for the 8086, 8088, or related microprocessor.
- A system designer who needs a specific routine or technique for immediate use.
- A high-level language programmer who must debug or optimize programs at the assembly level, link a program written in a high-level language to one written in assembly language, or move the machine-dependent part of a program to a new computer.
- A maintenance programmer who must understand quickly how specific assembly language programs work.
- A microcomputer owner who wants to understand the operating system of a particular computer, or who wants to modify standard I/O routines or systems programs.
- A student, hobbyist, or teacher who wants to see examples of working assembly language programs.

This book should save the reader time and effort. He or she should not have to write, debug, test, or optimize standard routines, or search through a textbook for particular examples. The reader should instead be able to obtain easily the specific information, technique, or routine he or she needs.

Obviously, a book with such an aim demands feedback from its readers. We have, of course, tested all programs thoroughly and documented them carefully. If you find any errors, please inform the publisher. If you have suggestions for better methods or for additional topics, routines, or programming hints, please tell us about them. We have used our programming experience to develop this book, but we need your help to improve it. We would greatly appreciate your comments, criticisms, and suggestions.

Nomenclature

We have used the following nomenclature in this book to describe the architecture of the 8086/8088 processors and to specify operands.

8086 architecture

Figure N-1 shows the 8086's registers. The byte-length (8-bit) ones are:

AH(more significant byte of accumulator AX)
AL (less significant byte of accumulator AX, accumulator for byte-length operations)
BH (more significant byte of base register BX)
BL (less significant byte of base register BX)
CH (more significant byte of count register CX)
CL (less significant byte of count register CX)
DH(more significant byte of data register DX)
DL (less significant byte of data register DL)

The 8086's word-length (16-bit) data registers are:

AX(word-length accumulator)
BP (base pointer)
CX (count)
DI (destination index)
DX(data)
F or FL (flags)
SI (source index)
SP (stack pointer)

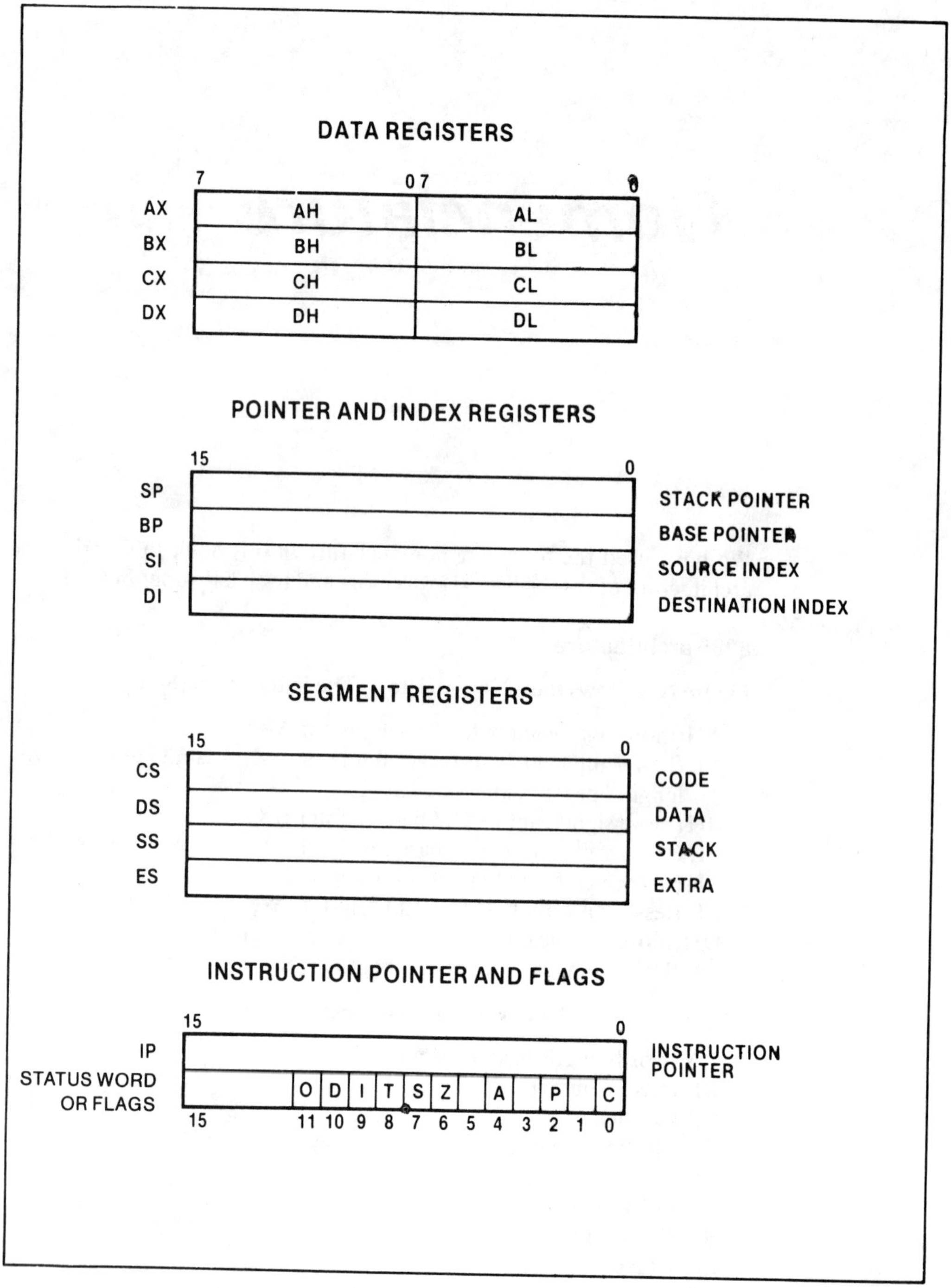
DATA REGISTERS
7
0 7
0
AX
BX
CX
DX
AH
AL
BH
BL
CH
CL
DH
DL
POINTER AND INDEX REGISTERS
15
0
SP
BP
SI
DI
STACK POINTER
BASE POINTER
SOURCE INDEX
DESTINATION INDEX
SEGMENT REGISTERS
15
0
CS
DS
SS
ES
CODE
DATA
STACK
EXTRA
INSTRUCTION POINTER AND FLAGS
15
0
IP
STATUS WORD OR FLAGS
INSTRUCTION POINTER
O D I T S Z A P C
15
11 10 9 8 7 6 5 4 3 2 1 0

Its word-length segment registers (used only in calculating memory addresses) are:

CS (code segment)
DS (data segment)
ES (extra data segment)
SS (stack segment)

The FL (flag) register consists of bits with independent functions and meanings, arranged as shown in Figure N-2.

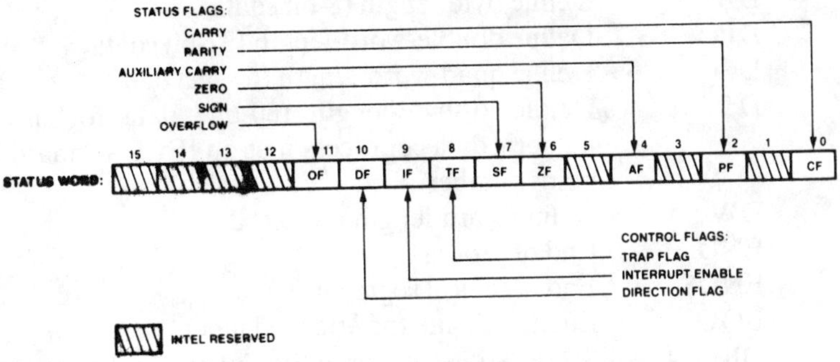

Figure N-2 8086 flag (F or FL) register

The 8086's flags (see Figure N-2) are:

AC AUXILIARY (HALF) CARRY, i.e., carry from bit 3 of a byte
C CARRY
D DIRECTION (autoincrement or autodecrement in string or block operations)
I INTERRUPT ENABLE
O OVERFLOW
P (EVEN) PARITY
S SIGN
T TRAP (single-step)
Z ZERO

8086 Assembler

Delimiters include

space	After an operation code
, (comma)	Between entries in the operand (address) field
[ ]	Around addresses to be used indirectly or as indexes (as a substitute for +)

;	Before a comment
:	After a label associated with an instruction statement, between segment register designations or segment numbers and address register designations or address values within a segment, and between segment register designations and their assigned values
' '	Around ASCII characters

Assembler directives (pseudo-operations) include

DB	Define byte-length (8-bit) data
DD	Define double-word-length (32-bit) data
DQ	Define quad-word-length (64-bit) data
DT	Define 10-byte-length (80-bit) data for use with 8087 numeric data coprocessor as an IEEE standard 754 floating point number
DW	Define word-length (16-bit) data
END	End of program
ENDS	End of logical segment
EQU	Equate; define the attached label
ORG	Set (location counter to) origin; place subsequent object code starting at the specified address within the current segment
SEGMENT	Start of logical segment

Designations include

Number Systems:

B (suffix)	Binary
D (suffix)	Decimal
H (suffix)	Hexadecimal
Q (suffix)	Octal

The default mode is decimal; hexadecimal numbers must start with a digit (i.e. you must add a leading zero if a number starts with a letter).

Others:

BYTE PTR	Indicates a byte-length (8-bit) memory reference
DUP	Repeated initialization, e.g., 3 DUP (2) indicates 3 items, each with a value of 2
DWORD PTR	Indicates a double-word length (32-bit) memory reference
FAR	Label type, indicating a label that will be accessed from another segment
NEAR	Label type, indicating a label that will be accessed from within the same segment

OFFSET	Offset of a variable or label from the base of the segment in which it is defined
WORD PTR	Indicates a word-length (16-bit) memory reference
?	Indeterminate initialization
$	Current value of location (program) counter

Defaults include

Unmarked values or expressions are taken to be immediate data (not addresses).
Unmarked numbers are decimal.
Unmarked memory references are assumed to be either byte-length or word-length according to the length of the register involved. An operation that does not involve a register must have its length indicated with a BYTE PTR or WORD PTR operator; there is no default.
Default segment registers are:

- [BX], [DI], and [SI], relative offsets from them, and combinations of them default to segment register DS.
- [BP], relative offsets from it, and combinations involving it default to segment register SS.
- Operations that reference the stack (i.e., PUSH, POP, CALL, INT, and IRET) always use SS and cannot be overriden.
- String instructions default to segment register ES for operands pointed to by DI. This cannot be overriden.
- All instruction fetches are relative to segment register CS and cannot be overriden.

Introduction

Each description of a subroutine contains the following information:

- Purpose
- Procedure
- Registers used
- Execution time
- Program size
- Data memory required
- Special cases
- Entry conditions
- Exit conditions
- Examples

The program listing repeats this information and provides section-by-section comments.

We have made each routine as general as possible. This is difficult for the I/O and interrupt service routines in Chapters 8 and 9 since they are always computer-dependent in practice. Our approach has been to limit the dependence to generalized input and output handlers and interrupt managers. We have drawn specific examples from the popular Microsoft MS-DOS operating system running on an IBM PC. The general principles apply to other 8086/8088-based computers as well.

All routines use the following parameter passing techniques, derived largely from the PL/M procedural interface defined by Intel:

1. A single data parameter is passed in register AX (16 bits) or AL (8 bits).

2. A single address parameter within the current data segment is passed in register BX.

3. Larger numbers of parameters are passed on the stack, either directly or indirectly.

We have generally assumed Intel's PL/M SMALL memory model as described in *An Introduction to ASM86* (Intel Corporation, Santa Clara, CA, 1981). This model assumes:

1. A single fixed code segment. The CS register thus is a constant, so jumps and calls need change only the instruction pointer.

2. A single fixed data and stack segment. The DS and SS registers are thus constants with the same value.

In this model, all subroutines are entered using intrasegment CALL instructions and exited using intrasegment RET instructions. That is, the return address is always a short (16-bit) pointer stored at the top of the stack. All data and stack addresses, as well as other pointers, are also 16-bit offsets within a segment. We have assumed that the ES and DS registers generally have the same value as well, so that we can use all string instructions without setting ES explicitly. Furthermore, we have followed Intel's PL/M procedural convention whereby all routines preserve the BP, CS, DS, SP, and SS registers. The subroutines can be modified easily to satisfy other memory models involving multiple code or data segments.

Where there have been trade-offs between execution time and memory usage, we have chosen to minimize execution time. For example, we have not used the multiple-bit shift instructions since they are slower than repeated single-bit shifts although they occupy less memory. We have also chosen to minimize repetitive calculations. For example, consider array indexing. The number of bytes between the starting addresses of elements differing only by one in a particular subscript (known as the *size* of that subscript) depends on the number of bytes per element and the bounds of the array. We can, therefore, calculate the sizes of all subscripts and use them as parameters in indexing routines. This saves us from having to recalculate them each time a given array is indexed.

We have specified the execution times for short routines. For long routines, we provide an approximate execution time. The execution time of programs with many branches obviously depends on which path the computer follows. Other complicating factors include the time required to fill the instruction pipeline, memory management (segment register) overhead, and the dependence of branch execution times on whether a branch actually occurs. Thus, a precise execution time is often impossible to define. The documentation always contains at least one typical example showing an approximate or maximum execution time.

The execution times also do not consider:

- Extra fetch cycles required by the 8088 because of its shorter pipeline and narrower data bus.
- Extra cycles required by the 8086 to fetch misaligned data words (i.e. words starting at odd addresses).

Our philosophy on error indicators and special cases has been the following:

1. Routines should provide an easily tested indicator (such as the Carry flag) of whether any errors or exceptions have occurred. More complex routines should return a status byte or result code. The common convention (established in UNIX and other operating systems) is for a zero value to indicate successful completion and other values to indicate types of errors.

2. Trivial cases, such as no elements in an array or strings of zero length, should result in immediate exits with minimal effect on the underlying data.

3. Misspecified data (such as a maximum string length of zero or an index beyond the end of an array) should result in immediate exits with minimal effect on the underlying data.

4. The documentation should include a summary of errors and exceptions (under the heading 'Special cases').

5. Exceptions that are convenient for the user (such as deleting more characters than could possibly be left in a string rather than counting the precise number) should be handled reasonably, but should still be indicated as errors.

Obviously, no method of handling errors or exceptions can ever be completely consistent or well-suited to all applications. Our approach is that a set of standard subroutines must deal with this issue, rather than ignoring it or assuming that the user will always provide properly formatted data.

1 Code conversion

1A Binary to BCD conversion (BN2BCD)

Converts one byte of binary data to two bytes of BCD data.

Procedure The program first divides the original data by 100 to obtain the hundreds digit, then divides the remainder by 10 to obtain the tens digit, and finally shifts the tens digit left four positions and combines it with the ones digit.

Entry conditions

Binary data in AL

Exit conditions

BCD data in AX

Examples

1. Data: $[AL] = 6D_{16}$ (109 decimal)
   Result: $[AX] = 0109_{16}$

2. Data: $[AL] = B7_{16}$ (183 decimal)
   Result: $[AX] = 0183_{16}$

Registers used AX, BX, F

Execution time 220 cycles maximum

Program size 25 bytes

Data memory required None

```
;
;
;
;
;       Title:                  Binary to BCD Conversion
;       Name:                   BN2BCD
;
;
;
;       Purpose:                Converts one byte of binary data to two
;                               bytes of BCD data
;
;       Entry:                  Register AL = Binary data
;
;       Exit:                   Register AX = BCD data
;
;       Registers Used:         AX,BX,F
;
;       Time:                   220 cycles maximum
;
;       Size:                   Program 25 bytes
;
;

BN2BCD:
        ;
        ;CALCULATE 100'S DIGIT
        ;DIVIDE DATA BY 100
        ;
        SUB     AH,AH           ;EXTEND 8-BIT DATA TO 16 BITS
        MOV     BL,100          ;DIVIDE BY 100
        DIV     BL
        MOV     BH,AL           ;SAVE QUOTIENT AS 100'S DIGIT
        ;
        ;CALCULATE TENS AND ONES DIGITS
        ;DIVIDE REMAINDER BY 10
```

```
;
MOV     AL,AH           ;NEW DIVIDEND = OLD REMAINDER
SUB     AH,AH           ;EXTEND REMAINDER TO 16 BITS
MOV     BL,10           ;DIVIDE BY 10
DIV     BL              ;QUOTIENT IS 10'S DIGIT,
                        ;  REMAINDER IS 1'S DIGIT
;
;COMBINE 1'S AND 10'S DIGITS
;SHIFT 10'S DIGIT LEFT 4 BITS AND ADD IT TO 1'S DIGIT
;
SHL     AL,1            ;SHIFT 10'S DIGIT LEFT 4 BITS
SHL     AL,1            ;NOTE THIS IS MUCH FASTER THAN
SHL     AL,1            ;  SHL AL,CL
SHL     AL,1
ADD     AL,AH           ;ADD 1'S DIGIT, SHIFTED 10'S DIGIT
MOV     AH,BH           ;GET 100'S DIGIT
RET


;
;
;       SAMPLE EXECUTION
;
;

SC1A:
        ;CONVERT 0A HEXADECIMAL TO 10 BCD
        MOV     AL,0AH
        CALL    BN2BCD          ;AX = 0010H (AH = 00, AL = 10H)

        ;CONVERT FF HEXADECIMAL TO 255 BCD
        MOV     AL,0FFH
        CALL    BN2BCD          ;AX = 0255H (AH = 02, AL = 55H)

        ;CONVERT 0 HEXADECIMAL TO 0 BCD
        SUB     AL,AL
        CALL    BN2BCD          ;AX = 0000 (AH = 00, AL = 00)

        END
```

1B BCD to binary conversion (BCD2BN)

Converts one byte of BCD data to one byte of binary data.

Procedure The program masks off the more significant digit and multiplies it by 10 using shifts. The program then adds the product to the less significant digit. We do not use MUL to multiply because of its long execution time.

Entry conditions

BCD data in AL

Exit conditions

Binary data in AL

Examples

1. Data: [AL] = 99_{16}
   Result: [AL] = $63_{16} = 99_{10}$
2. Data: [AL] = 23_{16}
   Result: [AL] = $17_{16} = 23_{10}$

Registers used AX, BL, F

Execution time 31 cycles

Program size 19 bytes

Data memory required None

1B BCD to binary conversion (BCD2BN)

```
;
;
;
;
;       Title:                  BCD to Binary Conversion
;       Name:                   BCD2BN
;
;
;
;       Purpose:                Converts one byte of BCD data to one
;                               byte of binary data
;
;       Entry:                  Register AL = BCD data
;
;       Exit:                   Register AL = Binary data
;
;       Registers Used:         AX, BL, F
;
;       Time:                   31 cycles
;
;       Size:                   Program 19 bytes
;
;

BCD2BN:
        ;
        ;MULTIPLY UPPER DIGIT TIMES TEN BY SHIFTING
        ;
        MOV     BL,AL           ;SAVE ORIGINAL BCD VALUE
        AND     AL,0F0H         ;MASK OFF UPPER DIGIT
        SHR     AL,1            ;CALCULATE UPPER DIGIT TIMES 8
                                ;REMEMBER DIGIT IN UPPER 4 BITS
                                ;  IS EQUIVALENT TO DIGIT VALUE
                                ;  MULTIPLIED BY 16
        MOV     AH,AL           ;SAVE UPPER DIGIT TIMES 8
        SHR     AL,1            ;CALCULATE UPPER DIGIT TIMES 2
        SHR     AL,1            ;THIS IS UPPER DIGIT TIMES 8
                                ;  DIVIDED BY 4 (2 RIGHT SHIFTS)
        ADD     AL,AH           ;CALCULATE UPPER DIGIT TIMES 10
                                ;  USING 10 = 8 + 2
        ;
        ;ADD PRODUCT TO LOWER DIGIT
        ;
        AND     BL,0FH          ;MASK OFF LOWER DIGIT
        ADD     AL,BL           ;ADD LOWER DIGIT TO PRODUCT
        RET

;
;
;       SAMPLE EXECUTION
;
;

SC1B:
        ;CONVERT 0 BCD TO 0 HEXADECIMAL
        SUB     AL,AL
```

```
CALL      BCD2BN          ;AL = 00

;CONVERT 99 BCD TO 63 HEXADECIMAL
MOV       AL,99H
CALL      BCD2BN          ;AL = 63H

;CONVERT 23 BCD TO 17 HEXADECIMAL
MOV       AL,23H
CALL      BCD2BN          ;AL = 17H

END
```

1C Binary to hexadecimal ASCII conversion (BN2HEX)

Converts one byte of binary data to two hexadecimal digits represented as ASCII characters.

Procedure The program masks off each hexadecimal digit separately and converts it to its ASCII equivalent. This involves a simple addition of 30_{16} (ASCII 0) if the digit is decimal. If the digit is non-decimal, we must add an extra 7 to bridge the gap between ASCII 9 (39_{16}) and ASCII A (41_{16}).

Entry conditions

Binary data in AL

Exit conditions

ASCII version of more significant hexadecimal digit in AH
ASCII version of less significant hexadecimal digit in AL

Examples

1. Data: [AL] = FB_{16}
   Result: [AH] = 46_{16} (ASCII F)
   [AL] = 42_{16} (ASCII B)
2. Data: [AL] = 59_{16}
   Result: [AH] = 35_{16} (ASCII 5)
   [AL] = 39_{16} (ASCII 9)

Registers used AX, F

Execution time 75 cycles minus 8 cycles for each non-decimal digit

Program size 29 bytes

Data memory required None

```
;
;
;
;
;       Title:                  Binary to Hexadecimal ASCII
;       Name:                   BN2HEX
;
;
;
;
;       Purpose:                Converts one byte of binary data to two
;                               ASCII characters
;
;       Entry:                  Register AL = Binary data
;
;       Exit:                   Register AH = ASCII more significant digit
;                               Register AL = ASCII less significant digit
;
;       Registers Used:         AX, F
;
;       Time:                   Approximately 75 cycles
;
;       Size:                   Program 29 bytes
;
;

BN2HEX:
        ;
        ;CONVERT MORE SIGNIFICANT DIGIT TO ASCII
        ;
        MOV     AH,AL           ;SAVE ORIGINAL BINARY VALUE
        SHR     AH,1            ;MOVE HIGH DIGIT TO LOW DIGIT
        SHR     AH,1
        SHR     AH,1
        SHR     AH,1
        CMP     AH,9
        JBE     ADASCH          ;BRANCH IF HIGH DIGIT IS DECIMAL
        ADD     AH,7            ;ELSE ADD 7 SO AFTER ADDING '0' THE
                                ; CHARACTER WILL BE IN 'A'..'F'
ADASCH: ADD     AH,'0'          ;ADD ASCII 0 TO MAKE A CHARACTER
        ;
        ;CONVERT LESS SIGNIFICANT DIGIT TO ASCII
        ;
        AND     AL,0FH          ;MASK OFF LOW DIGIT
        CMP     AL,9
        JBE     ADASCL          ;BRANCH IF LOW DIGIT IS DECIMAL
        ADD     AL,7            ;ELSE ADD 7 SO AFTER ADDING '0' THE
                                ; CHARACTER WILL BE IN 'A'..'F'
ADASCL: ADD     AL,'0'          ;ADD ASCII 0 TO MAKE A CHARACTER
        RET
;
;
;       SAMPLE EXECUTION
;
;
```

```
SC1C:
        ;CONVERT 0 TO ASCII '00'
        SUB     AL,AL
        CALL    BN2HEX          ;AH='0'=30H, AL='0'=30H

        ;CONVERT FF HEXADECIMAL TO ASCII 'FF'
        MOV     AL,0FFH
        CALL    BN2HEX          ;AH='F'=46H, AL='F'=46H

        ;CONVERT 23 HEXADECIMAL TO ASCII '23'
        MOV     AL,23H
        CALL    BN2HEX          ;AH='2'=32H, AL='3'=33H

        END
```

1D Hexadecimal ASCII to binary conversion (HEX2BN)

Converts two ASCII characters (representing two hexadecimal digits) to one byte of binary data.

Procedure The program converts each ASCII character separately to a hexadecimal digit. This involves a simple subtraction of 30_{16} (ASCII 0) if the digit is decimal. If the digit is non-decimal, the program must subtract another 7 to account for the gap between ASCII 9 (39_{16}) and ASCII A (41_{16}). The program then shifts the more significant digit left four bit positions and combines it with the less significant digit. The program does not check whether the ASCII characters represent valid hexadecimal digits.

Entry conditions

More significant ASCII digit in AH, less significant ASCII digit in AL

Exit conditions

Binary data in AL

Examples

1. Data: [AH] = 44_{16} (ASCII D)
   [AL] = 37_{16} (ASCII 7)
   Result: [AL] = $D7_{16}$
2. Data: [AH] = 31_{16} (ASCII 1)
   [AL] = 42_{16} (ASCII B)
   Result: [AL] = $1B_{16}$

Registers used AX, F

Execution time 80 cycles minus 8 cycles for each non-decimal digit

Program size 27 bytes

Data memory required None

```
;
;
;
;
;       Title:                  Hexadecimal ASCII to Binary
;       Name:                   HEX2BN
;
;
;
;       Purpose:                Converts two ASCII characters to one
;                               byte of binary data
;
;       Entry:                  Register AH = ASCII more significant digit
;                               Register AL = ASCII less significant digit
;
;       Exit:                   Register AL = Binary data
;
;       Registers Used:         AX,F
;
;       Time:                   Approximately 80 cycles
;
;       Size:                   Program 27 bytes
;
;

;
;       CONVERT MORE SIGNIFICANT DIGIT TO BINARY
;
HEX2BN:
        SUB     AH,'0'      ;SUBTRACT ASCII OFFSET (ASCII 0)
        CMP     AH,9        ;CHECK IF DIGIT DECIMAL
        JBE     SHFTMS      ;BRANCH IF DIGIT IS DECIMAL
        SUB     AH,7        ;ELSE SUBTRACT OFFSET FOR LETTERS
SHFTMS: SHL     AH,1        ;SHIFT DIGIT TO MORE SIGNIFICANT BITS
        SHL     AH,1
        SHL     AH,1
        SHL     AH,1
;
;       CONVERT LESS SIGNIFICANT DIGIT TO BINARY
;
        SUB     AL,'0'      ;SUBTRACT ASCII OFFSET (ASCII 0)
        CMP     AL,9        ;CHECK IF DIGIT DECIMAL
        JBE     CMBDIG      ;BRANCH IF DIGIT IS DECIMAL
        SUB     AL,7        ;ELSE SUBTRACT OFFSET FOR LETTERS
;
;       COMBINE LESS SIGNIFICANT, MORE SIGNIFICANT DIGITS
;
CMBDIG:
        ADD     AL,AH       ;ADD DIGITS
        RET
```

```
;
;
;       SAMPLE EXECUTION
;
;

SC1D:
        ;CONVERT ASCII 'C7' TO C7 HEXADECIMAL
        MOV     AX,'C7'
        CALL    HEX2BN   ;AL=C7H

        ;CONVERT ASCII '2F' TO 2F HEXADECIMAL
        MOV     AX,'2F'
        CALL    HEX2BN   ;AL=2FH

        ;CONVERT ASCII '2A' TO 2A HEXADECIMAL
        MOV     AX,'2A'
        CALL    HEX2BN   ;AL=2AH

        END
```

1E Conversion of a binary number to decimal ASCII (BN2DEC)

Converts a 16-bit signed binary number into an ASCII string. The string consists of the length of the number in bytes, an ASCII minus sign (if needed), and the ASCII digits. Note that the length is in binary, not in ASCII.

Procedure If the number is negative, the program takes its absolute value and places an ASCII minus sign in the buffer. It then divides the absolute value by 10 000. If the quotient is non-zero, the program converts it to ASCII (by adding ASCII 0) and saves it in the buffer. It continues through the rest of the digits, replacing the quotient with the remainder each time. It saves the ASCII version of each digit except for leading zeros. Finally, the program converts the remainder from the division by 10 to ASCII and saves it as the ones digit. This digit always appears in the buffer; i.e. it is not dropped even if its value is 0.

Entry conditions

Base address of output buffer in BX
Value to convert in AX (between −32 767 and +32 767)

Exit conditions

Order in buffer:
  Length of the string in bytes (a binary number)
  ASCII − (if value to convert is negative)
  ASCII digits (most significant digit first)

Examples

1. Data: Value to convert = $3EB7_{16}$
Result (in output buffer):
05 (number of bytes in buffer)
31 (ASCII 1)
36 (ASCII 6)
30 (ASCII 0)
35 (ASCII 5)

35 (ASCII 5)
i.e. $3EB7_{16} = 16055_{10}$

2. Data: Value to convert = $FFC8_{16}$
Result (in output buffer):
03 (number of bytes in buffer)
2D (ASCII −)
35 (ASCII 5)
36 (ASCII 6)
i.e. $FFC8_{16} = -56_{10}$, when considered as a signed two's complement number

---

Registers used AX, BX, CX, DI, DX, SI

Execution time Approximately 700 cycles

Program size 67 bytes

Data memory required None except for the output buffer, which should be 7 bytes long.

```
;
;
;
;
;       Title:                  Binary to Decimal ASCII
;       Name:                   BN2DEC
;
;
;
;       Purpose:                Converts a 16-bit signed binary number
;                               to ASCII data
;
;       Entry:                  Register AX = Value to convert
;                               Register BX = Output buffer address
;
;       Exit:                   The first byte of the buffer is the
;                               length of the string in bytes, followed
;                               by the characters
;
;       Registers Used:         AX, BX, CX, DI, DX, SI
;
;       Time:                   Approximately 700 cycles
;
;       Size:                   Program  67 bytes
```

```
;
;
;
;
BN2DEC:
;
;       SET D FLAG FOR AUTOINCREMENTING, SAVE OLD VALUE
;
        PUSHF                   ;SAVE FLAGS (INCLUDING D FLAG)
        CLD                     ;SELECT AUTOINCREMENTING
;
;       SAVE ORIGINAL BUFFER POINTER FOR LATER USE
;         WHEN STORING LENGTH
;       SET BUFFER POINTER, NUMBER OF DIGITS, LEADING
;         NON-ZERO DIGIT FLAG
;
        MOV     SI,BX           ;SAVE ORIGINAL BUFFER POINTER
        MOV     DI,SI           ;STRING POINTER = BUFFER POINTER
        INC     DI              ;POINT BEYOND LENGTH BYTE
        SUB     CX,CX           ;NUMBER OF DIGITS (CL) = 0
                                ;  NO LEADING NON-ZERO DIGIT FOUND (CH=0)
;
;       TAKE ABSOLUTE VALUE AND STORE MINUS SIGN IN
;         BUFFER IF DATA NEGATIVE
;
        AND     AX,AX           ;CHECK SIGN OF DATA
        JNS     CALCDG          ;BRANCH IF SIGN POSITIVE
        NEG     AX              ;NEGATIVE, TAKE ABSOLUTE VALUE
        MOV     BYTE PTR [DI],'-'  ;SAVE MINUS SIGN IN BUFFER
        INC     DI              ;MOVE BUFFER POINTER
        INC     CL              ;ADD 1 TO STRING LENGTH FOR MINUS SIGN
;
;       DIVIDE BINARY DATA BY POWERS OF 10 TO GET DIGITS
;         STARTING WITH TEN THOUSAND
;       DO NOT SAVE LEADING ZEROS IN BUFFER
;
CALCDG:
        MOV     BX,10000        ;DIVISOR = 10,000
        CALL    DIVS16          ;DIVIDE AND SAVE DIGIT IF NECESSARY
        MOV     BX,1000         ;DIVISOR = 1000
        CALL    DIVS16          ;DIVIDE AND SAVE DIGIT IF NECESSARY
        MOV     BX,100          ;DIVISOR = 100
        CALL    DIVS8           ;DIVIDE AND SAVE DIGIT IF NECESSARY
        MOV     BX,10           ;DIVISOR = 10
        CALL    DIVS8           ;DIVIDE AND SAVE DIGIT IF NECESSARY
        ADD     AL,'0'          ;CONVERT ONES DIGIT TO ASCII
        STOSB                   ;ALWAYS SAVE ONES DIGIT
        INC     CL              ;ADD 1 TO STRING LENGTH FOR ONES DIGIT
;
;       SAVE LENGTH OF STRING AT HEAD OF BUFFER
;
        MOV     [SI],CL         ;SAVE STRING LENGTH AT HEAD OF BUFFER
        POPF                    ;RESTORE FLAGS (PARTICULARLY D FLAG)
        RET
```

```
;*****************************************************
;ROUTINE: DIVS16, DIVS8
;PURPOSE: DIVIDE DX:AX BY BX (DIVS16) OR AX BY BL (DIVS8)
;         SAVE ASCII QUOTIENT AT DI IF NON-ZERO OR NON-LEADING
;         FLAG LEADING NON-ZERO DIGIT WITH 1 IN REGISTER CH
;         MOVE BUFFER POINTER UP 1 IF DIGIT SAVED IN BUFFER
;ENTRY:   DX:AX CONTAINS DIVIDEND FOR DIVS16, BX DIVISOR
;         AX CONTAINS DIVIDEND FOR DIVS8, BL DIVISOR
;EXIT:    REMAINDER IN AX
;REGISTERS USED: AX,CX,DI,DX,F
;*****************************************************

DIVS16:   SUB     DX,DX      ;SET UPPER WORD OF DATA TO ZERO, THUS
                             ;  EXTENDING IT TO 32 BITS FOR DIVISION
          DIV     BX         ;PERFORM 16-BIT DIVISION
          JMP     CHKSV      ;SAVE QUOTIENT IN STRING IF NECESSARY
DIVS8:    DIV     BL         ;PERFORM 8-BIT DIVISION
          SUB     DX,DX      ;MOVE REMAINDER TO DX WITH UPPER
          MOV     DL,AH      ;  BYTE = 0
CHKSV:    AND     CH,CH      ;HAS A LEADING NON-ZERO DIGIT
                             ;  ALREADY BEEN FOUND?
          JNE     SVDIG      ;IF SO, SAVE THIS DIGIT FOR SURE
          AND     AL,AL      ;IF NOT, IS THIS DIGIT NON-ZERO?
          JE      ENDDIV     ;NO, BRANCH TO AVOID SAVING LEADING
                             ;  ZERO
          INC     CH         ;YES, INDICATE LEADING NON-ZERO
                             ;  DIGIT FOUND (SET CH TO 1)
SVDIG:    INC     CL         ;ADD 1 TO STRING LENGTH
          ADD     AL,'0'     ;CONVERT DIGIT TO ASCII
          STOSB              ;SAVE ASCII DIGIT IN BUFFER
ENDDIV:   MOV     AX,DX      ;REPLACE QUOTIENT WITH REMAINDER
                             ;  FOR NEXT DIVISION
          RET

;
;
;         SAMPLE EXECUTION
;
;

SC1E:
          ;CONVERT 0 TO ASCII '0'
          SUB     AX,AX          ;DATA VALUE = 0
          MOV     BX,BUFFER      ;GET BASE ADDRESS OF BUFFER
          CALL    BN2DEC         ;CONVERT TO ASCII
                                 ; BUFFER SHOULD CONTAIN
                                 ;    BINARY 1 (LENGTH)
                                 ;    ASCII 0 (STRING)
          ;CONVERT 32767 TO ASCII '32767'
          MOV     AX,32767       ;DATA VALUE = 32767
          MOV     BX,BUFFER      ;GET BASE ADDRESS OF BUFFER
          CALL    BN2DEC         ;CONVERT TO ASCII
                                 ; BUFFER SHOULD CONTAIN
                                 ;    BINARY 5 (LENGTH)
                                 ;    ASCII 32767 (STRING)
          ;CONVERT -32767 TO ASCII '-32767'
```

```
         MOV       AX,-32767          ;DATA VALUE = -32767
         MOV       BX,BUFFER          ;GET BASE ADDRESS OF BUFFER
         CALL      BN2DEC             ;CONVERT TO ASCII
                                      ; BUFFER SHOULD CONTAIN
                                      ;     BINARY 6 (LENGTH)
                                      ;     ASCII - (SIGN)
                                      ;     ASCII 32767 (STRING)
BUFFER:  DB       7 DUP(0)            ;7-BYTE BUFFER
         END
```

1F Conversion of ASCII decimal to binary (DEC2BN)

Converts an ASCII string consisting of the length of the number (in bytes), a possible ASCII + or − sign, and a series of ASCII digits to two bytes of binary data. Note that the length is in binary, not in ASCII.

Procedure The program checks whether the first byte is a sign and skips over it if it is. The program then uses the length of the string to determine the leftmost digit position. Moving left to right, it converts each digit to decimal (by subtracting ASCII 0), validates it, multiplies it by the corresponding power of 10, and adds the product to the running total. Finally, the program subtracts the binary value from zero if the string started with a minus sign. The program exits immediately, setting the Carry flag, if it finds something other than a leading sign or a decimal digit in the string.

Entry conditions

Base address of string in BX

Exit conditions

Binary value in AX
The Carry flag is 0 if the string is valid, and 1 otherwise. Note that the result is a signed two's complement 16-bit number.

Examples

1. Data: String consists of
   04 (number of bytes in string)
   31 (ASCII 1)
   32 (ASCII 2)
   33 (ASCII 3)
   34 (ASCII 4)
   i.e. the number is $+1234_{10}$

   Result: [AX] = $04D2_{16}$ (binary data)
   i.e. $+1234_{10} = 04D2_{16}$

2. Data: String consists of

06 (number of bytes in string)
2D (ASCII −)
33 (ASCII 3)
32 (ASCII 2)
37 (ASCII 7)
35 (ASCII 5)
30 (ASCII 0)
i.e. the number is $-32\,750_{10}$

Result: $[AX] = 8016_{16}$ (binary data)
i.e. $-23\,750_{10} = 8012_{16}$

Registers used AX, BX, CX, DI, DX, F, SI

Execution time Approximately 125 cycles per ASCII digit plus 100 cycles overhead

Program size 155 bytes

Data memory required None

Special cases

1. If the string contains something other than a leading sign or a decimal digit, the program returns with the Carry flag set to 1. The result in AX is invalid.

2. If the string contains only a leading sign (ASCII + or ASCII −), the program returns with the Carry flag set to 1 and a result of 0.

```
;
;
;
;
;       Title:                  Decimal ASCII to Binary
;       Name:                   DEC2BN
;
;
;
;       Purpose:                Converts ASCII characters to two bytes
;                               of binary data
;
```

```
;       Entry:                  Register BX = Input buffer address
;
;       Exit:                   Register AX = Binary data
;                               If no errors then
;                                 Carry = 0
;                               else
;                                 Carry = 1
;
;       Registers Used:         AX,BX,CX,DI,DX,F,SI
;
;       Time:                   Approximately 125 cycles per ASCII digit
;                               plus 100 cycles overhead
;
;       Size:                   Program 155 bytes
;
;
;
;               SAVE BUFFER POINTER, INITIALIZE BINARY VALUE TO ZERO
;
DEC2BN:
                CLD                     ;SELECT AUTOINCREMENTING
                MOV     SI,BX           ;STRING POINTER = BUFFER POINTER
                MOV     DI,SI           ;SAVE BUFFER POINTER TO EXAMINE SIGN LATER
                SUB     BX,BX           ;INITIALIZE BINARY VALUE TO ZERO
                LODSB                   ;GET BYTE COUNT
                MOV     CL,AL           ;SAVE BYTE COUNT
                SUB     CH,CH           ;INDICATE THERE IS A SIGN IN BUFFER
;
;               CHECK IF FIRST BYTE OF ACTUAL STRING IS SIGN
;               IF SO, INDICATOR IN CH IS CORRECT AND DIGIT COUNTS
;                 ARE CORRECT SINCE THEY ASSSUME A SIGN BYTE
;
                LODSB                   ;GET FIRST BYTE OF ACTUAL STRING
                CMP     AL,'-'          ;CHECK IF IT IS ASCII -
                JE      STMSD           ;BRANCH IF IT IS
                CMP     AL,'+'          ;CHECK IF IT IS ASCII +
                JE      STMSD           ;BRANCH IF IT IS
;
;               FIRST BYTE IS NOT A SIGN
;               SET A FLAG, MOVE POINTER BACK TO START AT FIRST DIGIT
;               INCREASE BYTE COUNT BY 1 SINCE NO SIGN INCLUDED
;
                INC     CH              ;INDICATE NO SIGN IN BUFFER
                DEC     SI              ;MOVE POINTER BACK TO FIRST DIGIT
                INC     CL              ;ADD 1 TO BYTE COUNT
;
;               START CONVERSION AT MOST SIGNIFICANT DIGIT IN BUFFER
;               COULD BE UP TO SIX BYTES INCLUDING SIGN
;
STMSD:
                CMP     CL,6            ;LOOK FOR 10000'S DIGIT
                JE      TENKD           ;BRANCH IF FOUND
                CMP     CL,5            ;LOOK FOR 1000'S DIGIT
                JE      ONEKD           ;BRANCH IF FOUND
                CMP     CL,4            ;LOOK FOR 100'S DIGIT
                JE      HUNDD           ;BRANCH IF FOUND
```

```
        CMP     CL,3        ;LOOK FOR TENS DIGIT
        JE      TENSD       ;BRANCH IF FOUND
        CMP     CL,2        ;LOOK FOR ONES DIGIT
        JE      ONESD       ;BRANCH IF FOUND
        JMP     ERREXIT     ;NO DIGITS, INDICATE ERROR
;
;       CONVERT 10000'S DIGIT TO BINARY
;
TENKD:
        LODSB               ;GET 10000'S ASCII DIGIT
        CALL    ASCDEC      ;CONVERT TO BINARY, CHECK VALIDITY
        JC      ERREXIT     ;JUMP IF ERROR RETURN
        CMP     AL,3        ;CHECK IF DIGIT TOO LARGE
        JA      ERREXIT     ;TAKE ERROR EXIT IF IT IS
        SUB     AH,AH       ;EXTEND DIGIT TO 16 BITS
        MOV     DX,10000    ;MULTIPLY TIMES 10,000
        MUL     DX
        MOV     BX,AX       ;SAVE PRODUCT
;
;       CONVERT 1000'S DIGIT TO BINARY
;
ONEKD:
        LODSB               ;GET 1000'S ASCII DIGIT
        CALL    ASCDEC      ;CONVERT TO BINARY, CHECK VALIDITY
        JC      ERREXIT     ;JUMP IF ERROR RETURN
        SUB     AH,AH       ;EXTEND DIGIT TO 16 BITS
        MOV     DX,1000     ;MULTIPLY TIMES 1,000
        MUL     DX
        ADD     BX,AX       ;ADD PRODUCT TO PREVIOUS DIGITS
;
;       CONVERT 100'S DIGIT TO BINARY
;
HUNDD:
        LODSB               ;GET 100'S ASCII DIGIT
        CALL    ASCDEC      ;CONVERT TO BINARY, CHECK VALIDITY
        JC      ERREXIT     ;JUMP IF ERROR RETURN
        MOV     DL,100      ;MULTIPLY TIMES 100
        MUL     DL
        ADD     BX,AX       ;ADD PRODUCT TO PREVIOUS DIGITS
;
;       CONVERT TENS DIGIT TO BINARY
;
TENSD:
        LODSB               ;GET 10'S ASCII DIGIT
        CALL    ASCDEC      ;CONVERT TO BINARY, CHECK VALIDITY
        JC      ERREXIT     ;JUMP IF ERROR RETURN
        MOV     DL,10       ;MULTIPLY TIMES 10
        MUL     DL
        ADD     BX,AX       ;ADD PRODUCT TO PREVIOUS DIGITS
;
;       CONVERT ONES DIGIT TO BINARY
;
ONESD:
        LODSB               ;GET 1'S ASCII DIGIT
        JSR     ASCDEC      ;CONVERT TO BINARY, CHECK VALIDITY
        JC      ERREXIT     ;JUMP IF ERROR RETURN
```

```
          SUB       AH,AH      ;EXTEND TO 16 BITS
          ADD       BX,AX      ;ADD TO PREVIOUS DIGITS
;
;         CHECK FOR MINUS SIGN
;
          AND       CH,CH      ;WAS THERE A SIGN BYTE?
          JNE       VALEXIT    ;BRANCH IF NO SIGN
          MOV       AL,[DI]    ;GET SIGN BYTE
          CMP       AL,'-'     ;CHECK IF IT IS ASCII -
          JNE       VALEXIT    ;BRANCH IF IT ISN'T
;
;         NEGATIVE NUMBER, SO SUBTRACT VALUE FROM ZERO
;
          NEG       BX         ;SUBTRACT VALUE FROM ZERO
;
;         EXIT WITH BINARY VALUE IN AX
;
VALEXIT:
          MOV       AX,BX      ;RETURN TOTAL IN AX
          CLC                  ;CLEAR CARRY, INDICATING NO ERRORS
          RET
;
;         ERROR EXIT - SET CARRY FLAG TO RETURN ERROR CONDITION
;
ERREXIT:
          MOV       AX,BX      ;RETURN TOTAL IN AX
          STC                  ;SET CARRY TO INDICATE ERROR
          RET

;**************************************************************
;ROUTINE: ASCDEC
;PURPOSE: CONVERTS ASCII TO DECIMAL, CHECKS VALIDITY OF DIGITS
;ENTRY: ASCII DIGIT IN AL
;EXIT: DECIMAL DIGIT IN AL, CARRY = 0 IF DIGIT VALID, 1 IF NOT VALID
;REGISTERS USED: AL, F
;**************************************************************
ASCDEC:   SUB       AL,'0'     ;CONVERT TO DECIMAL BY SUBTRACTING ASCII 0
          JB        EREXIT     ;BRANCH IF ERROR (VALUE TOO SMALL)
          CMP       AL,9       ;CHECK IF RESULT IS DECIMAL DIGIT
          JA        EREXIT     ;BRANCH IF ERROR (VALUE TOO LARGE)
          CLC                  ;ELSE RETURN DECIMAL DIGIT AND CLEAR
                               ;  CARRY TO INDICATE VALID RESULT
          RET                  ;
EREXIT:   STC                  ;SET CARRY TO INDICATE INVALID RESULT
          RET

;
;
;     SAMPLE EXECUTION
;
;

SC1F:
          ;CONVERT ASCII '1234' TO 04D2 HEX
          MOV       BX,S1      ;GET BASE ADDRESS OF S1
          CALL      DEC2BN     ;AX=04D2 HEX
```

```
        ;CONVERT ASCII '+32767' TO 7FFF HEX
        MOV     BX,S2       ;GET BASE ADDRESS OF S2
        CALL    DEC2BN      ;AX=7FFF HEX

        ;CONVERT ASCII '-32768' TO 8000 HEX
        MOV     BX,S3       ;GET BASE ADDRESS OF S3
        CALL    DEC2BN      ;AX=8000 HEX

S1:     DB      4
        DB      '1234'
S2:     DB      6
        DB      '+32767'
S3:     DB      6
        DB      '-32768'
        END
```

2 Array manipulation and indexing

2A Two-dimensional byte array indexing (D2BYTE)

Calculates the address of an element of a two-dimensional byte-length array, given the array's base address, the element's two subscripts, and the size of a row (i.e. the number of columns). The array is assumed to be stored in row major order (i.e. by rows), and both subscripts are assumed to begin at 0. The array is also assumed to be contained entirely within the current data segment.

Procedure The program multiplies the row size (number of columns in a row) times the row subscript (since the elements are stored by rows) and adds the product to the column subscript. It then adds the sum to the base address.

Entry conditions

Order in stack (starting from the top)

Low byte of return address
High byte of return address

Low byte of column subscript
High byte of column subscript

Low byte of the size of a row (in bytes)
High byte of the size of a row (in bytes)

Low byte of row subscript
High byte of row subscript

Low byte of base address of array
High byte of base address of array

Exit conditions

Address of element in BX

Examples

1. Data: Base address = $3C00_{16}$
   Column subscript = 0004_{16}
   Size of row (number of columns) = 0018_{16}
   Row subscript = 0003_{16}

   Result: Element address = $3C00_{16} + 0003_{16} \times 0018_{16} + 0004_{16}$
   $= 3C00_{16} + 0048_{16} + 0004_{16}$
   $= 3C4C_{16}$

   i.e. the address of ARRAY(3,4) is $3C4C_{16}$

2. Data: Base address = $6A4A_{16}$
   Column subscript = 0037_{16}
   Size of row (number of columns) = 0050_{16}
   Row subscript = 0002_{16}

   Result: Element address = $6A4A_{16} + 0002_{16} \times 0050_{16} + 0037_{16}$
   $= 6A4A_{16} + 00A0_{16} + 0037_{16}$
   $= 6B21_{16}$

   i.e. the address of ARRAY(2,35) is $6B21_{16}$

Note that all subscripts are hexadecimal (e.g. $37_{16} = 55_{10}$).

The general formula is

ELEMENT ADDRESS = ARRAY BASE ADDRESS + ROW SUBSCRIPT × ROW SIZE + COLUMN SUBSCRIPT

Note that we refer to the *size* of the row subscript; this is the number of consecutive memory addresses for which the subscript has the same value. It is also the distance in bytes from the address of an element to the address of the element with the same column subscript but a row subscript 1 larger.

Registers used AX, BX, DX, F

Execution time Approximately 223 cycles

Program size 22 bytes

Data memory required None

```
;
;
;
;
;       Title:                  Two-Dimensional Byte Array Indexing
;       Name:                   D2BYTE
;
;
;
;       Purpose:                Given the base address of a byte array,
;                               two subscripts 'I' and 'J', and the size
;                               of the first subscript in bytes, calculate
;                               the address of A[I,J].  The array is assumed
;                               to be stored in row major order (A[0,0],
;                               A[0,1],...,A[K,L]), and both dimensions
;                               are assumed to begin at zero as in the
;                               C language or in the following Pascal
;                               declaration:
;                                 A:ARRAY[0..2,0..7] OF BYTE;
;
;       Entry:                  TOP OF STACK
;                                 Low byte of return address
;                                 High byte of return address
;                                 Low byte of second subscript (column number)
;                                 High byte of second subscript (column number)
;                                 Low byte of first subscript size, in bytes
;                                 High byte of first subscript size, in bytes
;                                 Low byte of first subscript (row number)
;                                 High byte of first subscript (row number)
;                                 Low byte of array base address
;                                 High byte of array base address
;                               NOTE:
;                                 The first subscript size is the length of
;                                 a row in bytes (number of columns).
;
;       Exit:                   Register BX = Element address
;
;       Registers Used:         AX,BX,DX,F
;
;       Time:                   Approximately 223 cycles
;
;       Size:                   Program 22 bytes
```

```
;
;
;
D2BYTE:
        ;
        ;ELEMENT ADDRESS = ROW SIZE X ROW SUBSCRIPT + COLUMN
        ;  SUBSCRIPT + BASE ADDRESS
        ;
        PUSH    BP              ;SAVE BASE POINTER
        MOV     BP,SP           ;GET BASE ADDRESS OF PARAMETERS
        MOV     AX,[BP+4]       ;GET ROW SIZE
        MOV     DX,[BP+6]       ;GET ROW SUBSCRIPT
        MUL     DX              ;ROW SIZE X ROW SUBSCRIPT
        ;
        ;ADD COLUMN SUBSCRIPT AND BASE ADDRESS
        ;
        ADD     AX,[BP+2]       ;ADD COLUMN SUBSCRIPT
        ADD     AX,[BP+8]       ;ADD BASE ADDRESS
        ;
        ;SAVE ELEMENT ADDRESS IN BX
        ;REMOVE PARAMETERS FROM STACK AND EXIT
        ;
        MOV     BX,AX           ;SAVE ELEMENT ADDRESS
        POP     BP              ;RESTORE BASE POINTER
        RET     8               ;EXIT, REMOVING PARAMETERS
                                ;  FROM STACK
;
;
;       SAMPLE EXECUTION
;
;

SC2A:
        MOV     BX,OFFSET ARY   ;GET BASE ADDRESS OF ARRAY
        PUSH    BX
        MOV     AX,[SUBS1]      ;GET FIRST (ROW) SUBSCRIPT
        PUSH    AX
        MOV     AX,[SSUBS1]     ;GET SIZE OF FIRST SUBSCRIPT
        PUSH    AX
        MOV     AX,[SUBS2]      ;GET SECOND (COLUMN) SUBSCRIPT
        PUSH    AX
        CALL    D2BYTE  ;CALCULATE ADDRESS OF ELEMENT
                        ;FOR THE INITIAL TEST DATA
                        ;BX = ADDRESS OF ARY(2,4)
                        ;   = ARY + (2 X 8) + 4
                        ;   = ARY + 20 (CONTENTS ARE 21)
                        ;NOTE BOTH SUBSCRIPTS START AT 0
        JMP     SC2A    ;REPEAT TEST
;
;DATA
;
SUBS1   DW      2       ;SUBSCRIPT 1 (ROW NUMBER)
SSUBS1  DW      8       ;SIZE OF SUBSCRIPT 1 (NUMBER OF BYTES
                        ; PER ROW)
SUBS2   DW      4       ;SUBSCRIPT 2 (COLUMN NUMBER)
```

```
;THE ARRAY (3 ROWS OF 8 COLUMNS)
ARY       DB        1,2,3,4,5,6,7,8
          DB        9,10,11,12,13,14,15,16
          DB        17,18,19,20,21,22,23,24

          END
```

2B Two-dimensional word array indexing (D2WORD)

Calculates the address of an element of a two-dimensional word-length (16-bit) array, given the array's base address, the element's two subscripts, and the size of a row (i.e. the number of columns). The array is assumed to be stored in row major order (i.e. by rows), and both subscripts are assumed to begin at 0.

Procedure The program multiplies the row size (number of bytes in a row) times the row subscript (since the elements are stored by rows), adds the product to the doubled column subscript (doubled because each element occupies two bytes), and adds the sum to the base address.

Entry conditions

Order in stack (starting from the top)

Low byte of return address
High byte of return address

Low byte of column subscript
High byte of column subscript

Low byte of the size of a row (in bytes)
High byte of the size of a row (in bytes)

Low byte of row subscript
High byte of row subscript

Low byte of base address of array
High byte of base address of array

Exit conditions

Base address of element in BX
The element occupies the address in BX and the next higher address

Examples

1. Data: Base address = $5E14_{16}$

Column subscript = 0008_{16}
Size of row (in bytes) = $001C_{16}$ (i.e. each row has 0014_{10} or $000E_{16}$ word-length elements)
Row subscript = 0005_{16}

Result: Element base address = $5E14_{16} + 0005_{16} \times 001C_{16} + 0008_{16} \times 2$
$= 5E14_{16} + 008C_{16} + 0010_{16}$
$= 5EB0_{16}$

i.e. the base address of ARRAY(5,8) is $5EB0_{16}$ and the element occupies addresses $5EB0_{16}$ and $5EB1_{16}$

2. Data: Base address = $B100_{16}$
Column subscript = 0002_{16}
Size of row (in bytes) = 0008_{16} (i.e. each row has four word-length elements)
Row subscript = 0006_{16}

Result: Element's base address = $B100_{16} + 0006_{16} \times 0008_{16} + 0002_{16} \times 2$
$= B100_{16} + 0030_{16} + 0004_{16}$
$= B134_{16}$

i.e. the base address of ARRAY(6,2) is $B134_{16}$ and the element occupies addresses $B134_{16}$ and $B135_{16}$

The general formula is

ELEMENT'S BASE ADDRESS = ARRAY BASE ADDRESS + ROW SUBSCRIPT × ROW SIZE + COLUMN SUBSCRIPT × 2

Note that one parameter of this routine is the size of a row in bytes. The size for word-length elements is the number of columns per row times 2 (the size of an element in bytes). The reason for choosing this parameter rather than the number of columns or the maximum column index is that it can be calculated once (when the array bounds are determined) and used whenever the array is accessed. The alternative parameters (number of columns or maximum column index) would require extra calculations during each indexing operation.

Registers used AX, BX, DX, F

Execution time Approximately 228 cycles

Program size 26 bytes

Data memory required None

```
;
;
;
;       Title:                 Two-Dimensional Word Array Indexing
;       Name:                  D2WORD
;
;
;
;       Purpose:               Given the base address of a word array,
;                              two subscripts 'I' and 'J', and the size
;                              of the first subscript in bytes, calculate
;                              the address of A[I,J].  The array is assumed
;                              to be stored in row major order (A[0,0],
;                              A[0,1],...,A[K,L]), and both dimensions
;                              are assumed to begin at zero as in the C
;                              language or the following Pascal declaration:
;                                A:ARRAY[0..2,0..7] OF WORD;
;
;       Entry:                 TOP OF STACK
;                                Low byte of return address
;                                High byte of return address
;                                Low byte of second subscript (column element)
;                                High byte of second subscript (column element)
;                                Low byte of first subscript size, in bytes
;                                High byte of first subscript size, in bytes
;                                Low byte of first subscript (row element)
;                                High byte of first subscript (row element)
;                                Low byte of array base address
;                                High byte of array base address
;                              NOTE:
;                                The first subscript's size is the length of
;                                a row in words times 2.
;
;       Exit:                  Register BX = Element's base address
;
;       Registers Used:        AX,BX,DX,F
;
;       Time:                  Approximately 228 cycles
;
;       Size:                  Program 26 bytes
;
;
;

D2WORD:
        ;
        ;ELEMENT ADDRESS = ROW SIZE X ROW SUBSCRIPT + 2 X COLUMN
        ;  SUBSCRIPT + BASE ADDRESS
        ;
        PUSH    BP                      ;SAVE BASE POINTER
```

```
        MOV     BP,SP           ;GET BASE ADDRESS OF PARAMETERS
        MOV     AX,[BP+4]       ;GET ROW SIZE
        MOV     DX,[BP+6]       ;GET ROW SUBSCRIPT
        MUL     DX              ;ROW SIZE X ROW SUBSCRIPT
        ;
        ;ADD DOUBLED COLUMN SUBSCRIPT AND BASE ADDRESS
        ;
        MOV     DX,[BP+2]       ;GET COLUMN SUBSCRIPT
        SHL     DX,1            ;DOUBLE COLUMN SUBSCRIPT SINCE
                                ;  ELEMENTS EACH OCCUPY 2 BYTES
        ADD     AX,DX           ;ADD DOUBLED COLUMN SUBSCRIPT
        ADD     AX,[BP+8]       ;ADD BASE ADDRESS
        ;
        ;REMOVE PARAMETERS FROM STACK AND EXIT
        ;
        MOV     BX,AX           ;SAVE ELEMENT ADDRESS
        POP     BP              ;RESTORE BASE POINTER
        RET     8               ;EXIT, REMOVING PARAMETERS FROM
                                ;  STACK
;
;
;       SAMPLE EXECUTION
;
;

SC2B:
        MOV     BX,OFFSET ARY   ;GET BASE ADDRESS OF ARRAY
        PUSH    BX
        MOV     AX,[SUBS1]      ;GET FIRST SUBSCRIPT (ROW
                                ;  NUMBER)
        PUSH    AX
        MOV     AX,[SSUBS1]     ;GET SIZE OF FIRST SUBSCRIPT
        PUSH    AX
        MOV     AX,[SUBS2]      ;GET SECOND SUBSCRIPT (COLUMN
                                ;  NUMBER)
        PUSH    AX
        CALL    D2WORD      ;CALCULATE ADDRESS OF ELEMENT
                            ;FOR THE INITIAL TEST DATA
                            ;BX = ADDRESS OF ARY(2,4)
                            ;   = ARY + (2 X 16) + 4 X 2
                            ;   = ARY + 40 (CONTENTS ARE 2100H)
                            ;NOTE BOTH SUBSCRIPTS START AT 0
        JMP     SC2B        ;REPEAT TEST
;
;DATA
;
SUBS1   DW      2           ;SUBSCRIPT 1 (ROW NUMBER)
SSUBS1  DW      16          ;SIZE OF SUBSCRIPT 1 (NUMBER OF BYTES
                            ; PER ROW)
SUBS2   DW      4           ;SUBSCRIPT 2 (COLUMN NUMBER)

;THE ARRAY (3 ROWS OF 8 COLUMNS)
ARY     DW      0100H,0200H,0300H,0400H,0500H,0600H,0700H,0800H
        DW      0900H,1000H,1100H,1200H,1300H,1400H,1500H,1600H
        DW      1700H,1800H,1900H,2000H,2100H,2200H,2300H,2400H
        END
```

2C Two-dimensional array indexing with a dope vector (CRDVEC, D2BYDV)

Calculates the address of an element of a two-dimensional byte-length (8-bit) array, given the array's base address, the element's two subscripts, and the size of a row (i.e. the number of columns). The array is assumed to be stored in row major order (i.e. by rows), and both subscripts are assumed to begin at 0.

Consists of two subroutines: CRDVEC, which creates a 'dope vector' consisting of the addresses of the 0th elements of each row; and D2BYDV, which calculates the address of an element using the dope vector. This approach saves indexing time (since no multiplications are necessary); the cost is the extra storage required for the dope vector.

Procedure Subroutine CRDVEC creates the dope vector by starting with the base address and adding the row size repeatedly to determine the remaining elements. Subroutine D2BYDV calculates the address of a particular byte-length element by adding the column subscript to the selected element of the dope vector. This routine can be modified easily to handle elements of different sizes. Note that the dope vector's elements are 16-bit offset addresses (i.e. addresses within the current data segment).

Entry conditions

Order in stack (starting from the top)

1. CRDVEC
Low byte of return address
High byte of return address

Low byte of the size of a row (in bytes)
High byte of the size of a row (in bytes)

Low byte of number of rows in array
High byte of number of rows in array

Low byte of base address of dope vector
High byte of base address of dope vector

Low byte of base address of array
High byte of base address of array

2. D2BYDV
Low byte of return address
High byte of return address

Low byte of column subscript
High byte of column subscript

Low byte of row subscript
High byte of row subscript

Low byte of base address of dope vector
High byte of base address of dope vector

Exit conditions

1. CRDVEC
Dope vector stored in memory

2. D2BYDV
Base address of element in BX

Examples

1. Creating a dope vector:

Base address = $5E14_{16}$
Size of row (in bytes) = $001C_{16}$
Number of rows = 0005_{16}

Result: Dope vector has the following elements:

$5E14_{16}$ (address of element in row 0, column 0)
$5E30_{16}$ (address of element in row 1, column 0)
$5E4C_{16}$ (address of element in row 2, column 0)
$5E68_{16}$ (address of element in row 3, column 0)
$5E84_{16}$ (address of element in row 4, column 0)

2. Using a dope vector (created in part 1) with byte-length elements:

Column subscript = $0B_{16}$
Row subscript = 2

Result: Element's address = Element 2 of dope vector + column subscript = $5E4C_{16}$ + 0B = $5E57_{16}$
i.e. ARRAY(2,11) is in address $5E57_{16}$

The general formula is

ELEMENT'S ADDRESS = DOPE VECTOR (ROW SUBSCRIPT) + COLUMN SUBSCRIPT

Note that one parameter of CRDVEC is the size of a row in bytes. For example, the size for word-length elements would be the number of columns per row times 2 (the size of an element in bytes). However, D2BYDV assumes byte-length elements; you would have to adjust either the routine or the column subscript to handle elements of other sizes.

Registers used

1. CRDVEC: AX, CX, DI, DX
2. D2BYDV: BX, DX, F, SI

Execution time

1. CRDVEC: 120 cycles overhead plus 31 cycles per row
2. D2BYDV: 116 cycles

Program size

1. CRDVEC: 27 bytes
2. D2BYDV: 20 bytes

Data memory required

1. CRDVEC: None
2. D2BYDV: None

```
;
;
;
;
;       Title:                  Two-Dimensional Array Indexing
;                               with a Dope Vector
;       Name:                   CRDVEC, D2BYDV
;
;
;
;       Purpose:                Given the base address of an array,
;                               and two subscripts 'I' and 'J', calculate
```

```
;                               the address of A[I,J], using a  dope
;                               vector containing the addresses of the
;                               first element in each row.
;                               The array is assumed to be stored
;                               in row major order (A[0,0], A[0,1],
;                               A[0,2],...,A[K,L]), and both dimensions
;                               are assumed to begin at zero as in the C
;                               language or the following Pascal declaration:
;                                 A:ARRAY[0..2,0..7] OF BYTE;
;
;                               D2BYDV assumes that the array consists of
;                               byte-length elements
;
;       Entry:                  TOP OF STACK
;
;                                 1) CRDVEC
;                                 Low byte of return address
;                                 High byte of return address
;                                 Low byte of row size, in bytes
;                                 High byte of row size, in bytes
;                                 Low byte of number of rows
;                                 High byte of number of rows
;                                 Low byte of base address of dope vector
;                                 High byte of base address of dope vector
;                                 Low byte of array base address
;                                 High byte of array base address
;
;                                 2) D2BYDV
;                                 Low byte of return address
;                                 High byte of return address
;                                 Low byte of column subscript
;                                 High byte of column subscript
;                                 Low byte of row subscript
;                                 High byte of row subscript
;                                 Low byte of base address of dope vector
;                                 High byte of base address of dope vector
;
;       Exit:                   CRDVEC - Dope vector in memory
;                               D2BYDV - Base address of element in BX
;
;       Registers Used:         CRDVEC - AX,CX,DI,DX
;                               D2BYDV - BX,DX,F,SI
;
;       Time:                   CRDVEC - 120 cycles overhead plus 31
;                                 cycles per row
;                               D2BYDV - Approximately 116 cycles
;
;       Size:                   CRDVEC - Program 27 bytes
;                               D2BYDV - Program 20 bytes
;
;
;

;
;CREATE A DOPE VECTOR IN MEMORY
;IT CONTAINS THE ADDRESS OF THE ZEROTH ELEMENT
```

```
;  OF EACH ROW OF THE ARRAY
;
CRDVEC:
        PUSH    BP              ;SAVE BASE POINTER
        PUSHF                   ;SAVE FLAGS (PARTICULARLY D)
        MOV     BP,SP           ;GET BASE ADDRESS OF PARAMETERS
        MOV     CX,[BP+6]       ;GET NUMBER OF ROWS
        MOV     AX,[BP+10]      ;GET ARRAY BASE ADDRESS
        MOV     DI,[BP+8]       ;GET DOPE VECTOR BASE ADDRESS
        MOV     DX,[BP+4]       ;GET SIZE OF SUBSCRIPT
        CLD                     ;SET AUTOINCREMENTING
        ;
        ;BUILD DOPE VECTOR STARTING WITH ARRAY BASE ADDRESS
        ;  AND ADDING ROW SIZE FOR EACH SUCCESSIVE ELEMENT
        ;
STVEC:  STOSW                   ;SAVE ELEMENT OF VECTOR
        ADD     AX,DX           ;ADD ROW SIZE TO GET NEXT
        LOOP    STVEC           ;CONTINUE THROUGH NUMBER
                                ;  OF ROWS
        ;
        ;REMOVE PARAMETERS FROM STACK AND EXIT
        ;
        POPF                    ;RESTORE D FLAG
        POP     BP              ;RESTORE BASE POINTER
        RET     8               ;EXIT, REMOVING PARAMETERS FROM
                                ;  STACK
;
;
;ACCESS AN ELEMENT GIVEN ITS ROW AND COLUMN SUBSCRIPTS AND
;  THE DOPE VECTOR
;THIS ROUTINE ASSUMES BYTE-LENGTH ELEMENTS
;
D2BYDV:
        ;
        ;GET ELEMENT OF DOPE VECTOR BASED ON ROW SUBSCRIPT
        ;
        PUSH    BP              ;SAVE BASE POINTER
        MOV     BP,SP           ;GET BASE ADDRESS OF PARAMETERS
        MOV     BX,[BP+6]       ;GET DOPE VECTOR BASE ADDRESS
        MOV     SI,[BP+4]       ;GET ROW SUBSCRIPT
        SHL     SI,1            ;DOUBLE SUBSCRIPT SINCE DOPE
                                ;  VECTOR ELEMENTS ARE 16-BIT
                                ;  ADDRESSES
        MOV     BX,[BX+SI]      ;GET ELEMENT OF DOPE VECTOR
        ;
        ;ADD COLUMN SUBSCRIPT TO ELEMENT OF DOPE VECTOR
        ;
        ADD     BX,[BP+2]       ;ADD COLUMN SUBSCRIPT
        ;
        ;REMOVE PARAMETERS FROM STACK AND EXIT
        ;
        POP     BP              ;RESTORE BASE POINTER
        RET     6               ;EXIT, REMOVING PARAMETERS FROM
                                ;  STACK
;
;
```

```
;           SAMPLE EXECUTION
;
;

SC2C:
            MOV         BX,OFFSET ARY       ;GET BASE ADDRESS OF ARRAY
            PUSH        BX
            MOV         BX,OFFSET DPVECT    ;GET BASE ADDRESS OF DOPE VECTOR
            PUSH        BX
            MOV         AX,[NROWS]          ;GET NUMBER OF ROWS
            PUSH        AX
            MOV         AX,[SIZEROW]        ;GET SIZE OF ROW IN BYTES
            PUSH        AX
            CALL        CRDVEC              ;CREATE DOPE VECTOR
                                            ;IT CONTAINS THE ADDRESS
                                            ;  OF THE ZEROTH ELEMENT OF
                                            ;  EACH ROW
            MOV         BX,OFFSET DPVECT    ;GET BASE ADDRESS OF DOPE VECTOR
            PUSH        BX
            MOV         AX,[ROWNO]          ;GET ROW SUBSCRIPT
            PUSH        AX
            MOV         AX,[COLNO]          ;GET COLUMN SUBSCRIPT
            PUSH        AX
            CALL        D2BYDV              ;CALCULATE ADDRESS FOR TEST
                                            ;  DATA
                                            ;BX = ADDRESS OF ARY(2,4)
                                            ;   = ARY + (2 X 16) + 4 X 2
                                            ;   = ARY + 40
                                            ;CONTENTS ARE 41
            JMP         SC2C                ;REPEAT TEST

;
;DATA
;
COLNO       DW          4           ;COLUMN SUBSCRIPT (COLUMN NUMBER)
NROWS       DW          5           ;NUMBER OF ROWS IN ARRAY
ROWNO       DW          2           ;ROW SUBSCRIPT (ROW NUMBER)
SIZEROW     DW          16          ;SIZE OF A ROW IN BYTES

DPVECT      DW          5 DUP(0)    ;DOPE VECTOR (ADDRESS OF ZEROTH
                                    ;  ELEMENT IN EACH ROW)

;THE ARRAY (5 ROWS OF 16 COLUMNS) - ONE BYTE PER ELEMENT
ARY         DB          1,2,3,4,5,6,7,8,9,10,11,12,13,14,15,16
            DB          17,18,19,20,21,22,23,24,25,26,27,28,29,30,31,32
            DB          33,34,35,36,37,38,39,40,41,42,43,44,45,46,47,48
            DB          49,50,51,52,53,54,55,56,57,58,59,60,61,62,63,64
            DB          65,66,67,68,69,70,71,72,73,74,75,76,77,78,79,80
            END
```

2D *N*-dimensional array indexing (NDIM)

Calculates the base address of an element of an *N*-dimensional array, given the array's base address and *N* pairs of sizes and subscripts. The size of a dimension is the number of bytes from the base address of an element to the base address of the element with an index 1 larger in the dimension but the same in all other dimensions. The array is assumed to be stored in row major order (i.e. organized so that subscripts to the right change before ones to the left). All subscripts are assumed to begin at 0.

Note that the size of the rightmost subscript is simply the size of an element in bytes; the size of the next subscript is the size of an element times the maximum value of the rightmost subscript plus 1, and so on. All subscripts are assumed to begin at 0. Otherwise, the user must normalize them (see the second example at the end of the listing).

Procedure The program loops on each dimension, calculating the offset in it as the subscript times the size. After calculating the overall offset, the program adds it to the array's base address to obtain the element's base address.

Entry conditions

Order in stack (starting from the top)

Low byte of return address
High byte of return address

Low byte of number of dimensions
High byte of number of dimensions

Low byte of size of rightmost dimension
High byte of size of rightmost dimension

Low byte of rightmost subscript
High byte of rightmost subscript

.
.
.

Low byte of size of leftmost dimension
High byte of size of leftmost dimension

Low byte of leftmost subscript

High byte of leftmost subscript

Low byte of base address of array
High byte of base address of array

Note that the number of parameters in the stack depends on the number of dimensions.

Exit conditions

Base address of element in BX
The element occupies memory addresses START through START + SIZE − 1, where START is the calculated address and SIZE is the size of an element in bytes.

Example

Data: Base address = $3C00_{16}$
Number of dimensions = 0003_{16}
Rightmost subscript = 0005_{16}
Rightmost size = 0003_{16} (3-byte entries)
Middle subscript = 0003_{16}
Middle size = 0012_{16} (six 3-byte entries)
Leftmost subscript = 0004_{16}
Leftmost size = $007E_{16}$ (seven sets of six 3-byte entries)

Result: Element base address = $3C00_{16} + 0005_{16} \times 0003_{16} + 0003_{16} \times 0012_{16} + 0004_{16} \times 007E_{16}$
$= 3C00_{16} + 000F_{16} + 0036_{16} + 01F8_{16}$
$= 3E3D_{16}$

i.e. the element is ARRAY(4,3,5); it occupies addresses $3E3D_{16}$ through $3E3F_{16}$. [The maximum values of the various subscripts are 6 (leftmost) and 5 (middle), with each element occupying 3 bytes.]

The general formula is

$$\text{ELEMENT ADDRESS} = \text{ARRAY ADDRESS} + \sum_{i=1}^{N} \text{SUBSCRIPT}_i \times \text{SIZE}_i$$

where:

N is the number of dimensions
SUBSCRIPT_i is the ith subscript
SIZE_i is the size of the ith dimension

Note that we use the size of each dimension as a parameter to reduce the number of repetitive multiplications and to generalize the procedure. The sizes can be calculated and saved as soon as the bounds of the array are known. Those sizes can then be used whenever indexing is performed on the array. Obviously, the sizes do not change if the bounds are fixed, and they should not be recalculated as part of each indexing operation. The sizes are also general, since the elements can themselves consist of any number of bytes.

Registers used AX, BX, CX, DI, DX, F

Execution time Approximately 161 cycles per dimension plus 42 cycles overhead

Program size 21 bytes

Data memory required None

Special case

If the number of dimensions is 0, the program returns with the base address in BX.

```
;
;
;
;
;       Title:              N-Dimensional Array Indexing
;       Name:               NDIM
;
;
;
;       Purpose:            Calculate the address of an element in an
;                           N-dimensional array given the base address,
;                           N pairs of size in bytes and subscripts, and
;                           the number of dimensions of the array.  The
;                           array is assumed to be stored in row major
;                           order (e.g., A[0,0,0],A[0,0,1],...,A[0,1,0],
;                           A[0,1,1],...).  Also, it is assumed that all
;                           dimensions begin at 0 as in the C language or
;                           in the following Pascal declaration:
;                             A:ARRAY[0..10,0..3,0..5] OF SOMETHING
;
;       Entry:              TOP OF STACK
;                             Low byte of return address
;                             High byte of return address
;                             Low byte of number of dimensions
```

```
;                                High byte of number of dimensions
;                                Low byte of dim N size
;                                High byte of dim N size
;                                Low byte of dim N subscript
;                                High byte of dim N subscript
;                                Low byte of dim N-1 size
;                                High byte of dim N-1 size
;                                Low byte of dim N-1 subscript
;                                High byte of dim N-1 subscript
;                                    .
;                                    .
;                                    .
;
;                                Low byte of array base address
;                                High byte of array base address
;                              NOTE:
;                                All sizes are in bytes.
;
;       Exit:                  Register BX = Element's base address
;
;       Registers Used:        AX,BX,CX,DI,DX,F
;
;       Time:                  Approximately 161 cycles per dimension plus
;                              42 cycles overhead
;
;       Size:                  Program  21 bytes
;
;
;


;
;       EXIT IMMEDIATELY IF NUMBER OF DIMENSIONS IS ZERO
;
NDIM:
        POP     DI                      ;SAVE RETURN ADDRESS
        POP     CX                      ;GET NUMBER OF DIMENSIONS
        POP     BX                      ;GET BASE ADDRESS IF ZERO
                                        ;  DIMENSIONS
        JCXZ    EXITND                  ;BRANCH IF NUMBER OF DIMENSIONS
                                        ;  IS ZERO
        MOV     AX,BX                   ;IF NO. DIMENSIONS NOT ZERO,
                                        ;  PARAMETER IS FIRST SIZE
        ;
        ;ELEMENT ADDRESS = BASE ADDRESS + SIZE(I) X SUBSCRIPT(I) FOR
        ;  I = 1 TO N
        ;
        SUB     BX,BX                   ;START ELEMENT ADDRESS AT ZERO
        ;
        ;MULTIPLY ROW SUBSCRIPT X ROW SIZE AND ADD TO PREVIOUS
        ;  ACCUMULATION
        ;
NXTDIM: POP     DX                      ;GET NEXT SUBSCRIPT
        MUL     DX                      ;SIZE X SUBSCRIPT
        ADD     BX,AX                   ;ADD TO ACCUMULATED ELEMENT
                                        ;  ADDRESS
        POP     AX                      ;GET NEXT SIZE OR BASE ADDRESS
                                        ;  IF ON LAST DIMENSION
```

```
        LOOP    NXTDIM              ;COUNT DIMENSIONS
        ;
        ;ADD TOTAL OFFSET TO BASE ADDRESS OF ARRAY
        ;
        ADD     BX,AX               ;ADD BASE ADDRESS OF ARRAY
        ;
        ;EXIT
        ;
EXITND: JMP     DI                  ;EXIT TO RETURN ADDRESS

;
;       SAMPLE EXECUTION
;
;

SC2D:
        ;
        ;CALCULATE ADDRESS OF AY1[1,3,0]
        ;SINCE LOWER BOUNDS OF ARRAY 1 ARE ALL ZERO IT IS
        ;  NOT NECESSARY TO NORMALIZE THEM
        ;
        MOV     BX,OFFSET AY1       ;BASE ADDRESS OF ARRAY
        PUSH    BX
        MOV     AX,1                ;FIRST SUBSCRIPT
        PUSH    AX
        MOV     AX,A1SZ1            ;SIZE OF FIRST SUBSCRIPT
        PUSH    AX
        MOV     AX,3                ;SECOND SUBSCRIPT
        PUSH    AX
        MOV     AX,A1SZ2            ;SIZE OF SECOND SUBSCRIPT
        PUSH    AX
        SUB     AX,AX               ;THIRD SUBSCRIPT = 0
        PUSH    AX
        MOV     AX,A1SZ3            ;SIZE OF THIRD SUBSCRIPT
        PUSH    AX
        MOV     AX,A1DIM            ;NUMBER OF DIMENSIONS
        PUSH    AX
        CALL    NDIM        ;CALCULATE ADDRESS OF ELEMENT
                            ;BX = STARTING ADDRESS OF AY1(1,3,0)
                            ;   = AY1 + (1 X 126) + (3 X 21) + (0 X 3)
                            ;   = AY1 + 189

        ;
        ;CALCULATE ADDRESS OF AY2[-1,6]
        ; SINCE LOWER BOUNDS OF ARRAY 2 DO NOT START AT 0, SUBSCRIPTS
        ; MUST BE NORMALIZED
        ;
        MOV     BX,OFFSET AY2       ;BASE ADDRESS OF ARRAY
        PUSH    BX
        MOV     AX,-1               ;UNNORMALIZED FIRST SUBSCRIPT
        SUB     AX,A2D1L            ;NORMALIZE FIRST SUBSCRIPT BY
                                    ; SUBTRACTING LOWER BOUND

        PUSH    AX
        MOV     AX,A2SZ1            ;SIZE OF FIRST SUBSCRIPT
        PUSH    AX
        MOV     AX,6                ;UNNORMALIZED SECOND SUBSCRIPT
        SUB     AX,A2D2L            ;NORMALIZE SECOND SUBSCRIPT BY
```

```
                                                ; SUBTRACTING LOWER BOUND
          PUSH      AX
          MOV       AX,A2SZ2                    ;SIZE OF SECOND SUBSCRIPT
          PUSH      AX
          MOV       AX,A2DIM                    ;NUMBER OF DIMENSIONS
          PUSH      AX
          CALL      NDIM          ;CALCULATE ADDRESS
                                  ;BX = STARTING ADDRESS OF AY2(-1,6)
                                  ;   = AY2+(((-1)-(-5)) X 18)+((6-2) X 2)
                                  ;   = AY2+80
          JMP       SC2D          ;REPEAT TEST
;DATA
;AY1 ARRAY[A1D1L..A1D1H,A1D2L..A1D2H,A1D3L..A1D3H] 3-BYTE ELEMENTS
;          [ 0  . .  3  ,  0  .  . 5  ,  0  . . 6  ]
A1DIM     EQU       3             ;NUMBER OF DIMENSIONS
A1D1L     EQU       0             ;LOW BOUND OF DIMENSION 1
A1D1H     EQU       3             ;HIGH BOUND OF DIMENSION 1
A1D2L     EQU       0             ;LOW BOUND OF DIMENSION 2
A1D2H     EQU       5             ;HIGH BOUND OF DIMENSION 2
A1D3L     EQU       0             ;LOW BOUND OF DIMENSION 3
A1D3H     EQU       6             ;HIGH BOUND OF DIMENSION 3
A1SZ3     EQU       3             ;SIZE OF ELEMENT IN DIMENSION 3
A1SZ2     EQU       ((A1D3H-A1D3L)+1)*A1SZ3  ;SIZE OF ELEMENT IN D2
A1SZ1     EQU       ((A1D2H-A1D2L)+1)*A1SZ2  ;SIZE OF ELEMENT IN D1
AY1       DB        ((A1D1H-A1D1L)+1)*A1SZ1 DUP(0) ;ARRAY

;AY2 ARRAY [A2D1L..A2D1H,A2D2L..A2D2H] OF WORD
;           [  -5 .. -1  ,  2  .. 10  ]
A2DIM     EQU       2             ;NUMBER OF DIMENSIONS
A2D1L     EQU       -5            ;LOW BOUND OF DIMENSION 1
A2D1H     EQU       -1            ;HIGH BOUND OF DIMENSION 1
A2D2L     EQU       2             ;LOW BOUND OF DIMENSION 2
A2D2H     EQU       10            ;HIGH BOUND OF DIMENSION 2
A2SZ2     EQU       2                        ;SIZE OF ELEMENT IN D2
A2SZ1     EQU       ((A2D2H-A2D2L)+1)*A2SZ2  ;SIZE OF ELEMENT IN D1
AY2       DB        ((A2D1H-A2D1L)+1)*A2SZ1 DUP(0) ;ARRAY
          END
```

3 Arithmetic

3A Multiple-precision binary addition (MPBADD)

Adds two multi-byte unsigned binary numbers. Both are stored with their least significant bytes at the lowest address. The sum replaces the number with the base address lower in the stack.

Procedure The program clears the Carry flag initially and adds the operands one byte at a time, starting with the least significant bytes. The final Carry flag indicates whether the overall addition produced a carry. A length of 0 causes an immediate exit with no addition.

Entry conditions

Order in stack (starting from the top)

Low byte of return address
High byte of return address

Low byte of length of operands in bytes
High byte of length of operands in bytes

Low byte of base address of second operand (address containing the least significant byte of array 2)
High byte of base address of second operand (address containing the least significant byte of array 2)

Low byte of base address of first operand and sum (address containing the least significant byte of array 1)
High byte of base address of first operand and sum (address containing the least significant byte of array 1)

Exit conditions

First operand (array 1) replaced by first operand (array 1) plus second operand (array 2)

Example

Data: Length of operands (in bytes) = 6
Top operand (array 2) = $19D028A193EA_{16}$
Bottom operand (array 1) = $293EABF059C7_{16}$
Result: Bottom operand (array 1) = Bottom operand (array 1) + Top operand (array 2)
= $430ED491EDB1_{16}$
Carry = 0

Registers used AX, CX, DI, DX, F (clears D flag), SI

Execution time 54 cycles per byte plus 51 cycles overhead. For example, adding two 6-byte operands takes

$$54 \times 6 + 51 = 375 \text{ cycles}$$

Program size 16 bytes

Data memory required None

Special case A length of 0 causes an immediate exit with the sum equal to the bottom operand (i.e. array 1 is unchanged). The Carry flag is cleared.

```
;
;
;
;
;       Title:                   Multiple-Precision Binary Addition
;       Name:                    MPBADD
;
;
;
;       Purpose:                 Add 2 arrays of binary bytes
;                                Array1 := Array 1 + Array 2
;
;       Entry:                   TOP OF STACK
;                                  Low byte of return address
;                                  High byte of return address
;                                  Low byte of array length in bytes
;                                  High byte of array length in bytes
;                                  Low byte of array 2 address
;                                  High byte of array 2 address
;                                  Low byte of array 1 address
;                                  High byte of array 1 address
;
;                                  The arrays are unsigned binary numbers
;                                  with a maximum length of 65,535 bytes,
;                                  ARRAY[0] is the least significant
;                                  byte, and ARRAY[LENGTH-1] is the
;                                  most significant byte.
;
;       Exit:                    Array1 := Array1 + Array2
;
;       Registers Used:          AX,CX,DI,DX,F (clears D flag),SI
;
;       Time:                    54 cycles per byte plus 51 cycles overhead
;
;       Size:                    Program 16 bytes
;
;
;

MPBADD:
        ;
        ;CHECK IF LENGTH OF ARRAYS IS ZERO
        ;EXIT WITH CARRY CLEARED IF IT IS
        ;
        POP     DX              ;SAVE RETURN ADDRESS
        POP     CX              ;GET LENGTH OF ARRAYS
        POP     SI              ;GET BASE ADDRESS OF ARRAY 2
        POP     DI              ;GET BASE ADDRESS OF ARRAY 1
        CLC                     ;CLEAR CARRY TO START
        JCXZ    ADEXIT          ;BRANCH (EXIT) IF ARRAY LENGTH IS ZERO
        ;
        ;ADD ARRAYS ONE BYTE AT A TIME
        ;
        CLD                     ;SET AUTOINCREMENTING
ADDBYT:
        LODSB                   ;GET BYTE FROM ARRAY 2
```

```
        ADC     AL,[DI]    ;ADD WITH CARRY TO BYTE FROM ARRAY 1
        STOSB              ;SAVE SUM IN ARRAY 1
        LOOP    ADDBYT     ;CONTINUE UNTIL ALL BYTES SUMMED
        ;
        ;EXIT TO RETURN ADDRESS
        ;
ADEXIT:
        JMP     DX         ;EXIT TO RETURN ADDRESS


;
;
;       SAMPLE EXECUTION
;
;

SC3A:
        MOV     BX,[AY1ADR]     ;GET FIRST OPERAND
        PUSH    BX
        MOV     BX,[AY2ADR]     ;GET SECOND OPERAND
        PUSH    BX
        MOV     AX,SZAYS        ;LENGTH OF ARRAYS IN BYTES
        PUSH    AX
        CALL    MPBADD     ;MULTIPLE-PRECISION BINARY ADDITION
                           ;RESULT OF 12345678H + 9ABCDEF0H
                           ;  = ACF13568H
                           ; IN MEMORY AY1      = 68H
                           ;           AY1+1    = 35H
                           ;           AY1+2    = F1H
                           ;           AY1+3    = ACH
                           ;           AY1+4    = 00H
                           ;           AY1+5    = 00H
                           ;           AY1+6    = 00H
        JMP     SC3A       ;REPEAT TEST
;
;  DATA
;
SZAYS   EQU     7          ;LENGTH OF ARRAYS IN BYTES

AY1ADR  DW      AY1        ;BASE ADDRESS OF ARRAY 1
AY2ADR  DW      AY2        ;BASE ADDRESS OF ARRAY 2

AY1     DB      78H,56H,34H,12H,0,0,0        ;FIRST OPERAND
AY2     DB      0F0H,0DEH,0BCH,9AH,0,0,0     ;SECOND OPERAND

        END
```

3B Multiple-precision binary subtraction (MPBSUB)

Subtracts two multi-byte unsigned binary numbers. Both are stored with their least significant bytes at the lowest address. The subtrahend (number to be subtracted) is stored on top of the minuend (number from which it is subtracted). The difference replaces the minuend.

Procedure The program clears the Carry flag initially and subtracts the subtrahend from the minuend one byte at a time, starting with the least significant bytes. The final Carry flag indicates whether the overall subtraction required a borrow. A length of 0 causes an immediate exit with no subtraction.

Entry conditions

Order in stack (starting from the top)

Low byte of return address
High byte of return address

Low byte of operand length in bytes
High byte of operand length in bytes

Low byte of base address of subtrahend
High byte of base address of subtrahend

Low byte of base address of minuend
High byte of base address of minuend

Exit conditions

Minuend replaced by minuend minus subtrahend

Example

Data: Length of operands (in bytes) = 4
Minuend = $2F5BA7C3_{16}$
Subtrahend = $14DF35B8_{16}$

Result: Minuend = $1A7C720B_{16}$
Carry = 0, since no borrow is necessary.

Registers used AX, CX, DI, DX, F (clears D flag), SI

Execution time 57 cycles per byte plus 51 cycles overhead. For example, subtracting two 6-byte operands takes

$$57 \times 6 + 51 = 393 \text{ cycles}$$

Program size 17 bytes

Data memory required None

Special case A length of 0 causes an immediate exit with the minuend unchanged (i.e. the difference is equal to the minuend). The Carry flag is cleared.

```
;
;
;
;
;       Title:                  Multiple-Precision Binary Subtraction
;       Name:                   MPBSUB
;
;
;
;       Purpose:                Subtract 2 arrays of binary bytes
;                               Minuend := Minuend - Subtrahend
;
;       Entry:                  TOP OF STACK
;                                 Low byte of return address
;                                 High byte of return address
;                                 Low byte of array length in bytes
;                                 High byte of array length in bytes
;                                 Low byte of subtrahend address
;                                 High byte of subtrahend address
;                                 Low byte of minuend address
;                                 High byte of minuend address
;
;                                 The arrays are unsigned binary numbers,
;                                 ARRAY[0] is the least significant
;                                 byte, and ARRAY[LENGTH-1] is the
;                                 most significant byte.
;
;       Exit:                   Minuend := Minuend - Subtrahend
;
;       Registers Used:         AX,CX,DI,DX,F (clears D flag),SI
;
;       Time:                   57 cycles per byte plus 51 cycles overhead
```

```
;
;    Size:              Program 17 bytes
;
;
;

MPBSUB:
        ;
        ;CHECK IF LENGTH OF ARRAYS IS ZERO
        ;EXIT WITH CARRY CLEARED IF IT IS
        ;
        POP     DX          ;SAVE RETURN ADDRESS
        POP     CX          ;GET LENGTH OF ARRAYS
        POP     SI          ;GET BASE ADDRESS OF SUBTRAHEND
        POP     DI          ;GET BASE ADDRESS OF MINUEND
        CLC                 ;NO BORROW INITIALLY
        JCXZ    SBEXIT      ;BRANCH (EXIT) IF LENGTH IS ZERO
        ;
        ;SUBTRACT ARRAYS ONE BYTE AT A TIME
        ;
        CLD                 ;SET AUTOINCREMENTING
SUBBYT:
        MOV     AL,[DI]     ;GET BYTE OF MINUEND
        SBB     AL,[SI]     ;SUBTRACT BYTE OF SUBTRAHEND WITH BORROW
        STOSB               ;SAVE DIFFERENCE IN MINUEND
        INC     SI
        LOOP    SUBBYT      ;CONTINUE UNTIL ALL BYTES SUBTRACTED
        ;
        ;EXIT TO RETURN ADDRESS
        ;
SBEXIT: JMP     DX          ;EXIT TO RETURN ADDRESS

;
;
;       SAMPLE EXECUTION
;
;

SC3B:
        MOV     BX,[AY1ADR]     ;GET BASE ADDRESS OF MINUEND
        PUSH    BX
        MOV     BX,[AY2ADR]     ;GET BASE ADDRESS OF SUBTRAHEND
        PUSH    BX
        MOV     AX,SZAYS        ;GET LENGTH OF ARRAYS IN BYTES
        PUSH    AX
        CALL    MPBSUB      ;MULTIPLE-PRECISION BINARY SUBTRACTION
                            ;RESULT OF 2F3E4D5CH-175E809FH
                            ;  = 17DFCCBDH
                            ; IN MEMORY AY1     = BDH
                            ;           AY1+1   = CCH
                            ;           AY1+2   = DFH
                            ;           AY1+3   = 17H
                            ;           AY1+4   = 00H
                            ;           AY1+5   = 00H
                            ;           AY1+6   = 00H

;
```

```
;  DATA
;
SZAYS      EQU      7              ;LENGTH OF ARRAYS IN BYTES

AY1ADR     DW       AY1            ;BASE ADDRESS OF ARRAY 1
AY2ADR     DW       AY2            ;BASE ADDRESS OF ARRAY 2

AY1        DB       5CH,4DH,3EH,2FH,0,0,0     ;MINUEND
AY2        DB       9FH,80H,5EH,17H,0,0,0     ;SUBTRAHEND

           END
```

3C Multiple-precision binary multiplication (MPBMUL)

Multiplies two multi-byte unsigned binary numbers. Both are stored with their least significant bytes at the lowest address. The product replaces the multiplicand. The length of the numbers (in bytes) is 255 or less. Only the less significant bytes of the product are returned to provide compatibility with other multiple-precision binary operations.

Procedure The program multiplies the numbers one byte at a time, starting with the least significant bytes. It keeps a full double-length unsigned partial product in memory locations starting at PROD (more significant bytes) and in the multiplicand (less significant bytes). The less significant bytes of the product replace the multiplicand as it is shifted. A 0 length causes an exit with no multiplication.

Entry conditions

Order in stack (starting from the top)

Low byte of return address
High byte of return address

Low byte of length of operands in bytes
High byte of length of operands in bytes (always 0)

Low byte of base address of multiplicand
High byte of base address of multiplicand

Low byte of base address of multiplier
High byte of base address of multiplier

Exit conditions

Multiplicand replaced by multiplicand times multiplier

Example

Data: Length of operands (in bytes) = 4
Multiplicand = $0005D1F7_{16} = 381\,431_{10}$
Multiplier = $00000AB1_{16} = 2737_{10}$

Result: Multiplicand = $3E39D1C7_{16} = 1\,043\,976\,647_{10}$

Note that MPBMUL returns only the less significant bytes (i.e. the number of bytes in the multiplicand and multiplier) of the product to maintain compatibility with other multiple-precision binary arithmetic operations. The more significant bytes of the product are available starting with their least significant byte at address PROD. The user may need to check those bytes for a possible overflow.

Registers used AX, BX, CX, DI, DX, F (clears D flag), SI

Execution time Depends on the length of the operands and on the number of non-zero bytes in the multiplicand. If all the multiplicand's bytes are non-zero, the execution time is approximately

$$179 \times \text{LENGTH}^2 + 115 \times \text{LENGTH} + 84$$

If, for example, the operands are 4 bytes (32 bits) long, the execution time is approximately

$$179 \times 16 + 115 \times 4 + 84 = 2864 + 460 + 84 = 3408 \text{ cycles}$$

There is a savings of 179 × LENGTH cycles for each multiplicand byte that is 0.

Program size 76 bytes

Data memory required 256 bytes anywhere in RAM for the more significant bytes of the partial product (starting at address PROD). This includes an overflow byte. Also 4 stack bytes.

Special case A length of 0 causes an immediate exit with the product equal to the multiplicand. The Carry flag is cleared.

```
;
;
;
;
;       Title:                  Multiple-Precision Binary Multiplication
;       Name:                   MPBMUL
;
;
```

```
;
;       Purpose:                Multiply 2 arrays of binary bytes
;                               Multiplicand := Multiplicand X multiplier
;
;       Entry:                  TOP OF STACK
;                                 Low byte of return address
;                                 High byte of return address
;                                 Low byte of array length in bytes
;                                 High byte of array length in bytes (always 0)
;                                 Low byte of multiplicand address
;                                 High byte of multiplicand address
;                                 Low byte of multiplier address
;                                 High byte of multiplier address
;
;                                 The arrays are unsigned binary numbers
;                                 with a maximum length of 255 bytes,
;                                 ARRAY[0] is the least significant
;                                 byte, and ARRAY[LENGTH-1] is the
;                                 most significant byte.
;
;       Exit:                   Multiplicand := Multiplicand X multiplier
;
;       Registers Used:         AX,BX,CX,DI,DX,F (clears D flag),SI
;
;       Time:                   Assuming all multiplicand bytes are non-zero,
;                               then the time is approximately:
;                                (179 X length^2) + (115 X length) + 84 cycles
;
;       Size:                   Program  76 bytes
;                               Data     256 bytes plus 2 stack bytes
;
;
;

MPBMUL:
;
;       CHECK LENGTH OF OPERANDS
;       EXIT IF LENGTH IS ZERO
;       SAVE LENGTH FOR USE AS LOOP COUNTER
;
        PUSH    BP              ;SAVE BASE POINTER
        MOV     BP,SP           ;GET START OF PARAMETER AREA
        MOV     CX,[BP+4]       ;GET ARRAY LENGTH
        JCXZ    EXITML          ;EXIT (RETURN) IF LENGTH IS ZERO
        MOV     DX,CX           ;SAVE LENGTH AS LOOP COUNTER
;
;       CLEAR PARTIAL PRODUCT AREA, SIZE IS OPERAND LENGTH
;         PLUS 1 BYTE FOR OVERFLOW
;
        CLD                     ;SET AUTOINCREMENTING
        MOV     DI,OFFSET PROD  ;POINT TO PARTIAL PRODUCT
        INC     CX              ;AREA SIZE IS OPERAND LENGTH PLUS 1
        SUB     AL,AL           ;GET ZERO FOR CLEARING
REP     STOSB                   ;CLEAR PARTIAL PRODUCT AREA
;
;       LOOP OVER ALL MULTIPLICAND BYTES
;       MULTIPLYING EACH ONE BY ALL MULTIPLIER BYTES
;
```

```
;
          MOV       BX,[BP+6]       ;GET MULTIPLICAND ADDRESS
MCNDLP:
          TEST      BYTE PTR [BX],0FFH  ;CHECK MULTIPLICAND DIGIT
          JZ        SKIP            ;NO NEED TO MULTIPLY IF DIGIT IS 0
          MOV       SI,[BP+8]       ;GET MULTIPLIER ADDRESS
          MOV       DI,OFFSET PROD  ;POINT TO PARTIAL PRODUCT
          MOV       CX,[BP+4]       ;GET ARRAY LENGTH
;
;         MULTIPLY BYTE OF MULTIPLICAND TIMES EACH BYTE OF
;          MULTIPLIER
;
MPLRLP:   LODSB                     ;GET MULTIPLIER BYTE
          MUL       [BX]            ;MULTIPLY TIMES MULTIPLICAND BYTE
          ADD       [DI],AX         ;ADD RESULT TO PARTIAL PRODUCT
          INC       DI              ;INCREMENT PRODUCT POINTER
          JNC       PLREND          ;JUMP IF NO CARRY
          PUSH      DI              ;ELSE SAVE PRODUCT POINTER
CRYTHR:
          INC       DI              ;POINT TO NEXT BYTE OF PRODUCT
          INC       BYTE PTR [DI]   ;ADD CARRY TO NEXT BYTE
          JZ        CRYTHR          ;LOOP WHILE CARRY PROPAGATES
          POP       DI              ;RESTORE PRODUCT POINTER
PLREND:
          LOOP      MPLRLP          ;LOOP THROUGH ALL MULTIPLIER BYTES
;
;         MOVE LOW BYTE OF PARTIAL PRODUCT INTO RESULT AREA
;         THIS OVERWRITES THE MULTIPLICAND BYTE USED IN THE
;           LATEST MULTIPLICATION LOOP
;
SKIP:
          MOV       CX,[BP+4]       ;GET ARRAY LENGTH
          MOV       DI,OFFSET PROD  ;DESTINATION IS PARTIAL PRODUCT
          MOV       SI,DI           ;SOURCE IS ONE BYTE HIGHER
          INC       SI              ;  THAN DESTINATION
          MOV       AL,[DI]         ;GET LOWEST PRODUCT BYTE
          MOV       [BX],AL         ;STORE IN MULTIPLICAND
          INC       BX              ;POINT TO NEXT MULTIPLICAND BYTE
;
;         SHIFT PARTIAL PRODUCT RIGHT ONE BYTE
;
    REP   MOVSB                     ;SHIFT PRODUCT RIGHT ONE BYTE
;
;         COUNT MULTIPLICAND DIGITS
;
          DEC       DX              ;DECREMENT MULTIPLICAND DIGIT COUNT
          JNZ       MCNDLP          ;LOOP UNTIL ALL BYTES MULTIPLIED
;
;         REMOVE PARAMETERS FROM STACK AND EXIT
;
EXITML:
          POP       BP              ;RESTORE BASE POINTER
          RET       6               ;RETURN, REMOVING PARAMETERS FROM
                                    ;  STACK
;
;         DATA
```

```
;
PROD      DB        256 DUP(0)    ;PARTIAL PRODUCT BUFFER WITH OVERFLOW
                                  ;BYTE
;
;
;         SAMPLE EXECUTION
;
;

SC3C:
          MOV       BX,[AY2ADR]   ;GET MULTIPLIER
          PUSH      BX
          MOV       BX,[AY1ADR]   ;GET MULTIPLICAND
          PUSH      BX
          MOV       AX,SZAYS      ;GET LENGTH OF OPERAND IN BYTES
          PUSH      AX
          JSR       MPBMUL    ;MULTIPLE-PRECISION BINARY MULTIPLICATION
                              ;RESULT OF 12345H X 1234H = 14B60404H
                              ; IN MEMORY AY1      = 04H
                              ;           AY1+1    = 04H
                              ;           AY1+2    = B6H
                              ;           AY1+3    = 14H
                              ;           AY1+4    = 00H
                              ;           AY1+5    = 00H
                              ;           AY1+6    = 00H
          JMP       SC3C      ;REPEAT TEST
;
;  DATA
;
SZAYS     EQU       7         ;LENGTH OF OPERANDS IN BYTES

AY1ADR    DW        AY1       ;BASE ADDRESS OF ARRAY 1
AY2ADR    DW        AY2       ;BASE ADDRESS OF ARRAY 2

AY1       DB        45H,23H,1,0,0,0,0         ;MULTIPLICAND
AY2       DB        34H,12H,0,0,0,0,0         ;MULTIPLIER

          END
```

3D Multiple-precision binary division (MPBDIV)

Divides two multi-byte unsigned binary numbers. Both are stored with their least significant bytes at the lowest address. The quotient replaces the dividend, and the address of the least significant byte of the remainder ends up in register BX. The length of the numbers (in bytes) is 255 or less. The Carry flag is cleared if no errors occur; if a divide by 0 is attempted, the Carry flag is set to 1, the dividend is left unchanged, and the remainder is set to 0.

Procedure The program divides using the standard shift-and-subtract algorithm, shifting quotient and dividend and placing a 1 bit in the quotient each time a trial subtraction succeeds. An extra buffer holds the result of the trial subtraction; that buffer is simply switched with the buffer holding the dividend if the subtraction succeeds. The program sets the Carry flag if the divisor is 0 and clears Carry otherwise.

Entry conditions

Order in stack (starting from the top)

Low byte of return address
High byte of return address

Low byte of operand length in bytes
High byte of operand length in bytes (always 0)

Low byte of base address of divisor
High byte of base address of divisor

Low byte of base address of dividend
High byte of base address of dividend

Exit conditions

Dividend replaced by quotient (dividend divided by divisor)
If the divisor is non-zero, Carry = 0 and the result is normal
If the divisor is 0, Carry = 1, the dividend is unchanged, and the remainder is 0
The remainder is stored starting with its least significant byte at the address in BX

Example

Data: Length of operands (in bytes) = 3
Top operand (array 2 or divisor) = $000F45_{16} = 3\,909_{10}$
Bottom operand (array 1 or dividend) = $35A2F7_{16}$ = $3\,515\,127_{10}$

Result: Bottom operand (array 1) = Bottom operand (array 1)/Top operand (array 2) = $000383_{16} = 899_{10}$
Remainder (starting at address in BX) = $0003A8_{16} = 936_{10}$
Carry flag = 0 to indicate no divide-by-zero error

Registers used AX, BX, CX, DI, DX, F (clears D flag), SI

Execution time Depends on the length of the operands and on the number of 1 bits in the quotient (requiring a replacement of the dividend by the remainder). If the average number of 1 bits in the quotient is four per byte, the execution time is approximately

$$1072 \times \text{LENGTH}^2 + 1142 \times \text{LENGTH} + 165 \text{ cycles}$$

where LENGTH is the length of the operands in bytes. If, for example, LENGTH = 4 (32-bit division), the approximate execution time is

$$1072 \times 4^2 + 1142 \times 4 + 165 = 21\,885 \text{ cycles}$$

Program size 133 bytes

Data memory required 514 bytes anywhere in RAM for the buffers holding either the high dividend or the result of the trial subtraction (255 bytes starting at addresses HIDE1 and HIDE2, respectively), and for the pointers that assign the buffers to specific purposes (2 bytes starting at addresses HDEPTR and DIFPTR, respectively). Also 2 stack bytes.

Special cases

1. A length of 0 causes an immediate exit with the Carry flag cleared, the quotient equal to the original dividend, and the remainder undefined.

2. A divisor of 0 causes an exit with the Carry flag set to 1, the quotient equal to the original dividend, and the remainder equal to 0.

```
;
;
;
;
;       Title:                  Multiple-Precision Binary Division
;       Name:                   MPBDIV
;
;
;
;       Purpose:                Divide 2 arrays of binary bytes
;                               Array1 := Array 1 / Array 2
;
;       Entry:                  TOP OF STACK
;                                 Low byte of return address
;                                 High byte of return address
;                                 Low byte of array length in bytes
;                                 High byte of array length in bytes (always 0)
;                                 Low byte of divisor address
;                                 High byte of divisor address
;                                 Low byte of dividend address
;                                 High byte of dividend address
;
;                                 The arrays are unsigned binary numbers
;                                 with a maximum length of 255 bytes,
;                                 ARRAY[0] is the least significant
;                                 byte, and ARRAY[LENGTH-1] is the
;                                 most significant byte.
;
;       Exit:                   Array1 := Array1 / Array2
;                               Register BX = Base address of remainder
;                               If no errors then
;                                 Carry := 0
;                               else
;                                 divide-by-zero error
;                                 Carry := 1
;                                 quotient := array 1 unchanged
;                                 remainder := 0
;
;       Registers Used:         AX,BX,CX,DI,DX,F (clears D flag),SI
;
;       Time:                   Assuming there are length/2 1 bits in the
;                               quotient, then the time is approximately
;                                 (1072 X length^2) + (1142 X length) +
;                                  165 cycles
;
;       Size:                   Program  133 bytes
;                               Data     514 bytes plus 2 stack bytes
;
;
;

MPBDIV:
;
```

```
;
;       EXIT INDICATING NO ERROR IF LENGTH OF OPERANDS IS ZERO
;
        PUSH    BP              ;SAVE BASE POINTER
        MOV     BP,SP           ;GET BASE ADDRESS OF PARAMETERS
        MOV     CX,[BP+4]       ;GET LENGTH OF OPERANDS
        JCXZ    GOODRT          ;BRANCH (GOOD EXIT) IF LENGTH IS ZERO
        MOV     DX,CX           ;SAVE LENGTH
;
;       SET UP HIGH DIVIDEND AND DIFFERENCE POINTERS
;       CLEAR HIGH DIVIDEND AND DIFFERENCE ARRAYS
;       ARRAYS 1 AND 2 ARE USED INTERCHANGEABLY FOR THESE TWO
;         PURPOSES.  THE POINTERS ARE SWITCHED WHENEVER A
;         TRIAL SUBTRACTION SUCCEEDS
;
        CLD                     ;SET AUTOINCREMENTING
        MOV     SI,OFFSET HIDE1  ;GET BASE ADDRESS OF ARRAY 1
        MOV     [HDEPTR],SI     ;DIVIDEND POINTER = ARRAY 1
        MOV     DI,OFFSET HIDE2  ;GET BASE ADDRESS OF ARRAY 2
        MOV     [DIFPTR],SI     ;DIFFERENCE POINTER = ARRAY 2
        SUB     AL,AL           ;GET ZERO FOR CLEARING ARRAYS
CLRHI:
        MOV     [SI],AL         ;CLEAR BYTE OF ARRAY 1
        STOSB                   ;CLEAR BYTE OF ARRAY 2
        INC     SI
        LOOP    CLRHI           ;CONTINUE THROUGH ALL BYTES
;
;       CHECK WHETHER DIVISOR IS ZERO
;       IF IT IS, EXIT INDICATING DIVIDE-BY-ZERO ERROR
;
        MOV     CX,DX           ;GET LENGTH OF OPERANDS
        MOV     SI,[BP+6]       ;GET BASE ADDRESS OF DIVISOR
        SUB     AL,AL           ;START INDICATOR AT ZERO
   REPE SCASB                   ;SCAN DIVISOR UNTIL ALL BYTES
                                ;  EXAMINED OR NON-ZERO BYTE FOUND
        JNE     INITDV          ;BRANCH IF NON-ZERO BYTE FOUND
        STC                     ;ALL BYTES ARE ZERO - INDICATE
                                ;  DIVIDE-BY-ZERO ERROR
        JMP     DVEXIT          ;EXIT INDICATING ERROR
;
;       DIVIDE USING TRIAL SUBTRACTIONS
;
INITDV:
;
;       BIT COUNT = 8 X ARRAY LENGTH + 1
;
        MOV     CX,DX           ;GET ARRAY LENGTH
        SHL     CX,1            ;MULTIPLY LENGTH TIMES 8 TO GET
        SHL     CX,1            ;  THE NUMBER OF BITS IN THE
        SHL     CX,1            ;  DIVIDEND ARRAY
        INC     CX              ;MUST DO 1 EXTRA SHIFT
        MOV     [BP+4],CX       ;SAVE SHIFT COUNT ON STACK

;
;       SHIFT QUOTIENT AND UPPER DIVIDEND LEFT 1 BIT
;       CARRY IN IS 1 IF PREVIOUS SUBTRACTION WAS SUCCESSFUL
;
```

```
;         POINTER TO UPPER DIVIDEND IS IN HDEPTR
;
          CLC                              ;CLEAR CARRY INITIALLY
DIVLOOP:
          MOV       CX,DX                  ;GET ARRAY LENGTH
          MOV       DI,[BP+8]              ;GET QUOTIENT ADDRESS
;
;         SHIFT QUOTIENT LEFT 1 BIT
;         CARRY IN IS RESULT OF PREVIOUS TRIAL SUBTRACTION
;
SHFTQT:
          RCL       BYTE PTR [DI],1        ;SHIFT QUOTIENT BYTE LEFT
          INC       DI                     ;POINT TO NEXT BYTE
          LOOP      SHFTQT                 ;SHIFT ALL BYTES OF QUOTIENT
;
;         SHIFT UPPER DIVIDEND LEFT WITH CARRY FROM LOWER DIVIDEND
;
          MOV       CX,DX                  ;GET ARRAY LENGTH
          MOV       DI,[HDEPTR]            ;GET ADDRESS OF UPPER DIVIDEND
SHFTDV:
          RCL       BYTE PTR [DI],1        ;SHIFT UPPER DIVIDEND BYTE LEFT
          INC       DI                     ;POINT TO NEXT BYTE
          LOOP      SHFTDV                 ;COUNT BYTES
;
;         CHECK IF FINAL SHIFT OF QUOTIENT HAS BEEN DONE
;         EXIT WITH RESULT IF SO, ELSE DO NEXT SUBTRACTION
;
          DEC       WORD PTR [BP+4]        ;DECREMENT SHIFT COUNT
          JZ        GOODRT                 ;EXIT IF DONE
;
;         TRIAL SUBTRACTION OF DIVISOR FROM DIVIDEND
;         SAVE DIFFERENCE IN CASE IT IS NEEDED LATER
;
          MOV       SI,[HDEPTR]            ;POINT TO UPPER DIVIDEND
          MOV       BX,[BP+6]              ;POINT TO DIVISOR
          MOV       DI,[DIFPTR]            ;POINT TO BUFFER FOR DIFFERENCE
          CLC                              ;CLEAR BORROW INITIALLY
          MOV       CX,DX                  ;GET ARRAY LENGTH
SUBDVS:
          LODSB                            ;GET BYTE OF DIVIDEND
          SBB       AL,[BX]                ;SUBTRACT BYTE OF DIVISOR
          STOSB                            ;SAVE DIFFERENCE IN BUFFER
          INC       BX                     ;INCREMENT DIVISOR POINTER
          LOOP      SUBDVS                 ;COUNT BYTES
;
;         NEXT BIT OF QUOTIENT IS 1 IF SUBTRACTION WAS SUCCESSFUL,
;          0 IF IT WAS NOT
;         THIS IS COMPLEMENT OF FINAL BORROW FROM SUBTRACTION
;
          CMC                              ;NEXT BIT OF QUOTIENT = COMPLEMENT
                                           ;  OF FINAL BORROW
          JNC       DIVLOOP                ;DO NEXT SHIFT IF TRIAL SUBTRACTION
                                           ;  FAILED
;
;         TRIAL SUBTRACTION SUCCEEDED, SO REPLACE UPPER DIVIDEND
;           WITH DIFFERENCE BY SWITCHING POINTERS
```

```
;
        MOV     AX,[HDEPTR]         ;GET OLD DIVIDEND POINTER
        XCHG    AX,[DIFPTR]         ;DIVIDEND POINTER BECOMES NEW
                                    ;  DIFFERENCE POINTER FOR NEXT
                                    ;  ITERATION
        MOV     [HDEPTR],AX         ;DIFFERENCE BECOMES DIVIDEND FOR
                                    ;  NEXT ITERATION
        JMP     DIVLOOP             ;DO NEXT SHIFT
;
;       CLEAR CARRY TO INDICATE NO ERRORS
;
GOODRT:
        CLC                         ;CLEAR CARRY - NO DIVIDE-BY-ZERO ERROR
;
;       REMOVE PARAMETERS FROM STACK AND EXIT
;
DVEXIT:
        MOV     BX,[HDEPTR]         ;GET BASE ADDRESS OF REMAINDER
        POP     BP                  ;RESTORE BASE POINTER
        RET     6                   ;RETURN, DISCARDING PARAMETERS
                                    ;  FROM STACK

;
;       DATA
;
HDEPTR  DW      0           ;POINTER TO HIGH DIVIDEND
DIFPTR  DW      0           ;POINTER TO DIFFERENCE BETWEEN HIGH
                            ; DIVIDEND AND DIVISOR
HIDE1   DB      255 DUP(0)      ;HIGH DIVIDEND BUFFER 1
HIDE2   DB      255 DUP(0)      ;HIGH DIVIDEND BUFFER 2

;
;       SAMPLE EXECUTION
;
;

SC3D:
        MOV     BX,[AY1ADR]     ;GET DIVIDEND
        PUSH    BX
        MOV     BX,[AY2ADR]     ;GET DIVISOR
        PUSH    BX
        MOV     AX,SZAYS        ;LENGTH OF ARRAYS IN BYTES
        PUSH    AX
        JSR     MPBDIV      ;MULTIPLE-PRECISION BINARY DIVISION
                            ;RESULT OF 14B60404H / 1234H = 12345H
                            ; IN MEMORY AY1       = 45H
                            ;           AY1+1     = 23H
                            ;           AY1+2     = 01H
                            ;           AY1+3     = 00H
                            ;           AY1+4     = 00H
                            ;           AY1+5     = 00H
                            ;           AY1+6     = 00H
        JMP     SC3D

;
;  DATA
```

```
;
SZAYS   EQU  7                        ;LENGTH OF ARRAYS IN BYTES

AY1ADR  DW   AY1                      ;BASE ADDRESS OF ARRAY 1 (DIVIDEND)
AY2ADR  DW   AY2                      ;BASE ADDRESS OF ARRAY 2 (DIVISOR)

AY1     DB   04H,04H,B6H,14H,0,0,0,0          ;DIVIDEND
AY2     DB   34H,12H,0,0,0,0,0,0              ;DIVISOR

        END
```

3E Multiple-precision binary comparison (MPBCMP)

Compares two multi-byte unsigned binary numbers and sets the Carry and Zero flags. Both numbers are stored with their least significant bytes at the lowest address. Sets the Zero flag to 1 if the operands are equal and to 0 otherwise. Sets the Carry flag to 1 if the subtrahend (the number stored higher in the stack) is larger than the minuend and to 0 otherwise. Thus, it sets the flags as if it had subtracted the subtrahend from the minuend.

Procedure The program compares the operands one byte at a time, starting with the most significant bytes and continuing until it finds corresponding bytes that are not equal. If all the bytes are equal, it exits with the Zero flag set to 1. Note that the comparison starts with the operands' most significant bytes, whereas the subtraction (Subroutine 3B) starts with the least significant bytes.

Entry conditions

Order in stack (starting from the top)

Low byte of return address
High byte of return address

Low byte of operand length in bytes
High byte of operand length in bytes

Low byte of base address of subtrahend
High byte of base address of subtrahend

Low byte of base address of minuend
High byte of base address of minuend

Exit conditions

Flags set as if subtrahend had been subtracted from minuend

Zero flag = 1 if subtrahend and minuend are equal, 0 if they are not equal

Carry flag = 1 if subtrahend is larger than minuend in the unsigned sense, 0 if it less than or equal to the minuend

Examples

1. Data: Length of operands (in bytes) = 6
   Top operand (subtrahend) = $19D028A193EA_{16}$
   Bottom operand (minuend) = $4E67BC15A266_{16}$
   Result: Zero flag = 0 (operands are not equal)
   Carry flag = 0 (subtrahend is not larger than minuend)
2. Data: Length of operands (in bytes) = 6
   Top operand (subtrahend) = $19D028A193EA_{16}$
   Bottom operand (minuend) = $19D028A193EA_{16}$
   Result: Zero flag = 1 (operands are equal)
   Carry flag = 0 (subtrahend is not larger than minuend)
3. Data: Length of operands (in bytes) = 6
   Top operand (subtrahend) = $19D028A193EA_{16}$
   Bottom operand (minuend) = $0F37E5991D7C_{16}$
   Result: Zero flag = 0 (operands are not equal)
   Carry flag = 1 (subtrahend is larger than minuend)

Registers used AX, CX, DI, DX, F (sets D flag), SI

Execution time 24 cycles per byte that must be examined plus approximately 64 cycles overhead. That is, the program continues until it finds corresponding bytes that are not the same; each pair of bytes it must examine requires 24 cycles.

Examples

1. Comparing two 6-byte numbers that are equal takes

   $24 \times 6 + 64 = 208$ cycles

2. Comparing two 8-byte numbers that differ in the next to most significant bytes takes

   $24 \times 2 + 64 = 112$ cycles

Program size 20 bytes

Data memory required None

Special case A length of 0 causes an immediate exit with both the Carry flag and the Zero flag set to 1.

```
;
;
;
;       Title:              Multiple-Precision Binary Comparison
;       Name:               MPBCMP
;
;
;
;       Purpose:            Compare 2 arrays of binary bytes and
;                           return the Carry and Zero flags set or
;                           cleared
;
;       Entry:              TOP OF STACK
;                             Low byte of return address
;                             High byte of return address
;                             Low byte of operand length in bytes
;                             High byte of operand length in bytes
;                             Low byte of subtrahend address
;                             High byte of subtrahend address
;                             Low byte of minuend address
;                             High byte of minuend address
;
;                             The arrays are unsigned binary numbers,
;                             ARRAY[0] is the least significant
;                             byte, and ARRAY[LENGTH-1] is the
;                             most significant byte.
;
;       Exit:                IF minuend = subtrahend THEN
;                              C=0,Z=1
;                            IF minuend > subtrahend THEN
;                              C=0,Z=0
;                            IF minuend < subtrahend THEN
;                              C=1,Z=0
;                            IF array length = 0 THEN
;                              C=1,Z=1
;
;       Registers Used:      AX,CX,DI,DX,F (sets D flag),SI
;
;       Time:                24 cycles per byte that must be examined plus
;                              64 cycles overhead
;
;
;       Size:                Program  20 bytes
;


;
;       CHECK IF LENGTH OF ARRAYS IS ZERO
;       EXIT WITH SPECIAL FLAG SETTING (C=1, Z=1) IF IT IS
;
MPBCMP:
```

```
        POP     DX          ;SAVE RETURN ADDRESS
        POP     CX          ;GET LENGTH OF ARRAYS IN BYTES
        POP     DI          ;GET BASE ADDRESS OF SUBTRAHEND
        POP     SI          ;GET BASE ADDRESS OF MINUEND
        AND     CX,CX       ;TEST ARRAY LENGTH
        STC                 ;SET CARRY IN CASE LENGTH IS 0
        JZ      EXITCP      ;BRANCH (EXIT) IF LENGTH IS ZERO
                            ; C=1,Z=1 IN THIS CASE
                            ;NOTE: CANNOT USE JCXZ HERE SINCE
                            ; ROUTINE MUST RETURN WITH FLAGS
                            ; SET.
;
;       COMPARE ARRAYS BYTE AT A TIME UNTIL UNEQUAL BYTES
;        ARE ENCOUNTERED
;
        ADD     DI,CX       ;CALCULATE ADDRESS JUST BEYOND END
                            ;  OF SUBTRAHEND
        ADD     SI,CX       ;CALCULATE ADDRESS JUST BEYOND END
                            ;  OF MINUEND
        DEC     DI          ;GO BACK TO LAST BYTE OF SUBTRAHEND
        DEC     SI          ;GO BACK TO LAST BYTE OF MINUEND
        STD                 ;SET AUTODECREMENTING
  REPNE CMPSB               ;COMPARE MINUEND AND SUBTRAHEND THROUGH
                            ;  ALL BYTES OR UNTIL UNEQUAL BYTES
                            ;  ARE FOUND
;
;       EXIT TO RETURN ADDRESS
;
EXITCP:
        JMP     DX          ;EXIT TO RETURN ADDRESS

;
;
;       SAMPLE EXECUTION
;
;

SC3E:
        MOV     BX,[AY1ADR]     ;GET BASE ADDRESS OF MINUEND
        PUSH    BX
        MOV     BX,[AY2ADR]     ;GET BASE ADDRESS OF SUBTRAHEND
        PUSH    BX
        MOV     AX,SZAYS        ;GET LENGTH OF OPERANDS IN BYTES
        PUSH    AX
        JSR     MPBCMP      ;MULTIPLE-PRECISION BINARY COMPARISON
                            ;RESULT OF COMPARE (2F3E4D5CH,175E809FH)
                            ;  IS C=0,Z=0
        JMP     SC3E        ;REPEAT TEST
;
;  DATA
;
SZAYS   EQU     7           ;LENGTH OF OPERANDS IN BYTES

AY1ADR  DW      AY1         ;BASE ADDRESS OF ARRAY 1
AY2ADR  DW      AY2         ;BASE ADDRESS OF ARRAY 2
```

```
AY1     DB      5CH,4DH,3EH,2FH,0,0,0    ;MINUEND
AY2     DB      9FH,80H,5EH,17H,0,0,0    ;SUBTRAHEND

        END
```

3F Multiple-precision decimal addition (MPDADD)

Adds two multi-byte unsigned decimal (BCD) numbers. Both numbers are stored with their least significant digits at the lowest address. The sum replaces the number with the base address lower in the stack.

Procedure The program clears the Carry flag initially and then adds the operands one byte (two digits) at a time, starting with the least significant digits. The final Carry flag indicates whether the overall addition produced a carry. The sum replaces the operand with the base address lower in the stack (array 1 in the listing). A length of 0 causes an immediate exit with no addition.

Entry conditions

Order in stack (starting from the top)

Low byte of return address
High byte of return address

Low byte of length of operands in bytes
High byte of length of operands in bytes

Low byte of base address of second operand (address containing the least significant byte of array 2)
High byte of base address of second operand (address containing the least significant byte of array 2)

Low byte of base address of first operand and sum (address containing the least significant byte of array 1)
High byte of base address of first operand and sum (address containing the least significant byte of array 1)

Exit conditions

First operand (array 1) replaced by first operand (array 1) plus second operand (array 2)

Example

Data: Length of operands (in bytes) = 6
Top operand (array 2) = 196028819315_{16}
Bottom operand (array 1) = 293471605987_{16}

Result: Bottom operand (array 1) = Bottom operand (array 1) + Top operand (array 2) = 489500425302_{16}
Carry = 0

Registers used AX, CX, DI, DX, F (clears D flag), SI

Execution time 58 cycles per byte plus 53 cycles overhead. For example, adding two 6-byte operands takes

$58 \times 6 + 53 = 401$ cycles

Program size 17 bytes

Data memory required None

Special case A length of 0 causes an immediate exit with the sum equal to the bottom operand (i.e. array 1 is unchanged). The Carry flag is cleared.

```
;
;
;
;
;       Title:                  Multiple-Precision Decimal Addition
;       Name:                   MPDADD
;
;
;
;       Purpose:                Add 2 arrays of BCD bytes
;                               Array1 := Array 1 + Array 2
;
;
;       Entry:                  TOP OF STACK
;                                 Low byte of return address
;                                 High byte of return address
;                                 Low byte of array length in bytes
;                                 High byte of array length in bytes
;                                 Low byte of array 2 address
```

```
;                               High byte of array 2 address
;                               Low byte of array 1 address
;                               High byte of array 1 address
;
;                               The arrays are unsigned BCD numbers,
;                               ARRAY[0] is the least significant
;                               byte, and ARRAY[LENGTH-1] is the
;                               most significant byte
;
;       Exit:                   Array1 := Array1 + Array2
;
;       Registers Used:         AX,CX,DI,DX,F (clears D flag),SI
;
;       Time:                   58 cycles per byte plus 53 cycles overhead
;
;       Size:                   Program  17 bytes
;
;
;

MPDADD:
        ;
        ;CHECK IF LENGTH OF ARRAYS IS ZERO
        ;EXIT WITH CARRY CLEARED IF IT IS
        ;
        POP     DX              ;SAVE RETURN ADDRESS
        POP     CX              ;CHECK LENGTH OF ARRAYS
        POP     SI              ;GET BASE ADDRESS OF ARRAY 2
        POP     DI              ;GET BASE ADDRESS OF ARRAY 1
        CLC                     ;CLEAR CARRY TO START
        JCXZ    ADEXIT          ;BRANCH (EXIT) IF LENGTH IS ZERO
        ;
        ;ADD OPERANDS 2 DIGITS AT A TIME
        ;
        CLD                     ;SELECT AUTOINCREMENTING
ADDBYT:
        LODSB                   ;GET 2 DIGITS FROM ARRAY 2
        ADC     AL,[DI]         ;ADD 2 DIGITS FROM ARRAY 1 WITH CARRY
        DAA                     ;MAKE ADDITION DECIMAL
        STOSB                   ;SAVE SUM IN ARRAY 1
        LOOP    ADDBYT          ;CONTINUE UNTIL ALL DIGITS SUMMED
        ;
        ;EXIT TO RETURN ADDRESS
        ;
ADEXIT:
        JMP     DX              ;EXIT TO RETURN ADDRESS

;
;
;       SAMPLE EXECUTION
;
;

SC3F:
        MOV     BX,[AY1ADR]     ;GET FIRST OPERAND
        PUSH    BX
```

```
        MOV     BX,[AY2ADR]     ;GET SECOND OPERAND
        PUSH    BX
        MOV     AX,SZAYS        ;LENGTH OF OPERANDS IN BYTES
        PUSH    AX
        CALL    MPDADD          ;MULTIPLE-PRECISION BCD ADDITION
                                ;RESULT OF 12345678H + 35914028H
                                ;   = 48259706H
                                ; IN MEMORY AY1      = 06H
                                ;           AY1+1    = 97H
                                ;           AY1+2    = 25H
                                ;           AY1+3    = 48H
                                ;           AY1+4    = 00H
                                ;           AY1+5    = 00H
                                ;           AY1+6    = 00H
        JMP     SC3F            ;REPEAT TEST
;
;  DATA
;
SZAYS   EQU     7               ;LENGTH OF OPERANDS IN BYTES

AY1ADR  DW      AY1             ;BASE ADDRESS OF ARRAY 1
AY2ADR  DW      AY2             ;BASE ADDRESS OF ARRAY 2

AY1     DB      78H,56H,34H,12H,0,0,0   ;FIRST OPERAND
AY2     DB      28H,40H,91H,35H,0,0,0   ;SECOND OPERAND

        END
```

3G Multiple-precision decimal subtraction (MPDSUB)

Subtracts two multi-byte unsigned decimal (BCD) numbers. Both are stored with their least significant digits at the lowest address. The subtrahend (number to be subtracted) is stored on top of the minuend (number from which it is subtracted). The difference replaces the minuend.

Procedure The program clears the Carry flag initially and then subtracts the subtrahend from the minuend one byte (two digits) at a time, starting with the least significant digits. The final Carry flag indicates whether the overall subtraction required a borrow. A length of 0 causes an immediate exit with no subtraction.

Entry conditions

Order in stack (starting from the top)

Low byte of return address
High byte of return address

Low byte of length of operands in bytes
High byte of length of operands in bytes

Low byte of base address of subtrahend
High byte of base address of subtrahend

Low byte of base address of minuend
High byte of base address of minuend

Exit conditions

Minuend replaced by minuend minus subtrahend

Example

Data: Length of operands (in bytes) = 6
Minuend = 293471605987_{16}
Subtrahend = 196028819315_{16}
Result: Minuend = 097442786672_{16}
Carry = 1, since no borrow is necessary

Registers used AX, CX, DI, DX, F (clears D flag), SI

Execution time 61 cycles per byte plus 51 cycles overhead. For example, subtracting two 6-byte operands takes

$$61 \times 6 + 51 = 417 \text{ cycles}$$

Program size 18 bytes

Data memory required None

Special case A length of 0 causes an immediate exit with the minuend unchanged (i.e. the difference is equal to the minuend). The Carry flag is cleared.

```
;
;
;
;
;       Title:                  Multiple-Precision Decimal Subtraction
;       Name:                   MPDSUB
;
;
;
;       Purpose:                Subtract 2 arrays of BCD bytes
;                               Minuend := Minuend - Subtrahend
;
;       Entry:                  TOP OF STACK
;                                 Low byte of return address
;                                 High byte of return address
;                                 Low byte of array length in bytes
;                                 High byte of array length in bytes
;                                 Low byte of subtrahend address
;                                 High byte of subtrahend address
;                                 Low byte of minuend address
;                                 High byte of minuend address
;
;                                 The arrays are unsigned BCD numbers,
;                                 ARRAY[0] is the Ieast significant byte, and
;                                 ARRAY[LENGTH-1] is the most significant byte.
;
;       Exit:                   Minuend : = Minuend - Subtrahend
;
;       Registers Used:         AX,CX,DI,DX,F (clears D flag),SI
;
;       Time:                   61 cycles per byte plus 51 cycles overhead
;
```

```
;     Size:                   Program 18 bytes
;
;
;

MPDSUB:
        ;
        ;CHECK IF LENGTH OF ARRAYS IS ZERO
        ;EXIT WITH CARRY CLEARED IF IT IS
        ;
        POP       DX          ;SAVE RETURN ADDRESS
        POP       CX          ;CHECK LENGTH OF ARRAYS
        POP       SI          ;GET BASE ADDRESS OF SUBTRAHEND
        POP       DI          ;GET BASE ADDRESS OF MINUEND
        CLC                   ;CLEAR CARRY TO START
        JCXZ      SBEXIT      ;BRANCH (EXIT) IF LENGTH IS ZERO
        ;
        ;SUBTRACT OPERANDS 2 DIGITS AT A TIME
        ;
        CLD                   ;SET AUTOINCREMENTING
SUBBYT:
        MOV       AX,[DI]     ;GET BYTE OF MINUEND
        SBB       AL,[SI]     ;SUBTRACT BYTE OF SUBTRAHEND WITH BORROW
        DAS                   ;MAKE DIFFERENCE DECIMAL
        STOSB                 ;SAVE DIFFERENCE IN MINUEND
        INC       SI
        LOOP      SUBBYT      ;CONTINUE UNTIL ALL DIGITS SUBTRACTED
        ;
        ;EXIT TO RETURN ADDRESS
        ;
SBEXIT:
        JMP       DX          ;EXIT TO RETURN ADDRESS

;
;
;       SAMPLE EXECUTION
;
;

SC3G:
        MOV       BX,[AY1ADR]     ;GET BASE ADDRESS OF MINUEND
        PUSH      BX
        MOV       BX,[AY2ADR]     ;GET BASE ADDRESS OF SUBTRAHEND
        PUSH      BX
        MOV       AX,SZAYS        ;GET LENGTH OF OPERANDS IN BYTES
        PUSH      AX
        CALL      MPDSUB      ;MULTIPLE-PRECISION DECIMAL SUBTRACTION
                              ;RESULT OF 28364150H-17598093H
                              ;  = 10766057H
                              ; IN MEMORY AY1       = 57H
                              ;           AY1+1     = 60H
                              ;           AY1+2     = 76H
                              ;           AY1+3     = 10H
                              ;           AY1+4     = 00H
                              ;           AY1+5     = 00H
```

```
                           ;          AY1+6     = 00H
        JMP     SC3G       ;REPEAT TEST
;
;  DATA
;
SZAYS   EQU     7          ;LENGTH OF OPERANDS IN BYTES

AY1ADR  DW      AY1        ;BASE ADDRESS OF ARRAY 1
AY2ADR  DW      AY2        ;BASE ADDRESS OF ARRAY 2

AY1     DB      50H,41H,36H,28H,0,0,0          ;MINUEND
AY2     DB      93H,80H,59H,17H,0,0,0          ;SUBTRAHEND

        END
```

3H Multiple-precision decimal multiplication (MPDMUL)

Multiplies two multi-byte unsigned decimal (BCD) numbers. Both numbers are stored with their least significant digits at the lowest address. The product replaces the multiplicand. The length of the numbers (in bytes) is 255 or less. Only the less significant bytes of the product are returned to provide compatibility with other multiple-precision decimal operations.

Procedure The program handles each digit of the multiplicand separately. It masks the digit off, shifts it (if it is the upper digit of a byte), and then uses it as a counter to determine how many times to add the multiplier to the partial product. The least significant digit of the partial product is saved as the next digit of the full product, and the partial product is shifted right 4 bits. The program uses a flag to determine whether it is currently working with the upper or lower digit of a byte. A length of 0 causes an exit with no multiplication.

Entry conditions

Order in stack (starting from the top):

Low byte of return address
High byte of return address

Low byte of length of operands in bytes
High byte of length of operands in bytes

Low byte of base address of multiplicand
High byte of base address of multiplicand

Low byte of base address of multiplier
High byte of base address of multiplier

Exit conditions

Multiplicand replaced by multiplicand times multiplier.

Example

Data: Length of operands (in bytes) = 4
Multiplicand = = 00035118_{16}
Multiplier = 00006294_{16}
Result: Multiplicand = 22142826_{16}

Note that MPDMUL returns only the less significant bytes (i.e. the number of bytes in the multiplicand and multiplier) of the product to maintain compatibility with other multiple-precision decimal arithmetic operations. The more significant bytes of the product are available starting with their least significant byte at address PROD. The user may need to check those bytes for a possible overflow or extend the operands with additional zeros.

Registers used AX, BX, CX, DI, DX, F (clears D flag), SI

Execution time Depends on the length of the operands and on the size of the digits in the multiplicand (since those digits determine how many times the multiplier must be added to the partial product). If the average digit in the multiplicand has a value of 5, then the execution time is approximately

$$794 \times \text{LENGTH}^2 + 439 \times \text{LENGTH} + 84 \text{ cycles}$$

where LENGTH is the number of bytes in the operands. If, for example, LENGTH = 6 (12 digits), the approximate execution time is

$$\begin{aligned} 794 \times 6^2 + 439 \times 6 + 84 &= 794 \times 36 + 2634 + 84 \\ &= 28\,584 + 2718 \\ &= 31\,302 \text{ cycles} \end{aligned}$$

Program size 168 bytes

Data memory required 256 bytes anywhere in RAM. This is temporary storage for the high bytes of the partial product plus an overflow byte (starting at address PROD). Also 2 stack bytes.

Special case A length of 0 causes an immediate exit with the multiplicand unchanged. The more significant bytes of the product (starting at address PROD) are undefined.

```
;
;       Title:                  Multiple-Precision Decimal Multiplication
;       Name:                   MPDMUL
;
;
;       Purpose:                Multiply 2 arrays of BCD bytes
;                               Multiplicand := Multiplicand X multiplier
;
;       Entry:                  TOP OF STACK
;                                 Low byte of return address
;                                 High byte of return address
;                                 Low byte of length of arrays in bytes
;                                 High byte of length of arrays in bytes (0)
;                                 Low byte of multiplicand address
;                                 High byte of multiplicand address
;                                 Low byte of multiplier address
;                                 High byte of multiplier address
;
;                                 The arrays are unsigned BCD numbers
;                                 with a maximum length of 255 bytes,
;                                 ARRAY[0] is the least significant
;                                 byte, and ARRAY[LENGTH-1] is the
;                                 most significant byte.
;
;       Exit:                   Multiplicand := Multiplicand X multiplier
;
;       Registers Used:         AX,BX,CX,DI,DX,F (clears D flag),SI
;
;       Time:                   Assuming average digit value in multiplicand
;                               is 5, then the time is approximately
;                                 (794 X length^2)+(439 X length)+84 cycles
;
;       Size:                   Program   168 bytes
;                               Data      256 bytes plus 2 stack bytes
;
;

MPDMUL:
        PUSH    BP              ;SAVE BASE POINTER
        MOV     BP,SP           ;GET BASE ADDRESS OF PARAMETERS
        MOV     CX,[BP+4]       ;GET LENGTH OF OPERANDS IN BYTES
;
;       CALCULATE DIGIT COUNTER = ARRAY LENGTH X 2
;       BIT 0 SERVES AS A DIGIT FLAG - 0 INDICATES LOW DIGIT,
;         1 HIGH DIGIT
;
        MOV     BX,CX
        SHL     BX,1            ;ARRAY LENGTH X 2
;
;       CHECK LENGTH OF OPERANDS
;       EXIT IF LENGTH IS ZERO
;
```

```
        JNZ       NONZRO             ;CONTINUE IF LENGTH NOT ZERO
                                     ;NOTE: CANNOT USE JZ EXITML
                                     ;  BECAUSE EXITML IS TOO FAR AWAY
        JMP       EXITML             ;EXIT IF LENGTH IS ZERO
;
;       CLEAR PARTIAL PRODUCT, INCLUDING OVERFLOW BYTE
;
NONZRO:
        CLD                          ;SET AUTOINCREMENTING
        INC       CX                 ;AREA SIZE = ARRAY LENGTH PLUS 1
        MOV       DI,OFFSET PROD     ;POINT TO PARTIAL PRODUCT
        SUB       AL,AL              ;GET ZERO FOR CLEARING
   REP  STOSB                        ;CLEAR ENTIRE PARTIAL PRODUCT
;
;       LOOP THROUGH ALL BYTES OF MULTIPLICAND
;       USE EACH DIGIT TO DETERMINE HOW MANY TIMES TO ADD
;        MULTIPLIER TO PARTIAL PRODUCT
;
MCNDLP:
        MOV       DI,[BP+6]          ;GET MULTIPLICAND ADDRESS
        MOV       DL,[DI]            ;GET MULTIPLICAND BYTE
;
;       LOOP THROUGH 2 DIGITS PER BYTE
;       DURING LOWER DIGIT, DIGIT FLAG = 0
;       DURING UPPER DIGIT, DIGIT FLAG = 1
;
        TEST      BX,1               ;TEST DIGIT FLAG
        JZ        LOWDGT             ;JUMP IF WORKING ON LOW DIGIT
        SHR       DL,1               ;SHIFT HIGH DIGIT TO LOW DIGIT
        SHR       DL,1
        SHR       DL,1
        SHR       DL,1
LOWDGT:
        AND       DL,0FH             ;MASK OFF HIGH DIGIT OF MULTIPLICAND
                                     ;THIS IS UNNECESSARY IF HIGH DIGIT
                                     ;  WAS SHIFTED LOGICALLY, BUT IT
                                     ;  WOULD BE SLOWER TO BRANCH AROUND
                                     ;  IT THAN TO SIMPLY DO IT
        JZ        STRDGT             ;SKIP MULTIPLY LOOP IF DIGIT IS 0

;
;       ADD MULTIPLIER TO PRODUCT NUMBER OF TIMES GIVEN BY
;        DIGIT OF MULTIPLICAND
;
        MOV       SI,[BP+8]          ;GET MULTIPLIER ADDRESS
        MOV       DI,OFFSET PROD     ;GET PARTIAL PRODUCT ADDRESS
        MOV       CX,[BP+4]          ;GET ARRAY LENGTH
MPLRLP:
        MOV       AL,[DI]            ;GET PARTIAL PRODUCT BYTE
        MOV       DH,DL              ;SAVE MULTIPLICAND DIGIT
        SUB       AH,AH              ;CLEAR HIGH BYTE OF PRODUCT
ADDLP:
        ADD       AL,[SI]            ;ADD MULTIPLIER TO PARTIAL PRODUCT
        DAA                          ;MAKE SUM DECIMAL
        ADC       AH,0               ;ADD CARRY TO HIGH BYTE (NO DECIMAL
                                     ;  ADJUST NEEDED HERE SINCE HIGH BYTE
```

```
                                        ;  NEVER EXCEEDS 9)
        DEC     DH                      ;COUNT DOWN MULTIPLICAND DIGIT
        JNZ     ADDLP
        STOSB                           ;STORE RESULT IN PARTIAL PRODUCT
        MOV     AL,AH                   ;GET HIGH BYTE OF RESULT
        ADD     AL,[DI]                 ;ADD TO NEXT BYTE OF PRODUCT
        DAA                             ;MAKE SUM DECIMAL
        MOV     [DI],AL                 ;STORE RESULT IN PRODUCT
        JNC     MPLEND                  ;JUMP IF NO FURTHER CARRIES
        PUSH    DI                      ;SAVE PRODUCT POINTER
        INC     DI                      ;POINT TO NEXT BYTE OF PRODUCT
CRYTHR:
        MOV     AL,[DI]                 ;PROPAGATE CARRY TO NEXT BYTE
        ADD     AL,1
        DAA                             ;MAKE INCREMENT DECIMAL
        STOSB
        JC      CRYTHR                  ;CONTINUE PROPAGATING CARRY
        POP     DI                      ;RESTORE PRODUCT POINTER
MPLEND:
        INC     SI                      ;POINT TO NEXT MULTIPLIER BYTE
        LOOP    MPLRLP                  ;RESTORE PRODUCT POINTER
;
;       STORE LEAST SIGNIFICANT DIGIT OF UPPER PRODUCT AS
;         NEXT DIGIT OF MULTIPLICAND
;
STRDGT:
        MOV     SI,[BP+6]               ;POINT TO MULTIPLICAND
        MOV     AH,[SI]                 ;GET MULTIPLICAND BYTE
        MOV     DI,OFFSET PROD          ;POINT TO PARTIAL PRODUCT
        MOV     AL,[DI]                 ;GET LEAST SIGNIFICANT BYTE OF
                                        ;  PARTIAL PRODUCT
        AND     AL,0FH                  ;MASK OFF HIGH DIGIT OF PRODUCT
        TEST    BX,1                    ;TEST DIGIT FLAG
        JNZ     HIGHDGT                 ;JUMP IF WORKING ON HIGH DIGIT
        AND     AH,0F0H                 ;MASK OFF LOW DIGIT OF MULTIPLICAND
        JMP     ORDIGT                  ;SKIP HIGH DIGIT MASKING
HIGHDGT:
        AND     AH,0FH                  ;MASK OFF HIGH DIGIT OF MULTIPLICAND
        SHL     AL,1                    ;SHIFT PRODUCT DIGIT TO HIGH DIGIT
        SHL     AL,1
        SHL     AL,1
        SHL     AL,1
        INC     WORD PTR [BP+6]         ;INCREMENT MULTIPLICAND POINTER
ORDIGT:
        OR      AL,AH                   ;OR DIGITS TOGETHER
        MOV     [SI],AL                 ;SAVE RESULT IN MULTIPLICAND
;
;       SHIFT PARTIAL PRODUCT RIGHT 1 DIGIT (4 BITS)
;
        MOV     CX,[BP+4]               ;GET ARRAY LENGTH
SHRDGT:
        MOV     AX,[DI]                 ;GET TWO BYTES OF PRODUCT
        SHR     AX,1                    ;SHIFT RIGHT 4 BITS
        SHR     AX,1
        SHR     AX,1
        SHR     AX,1
```

```
        STOSB                       ;STORE LOW BYTE IN PRODUCT
        LOOP    SHRDGT              ;LOOP TO SHIFT ALL BYTES
;
;       CHECK IF MORE MULTIPLICAND DIGITS LEFT
;
        DEC     BX                  ;DECREMENT DIGIT COUNTER
        JZ      EXITML              ;EXIT IF ALL MULTIPLICAND DIGITS
        JMP     MCNDLP              ;  ARE DONE - CANNOT USE JNZ HERE
                                    ;  SINCE MCNDLP IS TOO FAR AWAY
;
;       REMOVE PARAMETERS FROM STACK AND EXIT
;
EXITML:
        POP     BP                  ;RESTORE BASE POINTER
        RET     6                   ;RETURN, DISCARDING PARAMETERS FROM
                                    ;  STACK
;
;       DATA
;
PROD    DB      256 DUP(0)          ;PRODUCT BUFFER WITH OVERFLOW BYTE

;
;
;       SAMPLE EXECUTION
;
;

SC3H:
        MOV     BX,[AY2ADR]     ;GET MULTIPLIER
        PUSH    BX
        MOV     BX,[AY1ADR]     ;GET MULTIPLICAND
        PUSH    BX
        MOV     AX,SZAYS        ;GET LENGTH OF ARRAYS IN BYTES
        CALL    MPDMUL          ;MULTIPLE-PRECISION DECIMAL MULTIPLICATION
                                ;RESULT OF 1234H X 5718H = 7056012H
                                ; IN MEMORY AY1    = 12H
                                ;           AY1+1  = 60H
                                ;           AY1+2  = 05H
                                ;           AY1+3  = 07H
                                ;           AY1+4  = 00H
                                ;           AY1+5  = 00H
                                ;           AY1+6  = 00H
        JMP     SC3H            ;REPEAT TEST

SZAYS   EQU     7               ;LENGTH OF ARRAYS IN BYTES

AY1ADR  DB      AY1             ;BASE ADDRESS OF ARRAY 1
AY2ADR  DB      AY2             ;BASE ADDRESS OF ARRAY 2

AY1     DB      34H,12H,0,0,0,0,0       ;MULTIPLICAND
AY2     DB      18H,57H,0,0,0,0,0       ;MULTIPLIER

        END
```

3I Multiple-precision decimal division (MPDDIV)

Divides two multi-byte unsigned decimal (BCD) numbers. Both numbers are stored with their least significant digits at the lowest address. The quotient replaces the dividend; the base address of the remainder is also returned. The length of the numbers (in bytes) is 255 or less. The Carry flag is cleared if no errors occur; if a divide by 0 is attempted, the Carry flag is set to 1, the dividend is unchanged, and the remainder is set to 0.

Procedure The program divides by determining how many times the divisor can be subtracted from the dividend. It saves that number in the quotient, makes the remainder into the new dividend, and rotates the dividend and the quotient left one digit.

Entry conditions

Order in stack (starting from the top)

Low byte of return address
High byte of return address

Low byte of length of operands in bytes
High byte of length of operands in bytes (always 0)

Low byte of base address of divisor
High byte of base address of divisor

Low byte of base address of dividend
High byte of base address of dividend

Exit conditions

Dividend replaced by dividend divided by divisor
If the divisor is non-zero, Carry = 0 and the result is normal
If the divisor is zero, Carry = 1, the dividend is unchanged, and the remainder is zero
The base address of the remainder (i.e., the address of its least significant digits) is in register BX

Example

Data: Length of operands (in bytes) = 4
Dividend = 22142298_{16}
Divisor = 00006294_{16}

Result: Dividend = 00003518_{16}
Remainder (base address in BX) = 00000006_{16}
Carry = 0, indicating no divide-by-zero error

Registers used AX, BX, CX, DI, DX, F (clears D flag), SI

Execution time Depends on the length of the operands and on the size of the digits in the quotient (determining how many times the divisor must be subtracted from the dividend). If the average digit in the quotient has a value of 5, the execution time is approximately

$$1224 \times \text{LENGTH}^2 + 1185 \times \text{LENGTH} + 195 \text{ cycles}$$

where LENGTH is the length of the operands in bytes. If, for example, LENGTH = 6 (12 digits), the approximate execution time is

$$\begin{aligned} 1224 \times 6^2 + 1185 \times 6 + 195 &= 1224 \times 36 + 7110 + 195 \\ &= 44\,064 + 7305 \\ &= 51\,369 \text{ cycles} \end{aligned}$$

Program size 152 bytes

Data memory required 514 bytes anywhere in RAM. This includes the buffers holding either the high dividend or the result of the trial subtraction (255 bytes each starting at addresses HIDE1 and HIDE2, respectively), and for the pointers that assign the buffers to specific purposes (2 bytes each starting at addresses HDEPTR and DIFPTR, respectively). Also 2 stack bytes.

Special cases

1. A length of 0 causes an immediate exit with the Carry flag cleared, the quotient equal to the original dividend, and the remainder undefined.

2. A divisor of 0 causes an exit with the Carry flag set to 1, the quotient equal to the original dividend, and the remainder equal to 0.

```
;
;
;
;
;       Title:                  Multiple-Precision Decimal Division
;       Name:                   MPDDIV
;
;
;
;       Purpose:                Divide 2 arrays of BCD bytes
;                               Quotient := Dividend / divisor
;
;       Entry:                  TOP OF STACK
;                                 Low byte of return address
;                                 High byte of return address
;                                 Low byte of operand length in bytes
;                                 High byte of operand length in bytes (0)
;                                 Low byte of divisor address
;                                 High byte of divisor address
;                                 Low byte of dividend address
;                                 High byte of dividend address
;
;                                 The arrays are unsigned BCD numbers
;                                 with a maximum length of 255 bytes,
;                                 ARRAY[0] is the least significant
;                                 byte, and ARRAY[LENGTH-1] is the
;                                 most significant byte.
;
;       Exit:                   Dividend := dividend / divisor
;                               If no errors then
;                                 Carry := 0
;                                 Dividend unchanged
;                                 Remainder := 0
;
;       Registers Used:         AX,BX,CX,DI,DX,F (clears D flag),SI
;
;       Time:                   Assuming the average digit value in the
;                               quotient is 5, then the time is approximately
;                                  (1224 X length^2) + (1185 X length) +
;                                  195 cycles
;
;       Size:                   Program  151 bytes
;                               Data     514 bytes plus 3 stack bytes
;
;


;
;       CHECK LENGTH OF OPERANDS
;       EXIT WITH CARRY CLEARED IF LENGTH IS ZERO
;
MPDDIV:
```

```
        PUSH    BP              ;SAVE BASE POINTER
        MOV     BP,SP           ;GET BASE ADDRESS OF PARAMETER AREA
        MOV     CX,[BP+4]       ;GET LENGTH OF OPERANDS
        MOV     DX,CX           ;SAVE LENGTH
        TEST    CX,CX           ;CHECK FOR ZERO LENGTH
        JNZ     STRDIV          ;JUMP IF LENGTH NOT ZERO
        JMP     GOODRT          ;BRANCH (GOOD EXIT) IF LENGTH IS ZERO
                                ;CANNOT USE JCXZ OR JZ HERE BECAUSE
                                ;  GOODRT IS TOO FAR AWAY
;
;       SET UP HIGH DIVIDEND AND DIFFERENCE POINTERS
;       CLEAR HIGH DIVIDEND AND DIFFERENCE ARRAYS
;       ARRAYS 1 AND 2 ARE USED INTERCHANGEABLY FOR THESE TWO
;         PURPOSES.  THE POINTERS ARE SWITCHED WHENEVER A
;         TRIAL SUBTRACTION SUCCEEDS
;
STRDIV:
        CLD                     ;SET AUTOINCREMENTING
        MOV     SI,OFFSET HIDE1 ;GET BASE ADDRESS OF ARRAY 1
        MOV     [HDEPTR],SI     ;DIVIDEND POINTER = ARRAY 1
        MOV     DI,OFFSET HIDE2 ;GET BASE ADDRESS OF ARRAY 2
        MOV     [DIFPTR],DI     ;DIFFERENCE POINTER = ARRAY 2
        SUB     AL,AL           ;GET ZERO FOR CLEARING ARRAYS
CLRHI:
        MOV     [SI],AL         ;CLEAR BYTE OF DIVIDEND
        INC     SI              ;INCREMENT DIVIDEND POINTER
        STOSB                   ;CLEAR BYTE OF DIFFERENCE AND
                                ;  INCREMENT DIFFERENCE POINTER
        LOOP    CLRHI           ;CONTINUE THROUGH ALL BYTES
;
;       CHECK WHETHER DIVISOR IS ZERO
;       IF IT IS, EXIT INDICATING DIVIDE-BY-ZERO ERROR
;
        MOV     CX,DX           ;GET LENGTH OF OPERANDS
        MOV     DI,[BP+6]       ;GET BASE ADDRESS OF DIVISOR
        SUB     AL,AL           ;GET ZERO FOR COMPARISON
REPE    SCASB                   ;SCAN DIVISOR UNTIL ALL BYTES EXAMINED
                                ;  OR NON-ZERO BYTE FOUND
        JNE     INITDV          ;BRANCH IF NON-ZERO BYTE FOUND
        STC                     ;ALL BYTES ARE ZERO - INDICATE
                                ;  DIVIDE-BY-ZERO ERROR
        JMP     DVEXIT          ;EXIT INDICATING ERROR
;
;       DIVIDE USING TRIAL SUBTRACTIONS
;
INITDV:
;
;       SHIFT QUOTIENT AND UPPER DIVIDEND LEFT AND DO TRIAL
;         SUBTRACTION FOR EACH DIGIT IN THE ARRAY LENGTH
;
        MOV     CX,DX           ;GET ARRAY LENGTH
        SHL     CX,1            ;MULTIPLY LENGTH TIMES 2
        INC     CX              ;NEED TO DO 1 EXTRA SHIFT
        MOV     [BP+4],CX       ;SAVE SHIFT COUNT ON STACK
;
;       SHIFT QUOTIENT AND UPPER DIVIDEND LEFT 1 DIGIT (4 BITS)
```

```
;         CARRY IN IS THE RESULT FROM THE PREVIOUS SUBTRACTION
;         POINTER TO UPPER DIVIDEND IS IN HDEPTR
;
          MOV       AH,0            ;CLEAR RESULT TO START
DIVSET:
          MOV       BX,4            ;NUMBER OF SHIFTS = 4
DIVLUP:
          SHL       AH,1            ;SHIFT RESULT INTO CARRY
          MOV       CX,DX           ;GET ARRAY LENGTH
          MOV       DI,[BP+8]       ;GET QUOTIENT ADDRESS
;
;         SHIFT QUOTIENT LEFT 1 BIT, CARRY IN IS RESULT OF
;           PREVIOUS TRIAL SUBTRACTION
;
SHFTQT:
          RCL       BYTE PTR [DI],1     ;SHIFT QUOTIENT BYTE LEFT
          INC       DI              ;POINT TO NEXT BYTE
          LOOP      SHFTQT          ;SHIFT ALL BYTES OF QUOTIENT
;
;         SHIFT UPPER DIVIDEND LEFT WITH CARRY FROM LOWER DIVIDEND
;
          MOV       CX,DX           ;GET ARRAY LENGTH
          MOV       DI,[HDEPTR]     ;GET ADDRESS OF UPPER DIVIDEND
SHFTDV:
          RCL       BYTE PTR [DI],1 ;SHIFT UPPER DIVIDEND BYTE LEFT
          INC       DI              ;POINT TO NEXT BYTE
          LOOP      SHFTDV          ;SHIFT ARRAY LENGTH BYTES
          DEC       BX              ;CHECK IF MORE SHIFTS NEEDED
          JNZ       DIVLUP
;
;         CHECK IF QUOTIENT HAS BEEN SHIFTED ENOUGH TIMES
;         EXIT WITH RESULT IF SO, ELSE DO NEXT SUBTRACTION
;
          DEC       WORD PTR [BP+4] ;DECREMENT SHIFT COUNT
          JZ        GOODRT          ;EXIT IF DONE
;
;         TRIAL SUBTRACTION OF DIVISOR FROM DIVIDEND
;         SAVE DIFFERENCE IN CASE IT IS NEEDED LATER
;
;         NEXT DIGIT OF QUOTIENT IS RESULT OF SUBTRACTION
;         10 IS ADDED FOR EACH SUCCESSFUL SUBTRACTION
;         SUCCESSFUL SUBTRACTION GENERATES NO BORROW
;
          SUB       AH,AH           ;CLEAR RESULT STORAGE AREA
SUBSET:
          MOV       SI,[HDEPTR]     ;GET UPPER DIVIDEND POINTER
          MOV       BX,[BP+6]       ;GET DIVISOR POINTER
          MOV       DI,[DIFPTR]     ;GET DIFFERENCE POINTER
          CLC                       ;CLEAR BORROW INITIALLY
          MOV       CX,DX           ;GET ARRAY LENGTH
SUBDVS:
          LODSB                     ;GET BYTE OF DIVIDEND
          SBB       AL,[BX]         ;SUBTRACT BYTE OF DIVIDEND
          DAS                       ;MAKE SUBTRACTION DECIMAL
          STOSB                     ;SAVE DIFFERENCE IN BUFFER
          INC       BX              ;INCREMENT DIVISOR POINTER
```

```
        LOOP    SUBDVS          ;COUNT BYTES
        JNC     SUCSES          ;NO BORROW - TRIAL SUBTRACTION
                                ;  SUCCEEDED
        JMP     DIVSET          ;BORROW - TRIAL SUBTRACTION FAILED SO
                                ;  DO NEXT SHIFT
;
;       TRIAL SUBTRACTION SUCCEEDED
;       REPLACE UPPER DIVIDEND WITH DIFFERENCE BY SWITCHING POINTERS
;
SUCSES:
        ADD     AH,10H          ;ADD 10 FOR GOOD SUBTRACTION
                                ;NO NEED TO DECIMAL ADJUST HERE
                                ;  SINCE DIGIT NEVER EXCEEDS 9
        MOV     CX,[HDEPTR]     ;GET OLD DIVIDEND POINTER
        XCHG    CX,[DIFPTR]     ;DIVIDEND POINTER BECOMES NEW
                                ;  DIFFERENCE POINTER FOR NEXT
                                ;  ITERATION
        MOV     [HDEPTR],CX     ;DIFFERENCE BECOMES DIVIDEND
                                ;  FOR NEXT ITERATION
        JMP     SUBSET          ;DO NEXT TRIAL SUBTRACTION
;
;       CLEAR CARRY TO INDICATE NO ERRORS
;
GOODRT:
        CLC                     ;CLEAR CARRY - NO DIVIDE-BY-ZERO
                                ;  ERROR
;
;       REMOVE PARAMETERS FROM STACK AND EXIT
;
EXITDV:
        MOV     BX,[HDEPTR]     ;GET BASE ADDRESS OF REMAINDER
        POP     BP              ;RESTORE BASE POINTER
        RET     6               ;RETURN, DISCARDING PARAMETERS
                                ;  FROM STACK

;
;       DATA
;
HDEPTR  DW      0               ;POINTER TO HIGH DIVIDEND
DIFPTR  DW      0               ;POINTER TO DIFFERENCE BETWEEN HIGH
                                ;  DIVIDEND AND DIVISOR
HIDE1   DB      255 DUP(0)      ;HIGH DIVIDEND BUFFER 1
HIDE2   DB      255 DUP(0)      ;HIGH DIVIDEND BUFFER 2

;
;
;       SAMPLE EXECUTION
;
;

SC3I:
        MOV     BX,[AY1ADR]     ;GET DIVIDEND
        PUSH    BX
        MOV     BX,[AY2ADR]     ;GET DIVISOR
        PUSH    BX
```

```
MOV         AX,SZAYS                  ;GET LENGTH OF ARRAYS IN BYTES
            PUSH        AX
            CALL        MPDDIV        ;MULTIPLE-PRECISION DECIMAL DIVISION
                                      ;RESULT OF 3822756 / 1234 = 3097
                                      ; IN MEMORY AY1      = 97H
                                      ;           AY1+1    = 30H
                                      ;           AY1+2    = 00H
                                      ;           AY1+3    = 00H
                                      ;           AY1+4    = 00H
                                      ;           AY1+5    = 00H
                                      ;           AY1+6    = 00H
            JMP         SC3I          ;REPEAT TEST

SZAYS       EQU         7             ;LENGTH OF ARRAYS IN BYTES

AY1ADR      DW          AY1           ;BASE ADDRESS OF ARRAY 1 (DIVIDEND)
AY2ADR      DW          AY2           ;BASE ADDRESS OF ARRAY 2 (DIVISOR)

AY1         DB          56H,27H,82H,03H,0,0,0          ;DIVIDEND
AY2         DB          34H,12H,0,0,0,0,0,0            ;DIVISOR

            END
```

3J Multiple-precision decimal comparison

Compares two multi-byte unsigned decimal (BCD) numbers, setting the Carry and Zero flags. Both numbers are stored with their least significant bytes at the lowest address. Sets the Zero flag to 1 if the operands are equal and to 0 otherwise. Sets the Carry flag to 1 if the subtrahend is larger than the minuend and to 0 otherwise. It thus sets the flags as if it had subtracted the subtrahend from the minuend.

Note This program is exactly the same as Subroutine 3E, the multiple-precision binary comparison, since the form of the operands does not matter if they are only being compared. See Subroutine 3E for a listing and other details.

Entry conditions

Order in stack (starting from the top)

Low significant byte of return address
High significant byte of return address

Low byte of length of operands in bytes
High byte of length of operands in bytes

Low byte of base address of subtrahend
High byte of base address of subtrahend

Low byte of base address of minuend
High byte of base address of minuend

Exit conditions

Flags set as if subtrahend had been subtracted from minuend

Zero flag = 1 if subtrahend and minuend are equal, 0 if they are not equal

Carry flag = 1 if subtrahend is larger than minuend in the unsigned sense, 0 if it less than or equal to the minuend

Examples

1. Data: Length of operands (in bytes) = 6
   Top operand (subtrahend) = 196528719340_{16}
   Bottom operand (minuend) = 456780153266_{16}
   Result: Zero flag = 0 (operands are not equal)
   Carry flag = 0 (subtrahend is not larger than minuend)
2. Data: Length of operands (in bytes) = 6
   Top operand (subtrahend) = 196528719340_{16}
   Bottom operand (minuend) = 196528719340_{16}
   Result: Zero flag = 1 (operands are equal)
   Carry flag = 0 (subtrahend is not larger than minuend)
3. Data: Length of operands (in bytes) = 6
   Top operand (subtrahend) = 196528719340_{16}
   Bottom operand (minuend) = 073785991074_{16}
   Result: Zero flag = 0 (operands are not equal)
   Carry flag = 1 (subtrahend is larger than minuend)

3K 8087 interface package (INTADD, FPADD, FPSUB, FPMUL, FPDIV, FPCOM)

Provides six sample routines that add, subtract, multiply, divide, and compare using the 8087 numeric data processor (NDP). Two separate addition routines handle integers and real (floating point) numbers, respectively. The 8087 NDP acts as a coprocessor for the 8086, executing a set of instructions that the 8086 ignores. The two devices thus run in parallel with a special synchronizing connection through the 8086's TEST input; the WAIT or FWAIT instructions check this input before proceeding.

Procedure Each routine pushes the secondary operand onto the 8087's stack, performs the operation with the primary operand, and finally saves the result in place of the primary operand. The comparison, of course, does not produce a result; it merely sets the flags. No error or exception checking is provided. The primary operand is the minuend in subtraction and comparison, the multiplicand in multiplication, and the dividend in division. The secondary operand is the subtrahend in subtraction and comparison, the multiplier in multiplication, and the divisor in division.

The routines handle synchronization between the 8086 CPU and the 8087 NDP. Each 8087 data manipulation or data transfer instruction automatically begins with a test (FWAIT) of whether the NDP is ready (i.e. whether it has finished its previous operation). The actual instruction is not executed until this test is satisfied. A final FWAIT instruction waits for the NDP to complete its last operation, thus ensuring a valid result in memory.

Discussion

The 8087 numeric data processor performs arithmetic operations on the following data types:

Data type	Bits	Significant digits (decimal)	Approximate range
Word integer	16	4	−32 768 to +32 767
Short integer	32	9	-2×10^9 to 2×10^9
Long integer	64	18	-9×10^{19} to 9×10^{19}
Packed decimal	80	18	−99...99 to 99...99
Short real	32	6–7	8.43×10^{-37} to 3.37×10^{38}
Long real	64	15–16	4.19×10^{-307} to 1.67×10^{308}
Temporary real	80	19	3.4×10^{-4932} to 1.2×10^{4932}

Note The short real format corresponds to IEEE Standard 754's single-width floating point numbers, the long real format to double-width floating point numbers, and the temporary real format to double-width extended floating point numbers.

The 8087 NDP performs most operations on data from a stack consisting of eight 80-bit registers. It automatically converts all data to the temporary real (80-bit) format before pushing it onto the stack. The 8087 has separate push and pop instructions for three classes of data: real, integer, and packed decimal. A pop instruction transforms data from the stack's temporary real format into the specified format.

The ASM86 and similar assemblers provide the following storage allocation directives for numeric data types:

Directive	Bytes	Pointer type	Data type
DB—define byte	1	BYTE PTR	Byte
DW—define word	2	WORD PTR	Word integer
DD—define doubleword	4	DWORD PTR	Short integer, short real
DQ—define quadword	8	QWORD PTR	Long integer, long real
DT—define tenbyte	10	TBYTE PTR	Packed decimal, temporary real

The assembler accepts integers, decimal numbers, or numbers written in scientific notation (i.e. decimal fraction, the letter E, and an exponent or power of 10) as values in DD, DQ, and DT directives. Values that have no decimal point and are not in scientific notation are assumed to be integers.

Entry conditions

Order in stack (starting from the top)

Low byte of return address
High byte of return address

Low byte of address of secondary operand
High byte of address of secondary operand

Low byte of address of primary operand
High byte of address of primary operand

Exit conditions

Primary operand replaced by result of operation except for a comparison, which does not change either operand. The result is the sum in addition, the difference in subtraction, the product in multiplication, and the quotient in division. A comparison sets the flags as if the subtrahend (secondary operand) had been subtracted from the minuend (primary operand). That is:

Zero flag = 1 if operands are equal, 0 if they are not equal
Carry flag = 1 if subtrahend is larger than minuend in the unsigned sense, 0 if it is less than or equal to the minuend.

Examples

1. INTADD
   Data: Primary operand = 123456 (1E240 hex)
   Secondary operand = 121212 (1D97C hex)
   Result: Primary operand = Primary operand + Secondary operand = 244668 (3BBBC hex)

2. FPADD
   Data: Primary operand = 12.456
   Secondary operand = 121.12
   Result: Primary operand = Primary operand + Secondary operand = 133.576

3. FPSUB
   Data: Primary operand (minuend) = 546.123
   Secondary operand (subtrahend) = 121.12
   Result: Primary operand = Primary operand − Secondary operand = 425.003

4. FPMUL
   Data: Primary operand (multiplicand) = 546.123
   Secondary operand (multiplier) = 121.12
   Result: Primary operand = Primary operand × Secondary operand = 66146.418

5. FPDIV
   Data: Primary operand (dividend) = 1694.25
   Secondary operand (divisor) = 125.5
   Result: Primary operand = Primary operand/Secondary operand = 13.5

6. FPCOM

(a)

Data: Primary operand (minuend) = 15750.25
Secondary operand (subtrahend) = 125.5

Result: Zero flag = 0 (operands are not equal)
Carry flag = 0 (secondary operand is not larger than primary operand)

(b)

Data: Primary operand (minuend) = 121.5
Secondary operand (subtrahend) = 125.5

Result: Zero flag = 0 (operands are not equal)
Carry flag = 1 (secondary operand is larger than primary operand)

(c)

Data: Primary operand (minuend) = 546.123
Secondary operand (subtrahend) = 546.123

Result: Zero flag = 1 (operands are equal)
Carry flag = 0 (secondary operand is not larger than primary operand)

References

Binary Floating-Point Arithmetic, Standard for (IEEE Std 754-1985), IEEE, Piscataway, NJ, 1985.

G. W. Gorsline, *16-Bit Modern Microcomputers: The Intel I8086 Family*, Prentice-Hall, Englewood Cliffs, NJ, 1985, Chapter 6.

R. Startz, *8087 Applications and Programming for the IBM PC and Other PCs*, Brady/Prentice-Hall, Bowie, MD, 1984.

Registers used

1. INTADD: DI, DX
2. FPADD: DI, DX
3. FPSUB: DI, DX
4. FPMUL: DI, DX
5. FPDIV: DI, DX
6. FPCOM: AH, DI, DX, F, SI

Execution time

1. INTADD: approximately 330 cycles
2. FPADD: approximately 316 cycles
3. FPSUB: approximately 316 cycles
4. FPMUL: approximately 319 cycles
5. FPDIV: approximately 421 cycles
6. FPCOM: approximately 200 cycles

Program size

1. INTADD: 15 bytes
2. FPADD: 15 bytes
3. FPSUB: 15 bytes
4. FPMUL: 15 bytes
5. FPDIV: 15 bytes
6. FPCOM: 18 bytes

Data memory required 2 bytes at address STAT87 for FPCOM to hold the status of the 8087 chip.

Special cases None. The calling routine must handle all errors and exceptions.

```
;
;       Title:              32-Bit Integer Addition Using 8087 NDP
;
;       Name:               INTADD
;
;       Purpose:            Add two 32-bit integers using the 8087
;                           numeric data processor (NDP)
;
;
;       Entry:              TOP OF STACK
;                             Low byte of return address
;                             High byte of return address
;                             Low byte of address of operand 2
;                             High byte of address of operand 2
;                             Low byte of address of operand 1
;                             High byte of address of operand 1
;
```

```
;       Exit:                   Operand 1 := Operand 1 + Operand 2
;
;
;       Registers Used:         DI,DX
;
;       Time:                   Approximately 330 cycles
;
;       Size:                   Program  15 bytes
;

INTADD:
        ;
        ;ADD 2 32-BIT INTEGERS USING THE 8087 NDP
        ;
        POP     DX                      ;SAVE RETURN ADDRESS
        POP     DI                      ;GET ADDRESS OF OPERAND 2
        FILD    DWORD PTR [DI]          ;PUSH OPERAND 2 ON 8087 STACK
        POP     DI                      ;GET ADDRESS OF OPERAND 1
        FIADD   DWORD PTR [DI]          ;ADD OPERANDS
        FISTP   DWORD PTR [DI]          ;POP SUM INTO OPERAND 1
        FWAIT                           ;WAIT FOR 8087 TO FINISH
        JMP     DX                      ;RETURN

;
;       SAMPLE EXECUTION
;

SC3K1:
        MOV     DI,OFFSET OPER1         ;GET ADDRESS OF OPERAND 1
        PUSH    DI
        MOV     DI,OFFSET OPER2         ;GET ADDRESS OF OPERAND 2
        PUSH    DI
        CALL    INTSUM                  ;DO INTEGER ADDITION
                                        ;RESULT OF 1E240H + 1D973H
                                        ;  = 3BBBCH
                                        ; IN MEMORY OPER1      = BCH
                                        ;           OPER1+1    = BBH
                                        ;           OPER1+2    = 03H
                                        ;           OPER1+3    = 00H
        JMP     SC3K1                   ;REPEAT TEST
;
;DATA
;
OPER1   DD      123456                  ;OPERAND 1 (1E240 HEX)
OPER2   DD      121212                  ;OPERAND 2 (1D973 HEX)

        END


;
;       Title:                  Floating Point Addition Using 8087 NDP
;
;       Name:                   FPADD
;
;       Purpose:                Add 2 double-precision floating point (real)
;                               numbers using the 8087 numeric data processor
```

```
;                       (NDP)
;
;   Entry:              TOP OF STACK
;                         Low byte of return address
;                         High byte of return address
;                         Low byte of address of operand 2
;                         High byte of address of operand 2
;                         Low byte of address of operand 1
;                         High byte of address of operand 1
;
;   Exit:               Operand 1 := Operand 1 + Operand 2
;
;
;   Registers Used:     DI
;
;   Time:               Approximately 316 cycles
;
;   Size:               Program  15 bytes
;

FPADD:
        ;
        ;ADD 2 LONG (8-BYTE) REALS USING THE 8087 NDP
        ;
        POP   DX                    ;SAVE RETURN ADDRESS
        POP   DI                    ;GET ADDRESS OF OPERAND 2
        FLD   QWORD PTR [DI]        ;PUSH OPERAND 2 ON 8087 STACK
        POP   DI                    ;GET ADDRESS OF OPERAND 1
        FADD  QWORD PTR [DI]        ;ADD OPERANDS
        FSTP  QWORD PTR [DI]        ;POP SUM INTO OPERAND 1
        FWAIT                       ;WAIT FOR 8087 TO FINISH
        JMP   DX                    ;RETURN

;
        SAMPLE EXECUTION
;
;

SC3K2:
        MOV   DI,OFFSET OPER1       ;GET ADDRESS OF OPERAND 1
        PUSH  DI
        MOV   DI,OFFSET NUMB        ;GET ADDRESS OF OPERAND 2
        PUSH  DI
        CALL  FPADD                 ;DO LONG REAL ADDITION
                                    ;RESULT OF ADDING 12.456 AND
                                    ; 121.12 = 133.576
                                    ; IN MEMORY OPER1     = DFH
                                    ;           OPER1 + 1 = 4FH
                                    ;           OPER1 + 2 = 8DH
                                    ;           OPER1 + 3 = 97H
                                    ;           OPER1 + 4 = 63H
                                    ;           OPER1 + 5 = B2H
                                    ;           OPER1 + 6 = 93H
                                    ;           OPER1 + 7 = 05H
        JMP   SC3K2                 ;REPEAT TEST

;
```

```
;DATA
;DOUBLE PRECISION NUMBERS OCCUPY 4 WORDS (8 BYTES) OF MEMORY
;
OPER1     DQ     12.456              ;OPERAND 1
OPER2     DQ     121.12              ;OPERAND 2


;
;    Title:                 Floating Point Subtraction Using 8087 NDP
;
;    Name:                  FPSUB
;
;    Purpose:               Subtract 2 double-precision floating point
;                           (real) numbers using the 8087 numeric data
;                           processor (NDP)
;
;    Entry:                 TOP OF STACK
;                             Low byte of return address
;                             High byte of return address
;                             Low byte of address of subtrahend
;                             High byte of address of subtrahend
;                             Low byte of address of minuend
;                             High byte of address of minuend
;
;    Exit:                  Minuend := Minuend - Subtrahend
;
;
;    Registers Used:        DI,DX
;
;    Time:                  Approximately 316 cycles
;
;    Size:                  Program  15 bytes
;

FPSUB:
        ;
        ;SUBTRACT 2 LONG (8-BYTE) REALS USING THE 8087 NDP
        ;
        POP    DX                   ;SAVE RETURN ADDRESS
        POP    DI                   ;GET ADDRESS OF SUBTRAHEND
        FLD    QWORD PTR [DI]       ;PUSH SUBTRAHEND ON 8087 STACK
        POP    DI                   ;GET ADDRESS OF MINUEND
        FSUBR  QWORD PTR [DI]       ;MINUEND - SUBTRAHEND
        FSTP   QWORD PTR [DI]       ;POP DIFFERENCE INTO MINUEND
        FWAIT                       ;WAIT FOR 8087 TO FINISH
        JMP    DX                   ;RETURN

;
;       SAMPLE EXECUTION
;

SC3K3:
        MOV    DI,OFFSET OPER1      ;GET ADDRESS OF MINUEND
        PUSH   DI
        MOV    DI,OFFSET OPER2      ;GET ADDRESS OF SUBTRAHEND
        PUSH   DI
```

```
        CALL  FPSUB              ;DO LONG REAL SUBTRACTION
                                 ;RESULT OF 546.123 - 121.12
                                 ; = 425.003
                                 ; IN MEMORY OPER1      = 35H
                                 ;          OPER1 + 1 = 5EH
                                 ;          OPER1 + 2 = BAH
                                 ;          OPER1 + 3 = 49H
                                 ;          OPER1 + 4 = 0CH
                                 ;          OPER1 + 5 = 90H
                                 ;          OPER1 + 6 = 7AH
                                 ;          OPER1 + 7 = 40H
        JMP   SC3K3              ;REPEAT TEST

;
;DATA
;DOUBLE PRECISION NUMBERS OCCUPY 4 WORDS (8 BYTES) OF MEMORY
;
OPER1       DQ    546.123        ;MINUEND
OPER2       DQ    121.12         ;SUBTRAHEND

        END


;
;     Title:               Floating Point Multiplication Using 8087 NDP
;
;     Name:                FPMUL
;
;     Purpose:             Multiply 2 double-precision floating point
;                          (real) numbers using the 8087 numeric data
;                          processor (NDP)
;
;     Entry:               TOP OF STACK
;                            Low byte of return address
;                            High byte of return address
;                            Low byte of address of multiplier
;                            High byte of address of multiplier
;                            Low byte of address of multiplicand
;                            High byte of address of multiplicand
;
;     Exit:                Multiplicand := Multiplicand X Multiplier
;
;
;     Registers Used:      DI,DX
;
;     Time:                Approximately 319 cycles
;
;     Size:                Program  15 bytes
;

FPMUL:
        ;
        ;MULTIPLY 2 LONG (8-BYTE) REALS USING THE 8087 NDP
        ;
        POP   DX                 ;SAVE RETURN ADDRESS
        POP   DI                 ;GET ADDRESS OF MULTIPLIER
```

```
        FLD   QWORD PTR [DI]       ;PUSH MULTIPLIER ON 8087 STACK
        POP   DI                   ;GET ADDRESS OF MULTIPLICAND
        FMUL  QWORD PTR [DI]       ;MULTIPLICAND X MULTIPLIER
        FSTP  QWORD PTR [DI]       ;POP PRODUCT INTO MULTIPLICAND
        FWAIT                      ;WAIT FOR 8087 TO FINISH
        JMP   DX                   ;RETURN

;
;       SAMPLE EXECUTION

SC3K4:
        MOV   DI,OFFSET OPER1      ;GET ADDRESS OF MULTIPLICAND
        PUSH  DI
        MOV   DI,OFFSET OPER2      ;GET ADDRESS OF MULTIPLIER
        PUSH  DI
        CALL  FPMUL                ;DO LONG REAL MULTIPLICATION
                                   ;RESULT OF 546.123 X 121.12
                                   ; = 66146.41776
                                   ; IN MEMORY OPER1     = 1AH
                                   ;          OPER1 + 1 = 1CH
                                   ;          OPER1 + 2 = 25H
                                   ;          OPER1 + 3 = AFH
                                   ;          OPER1 + 4 = 26H
                                   ;          OPER1 + 5 = 26H
                                   ;          OPER1 + 6 = F0H
                                   ;          OPER1 + 7 = 40H
        JMP   SC3K4                ;REPEAT TEST

;
;DATA
;DOUBLE PRECISION NUMBERS OCCUPY 4 WORDS (8 BYTES) OF MEMORY
;
OPER1   DQ    546.123              ;MULTIPLICAND
OPER2   DQ    121.12               ;MULTIPLIER

        END

;
;    Title:               Floating Point Division Using 8087 NDP
;
;    Name:                FPDIV
;
;    Purpose:             Divide 2 double-precision floating point
;                         (real) numbers using the 8087 numeric data
;                         processor (NDP)
;
;    Entry:               TOP OF STACK
;                           Low byte of return address
;                           High byte of return address
;                           Low byte of address of divisor
;                           High byte of address of divisor
;                           Low byte of address of dividend
;                           High byte of address of dividend
;
;    Exit:                Dividend := Dividend / Divisor
;
```

```
;
;    Registers Used:         DI,DX
;
;    Time:                   Approximately 421 cycles
;
;    Size:                   Program  15 bytes
;

FPDIV:
        ;
        ;DIVIDE 2 LONG (8-BYTE) REALS USING THE 8087 NDP
        ;
        POP   DX                  ;SAVE RETURN ADDRESS
        POP   DI                  ;GET ADDRESS OF DIVISOR
        FLD   QWORD PTR [DI]      ;PUSH DIVISOR ON 8087 STACK
        POP   DI                  ;GET ADDRESS OF DIVIDEND
        FDIVR QWORD PTR [DI]      ;DIVIDEND / DIVISOR
        FSTP  QWORD PTR [DI]      ;POP QUOTIENT INTO DIVIDEND
        FWAIT                     ;WAIT FOR 8087 TO FINISH
        JMP   DX                  ;RETURN

;
;       SAMPLE EXECUTION

SC3K5:
        MOV   DI,OFFSET OPER1     ;GET ADDRESS OF DIVIDEND
        PUSH  DI
        MOV   DI,OFFSET OPER2     ;GET ADDRESS OF DIVISOR
        PUSH  DI
        CALL  FPDIV               ;DO LONG REAL DIVISION
                                  ;RESULT OF 1694.25 / 125.5
                                  ; = 13.5
                                  ; IN MEMORY OPER1     = 00H
                                  ;         OPER1 + 1 = 00H
                                  ;         OPER1 + 2 = 00H
                                  ;         OPER1 + 3 = 00H
                                  ;         OPER1 + 4 = 00H
                                  ;         OPER1 + 5 = 00H
                                  ;         OPER1 + 6 = 2BH
                                  ;         OPER1 + 7 = 40H
        JMP   SC3K5               ;REPEAT TEST

;
;DATA
;DOUBLE PRECISION NUMBERS OCCUPY 4 WORDS (8 BYTES) OF MEMORY
;
OPER1   DQ    1694.25             ;DIVIDEND
OPER2   DQ    125.5               ;DIVISOR

        END


;
;    Title:                  Floating Point Comparison Using 8087 NDP
;
;    Name:                   FPCOM
;
```

```
;       Purpose:                Compare 2 single-precision floating point
;                               (real) numbers using the 8087 numeric data
;                               processor (NDP).  Return the Carry and
;                               Zero flags set or cleared.
;
;       Entry:                  TOP OF STACK
;                                 Low byte of return address
;                                 High byte of return address
;                                 Low byte of address of subtrahend
;                                 High byte of address of subtrahend
;                                 Low byte of address of minuend
;                                 High byte of address of minuend
;
;       Exit:                   IF minuend = subtrahend THEN
;                                 C=0,Z=1
;                               IF minuend > subtrahend THEN
;                                 C=0,Z=0
;                               IF minuend < subtrahend THEN
;                                 C=1,Z=0
;                               IF minuend and subtrahend cannot be compared,
;                                 THEN C=1,Z=1 (i.e., one operand is infinite
;                                 or has an illegal or improper value)
;
;
;       Registers Used:         AH,DI,DX,F,SI
;
;       Time:                   Approximately 200 cycles
;
;       Size:                   Program  18 bytes
;                               Data      2 bytes
;

FPCOM:
        ;
        ;COMPARE 2 LONG (8-BYTE) REALS USING THE 8087 NDP
        ;
        POP     DX                      ;SAVE RETURN ADDRESS
        POP     DI                      ;GET ADDRESS OF SUBTRAHEND
        POP     SI                      ;GET ADDRESS OF MINUEND
        FLD     QWORD PTR [SI]          ;PUSH MINUEND ON 8087 STACK
        FCOM    QWORD PTR [DI]          ;COMPARE MINUEND TO SUBTRAHEND
                                        ;  I.E., MINUEND-SUBTRAHEND
        FSTSW   STAT87                  ;GET STATUS FLAGS FROM 8087
        FWAIT                           ;WAIT FOR 8087 TO FINISH
        MOV     AH,[STAT87+1]           ;SET PROCESSOR FLAGS FROM 8087
        SAHF
        JMP     DX                      ;RETURN


;
;       SAMPLE EXECUTION

SC3K6:
        MOV     DI,OFFSET OPER1         ;GET ADDRESS OF MINUEND
        PUSH    DI
        MOV     DI,OFFSET OPER2         ;GET ADDRESS OF SUBTRAHEND
```

```
        PUSH  DI
        CALL  FPCOM                   ;DO LONG REAL COMPARISON
                                      ;RESULT OF COMPARE (15750.25,
                                      ; 125.5) IS C=0, Z=0
        JMP   SC3K6                   ;REPEAT TEST

;
;DATA
;DOUBLE PRECISION NUMBERS OCCUPY 8 BYTES (4 WORDS) OF MEMORY
;
OPER1   DD    15750.25                ;MINUEND
OPER2   DD    125.5                   ;SUBTRAHEND
STAT87  DW    0                       ;TEMPORARY STORAGE FOR 8087
                                      ;  STATUS
        END
```

4 Bit manipulation and shifts

4A Bit field extraction (BFE)

Extracts a field of bits from a word and returns it in the least significant bit positions. The width of the field and its lowest bit position are specified. This operation is useful in graphics, compilation, database management, and other applications where bit fields contain attributes such as colour, record type, or identifier type.

Procedure The program obtains a mask consisting of right-justified 1 bits covering the field's width. It shifts the mask left to align it with the specified lowest bit position and obtains the field by logically ANDing the mask with the data. It then normalizes the bit field by shifting it right until it starts in bit 0.

Entry conditions

Order in stack (starting from the top)

Low byte of return address
High byte of return address

Starting (lowest) bit position in the field (0–15)

Width of the field in bits (0–15)

Low byte of data
High byte of data

Exit conditions

Bit field in register AX (normalized to bit 0)

Examples

1\. Data: Value = $F67C_{16} = 1111011001111100_2$
Lowest bit position = 4
Width of field in bits = 8

Result: Bit field = $0067_{16} = 0000000001100111_2$
We have extracted 8 bits from the original data, starting with bit 4 (i.e. bits 4–11)

2\. Data: Value = $A2D4_{16} = 1010001011010100_2$
Lowest bit position = 6
Width of field in bits = 5

Result: Bit field = $000B_{16} = 0000000000001011_2$
We have extracted 5 bits from the original data, starting with bit 6 (i.e. bits 6–10)

Registers used AX, BX, CX, DX, F, SI

Execution time 8 × LOWEST BIT POSITION plus 89 cycles overhead. The lowest bit position determines how many times the program must shift the mask left and the bit field right. For example, if the field starts in bit 6, the execution time is

$$8 \times 6 + 89 = 48 + 89 = 137 \text{ cycles}$$

Program size 61 bytes (including the table of masks)

Data memory required None

Special cases

1. Requesting a field that would extend beyond the end of the word causes the program to return with only the bits through bit 15. That is, no wraparound is provided. If, for example, the user asks for a 10-bit field starting at bit 8, the program will return only 8 bits (bits 8–15).

2. Both the lowest bit position and the number of bits in the field are interpreted mod 16. For example, bit position 17 is equivalent to bit position 1 and a field of 20 bits is equivalent to a field of 4 bits.

3. Requesting a field of 0 width causes a return with a result of 0.

```
;
;
;
;
;       Title:                  Bit Field Extraction
;       Name:                   BFE
;
;
;
;       Purpose:                Extract a field of bits from a 16-bit
;                               word and return the field normalized
;                               to bit 0.
;                               NOTE: IF THE REQUESTED FIELD IS TOO
;                                     LONG, THEN ONLY THE BITS THROUGH
;                                     BIT 15 WILL BE RETURNED.  FOR
;                                     EXAMPLE, IF A 4 BIT FIELD IS
;                                     REQUESTED STARTING AT BIT 15 THEN
;                                     ONLY 1 BIT (BIT 15) WILL BE
;                                     RETURNED.
;
;       Entry:                  TOP OF STACK
;                                 Low byte of return address
;                                 High byte of return address
;                                 Lowest (starting) bit position in
;                                   the field (0..15)
;                                 Width of field in bits (0..15)
;                                 Low byte of data
;                                 High byte of data
;
;       Exit:                   Register AX = Field (normalized to bit 0)
;
;       Registers Used:         AX,BX,CX,DX,F,SI
;
;       Time:                   89 cycles overhead plus
;                                 (8 X lowest bit position) cycles
;
;       Size:                   Program  61 bytes (including the table
;                                 of masks)
;
;
```

```
BFE:
        POP     DX              ;SAVE RETURN ADDRESS
;
;       EXIT WITH ZERO RESULT IF WIDTH OF FIELD IS ZERO
;
        POP     CX              ;GET FIELD WIDTH, STARTING
                                ;  BIT POSITION
        AND     CX,0F0FH        ;BE SURE FIELD WIDTH, STARTING
                                ;  BIT POSITION ARE BOTH 0..15
        POP     BX              ;GET DATA
        SUB     AX,AX           ;INITIALIZE RESULT TO ZERO
        TEST    CH,CH           ;TEST FIELD WIDTH
        JZ      EXITBF          ;BRANCH (EXIT) IF FIELD WIDTH
                                ;  IS ZERO
                                ; NOTE: RESULT IN AX IS ZERO
;
;       USE FIELD WIDTH TO OBTAIN EXTRACTION MASK FROM ARRAY
;       MASK CONSISTS OF A 16-BIT RIGHT-JUSTIFIED SEQUENCE OF 1 BITS
;         WITH LENGTH GIVEN BY THE FIELD WIDTH
;
        MOV     AL,CH           ;CONSTRUCT A 16-BIT INDEX FROM
                                ;  FIELD WIDTH (REMEMBER AH=0)
        SHL     AX,1            ;DOUBLE INDEX TO ACCESS TABLE
                                ;  OF 16-BIT MASKS
        MOV     SI,AX
        MOV     AX,MSKARY-2[SI]  ;GET EXTRACTION MASK FROM TABLE
                                ;NOTE WIDTH IS 1 TO 15 ONLY SINCE
                                ; ZERO WIDTH CAUSED EARLIER EXIT
;
;       SHIFT MASK LEFT LOGICALLY TO ALIGN IT WITH LOWEST BIT
;         POSITION IN FIELD
;
        SHL     AX,CL           ;SHIFT MASK LEFT LOGICALLY
                                ;SHIFT OF 0 BITS DOES NOT AFFECT
                                ;  OPERAND
;
;       OBTAIN FIELD BY LOGICALLY ANDING SHIFTED MASK WITH VALUE
;
        AND     AX,BX           ;AND SHIFTED MASK WITH DATA
;
;       NORMALIZE FIELD TO BIT 0 BY SHIFTING RIGHT LOGICALLY FROM
;         LOWEST BIT POSITION
;
        SHR     AX,CL           ;SHIFT RESULT RIGHT LOGICALLY
                                ;SHIFT OF 0 BITS DOES NOT AFFECT
                                ;  OPERAND
;
;       EXIT TO RETURN ADDRESS
;
EXITBF:
        JMP     DX              ;EXIT TO RETURN ADDRESS
;
;       ARRAY OF MASKS WITH 1 TO 15 ONE BITS RIGHT-JUSTIFIED
;
MSKARY
        DW      0000000000000001B
```

```
        DW      0000000000000011B
        DW      0000000000000111B
        DW      0000000000001111B
        DW      0000000000011111B
        DW      0000000000111111B
        DW      0000000001111111B
        DW      0000000011111111B
        DW      0000000111111111B
        DW      0000001111111111B
        DW      0000011111111111B
        DW      0000111111111111B
        DW      0001111111111111B
        DW      0011111111111111B
        DW      0111111111111111B

;
;       SAMPLE EXECUTION
;
SC4A:
        MOV     AX,[VAL]        ;GET DATA
        PUSH    AX
        MOV     AH,[NBITS]      ;GET FIELD WIDTH IN BITS
        MOV     AL,[POS]        ;GET LOWEST BIT POSITION
        PUSH    AX
        CALL    BFE             ;EXTRACT BIT FIELD
                                ;RESULT FOR VAL=1234H, NBITS=4,
                                ;  POS=4 IS AX = 0003H
                                ;THIS OPERATION EXTRACTS 4 BITS
                                ;  STARTING AT BIT POSITION 4
                                ;  (THAT IS, BITS 4 THROUGH 7)
        JMP     SC4A            ;REPEAT TEST
;
;DATA
;
VAL     DW      1234H           ;DATA
NBITS   DB      4               ;FIELD WIDTH IN BITS
POS     DB      4               ;LOWEST BIT POSITION
        END
```

4B Bit field insertion (BFI)

Inserts a field of bits into a word. The width of the field and its lowest (starting) bit position are the parameters. This operation is useful in graphics, compilation, database management, and other applications where bit fields contain attributes such as colour, record type, or identifier type.

Procedure The program obtains a mask consisting of right-justified 0 bits covering the field's width. It then shifts the mask and the bit field left to align them with the specified lowest bit position. It logically ANDs the mask and the original data word, thus clearing the required bit positions, and then logically ORs the result with the shifted bit field.

Entry conditions

Order in stack (starting from the top)

Low byte of return address
High byte of return address

Starting (lowest) bit position in the field (0–15)
Width of the field in bits (0–15)

Low byte of bit field (value to insert)
High byte of bit field (value to insert)

Low byte of data
High byte of data

Exit conditions

Result in register AX

The result is the original data value with the bit field inserted, starting at the specified lowest bit position.

Examples

1. Data: Value = $F67C_{16} = 1111011001111100_2$

Lowest bit position = 4
Number of bits in the field = 8
Bit field = $008B_{16}$ = 0000000010001011_2

Result: Value with bit field inserted = $F8BC_{16}$
= 1111100010111100_2
The 8-bit field has been inserted into the original value starting at bit 4 (i.e. into bits 4–11)

2. Data: Value = $A2D4_{16}$ = 1010001011010100_2
Lowest bit position = 6
Number of bits in the field = 5
Bit field = 0015_{16} = 0000000000010101_2

Result: Value with bit field inserted = $A554_{16}$
= 1010010101010100_2
The 5-bit field has been inserted into the original value starting at bit 6 (i.e. into bits 6–10). Those five bits were 01011_2 ($0B_{16}$) and are now 10101_2 (15_{16})

Registers used AX, BX, CX, DI, DX, F, SI

Execution time 8 × LOWEST BIT POSITION plus 103 cycles overhead. The lowest bit position of the field determines how many times the program must shift the mask and the field left. For example, if the starting position is bit 10, the execution time is

$$8 \times 10 + 103 = 80 + 103 = 183 \text{ cycles}$$

Program size 65 bytes (including the table of masks)

Data memory required None

Special cases

1. Attempting to insert a field that would extend beyond the end of the word causes the program to insert only the bits through bit 15. That is, no wraparound is provided. If, for example, the user attempts to insert a 6-bit field starting at bit 14, only 2 bits (bits 14 and 15) are actually replaced.

2. Both the lowest bit position and the length of the bit field are interpreted mod 16. For example, bit position 17 is the same as bit position 1 and a 20-bit field is the same as a 4-bit field.

3. Attempting to insert a field of 0 width causes a return with a result equal to the initial data.

```
;
;
;
;
;       Title:                  Bit Field Insertion
;       Name:                   BFI
;
;
;
;       Purpose:                Inserts a field of bits which is
;                               normalized to bit 0 into a 16-bit word.
;                               NOTE: IF THE REQUESTED FIELD IS TOO LONG, THEN
;                                     ONLY THE BITS THROUGH BIT 15 WILL BE
;                                     INSERTED.  FOR EXAMPLE, IF A 4-BIT FIELD
;                                     IS TO BE INSERTED STARTING AT BIT 15,
;                                     THEN ONLY THE FIRST BIT WILL BE INSERTED
;                                     AT BIT 15.
;
;       Entry:                  TOP OF STACK
;                                 Low byte of return address
;                                 High byte of return address
;                                 Bit position at which inserted field will
;                                   start (0..15)
;                                 Width of field in bits (0..15)
;                                 Low byte of value to insert
;                                 High byte of value to insert
;                                 Low byte of value
;                                 High byte of value
;
;       Exit:                   Register AX = Value with field inserted
;
;       Registers Used:         AX,BX,CX,DI,DX,F,SI
;
;       Time:                   103 cycles overhead plus
;                                 (8 X lowest bit position) cycles
;
;       Size:                   Program  65 bytes (including the table
;                                 of masks)
;
;
;

BFI:
        POP     DI                      ;SAVE RETURN ADDRESS
;
;       EXIT WITH DATA AS RESULT IF FIELD WIDTH IS ZERO
;
        POP     CX                      ;GET NUMBER OF BITS IN FIELD,
                                        ;  LOWEST BIT POSITION
```

```
        AND     CX,0F0FH            ;BE SURE FIELD WIDTH, LOWEST BIT
                                    ;  POSITION ARE BOTH 0..15
        POP     DX                  ;GET VALUE TO INSERT
        POP     AX                  ;GET DATA VALUE
        TEST    CH,CH               ;TEST NUMBER OF BITS IN FIELD
        JZ      EXITBF              ;BRANCH (EXIT) IF FIELD WIDTH IS ZERO
                                    ;  RESULT IN AX IS ORIGINAL DATA
;
;       USE FIELD WIDTH TO OBTAIN MASK FROM ARRAY
;       16-BIT MASK HAS A NUMBER OF RIGHT-JUSTIFIED 0 BITS GIVEN
;         BY FIELD WIDTH
;
        MOV     BX,AX               ;SAVE DATA VALUE
        MOV     AL,CH               ;EXTEND FIELD WIDTH TO 16 BITS FOR
                                    ;  USE AS INDEX
        CBW                         ;CLEAR UPPER BYTE OF INDEX BY
                                    ;  EXTENSION (BIT 7 OF WIDTH IS 0)
        SHL     AX,1                ;DOUBLE FIELD WIDTH TO ACCESS INTO
                                    ;  TABLE OF 16-BIT MASKS
        MOV     SI,AX
        MOV     AX,MSKARY-2[SI]     ;GET MASK FROM ARRAY
                                    ;NOTE FIELD WIDTH IS 1..15 ONLY SINCE
                                    ;  ZERO WIDTH CAUSES EARLIER EXIT
;
;       SHIFT MASK AND FIELD TO BE INSERTED LEFT TO ALIGN THEM WITH
;         THE FIELD'S LOWEST BIT POSITION
;
        ROL     AX,CL               ;ROTATE MASK LEFT TO ALIGN IT,
                                    ;  FILLING EMPTY POSITIONS WITH 1S
        SHL     DX,CL               ;SHIFT FIELD TO BE INSERTED LEFT
                                    ;  TO ALIGN IT
                                    ;THESE OPERATIONS BOTH ASSUME THAT A
                                    ;  SHIFT OF 0 BITS DOES NOT AFFECT
                                    ;  OPERAND
;
;       USE MASK TO CLEAR FIELD, THEN OR IN INSERT VALUE
;
        AND     AX,BX               ;AND DATA VALUE WITH MASK
        OR      AX,DX               ;OR IN INSERT VALUE
;
;       EXIT TO RETURN ADDRESS
;
EXITBF:
        JMP     DI                  ;EXIT TO RETURN ADDRESS

;
;       MASK ARRAY USED TO CLEAR THE BIT FIELD INITIALLY
;       HAS 0 BITS RIGHT-JUSTIFIED IN 1 TO 15 BIT POSITIONS
;
MSKARY
        DW      1111111111111110B
        DW      1111111111111100B
        DW      1111111111111000B
        DW      1111111111110000B
        DW      1111111111100000B
        DW      1111111111000000B
```

```
        DW      1111111110000000B
        DW      1111111100000000B
        DW      1111111000000000B
        DW      1111110000000000B
        DW      1111100000000000B
        DW      1111000000000000B
        DW      1110000000000000B
        DW      1100000000000000B
        DW      1000000000000000B

;
;
;       SAMPLE EXECUTION
;
;

SC4B:
        MOV     AX,[VAL]        ;GET VALUE
        PUSH    AX
        MOV     AX,[VALINS]     ;GET VALUE TO INSERT
        PUSH    AX
        MOV     AH,[NBITS]      ;GET FIELD WIDTH IN BITS
        MOV     AL,[POS]        ;GET LOWEST BIT POSITION OF FIELD
        PUSH    AX
        CALL    BFI             ;INSERT BIT FIELD
                                ;RESULT FOR VAL=1234H, VALINS=0EH,
                                ;  NBITS = 4, POS = 0CH IS
                                ;  REGISTER AX = E234H
                                ;THIS OPERATION INSERTS 4 BITS (1110)
                                ;  STARTING IN BIT POSITION 12 (THAT
                                ;  IS, INTO BITS 12 THROUGH 15)
        JMP     SC4B            ;REPEAT TEST

;
;DATA
;
VAL     DW      1234H           ;DATA VALUE
VALINS  DW      000EH           ;VALUE TO INSERT
NBITS   DB      4               ;FIELD WIDTH IN BITS
POS     DB      0CH             ;LOWEST BIT POSITION IN FIELD

        END
```

4C Multiple-precision arithmetic shift right (MPASR)

Shifts a multi-byte operand right arithmetically by a specified number of bit positions. Sets the Carry flag from the last bit shifted out of the rightmost bit position. The length of the operand in bytes is 255 or less. The operand is stored with its least significant byte at the lowest address.

Procedure If the operand has an odd number of bytes, the program begins by shifting the most significant byte right arithmetically. Otherwise, it obtains the sign bit from the most significant byte and saves that bit in the Carry. It then rotates the entire remaining operand right 1 bit, starting with the most significant word. It repeats the operation for the specified number of shifts.

Entry conditions

Order in stack (starting from the top)

Low byte of return address
High byte of return address

Number of shifts (bit positions)

Length of the operand in bytes

Low byte of base address of operand (address of its least significant byte)
High byte of base address of operand (address of its least significant byte)

Exit conditions

Operand shifted right arithmetically by the specified number of bit positions. The original sign bit is extended to the right.

The Carry flag is set from the last bit shifted out of the rightmost bit position. It is cleared if either the number of shifts or the length of the operand is 0.

Examples

1. Data: Length of operand (in bytes) = 8
   Operand = $85A4C719FE06741E_{16}$
   Number of shifts = 4

   Result: Shifted operand = $F85A4C719FE06741_{16}$.
   This is the original operand shifted right 4 bits arithmetically. The four most significant bits thus all take on the value of the original sign bit (1)
   Carry = 1, since the last bit shifted from the rightmost bit position was 1.

2. Data: Length of operand (in bytes) = 4
   Operand = $3F6A42D3_{16}$
   Number of shifts = 3

   Result: Shifted operand = $07ED485A_{16}$
   This is the original operand shifted right 3 bits arithmetically. The three most significant bits thus all take on the value of the original sign bit (0)
   Carry = 0, since the last bit shifted from the rightmost bit position was 0.

Registers used AX, BX, CX, DI, DX, F, SI

Execution time NUMBER OF SHIFTS × (82 + 39 × LENGTH OF OPERAND IN BYTES/2) + 64 cycles.

If, for example, NUMBER OF SHIFTS = 6 and LENGTH OF OPERAND IN BYTES = 8, the execution time is

$$6 \times (82 + 39 \times 4) + 64 = 6 \times 238 + 64 = 1492 \text{ cycles}$$

Program size 55 bytes

Data memory required None

Special cases

1. If the length of the operand is 0, the program exits immediately with the operand unchanged and the Carry flag cleared.

2. If the number of shifts is 0, the program exits immediately with the operand unchanged and the Carry flag cleared.

```
;
;
;
;
;       Title:                  Multiple-Precision Arithmetic Shift Right
;       Name:                   MPASR
;
;
;
;       Purpose:                Arithmetic shift right a multi-byte operand
;                               N bits.
;
;       Entry:                  TOP OF STACK
;                                 Low byte of return address
;                                 High byte of return address
;                                 Number of bits to shift
;                                 Length of the operand in bytes
;                                 Low byte of operand base address
;                                 High byte of operand base address
;
;                                 The operand is stored with ARRAY[0] as its
;                                 least significant byte and ARRAY[LENGTH-1]
;                                 as its most significant byte
;
;       Exit:                   Operand shifted right with the most
;                               significant bit propagated.
;                               Carry := Last bit shifted from least
;                                        significant position.
;
;       Registers Used:         AX,BX,CX,DI,DX,F,SI
;
;       Time:                   64 cycles overhead plus
;                                 ((39 * length/2) + 82) cycles per shift
;
;       Size:                   Program  55 bytes
;
;
;

MPASR:
        POP     DX              ;SAVE RETURN ADDRESS
;
;       EXIT IF LENGTH OF OPERAND OR NUMBER OF BITS TO SHIFT
;         IS ZERO.  CARRY IS CLEARED (BY TEST) IN EITHER CASE
;
        POP     CX              ;GET OPERAND LENGTH, NUMBER OF BITS
                                ;  TO SHIFT
        POP     DI              ;GET OPERAND BASE ADDRESS
        TEST    CL,CL           ;TEST NUMBER OF BITS TO SHIFT
        JZ      EXITAS          ;EXIT IF NUMBER OF BITS TO SHIFT IS ZERO
        TEST    CH,CH           ;TEST LENGTH OF OPERAND
        JZ      EXITAS          ;EXIT IF LENGTH OF OPERAND IS ZERO
```

```
;
;       SAVE POINTER TO MOST SIGNIFICANT BYTE OF OPERAND
;
        MOV     BL,CH     ;MAKE OPERAND LENGTH INTO 16-BIT INDEX
        SUB     BH,BH
        ADD     DI,BX     ;FIND ADDRESSS JUST BEYOND END OF OPERAND
        DEC     DI        ;CALCULATE ADDRESS OF MOST SIGNIFICANT
                          ; BYTE OF OPERAND
        MOV     AL,CL     ;MAKE NUMBER OF BITS TO SHIFT INTO
                          ;  16-BIT COUNT
        SUB     AH,AH
;
;       SHIFT ENTIRE OPERAND RIGHT ONE BIT ARITHMETICALLY
;       IF LENGTH IS ODD, DO A BYTE-LENGTH ARITHMETIC SHIFT
;         RIGHT OF MOST SIGNIFICANT BYTE FIRST
;
;
ASRLP:
        MOV     SI,DI     ;GET ADDRESS OF MOST SIGNIFICANT BYTE
        MOV     CX,BX     ;GET OPERAND LENGTH IN BYTES
        SAR     CX,1      ;DIVIDE BY 2 TO GET LENGTH IN WORDS
        JNC     EVEN      ;JUMP IF LENGTH IN BYTES IS EVEN
        SAR     BYTE PTR [SI],1  ;IF LENGTH IS ODD, START WITH
                          ;  BYTE-LENGTH SHIFT OF MOST SIGNIFICANT
                          ;  BYTE
        DEC     SI        ;POINT TO NEXT BYTE
        JMP     STSHFT    ;NOW START WORD-LENGTH SHIFTS
;
;       IF LENGTH IS EVEN, USE SIGN OF MOST SIGNIFICANT BYTE
;         AS INITIAL CARRY INPUT TO PRODUCE ARITHMETIC SHIFT
;
;
EVEN:
        MOV     CH,[SI]   ;GET MOST SIGNIFICANT BYTE
        SHL     CH,1      ;MOVE SIGN BIT TO CARRY
        SUB     CH,CH     ;CLEAR HIGH BYTE OF SHIFT COUNT
;
;       SHIFT EACH REMAINING WORD OF OPERAND RIGHT ONE BIT
;       START WITH MOST SIGNIFICANT WORD IF LENGTH IS EVEN
;       START WITH WORD AFTER MOST SIGNIFICANT BYTE IF LENGTH IS ODD
;
;
ASRLP1:
        RCR     WORD PTR [SI],1     ;ROTATE NEXT WORD RIGHT
        DEC     SI
        DEC     SI
        LOOP    ASRLP1    ;CONTINUE THROUGH ALL WORDS
;
;       COUNT NUMBER OF SHIFTS
;
        DEC     AX        ;DECREMENT NUMBER OF SHIFTS
        JNZ     ASRLP     ;CONTINUE UNTIL DONE
;
;       EXIT TO RETURN ADDRESS
;
EXITAS:
        JMP     DX        ;EXIT TO RETURN ADDRESS

;
```

```
;           SAMPLE EXECUTION
;
;

SC4C:
            MOV         BX,[AYADR]        ;GET BASE ADDRESS OF OPERAND
            PUSH        BX
            MOV         AH,SZAY           ;GET LENGTH OF OPERAND IN BYTES
            MOV         AL,[SHIFTS]       ;GET NUMBER OF SHIFTS
            PUSH        AX
            CALL        MPASR                  ;ARITHMETIC SHIFT RIGHT
                                  ;RESULT OF SHIFTING AY=EDCBA987654321H
                                  ;4 BITS IS AY=FEDCBA98765432H, C=0
                                  ;  IN MEMORY AY   = 032H
                                  ;            AY+1 = 054H
                                  ;            AY+2 = 076H
                                  ;            AY+3 = 098H
                                  ;            AY+4 = 0BAH
                                  ;            AY+5 = 0DCH
                                  ;            AY+6 = 0FEH
            JMP         SC4C      ;REPEAT TEST

;
;DATA SECTION
;
SZAY        EQU         7         ;LENGTH OF OPERAND IN BYTES
SHIFTS      DB          4         ;NUMBER OF SHIFTS
AYADR       DW          AY        ;BASE ADDRESS OF OPERAND
AY          DB          21H,43H,65H,87H,0A9H,0CBH,0EDH  ;OPERAND

            END
```

4D Multiple-precision logical shift left (MPLSL)

Shifts a multi-byte operand left logically by a specified number of bit positions. The length of the operand (in bytes) is 255 or less. Sets the Carry flag from the last bit shifted out of the leftmost bit position. The operand is stored with its least significant byte at the lowest address.

Procedure If the operand has an odd number of bytes, the program begins by shifting the least significant byte left logically. Otherwise, it clears the Carry initially (to fill with a 0 bit). It then shifts the entire remaining operand left 1 bit, starting with the least significant word. It repeats the operation for the specified number of shifts.

Entry conditions

Order in stack (starting from the top)

Low byte of return address
High byte of return address

Number of shifts (bit positions)
Length of the operand in bytes

Low byte of base address of operand (address of its least significant byte)
High byte of base address of operand (address of its least significant byte)

Exit conditions

Operand shifted left logically by the specified number of bit positions. The least significant bit positions are filled with 0s.
The Carry flag is set from the last bit shifted out of the leftmost bit position. It is cleared if either the number of shifts or the length of the operand is 0.

Examples

1. Data: Length of operand (in bytes) = 8

Operand = $85A4C719FE06741E_{16}$
Number of shifts = 4

Result: Shifted operand = $5A4C719FE06741E0_{16}$.
This is the original operand shifted left 4 bits logically. The four least significant bits are all cleared.
Carry = 0, since the last bit shifted from the leftmost bit position was 0.

2. Data: Length of operand (in bytes) = 4
Operand = $3F6A42D3_{16}$
Number of shifts = 3

Result: Shifted operand = $FB521698_{16}$.
This is the original operand shifted left 3 bits logically. The three least significant bits are all cleared.
Carry = 1, since the last bit shifted from the leftmost bit position was 1.

Registers used AX, BX, CX, DI, DX, F, SI

Execution time NUMBER OF SHIFTS × (55 + 41 × LENGTH OF OPERAND IN BYTES/2) + 59 cycles.

If, for example, NUMBER OF SHIFTS = 6 and LENGTH OF OPERAND IN BYTES = 8, the execution time is

$$6 \times (55 + 41 \times 4) + 59 = 6 \times 219 + 59 = 1373 \text{ cycles}$$

Program size 41 bytes

Data memory required None

Special cases

1. If the length of the operand is 0, the program exits immediately with the operand unchanged and the Carry flag cleared.

2. If the number of shifts is 0, the program exits immediately with the operand unchanged and the Carry flag cleared.

```
;
;
;
;       Title:              Multiple-Precision Logical Shift Left
;       Name:               MPLSL
;
;
;
;
;       Purpose:            Logical shift left a multi-byte operand
;                           N bits.
;
;       Entry:              TOP OF STACK
;                             Low byte of return address
;                             High byte of return address
;                             Number of bits to shift
;                             Length of the operand in bytes
;                             Low byte of operand base address
;                             High byte of operand base address
;
;                             The operand is stored with ARRAY[0] as its
;                             least significant byte and ARRAY[LENGTH-1]
;                             as its most significant byte
;
;       Exit:               Operand shifted left filling the least
;                           significant bits with zeros.
;                           Carry := Last bit shifted from most
;                                    significant position
;
;       Registers Used:     AX,BX,CX,DI,DX,F,SI
;
;       Time:               59 cycles overhead plus
;                             ((41 X length/2) + 55) cycles per shift
;
;       Size:               Program  41 bytes
;
;
;

MPLSL:
        POP     DX              ;SAVE RETURN ADDRESS
;
;       EXIT IF LENGTH OF OPERAND OR NUMBER OF BITS TO SHIFT
;         IS ZERO.  CARRY IS CLEARED BY TEST IN EITHER CASE
;
        POP     CX              ;GET OPERAND LENGTH, NUMBER OF BITS
                                ; TO SHIFT
        POP     DI              ;GET OPERAND BASE ADDRESS
        TEST    CL,CL           ;TEST NUMBER OF BITS TO SHIFT
        JZ      EXITLS          ;EXIT IF NUMBER OF BITS TO SHIFT IS ZERO
        TEST    CH,CH           ;TEST LENGTH OF OPERAND
        JZ      EXITLS          ;EXIT IF LENGTH OF OPERAND IS ZERO
        MOV     BL,CH           ;MAKE OPERAND LENGTH INTO 16-BIT QUANTITY
        SUB     BH,BH
        MOV     AL,CL           ;MAKE NUMBER OF BITS TO SHIFT INTO 16-BIT
                                ; QUANTITY
        SUB     AH,AH
```

```
;
;       SHIFT ENTIRE OPERAND LEFT ONE BIT LOGICALLY
;       IF LENGTH IS ODD, DO A BYTE-LENGTH LOGICAL SHIFT
;         ON LEAST SIGNIFICANT BYTE FIRST
;       IF LENGTH IS EVEN, MAKE INITIAL CARRY INPUT ZERO TO
;         PRODUCE LOGICAL SHIFT
;
LSLLP:
        MOV     SI,DI           ;POINT TO LEAST SIGNIFICANT BYTE
        MOV     CX,BX           ;GET LENGTH OF OPERAND IN BYTES
        SAR     CX,1            ;DIVIDE BY 2 TO GET LENGTH IN WORDS
        JNC     LSLLP1          ;JUMP IF LENGTH IN BYTES IS EVEN
                                ; INITIAL CARRY INPUT IS ZERO TO
                                ; FILL WITH ZEROS
        SHL     BYTE PTR [SI],1 ;IF LENGTH IS ODD, START WITH
                                ; BYTE-LENGTH LOGICAL SHIFT OF LEAST
                                ; SIGNIFICANT BYTE
        INC     SI              ;POINT TO NEXT BYTE
;
;       ROTATE EACH WORD OF OPERAND LEFT ONE BIT
;       START WITH LEAST SIGNIFICANT WORD IF LENGTH IS EVEN
;       START WITH WORD AFTER LEAST SIGNIFICANT BYTE IF LENGTH IS ODD
;
LSLLP1:
        RCL     WORD PTR [SI],1         ;ROTATE NEXT WORD LEFT
        INC     SI
        INC     SI
        LOOP    LSLLP1          ;CONTINUE THROUGH ALL WORDS
;
;       COUNT NUMBER OF SHIFTS
;
        DEC     AX              ;DECREMENT NUMBER OF SHIFTS
        JNZ     LSLLP           ;CONTINUE UNTIL DONE
;
;       EXIT TO RETURN ADDRESS
;
EXITLS:
        JMP     DX              ;EXIT TO RETURN ADDRESS

;
;
;       SAMPLE EXECUTION
;
;

SC4D:
        MOV     BX,[AYADR]         ;GET BASE ADDRESS OF OPERAND
        PUSH    BX
        MOV     AH,SZAY            ;GET LENGTH OF OPERAND IN BYTES
        MOV     AL,[SHIFTS]        ;GET NUMBER OF SHIFTS
        PUSH    AX
        CALL    MPLSL              ;LOGICAL SHIFT LEFT
                        ;RESULT OF SHIFTING AY=EDCBA987654321H
                        ;4 BITS IS AY=DCBA9876543210H, C=0
                        ;  IN MEMORY AY    = 010H
                        ;            AY+1  = 032H
```

```
                                ;       AY+2 = 054H
                                ;       AY+3 = 076H
                                ;       AY+4 = 098H
                                ;       AY+5 = 0BAH
                                ;       AY+6 = 0DCH
        JMP     SC4D            ;REPEAT TEST

;
;DATA SECTION
;
SZAY    EQU     7               ;LENGTH OF OPERAND IN BYTES
SHIFTS  DB      4               ;NUMBER OF SHIFTS
AYADR   DW      AY              ;BASE ADDRESS OF OPERAND
AY      DB      21H,43H,65H,87H,0A9H,0CBH,0EDH  ;OPERAND

        END
```

4E Multiple-precision logical shift right (MPLSR)

Shifts a multi-byte operand right logically by a specified number of bit positions. The length of the operand (in bytes) is 255 or less. Sets the Carry flag from the last bit shifted out of the rightmost bit position. The operand is stored with its least significant byte at the lowest address.

Procedure If the operand has an odd number of bytes, the program begins by shifting the most significant byte right logically. Otherwise, it clears the Carry initially (to fill with a 0 bit). It then shifts the entire remaining operand right one bit, starting with the most significant word. It repeats the operation for the specified number of shifts.

Entry conditions

Order in stack (starting from the top)

Low byte of return address
High byte of return address

Number of shifts (bit positions)

Length of the operand in bytes

Low byte of base address of operand (address of its least significant byte)
High byte of base address of operand (address of its least significant byte)

Exit conditions

Operand shifted right logically by the specified number of bit positions. The most significant bit positions are filled with 0s.
The Carry flag is set from the last bit shifted out of the rightmost bit position. It is cleared if either the number of shifts or the length of the operand is 0.

Examples

1. Data: Length of operand (in bytes) = 8

Operand = $85A4C719FE06741E_{16}$
Number of shifts = 4

Result: Shifted operand = $085A4C719FE06741_{16}$.
This is the original operand shifted right 4 bits logically.
The four most significant bits are all cleared.
Carry = 1, since the last bit shifted from the rightmost bit position was 1.

2. Data: Length of operand (in bytes) = 4
Operand = $3F6A42D3_{16}$
Number of shifts = 3

Result: Shifted operand = $07ED485A_{16}$.
This is the original operand shifted right 3 bits logically.
The three most significant bits are all cleared.
Carry = 0, since the last bit shifted from the rightmost bit position was 0.

Registers used AX, BX, CX, DI, DX, F, SI

Execution time NUMBER OF SHIFTS × (55 + 41 × LENGTH OF OPERAND IN BYTES/2) + 64 cycles.

If, for example, NUMBER OF SHIFTS = 6 and LENGTH OF OPERAND IN BYTES = 8, the execution time is

$$6 \times (55 + 41 \times 4) + 64 = 6 \times 219 + 64 = 1378 \text{ cycles}$$

Program size 44 bytes

Data memory required None

Special cases

1. If the length of the operand is 0, the program exits immediately with the operand unchanged and the Carry flag cleared.

2. If the number of shifts is 0, the program exits immediately with the operand unchanged and the Carry flag cleared.

```
;
;
;
;
;   Title:              Multiple-Precision Logical Shift Right
;   Name:               MPLSR
;
;
;
;   Purpose:            Logical shift right a multi-byte operand
;                       N bits.
;
;   Entry:              TOP OF STACK
;                         Low byte of return address
;                         High byte of return address
;                         Number of bits to shift
;                         Length of the operand in bytes
;                         Low byte of operand base address
;                         High byte of operand base address
;
;                         The operand is stored with ARRAY[0] as its
;                         least significant byte and ARRAY[LENGTH-1]
;                         as its most significant byte
;
;   Exit:               Operand shifted right filling the most
;                       significant bits with zeros.
;                       Carry := Last bit shifted from least
;                                significant position.
;
;   Registers Used:     AX,BX,CX,DI,DX,F,SI
;
;   Time:               64 cycles overhead plus
;                       ((41 X length/2) + 55) cycles per shift
;
;   Size:               Program  44 bytes
;
;
;

MPLSR:
        POP     DX          ;SAVE RETURN ADDRESS
;
;       EXIT IF LENGTH OF OPERAND OR NUMBER OF BITS TO SHIFT
;         IS ZERO.  CARRY IS CLEARED BY TEST IN EITHER CASE
;
        POP     CX          ;GET OPERAND LENGTH, NUMBER OF BITS
                            ;  TO SHIFT
        POP     DI          ;GET OPERAND BASE ADDRESS
        TEST    CL,CL       ;TEST NUMBER OF BITS TO SHIFT
        JZ      EXITLS      ;EXIT IF NUMBER OF BITS TO SHIFT IS ZERO
        TEST    CH,CH       ;TEST LENGTH OF OPERAND
        JZ      EXITLS      ;EXIT IF LENGTH OF OPERAND IS ZERO
        MOV     BL,CH       ;MAKE OPERAND LENGTH INTO 16-BIT QUANTITY
        SUB     BH,BH
        MOV     AL,CL       ;MAKE NUMBER OF BITS TO SHIFT INTO 16-BIT
                            ;  QUANTITY
```

```
        SUB     AH,AH
;
;       SAVE POINTER TO END OF OPERAND
;
        ADD     DI,BX       ;FIND ADDRESS JUST BEYOND END OF OPERAND
        DEC     DI          ;CALCULATE ADDRESS OF MOST SIGNIFICANT
                            ;  BYTE OF OPERAND
;
;       SHIFT ENTIRE OPERAND RIGHT ONE BIT LOGICALLY
;       IF LENGTH IS ODD, START BY SHIFTING MOST SIGNIFICANT BYTE
;         RIGHT LOGICALLY
;       IF LENGTH IS EVEN, MAKE INITIAL CARRY INPUT ZERO TO
;         PRODUCE LOGICAL SHIFT
;
LSRLP:
        MOV     SI,DI       ;POINT TO END OF OPERAND
        MOV     CX,BX       ;GET LENGTH OF OPERAND IN BYTES
        SAR     CX,1        ;DIVIDE BY 2 TO GET LENGTH IN WORDS
        JNC     EVEN        ;JUMP IF LENGTH IN BYTES IS EVEN
                            ;  INITIAL CARRY INPUT IS ZERO TO
                            ;  FILL WITH ZEROS
        SHR     BYTE PTR [SI],1  ;IF LENGTH IS ODD, START WITH
                            ;  BYTE-LENGTH LOGICAL SHIFT OF MOST
                            ;  SIGNIFICANT BYTE
        DEC     SI          ;POINT TO NEXT BYTE
EVEN:
        DEC     SI          ;START WORD TRANSFERS BY POINTING TO
                            ;  LOW BYTE OF NEXT WORD
;
;       SHIFT EACH WORD OF OPERAND RIGHT ONE BIT
;       START WITH MOST SIGNIFICANT WORD IF LENGTH IS EVEN
;       START WITH WORD BEFORE MOST SIGNIFICANT BYTE IF LENGTH IS ODD
;
LSRLP1:
        RCR     WORD PTR [SI],1     ;ROTATE NEXT WORD RIGHT
        DEC     SI
        DEC     SI
        LOOP    LSRLP1      ;CONTINUE THROUGH ALL WORDS
;
;       COUNT NUMBER OF SHIFTS
;
        DEC     AX          ;DECREMENT NUMBER OF SHIFTS
        JNZ     LSRLP       ;CONTINUE UNTIL DONE
;
;       EXIT TO RETURN ADDRESS
;
EXITLS:
        JMP     DX          ;EXIT TO RETURN ADDRESS


;
;
;       SAMPLE EXECUTION
;
;

SC4E:
```

```
        MOV     BX,[AYADR]      ;GET BASE ADDRESS OF OPERAND
        PUSH    BX
        MOV     AH,SZAY         ;GET LENGTH OF OPERAND IN BYTES
        MOV     AL,[SHIFTS]     ;GET NUMBER OF SHIFTS
        PUSH    AX
        CALL    MPLSR           ;LOGICAL SHIFT LEFT
                                ;RESULT OF SHIFTING AY=EDCBA987654321H
                                ;4 BITS IS AY=0EDCBA98765432H, C=0
                                ;  IN MEMORY AY   = 032H
                                ;           AY+1 = 054H
                                ;           AY+2 = 076H
                                ;           AY+3 = 098H
                                ;           AY+4 = 0BAH
                                ;           AY+5 = 0DCH
                                ;           AY+6 = 00EH
        JMP     SC4E            ;REPEAT TEST

;
;DATA SECTION
;
SZAY    EQU     7               ;LENGTH OF OPERAND IN BYTES
SHIFTS  DB      4               ;NUMBER OF SHIFTS
AYADR   DW      AY              ;BASE ADDRESS OF OPERAND
AY      DB      21H,43H,65H,87H,0A9H,0CBH,0EDH  ;OPERAND

        END
```

4F Multiple-precision rotate right (MPRR)

Rotates a multi-byte operand right by a specified number of bit positions as if the most significant bit and least significant bit were connected. The length of the operand (in bytes) is 255 or less. Sets the Carry flag from the last bit shifted out of the rightmost bit position. The operand is stored with its least significant byte at the lowest address.

Procedure The program shifts bit 0 of the least significant byte of the operand to the Carry flag and shifts all the full words in the operand right 1 bit, starting with the most significant word. It then shifts the least significant byte right 1 bit, but saves the result only if the operand has an odd number of bytes. It repeats the operation for the specified number of rotates.

Entry conditions

Order in stack (starting from the top)

Low byte of return address
High byte of return address

Number of rotates (bit positions)

Length of the operand in bytes

Low byte of base address of operand (address of its least significant byte)
High byte of base address of operand (address of its least significant byte)

Exit conditions

Operand rotated right by the specified number of bit positions. The most significant bit positions are filled from the least significant bit positions.
The Carry flag is set from the last bit shifted out of the rightmost bit position. It is cleared if either the number of shifts or the length of the operand is 0).

Examples

1. Data: Length of operand (in bytes) = 8
   Operand = $85A4C719FE06741E_{16}$
   Number of rotates = 4
   Result: Shifted operand = $E85A4C719FE06741_{16}$.
   This is the original operand rotated right 4 bits. The four most significant bits are equivalent to the original 4 least significant bits.
   Carry = 1, since the last bit shifted from the rightmost bit position was 1.

2. Data: Length of operand (in bytes) = 4
   Operand = $3F6A42D3_{16}$
   Number of rotates = 3
   Result: Shifted operand = $67ED485A_{16}$.
   This is the original operand rotated right 3 bits. The three most significant bits (011) are equivalent to the original three least significant bits.
   Carry = 0, since the last bit shifted from the rightmost bit position was 0.

Registers used AX, BX, CX, DI, DX, F, SI

Execution time NUMBER OF ROTATES × (82 + 42 × LENGTH OF OPERAND IN BYTES/2) + 79 cycles.

If, for example, NUMBER OF ROTATES = 6 and LENGTH OF OPERAND IN BYTES = 8, the execution time is

$$6 \times (82 + 42 \times 4) + 79 = 6 \times 250 + 79 = 1579 \text{ cycles}$$

Program size 56 bytes

Data memory required None

Special cases

1. If the length of the operand is 0, the program exits immediately with the operand unchanged and the Carry flag cleared.

2. If the number of rotates is 0, the program exits immediately with the operand unchanged and the Carry flag cleared.

```
;
;
;
;
;       Title:              Multiple-Precision Rotate Right
;       Name:               MPRR
;
;
;
;       Purpose:            Rotate right a multi-byte operand
;                           N bits.
;
;       Entry:              TOP OF STACK
;                             Low byte of return address
;                             High byte of return address
;                             Number of bits to rotate
;                             Length of the operand in bytes
;                             Low byte of operand base address
;                             High byte of operand base address
;
;                             The operand is stored with ARRAY[0] as its
;                             least significant byte and ARRAY[LENGTH-1]
;                             as its most significant byte
;
;                           Operand rotated right
;                           Carry := Last bit shifted from least
;                                    significant position.
;
;       Registers Used:     AX,BX,CX,DI,DX,F,SI
;
;       Time:               79 cycles overhead plus
;                             ((42 X length/2) + 82) cycles per rotate
;
;       Size:               Program  56 bytes
;
;
;

MPRR:
        POP     DX              ;SAVE RETURN ADDRESS
;
;       EXIT IF LENGTH OF OPERAND OR NUMBER OF BITS TO ROTATE
;         IS ZERO.  CARRY IS CLEARED BY TEST IN EITHER CASE
;
        POP     CX              ;GET OPERAND LENGTH, NUMBER OF BITS
                                ;  TO ROTATE
        POP     DI              ;GET OPERAND BASE ADDRESS
        PUSH    DX              ;PUT RETURN ADDRESS BACK IN STACK
        TEST    CL,CL           ;TEST NUMBER OF BITS TO ROTATE
        JZ      EXITRR          ;EXIT IF NUMBER OF BITS TO ROTATE IS ZERO
        TEST    CH,CH           ;TEST LENGTH OF OPERAND
        JZ      EXITRR          ;EXIT IF LENGTH OF OPERAND IS ZERO
```

```
        MOV     BL,CH       ;MAKE OPERAND LENGTH INTO 16-BIT QUANTITY
        SUB     BH,BH
        LEA     DX,-2[DI+BX]    ;SAVE ADDRESS OF MOST SIGNIFICANT
                            ;  WORD OF OPERAND
        MOV     AL,CL       ;MAKE NUMBER OF BITS TO ROTATE INTO 16-BIT
                            ;  QUANTITY
        SUB     AH,AH
;
;       ROTATE ENTIRE OPERAND RIGHT ONE BIT
;       USE PREVIOUS LEAST SIGNIFICANT BIT AS INITIAL CARRY INPUT
;         TO PRODUCE ROTATION
;
RRLP:
        MOV     CX,BX       ;GET LENGTH OF OPERAND IN BYTES
        SAR     CX,1        ;DIVIDE BY 2 TO GET LENGTH IN WORDS
        MOV     CH,[DI]     ;GET LEAST SIGNIFICANT BYTE OF OPERAND
        SHR     CH,1        ;MOVE LEAST SIGNIFICANT BIT TO CARRY
        SUB     CH,CH       ;CLEAR HIGH BYTE OF COUNT
        MOV     SI,DX       ;POINT TO MOST SIGNIFICANT WORD
;
;       SHIFT EACH WORD OF OPERAND RIGHT ONE BIT
;       START WITH MOST SIGNIFICANT WORD
;
RRLP1:
        RCR     WORD PTR [SI],1     ;SHIFT NEXT WORD RIGHT
        DEC     SI
        DEC     SI
        LOOP    RRLP1       ;CONTINUE THROUGH ALL FULL WORDS
;
;       SHIFT LEAST SIGNIFICANT BYTE RIGHT ONE BIT
;       RETAIN SHIFTED BYTE ONLY IF OPERAND HAS ODD LENGTH
;
        MOV     CL,[DI]     ;GET LEAST SIGNIFICANT BYTE
        RCR     CL,1        ;SHIFT IT RIGHT IN CASE IT WAS NOT
                            ;  HANDLED AS PART OF A FULL WORD
                            ;NOTE: MUST DO THIS EVEN IF UNNECESSARY
                            ;  TO AVOID LOSING CARRY FROM LAST
                            ;  WORD-LENGTH SHIFT
        TEST    BL,1        ;CHECK IF LENGTH IN BYTES IS ODD (THIS
                            ;  CLEARS CARRY)
        JZ      CNTROT      ;JUMP IF LENGTH IN BYTES IS EVEN
        MOV     [DI],CL     ;SAVE SHIFTED LEAST SIGNIFICANT BYTE
                            ;  IF LENGTH IN BYTES IS ODD
;
;       COUNT NUMBER OF ROTATES
;
CNTROT:
        DEC     AX          ;DECREMENT NUMBER OF ROTATES
        JNZ     RRLP        ;CONTINUE UNTIL DONE
;
;       EXIT TO RETURN ADDRESS
;
EXITRR:
        RET                 ;EXIT TO RETURN ADDRESS

;
```

```
;
;       SAMPLE EXECUTION
;
;
SC4F:
        MOV     BX,[AYADR]      ;GET BASE ADDRESS OF OPERAND
        PUSH    BX
        MOV     AH,SZAY         ;GET LENGTH OF OPERAND IN BYTES
        MOV     AL,[ROTATS]     ;GET NUMBER OF ROTATES
        PUSH    AX
        CALL    MPRR            ;ROTATE RIGHT
                        ;RESULT OF ROTATING AY=EDCBA987654321H
                        ;4 BITS IS AY=1EDCBA98765432H, C=0
                        ;  IN MEMORY AY    = 032H
                        ;            AY+1  = 054H
                        ;            AY+2  = 076H
                        ;            AY+3  = 098H
                        ;            AY+4  = 0BAH
                        ;            AY+5  = 0DCH
                        ;            AY+6  = 01EH
        JMP     SC4F    ;REPEAT TEST

;
;DATA SECTION
;
SZAY    EQU     7       ;LENGTH OF OPERAND IN BYTES
ROTATS  DB      4       ;NUMBER OF ROTATES
AYADR   DW      AY      ;BASE ADDRESS OF OPERAND
AY      DB      21H,43H,65H,87H,0A9H,0CBH,0EDH  ;OPERAND
        END
```

4G Multiple-precision rotate left (MPRL)

Rotates a multi-byte operand left by a specified number of bit positions as if the most significant bit and least significant bit were connected. The length of the number (in bytes) is 255 or less. Sets the Carry flag from the last bit shifted out of the leftmost bit position. The operand is stored with its least significant byte at the lowest address.

Procedure The program shifts bit 7 of the most significant byte of the operand to the Carry flag and shifts all the full words in the operand left 1 bit, starting with the least significant word. It then shifts the byte after the most significant full word left 1 bit, but saves the result only if the operand has an odd number of bytes. It repeats the operation for the specified number of rotates.

Entry conditions

Order in stack (starting from the top)

Low byte of return address
High byte of return address

Number of rotates (bit positions)

Length of the operand in bytes

Low byte of base address of operand (address of its least significant byte)
High byte of base address of operand (address of its least significant byte)

Exit conditions

Operand rotated left by the specified number of bit positions (the least significant bit positions are filled from the most significant bit positions). The Carry flag is set from the last bit shifted out of the leftmost bit position. It is cleared if either the number of shifts or the length of the operand is 0.

Examples

1. Data: Length of operand (in bytes) = 8
Operand = $85A4C719FE06741E_{16}$
Number of rotates = 4

Result: Shifted operand = $5A4C719FE06741E8_{16}$.
This is the original operand rotated left 4 bits. The four least significant bits are equivalent to the original four most significant bits.
Carry = 0, since the last bit shifted from the leftmost bit position was 0.

2. Data: Length of operand (in bytes) = 4
Operand = $3F6A42D3_{16}$
Number of rotates = 3

Result: Shifted operand = $FB521699_{16}$.
This is the original operand rotated left 3 bits. The three least significant bits (001) are equivalent to the original three most significant bits.
Carry = 1, since the last bit shifted from the leftmost bit position was 0.

Registers used AX, BX, CX, DI, DX, F, SI

Execution time NUMBER OF ROTATES × (64 + 41 × LENGTH OF OPERAND IN BYTES/2) + 59 cycles.

If, for example, NUMBER OF ROTATES = 6 and LENGTH OF OPERAND IN BYTES = 8, the execution time is

$$6 \times (64 + 41 \times 4) + 59 = 6 \times 228 + 59 = 1427 \text{ cycles}$$

Program size 53 bytes

Data memory required None

Special cases

1. If the length of the operand is 0, the program exits immediately with the operand unchanged and the Carry flag cleared.

2. If the number of rotates is 0, the program exits immediately with the operand unchanged and the Carry flag cleared.

```
;
;
;
;
;       Title:                  Multiple-Precision Rotate Left
;       Name:                   MPRL
;
;
;
;       Purpose:                Rotate left a multi-byte operand
;                               N bits.
;
;       Entry:                  TOP OF STACK
;                                 Low byte of return address
;                                 High byte of return address
;                                 Number of bits to rotate
;                                 Length of the operand in bytes
;                                 Low byte of operand base address
;                                 High byte of operand base address
;
;                                 The operand is stored with ARRAY[0] as its
;                                 least significant byte and ARRAY[LENGTH-1]
;                                 as its most significant byte
;
;       Exit:                   Number rotated left
;                               Carry := Last bit shifted from the most
;                                         significant position.
;
;       Registers Used:         AX,BX,CX,DI,DX,F,SI
;
;       Time:                   59 cycles overhead plus
;                                 ((41 X length/2) + 64) cycles per rotate
;
;       Size:                   Program  53 bytes
;
;
;

MPRL:
        POP     DX              ;SAVE RETURN ADDRESS
;
;       EXIT IF LENGTH OF OPERAND OR NUMBER OF BITS TO ROTATE
;         IS ZERO.  CARRY IS CLEARED BY TEST IN EITHER CASE
;
        POP     CX              ;GET OPERAND LENGTH, NUMBER OF BITS
                                ;  TO ROTATE
        POP     DI              ;GET OPERAND BASE ADDRESS
        TEST    CL,CL           ;TEST NUMBER OF BITS TO ROTATE
        JZ      EXITRL          ;EXIT IF NUMBER OF BITS TO ROTATE IS ZERO
        TEST    CH,CH           ;TEST LENGTH OF OPERAND
        JZ      EXITRL          ;EXIT IF LENGTH OF OPERAND IS ZERO
        MOV     BL,CH           ;MAKE OPERAND LENGTH INTO 16-BIT QUANTITY
```

```
        SUB     BH,BH
        MOV     AL,CL       ;MAKE NUMBER OF BITS TO ROTATE INTO 16-BIT
                            ;  QUANTITY
        SUB     AH,AH
;
;       ROTATE ALL FULL WORDS IN OPERAND LEFT ONE BIT
;       USE PREVIOUS MOST SIGNIFICANT BIT AS INITIAL CARRY INPUT
;         TO PRODUCE ROTATION
;
RLLP:
        MOV     SI,DI       ;POINT TO LEAST SIGNIFICANT WORD
        MOV     CX,BX       ;GET LENGTH OF OPERAND IN BYTES
        SAR     CX,1        ;DIVIDE BY 2 TO GET LENGTH IN WORDS
        MOV     CH,-1[BX+DI]  ;GET MOST SIGNIFICANT BYTE
        SHL     CH,1        ;SHIFT BIT 7 TO CARRY FOR USE IN ROTATION
;
        SUB     CH,CH       ;CLEAR HIGH BYTE OF COUNT
;
;       SHIFT EACH FULL WORD OF OPERAND RIGHT ONE BIT
;       START WITH LEAST SIGNIFICANT WORD
;
RLLP1:
        RCL     WORD PTR [SI],1     ;SHIFT NEXT WORD LEFT
        INC     SI
        INC     SI
        LOOP    RLLP1       ;CONTINUE THROUGH ALL FULL WORDS
;
;       SHIFT BYTE AFTER MOST SIGNIFICANT WORD RIGHT ONE BIT
;       RETAIN SHIFTED BYTE ONLY IF OPERAND HAS ODD LENGTH
;       AND THIS BYTE IS ACTUALLY ITS MOST SIGNIFICANT BYTE
;
        MOV     CL,[SI]     ;GET POSSIBLE MOST SIGNIFICANT BYTE
        RCL     CL,1        ;SHIFT IT RIGHT IN CASE IT IS PART OF
                            ;  OPERAND
                            ;NOTE: MUST DO THIS EVEN IF UNNECESSARY
                            ;  TO AVOID LOSING CARRY FROM LAST
                            ;  WORD-LENGTH SHIFT
        TEST    BL,1        ;CHECK IF LENGTH IN BYTES IS ODD (THIS
                            ;  CLEARS CARRY)
        JZ      CNTROT      ;JUMP IF LENGTH IN BYTES IS EVEN
        MOV     [SI],CL     ;SAVE SHIFTED MOST SIGNIFICANT BYTE
                            ;  IF LENGTH IN BYTES IS EVEN
;
;       COUNT NUMBER OF ROTATES
;
CNTROT:
        DEC     AX          ;DECREMENT NUMBER OF ROTATES
        JNZ     RLLP        ;CONTINUE UNTIL DONE
;
;       EXIT TO RETURN ADDRESS
;
EXITRL:
        JMP     DX          ;EXIT TO RETURN ADDRESS

;
;
```

```
;          SAMPLE EXECUTION
;
;

SC4G:
           MOV       BX,[AYADR]      ;GET BASE ADDRESS OF OPERAND
           PUSH      BX
           MOV       AH,SZAY         ;GET LENGTH OF OPERAND IN BYTES
           MOV       AL,[ROTATS]     ;GET NUMBER OF ROTATES
           PUSH      AX
           CALL      MPRL            ;ROTATE LEFT
                                ;RESULT OF ROTATING AY=EDCBA987654321H
                                ;4 BITS IS AY=DCBA987654321EH, C=0
                                ;   IN MEMORY AY   = 01EH
                                ;             AY+1 = 032H
                                ;             AY+2 = 054H
                                ;             AY+3 = 076H
                                ;             AY+4 = 098H
                                ;             AY+5 = 0BAH
                                ;             AY+6 = 0DCH
           JMP       SC4G            ;REPEAT TEST

;
;DATA SECTION
;
SZAY       EQU       7          ;LENGTH OF OPERAND IN BYTES
ROTATS     DB        4          ;NUMBER OF ROTATES
AYADR      DW        AY         ;BASE ADDRESS OF OPERAND
AY         DB        21H,43H,65H,87H,0A9H,0CBH,0EDH   ;OPERAND

           END
```

5 String manipulation

5A String compare (STRCMP)

Compares two strings and sets the Carry and Zero flags accordingly. Sets the Zero flag to 1 if the strings are identical and to 0 otherwise. Sets the Carry flag to 1 if the string with the base address higher in the stack (string 2) is larger than the other string (string 1), and to 0 otherwise. Each string consists of at most 256 bytes, including an initial byte containing the length. That is, these are Pascal-style strings with a length byte, rather than C language-style strings with a terminating character. If the two strings are identical through the length of the shorter, the longer string is considered to be larger.

Procedure The program first determines which string is shorter. It then compares the strings a byte at a time through the length of the shorter one. It exits with the flags set if it finds corresponding bytes that differ. If the strings are the same through the length of the shorter one, the program sets the flags by comparing the lengths.

Entry conditions

Order in stack (starting from the top)

Low byte of return address

High byte of return address

Low byte of base address of string 2
High byte of base address of string 2

Low byte of base address of string 1
High byte of base address of string 1

Exit conditions

Flags set as if string 2 had been subtracted from string 1. If the strings are the same through the length of the shorter one, the flags are set as if the length of string 2 had been subtracted from the length of string 1.

Zero flag = 1 if the strings are identical, 0 if they are not identical.

Carry flag = 1 if string 2 is larger than string 1, 0 if they are identical or string 1 is larger. If the strings are the same through the length of the shorter one, the longer one is considered to be larger.

Examples

1. Data: String 1 = 05'PRINT' (05 is the length of the string)
String 2 = 03'END' (03 is the length of the string)
Result: Zero flag = 0 (strings are not identical)
Carry flag = 0 (string 2 is not larger than string 1)

2. Data: String 1 = 05'PRINT' (05 is the length of the string)
String 2 = 02'PR' (02 is the length of the string)
Result: Zero flag = 0 (strings are not identical)
Carry flag = 0 (string 2 is not larger than string 1)

The longer string (string 1) is considered to be larger. To determine whether string 2 is an abbreviation of string 1, use Subroutine 5C (Find the position of a substring). String 2 is an abbreviation if it is part of string 1 and starts at the first character.

3. Data: String 1 = 05'PRINT' (05 is the length of the string)
String 2 = 06'SYSTEM' (06 is the length of the string)
Result: Zero flag = 0 (strings are not identical)
Carry flag = 1 (string 2 is larger than string 1)

We are assuming here that the strings consist of ASCII characters. Note that the initial length byte is a hexadecimal number, not a character. We have represented this byte as two hexadecimal digits in front of the string; the string itself is surrounded by single quotation marks.

This routine treats spaces like other characters. Assuming ASCII strings, the routine will, for example, find that SPRINGMAID is larger than SPRING MAID, since an ASCII M ($4D_{16}$) is larger than an ASCII space (20_{16}).

Note that this routine does not order strings alphabetically as defined in common uses such as indexes and telephone directories. Instead, it uses the ASCII character order shown in Appendix 3. Note, in particular, that:

1. Spaces precede all printing characters.
2. Periods, commas, and dashes (hyphens) precede numbers.
3. Numbers precede letters.
4. Capital letters precede lower-case letters.

This ordering produces such non-standard results as the following:

1. 9TH AVENUE SCHOOL comes before CAPITAL CITY SCHOOL (or, in fact, any string starting with a letter). 9TH AVENUE is not treated as if it started with the letter N.

2. EZ8 Motel comes before East Street Motel since a capital Z precedes a lower-case a.

3. NEW YORK comes before NEWARK or NEWCASTLE since a space precedes any letter.

Registers used BX, CX, DI, DX, F (clears D flag), SI

Execution time

1. If the strings are not identical through the length of the shorter one, the execution time is approximately

$$124 + 24 \times \text{NUMBER OF CHARACTERS COMPARED}$$

If, for example, the routine compares five characters before finding a disparity, the execution time is approximately

$$124 + 24 \times 5 = 124 + 120 = 244 \text{ cycles}$$

2. If the strings are identical through the length of the shorter one, the execution time is approximately

115 + 24 × LENGTH OF SHORTER STRING

If, for example, the shorter string is 8 bytes long, the execution time is

115 + 24 × 8 = 115 + 192 = 307 cycles

Program size 25 bytes

Data memory required None

Special case If either string (but not both) has a 0 length, the program returns with the flags set as though the other string were larger. If both strings have 0 length, they are considered to be equal.

```
;       Title               String Compare
;       Name:               STRCMP
;
;
;       Purpose:            Compare 2 strings and return C and Z flags set
;                           or cleared.
;
;       Entry:              TOP OF STACK
;                             Low byte of return address
;                             High byte of return address
;                             Low byte of string 2 address
;                             High byte of string 2 address
;                             Low byte of string 1 address
;                             High byte of string 1 address
;
;                             Each string consists of a length byte
;                             followed by a maximum of 255 characters.
;
;       Exit:               IF string 1 = string 2 THEN
;                             Z=1,C=0
;                           IF string 1 > string 2 THEN
;                             Z=0,C=0
;                           IF string 1 < string 2 THEN
;                             Z=0,C=1
;
;       Registers Used: BX,CX,DI,DX,F (clears D flag),SI
;
;       Time:               124 cycles overhead plus 24 cycles per byte
;                           minus 9 cycles if the strings are identical
;                           through the length of the shorter one.
;
;       Size:               Program 25 bytes
;
;
STRCMP:
```

```
        ;
        ;REMOVE PARAMETERS FROM STACK
        ;
        POP     DX          ;SAVE RETURN ADDRESS
        POP     DI          ;GET BASE ADDRESS OF STRING 2
        POP     SI          ;GET BASE ADDRESS OF STRING 1
        ;
        ;DETERMINE WHICH STRING IS SHORTER
        ;LENGTH OF SHORTER = NUMBER OF BYTES TO COMPARE
        ;
        MOV     BH,[SI]     ;GET LENGTH OF STRING 1
        MOV     BL,[DI]     ;GET LENGTH OF STRING 2
        MOV     CL,BH       ;SAVE LENGTH OF STRING 1 AS BYTE COUNT
        CLD                 ;SELECT AUTOINCREMENTING
        CMPSB               ;COMPARE STRING LENGTHS
                            ;THIS ALSO INCREMENTS BOTH POINTERS
                            ;  SO THEY POINT TO FIRST ACTUAL
                            ;  CHARACTERS IN STRINGS
        JBE     BEGCMP      ;BRANCH IF STRING 1 IS SHORTER THAN
                            ;  STRING 2 OR THE SAME LENGTH
                            ;ITS LENGTH IS NUMBER OF BYTES TO COMPARE
        MOV     CL,BL       ;OTHERWISE, STRING 2 IS SHORTER
                            ;ITS LENGTH IS NUMBER OF BYTES TO COMPARE
        ;
        ;COMPARE STRINGS THROUGH LENGTH OF SHORTER
        ;EXIT AS SOON AS CORRESPONDING CHARACTERS DIFFER
        ;
BEGCMP:
        SUB     CH,CH       ;EXTEND LENGTH TO 16 BITS
                            ;SET ZERO FLAG IN CASE SHORTER STRING
                            ;  HAS ZERO LENGTH
   REPE CMPSB               ;COMPARE CHARACTERS ONE AT A TIME UNTIL
                            ;  UNEQUAL CHARACTERS FOUND OR SHORTER
                            ;  STRING EXHAUSTED
        JNE     EXITSC      ;BRANCH IF EXIT OCCURRED BECAUSE OF
                            ;  UNEQUAL CHARACTERS
                            ;  Z,C WILL BE PROPERLY SET OR CLEARED
                            ;FALL THROUGH IF EXIT OCCURRED BECAUSE
                            ;  ALL CHARACTERS WERE COMPARED
                            ;NOTE: LENGTH OF SHORTER STRING COULD
                            ;  BE ZERO IN WHICH CASE NO COMPARISON
                            ;  IS DONE AND ZERO FLAG IS 1 BECAUSE
                            ;  OF SUB CH,CH
        ;
        ;STRINGS SAME THROUGH LENGTH OF SHORTER
        ;SO USE LENGTHS TO SET FLAGS
        ;
        CMP     BH,BL       ;COMPARE STRING LENGTHS
        ;
        ;EXIT TO RETURN ADDRESS
        ;
EXITSC:
        JMP     DX          ;EXIT TO RETURN ADDRESS

;
;       SAMPLE EXECUTION:
```

```
;

SC5A:
        MOV     BX,OFFSET S1    ;GET BASE ADDRESS OF STRING 1
        PUSH    BX
        MOV     BX,OFFSET S2    ;GET BASE ADDRESS OF STRING 2
        PUSH    BX
        CALL    STRCMP          ;COMPARE STRINGS
                                ;COMPARING "STRING 1" AND "STRING 2"
                                ;  RESULTS IN STRING 1 LESS THAN
                                ;  STRING 2, SO Z=0,C=1
        JMP     SC5A            ;LOOP THROUGH TEST
;
;       TEST DATA
;
S1      DB      20H             ;LENGTH OF STRING 1 IN BYTES
        DB      'STRING 1                       '
S2      DB      20H             ;LENGTH OF STRING 2 IN BYTES
        DB      'STRING 2                       '

        END
```

5B String concatenation (CONCAT)

Combines (concatenates) two strings, placing the second immediately after the first in memory. If the concatenation would produce a string longer than a specified maximum, the program concatenates only enough of string 2 to give the combined string its maximum length. The Carry flag is cleared if all of string 2 can be concatenated. It is set to 1 if part of string 2 must be dropped. Each string consists of at most 256 bytes, including an initial byte containing the length. The strings are thus Pascal-style, rather than C language-style with a terminating character.

Procedure The program uses the length of string 1 to determine where to start adding characters, and the length of string 2 to determine how many characters to add. If the sum of the lengths exceeds the maximum, the program indicates an overflow. It then reduces the number of characters it must add to the maximum length minus the length of string 1. Finally, it moves the characters from string 2 to the end of string 1, updates the length of string 1, and sets the Carry flag to indicate whether characters were discarded.

Entry conditions

Order in stack (starting from the top)

Low byte of return address
High byte of return address

Low byte of maximum length of string 1
High byte of maximum length of string 1 (always 0)

Low byte of base address of string 2
High byte of base address of string 2

Low byte of base address of string 1
High byte of base address of string 1

Exit conditions

String 2 concatenated at the end of string 1 and the length of string 1 increased accordingly. If the combined string would exceed the maximum length, only the part of string 2 that would give string 1 its maximum length is concatenated. If any part of string 2 must be dropped, the Carry flag is set to 1. Otherwise, the Carry flag is cleared.

Examples

1. Data: Maximum length of string 1 = $0E_{16} = 14_{10}$
   String 1 = 07'JOHNSON' (07 is the length of the string)
   String 2 = 05', DON' (05 is the length of the string)
   Result: String 1 = 0C'JOHNSON, DON' ($0C_{16} = 12_{10}$ is the length of the combined string with string 2 placed after string 1)
   Carry = 0, since no characters were dropped

2. Data: String 1 = 07'JOHNSON' (07 is the length of the string)
   String 2 = 09', RICHARD' (09 is the length of the string)
   Result: String 1 = 0E'JOHNSON, RICHA' ($0E_{16} = 14_{10}$ is the maximum length allowed, so the last two characters of string 2 have been dropped)
   Carry = 1, since characters had to be dropped

Note that we are representing the initial byte (containing the string's length) as two hexadecimal digits in both examples.

Registers used AX, BX, CX, DI, DX, F (clears D flag), SI

Execution time Approximately

20 × NUMBER OF CHARACTERS CONCATENATED plus 185 cycles overhead

NUMBER OF CHARACTERS CONCATENATED is usually the length of string 2, but will be the maximum length of string 1 minus its current length if the combined string would be too long. If, for example, NUMBER OF CHARACTERS CONCATENATED is 14_{16} (20_{10}), the execution time is

$$20 \times 20 + 185 = 400 + 185 = 585 \text{ cycles}$$

The overhead is an extra 37 cycles if the string must be truncated.

Program size 53 bytes

Data memory required None

Special cases

1. If the concatenation would make the string exceed its specified maximum length, the program concatenates only enough of string 2 to reach the maximum. If any of string 2 must be truncated, the Carry flag is set to 1.

2. If string 2 has a length of 0, the program exits with the Carry flag cleared (no errors) and string 1 unchanged. That is, a length of 0 for either string is interpreted as 0, not as 256.

3. If the original length of string 1 exceeds the specified maximum, the program exits with the Carry flag set to 1 (indicating an error) and string 1 unchanged.

```
;
;       Title               String Concatenation
;       Name:               CONCAT
;
;
;       Purpose:            Concatenate 2 strings into one string.
;
;
;       Entry:              TOP OF STACK
;                             Low byte of return address
;                             High byte of return address
;                             Low byte of maximum length of string 1
;                             High byte of maximum length of string 1
;                               (always 0)
;                             Low byte of string 2 address
;                             High byte of string 2 address
;                             Low byte of string 1 address
;                             High byte of string 1 address
;
;                             Each string consists of a length byte
;                             followed by a maximum of 255 characters.
;
;       Exit:               String 1 := string 1 concatenated with string 2
;                           If no errors then
;                             Carry := 0
;                           else
;                             begin
;                               Carry := 1
;                               if the concatenation makes string 1 too
;                               long, concatenate only the part of string 2
;                               that results in string 1 having its maximum
;                               length
```

```
;                          if length(string1) > maximum length then
;                            no concatenation is done
;                        end
;
;       Registers Used: AX,BX,CX,DI,DX,F (clears D flag),SI
;
;       Time:           Approximately 20 X (length of string 2) cycles
;                       plus 185 cycles overhead
;
;       Size:           Program 53 bytes
;

CONCAT:
        ;
        ;REMOVE PARAMETERS FROM STACK
        ;SET MARKER TO INDICATE NO TRUNCATION NECESSARY
        ;
        POP     DX              ;SAVE RETURN ADDRESS
        POP     AX              ;GET MAXIMUM LENGTH OF STRING 1
        POP     SI              ;GET BASE ADDRESS OF STRING 2
        POP     DI              ;GET BASE ADDRESS OF STRING 1
        PUSH    DX              ;PUT RETURN ADDRESS BACK IN STACK
        MOV     DX,AX           ;SAVE MAXIMUM LENGTH OF STRING 1
        SUB     AX,AX           ;INDICATE NO TRUNCATION NECESSARY
        ;
        ;GET STRING LENGTHS AND EXTEND THEM TO 16 BITS
        ;NO CONCATENATION NECESSARY IF STRING 2 HAS ZERO LENGTH
        ;
        MOV     BL,[DI]         ;GET LENGTH OF STRING 1
        SUB     BH,BH           ;EXTEND LENGTH TO 16 BITS
        MOV     CL,[SI]         ;GET LENGTH OF STRING 2
        SUB     CH,CH           ;EXTEND LENGTH TO 16 BITS
        JCXZ    SETTRN          ;BRANCH (EXIT) IF STRING 2 HAS ZERO
                                ;  LENGTH - NO ERROR IN THIS CASE
        ;
        ;DETERMINE HOW MANY CHARACTERS TO CONCATENATE
        ;THIS IS LENGTH OF STRING 2 IF COMBINED STRING WOULD
        ;  NOT EXCEED MAXIMUM LENGTH
        ;OTHERWISE, IT IS THE NUMBER THAT WOULD BRING COMBINED
        ;  STRING TO ITS MAXIMUM LENGTH - THAT IS, MAXIMUM LENGTH
        ;  MINUS LENGTH OF STRING 1
        ;
        PUSH    CX              ;SAVE STRING 2'S LENGTH IN STACK
        ADD     CX,BX           ;COMPUTE LENGTH OF COMBINED STRING
        CMP     CX,DX           ;COMPARE LENGTH TO MAXIMUM LENGTH
        JBE     DOCAT           ;BRANCH IF LENGTH DOES NOT EXCEED
                                ;  MAXIMUM
        INC     AX              ;INDICATE TRUNCATION NECESSARY
        MOV     CX,DX           ;LIMIT COMBINED STRING TO MAXIMUM
                                ;  LENGTH
        SUB     DX,BX           ;COMPUTE MAXIMUM LENGTH MINUS LENGTH
                                ;  OF STRING 1
        JAE     RPLEN           ;BRANCH IF STRING 1 IS NOT ALREADY
                                ;  LONGER THAN ITS MAXIMUM LENGTH
        SUB     DX,DX           ;NUMBER OF CHARACTERS TO CONCATENATE
                                ;  IS ZERO SINCE STRING IS TOO LONG
```

```
RPLEN:  INC     SP              ;REMOVE STRING 2'S LENGTH FROM STACK
        INC     SP
        PUSH    DX              ;REPLACE IT WITH MAXIMUM LENGTH
                                ;  MINUS LENGTH OF STRING 1
        ;
        ;CONCATENATE STRINGS BY MOVING CHARACTERS FROM STRING 2
        ; TO THE AREA FOLLOWING STRING 1
        ;END OF STRING 1 = BASE 1 + LENGTH 1 + 1, WHERE THE EXTRA 1
        ; IS FOR THE LENGTH BYTE
        ;NEW CHARACTERS COME FROM STRING 2, STARTING AT BASE2+1
        ; (SKIPPING OVER LENGTH BYTE)
        ;
DOCAT:
        MOV     [DI],CL         ;SET LENGTH OF COMBINED STRING
        POP     CX              ;GET NUMBER OF CHARACTERS TO
                                ;  CONCATENATE
        JCXZ    SETTRN          ;BRANCH (EXIT) IF NO BYTES TO
                                ;  CONCATENATE
        ADD     DI,BX           ;POINT TO LAST BYTE OF STRING 1
        INC     DI              ;POINT BEYOND LAST BYTE OF STRING 1
                                ;  THIS IS WHERE ADDITION BEGINS
        INC     SI              ;POINT TO FIRST CHARACTER IN STRING 2
        CLD                     ;SELECT AUTOINCREMENTING
    REP MOVSB                   ;CONCATENATE STRINGS
        ;
        ;EXIT, SETTING CARRY FROM TRUNCATION INDICATOR
        ;CARRY = 1 IF CHARACTERS HAD TO BE TRUNCATED, 0 OTHERWISE
        ;
SETTRN:
        SHR     AX,1            ;CARRY = 1 IF TRUNCATION, 0 IF NOT
        RET                     ;EXIT TO RETURN ADDRESS

;
;       SAMPLE EXECUTION:
;

SC5B:
        MOV     BX,OFFSET S1    ;GET BASE ADDRESS OF STRING 1
        PUSH    BX
        MOV     BX,OFFSET S2    ;GET BASE ADDRESS OF STRING 2
        PUSH    BX
        MOV     AX,20H          ;GET MAXIMUM LENGTH OF STRING 1
        PUSH    AX
        CALL    CONCAT          ;CONCATENATE STRINGS
                                ;RESULT OF CONCATENATING
                                ; "LASTNAME" AND ", FIRSTNAME"
                                ; IS S1 = 13H,"LASTNAME, FIRSTNAME"
        JMP     SC5B            ;LOOP THROUGH TEST
;
;TEST DATA
;
S1      DB      8               ;LENGTH OF S1 IN BYTES
        DB      'LASTNAME                        ' ;32 BYTES
S2      DB      0BH             ;LENGTH OF S2 IN BYTES
        DB      ', FIRSTNAME                     ' ;32 BYTES

        END
```

5C Find the position of a substring (POS)

Searches for the first occurrence of a substring within a string. Returns the index at which the substring starts if it is found and 0 otherwise. The string and the substring each consist of at most 256 bytes, including an initial byte containing the length. Thus, if the substring is found, its starting index cannot be less than 1 or more than 255. These are Pascal-style strings with a length byte, rather than C language-style strings with a terminating character.

Procedure The program moves through the string searching for the substring. It continues until it finds a match or until the remaining part of the string is shorter than the substring and hence cannot possibly contain it. If the substring does not appear in the string, the program clears register AL; otherwise, the program places the substring's starting index in register AL.

Entry conditions

Order in stack (starting from the top)

Low byte of return address
High byte of return address

Low byte of base address of substring
High byte of base address of substring

Low byte of base address of string
High byte of base address of string

Exit conditions

Register AL contains index at which first occurrence of substring starts if it is found; register AL contains 0 if substring is not found.

Examples

1. Data: String = 1D'ENTER SPEED IN MILES PER HOUR'
($1D_{16} = 29_{10}$ is the length of the string)
Substring = 05'MILES' (05 is the length of the substring)

Result: Register AL contains 10_{16} (16_{10}), the index at which the substring 'MILES' starts.

2. Data: String = 1B'SALES FIGURES FOR JUNE 1989' ($1B_{16} = 27_{10}$ is the length of the string)
   Substring = 04'JUNE' (04 is the length of the substring)
   Result: Register AL contains 13_{16} (19_{10}), the index at which the substring 'JUNE' starts

3. Data: String = 10'LET Y1 = X1 + R7' ($10_{16} = 16_{10}$ is the length of the string)
   Substring = 02'R4' (02 is the length of the substring)
   Result: Register AL contains 0, since the substring 'R4' does not appear in the string LET Y1 = X1 + R7.

4. Data: String = 07'RESTORE' (07 is the length of the string)
   Substring = 03'RES' (03 is the length of the substring)
   Result: Register AL contains 1, the index at which the substring 'RES' starts. An index of 1 indicates that the substring could be an abbreviation of the string. Interactive programs, such as BASIC interpreters and word processors, often use abbreviations to save on typing and storage.

Registers used AX, BX, CX, DI, DX, F (clears D flag), SI

Execution time Data-dependent, but the overhead is approximately 147 cycles, each successful match of 1 character takes 24 cycles, and each unsuccessful match of 1 character takes 70 cycles. The worst case is when the string and substring always match except for the last character in the substring, such as

String = 'AAAAAAAAB'
Substring = 'AAB'

The execution time in that case is

(STRING LENGTH − SUBSTRING LENGTH + 1) × (24 × (SUBSTRING LENGTH − 1) + 70) + 147

If, for example, STRING LENGTH = 9 and SUBSTRING LENGTH = 3 (as in the example above), the execution time is

$$(9 - 3 + 1) \times (24 \times (3 - 1) + 70) + 147 = 7 \times 118 + 147$$

= 826 + 147
= 973 cycles

Program size 62 bytes

Data memory required None

Special cases

1. If either the string or the substring has a length of 0, the program exits with 0 in register AL, indicating that it did not find the substring.

2. If the substring is longer than the string, the program exits with 0 in register AL, indicating that it did not find the substring.

3. If the program returns an index of 1, the substring may be regarded as an abbreviation of the string. That is, the substring occurs in the string, starting at the first character. A typical example would be a string PRINT and a substring PR.

4. If the substring occurs more than once in the string, the program will return only the index to the first occurrence (the one with the smallest starting index).

```
;       Title               Find the Position of a Substring
;       Name:               POS
;
;
;       Purpose:            Search for the first occurrence of a substring
;                           in a string and return its starting index.
;                           If the substring is not found, a 0 is returned.
;
;       Entry:              TOP OF STACK
;                             Low byte of return address
;                             High byte of return address
;                             Low byte of substring address
;                             High byte of substring address
;                             Low byte of string address
;                             High byte of string address
;
;                             Each string consists of a length byte
;                             followed by a maximum of 255 characters.
;
;       Exit:               If the substring is found then
;                             Register AL = its starting index
;                           else
;                             Register AL = 0
```

```
;
;       Registers Used: AX,BX,CX,DI,DX,F (clears D flag),SI
;
;
;       Time:           Since the algorithm is so data dependent
;                       a simple formula is impossible but the
;                       following statements are true and a
;                       worst case is given below:
;
;                       147 cycles overhead.
;                       Each match of 1 character takes 24 cycles
;                       A mismatch takes 70 cycles
;
;                       Worst case timing occurs when the
;                       string and substring always match
;                       except for the last character of the
;                       substring, such as:
;                          string = 'AAAAAAAAAB'
;                          substring = 'AAB'
;
;       Size:           Program 62 bytes
;

POS:

        ;
        ;OBTAIN PARAMETERS FROM STACK
        ;
        POP     DX              ;SAVE RETURN ADDRESS
        POP     SI              ;GET BASE ADDRESS OF SUBSTRING
        POP     DI              ;GET BASE ADDRESS OF STRING
        PUSH    DX              ;PUT RETURN ADDRESS BACK IN STACK
        ;
        ;EXIT, INDICATING SUBSTRING NOT FOUND, IF STRING OR SUBSTRING
        ;  HAS ZERO LENGTH OR IF SUBSTRING IS LONGER THAN STRING
        ;
        SUB     AX,AX           ;INDICATE SUBSTRING NOT FOUND
        MOV     DL,[DI]         ;GET STRING LENGTH
        TEST    DL,DL           ;TEST STRING LENGTH
        JZ      EXITPO          ;BRANCH (EXIT) IF STRING LENGTH IS ZERO
        MOV     DH,[SI]         ;GET SUBSTRING LENGTH
        TEST    DH,DH           ;TEST SUBSTRING LENGTH
        JZ      EXITPO          ;BRANCH (EXIT) IF SUBSTRING LENGTH IS ZERO
        SUB     DL,DH           ;COMPARE STRING LENGTH, SUBSTRING LENGTH
        JB      EXITPO          ;BRANCH (EXIT) IF SUBSTRING IS LONGER THAN
                                ; STRING
        ;
        ;SET UP PARAMETERS FOR SEARCH
        ;
        MOV     AH,DH           ;SAVE SUBSTRING LENGTH
        SUB     DH,DH           ;EXTEND DIFFERENCE TO 16 BITS
        INC     DX              ;LENGTH OF PART THAT MUST BE EXAMINED IS
                                ; STRING LENGTH - SUBSTRING LENGTH + 1
                                ; REMAINDER IS TOO SHORT TO CONTAIN
                                ; SUBSTRING
        MOV     AL,DL           ;SAVE LENGTH OF PART THAT MUST BE
```

```
                                ; EXAMINED
        INC     SI              ;SAVE ADDRESS OF FIRST CHARACTER IN
        PUSH    SI              ; SUBSTRING
        MOV     BX,DI           ;CURRENT STARTING POSITION IN STRING IS
                                ; INITIALLY IN LENGTH BYTE
        CLD                     ;SELECT AUTOINCREMENTING
        ;
        ;SEARCH FOR SUBSTRING IN STRING
        ;START SEARCH AT BASE OF STRING
        ;CONTINUE UNTIL REMAINING STRING SHORTER THAN SUBSTRING
        ;
CMPPOS:
        INC     BX              ;MOVE CURRENT STARTING POSITION IN STRING
                                ; UP ONE CHARACTER
                                ;THIS STARTS FIRST ITERATION AT FIRST
                                ; CHARACTER IN STRING
        MOV     DI,BX           ;GET CURRENT STARTING POSITION IN STRING
        POP     SI              ;GET ADDRESS OF FIRST CHARACTER IN
                                ; SUBSTRING
        PUSH    SI              ;SAVE ADDRESS OF FIRST CHARACTER IN
                                ; SUBSTRING
        MOV     CL,AH           ;GET SUBSTRING LENGTH
        SUB     CH,CH           ;EXTEND SUBSTRING LENGTH TO 16 BITS
        ;
        ;COMPARE BYTES OF SUBSTRING WITH BYTES OF STRING,
        ; STARTING AT CURRENT POSITION IN STRING
        ;
  REPE  CMPSB                   ;COMPARE BYTES UNTIL DONE WITH SUBSTRING
                                ;  OR UNEQUAL CHARACTERS FOUND
        JNE     NOTFND          ;BRANCH IF UNEQUAL CHARACTERS FOUND -
                                ;  SUBSTRING NOT FOUND
        ;
        ;SUBSTRING FOUND - CALCULATE INDEX AT WHICH IT STARTS IN
        ; STRING (LENGTH OF PART THAT MUST BE EXAMINED - NUMBER
        ; OF COMPARISONS REMAINING + 1)

        ;
        SUB     AL,DL           ;LENGTH OF PART THAT MUST BE EXAMINED
                                ; - NUMBER OF COMPARISONS REMAINING
        SUB     AH,AH           ;EXTEND DIFFERENCE TO 16 BITS
        INC     AX              ;ADD 1 SINCE INDEXES BEGIN AT 1
        JMP     REMTMP          ;EXIT, REMOVING SUBSTRING STARTING
                                ; ADDRESS FROM STACK
        ;
        ;ARRIVE HERE IF SUBSTRING NOT FOUND
        ;COUNT NUMBER OF COMPARISONS
        ;
NOTFND:
        DEC     DX              ;SEARCH THROUGH SECTION OF STRING
        JNZ     CMPPOS          ;  THAT COULD CONTAIN SUBSTRING
        SUB     AX,AX           ;SUBSTRING NOT FOUND AT ALL - MAKE
                                ;  STARTING INDEX ZERO
        ;
        ;REMOVE TEMPORARY STORAGE AND EXIT
        ;
REMTMP:
```

```
        POP     SI              ;REMOVE TEMPORARY FROM STACK
EXITPO: RET                     ;EXIT TO RETURN ADDRESS

;
;       SAMPLE EXECUTION:
;

SC5C:
        MOV     BX,OFFSET STG   ;GET BASE ADDRESS OF STRING
        PUSH    BX
        MOV     BX,OFFSET SSTG  ;GET BASE ADDRESS OF SUBSTRING
        PUSH    BX
        CALL    POS                 ;FIND POSITION OF SUBSTRING
                                ; SEARCHING "AAAAAAAAAB" FOR "AAB"
                                ; RESULTS IN REGISTER A=8
        JMP     SC5C            ;LOOP THROUGH TEST
;
;       TEST DATA
;
STG     DB      0AH             ;LENGTH OF STRING
        DB      'AAAAAAAAAB                    ' ;32 BYTE MAX
SSTG    DB      3               ;LENGTH OF SUBSTRING
        DB      'AAB                           ' ;32 BYTE MAX

        END
```

5D Copy a substring from a string (COPY)

Copies a substring from a string, given a starting index and the number of bytes to copy. Each string consists of at most 256 bytes, including an initial byte containing the length. If the starting index of the substring is 0 (i.e. the substring would start in the length byte) or is beyond the end of the string, the substring is given a length of 0 and the Carry flag is set to 1. If the substring would exceed its maximum length or would extend beyond the end of the string, then only the maximum number or the available number of characters (up to the end of the string) are placed in the substring, and the Carry flag is set to 1. If the substring can be formed as specified, the Carry flag is cleared. The strings are Pascal-style with a length byte, rather than C language-style with a terminating character.

Procedure The program exits immediately if the number of bytes to copy, the maximum length of the substring, or the starting index is 0. It also exits immediately if the starting index exceeds the length of the string. If none of these conditions holds, the program checks whether the number of bytes to copy exceeds either the maximum length of the substring or the number of characters available in the string. If either is exceeded, the program reduces the number of bytes to copy accordingly. It then copies the bytes from the string to the substring. The program clears the Carry flag if the substring can be formed as specified and sets the Carry flag if it cannot.

Entry conditions

Order in stack (starting from the top)

Low byte of return address
High byte of return address

Number of bytes to copy

Starting index to copy from

Low byte of base address of substring
High byte of base address of substring

Low byte of base address of string
High byte of base address of string

Low byte of maximum length of substring
High byte of maximum length of substring (always 0)

Exit conditions

Substring contains characters copied from string. If the starting index is 0, the maximum length of the substring is 0, or the starting index is beyond the length of the string, the substring will have a length of 0 and the Carry flag will be set to 1. If the substring would extend beyond the end of the string or would exceed its specified maximum length, only the available characters from the string (up to the maximum length of the substring) are copied into the substring; the Carry flag is set in this case also. If no problems occur in forming the substring, the Carry flag is cleared.

Examples

1. Data: String = 10'LET Y1 = R7 + X4' ($10_{16} = 16_{10}$ is the length of the string)
Maximum length of substring = 2
Number of bytes to copy = 2
Starting index = 5

Result: Substring = 02'Y1' (2 is the length of the substring)
We have copied 2 bytes from the string starting at character #5 (that is, characters 5 and 6)
Carry = 0, since no problems occur in forming the substring

2. Data: String = 0E'8657 POWELL ST'
($0E_{16} = 14_{10}$ is the length of the string)
Maximum length of substring = $10_{16} = 16_{10}$
Number of bytes to copy = $0D_{16} = 13_{10}$
Starting index = 06

Result: Substring = 09'POWELL ST' (09 is the length of the substring)
Carry = 1, since there were not enough characters available in the string to provide the specified number of bytes to copy.

3. Data: String = 16'9414 HEGENBERGER DRIVE' ($16_{16} = 22_{10}$ is the length of the string)

Maximum length of substring = $10_{16} = 16_{10}$
Number of bytes to copy = $11_{16} = 17_{10}$
Starting index = 06

Result: Substring = 10'HEGENBERGER DRIV' ($10_{16} = 16_{10}$ is the length of the substring)
Carry = 1, since the number of bytes to copy exceeded the maximum length of the substring

---

Registers used AX, BX, CX, DI, DX, F (clears D flag), SI

Execution time Approximately

20 × NUMBER OF BYTES COPIED plus 196 cycles overhead

NUMBER OF BYTES COPIED is the number specified if no problems occur, or the number available or the maximum length of the substring if copying would extend beyond either the string or the substring. If, for example, NUMBER OF BYTES COPIED = 12_{10} ($0C_{16}$), the execution time is

$$20 \times 12 + 196 = 240 + 196 = 436 \text{ cycles.}$$

Program size 75 bytes

Data memory required None

Special Cases

1. If the number of bytes to copy is 0, the program assigns the substring a length of 0 and clears the Carry flag, indicating no error.

2. If the maximum length of the substring is 0, the program assigns the substring a length of 0 and sets the Carry flag to 1, indicating an error.

3. If the starting index of the substring is 0, the program assigns the substring a length of 0 and sets the Carry flag to 1, indicating an error.

4. If the source string does not even reach the specified starting index, the program assigns the substring a length of 0 and sets the Carry flag to 1, indicating an error.

5. If the substring would extend beyond the end of the source string, the program places all the available characters in the substring and sets the Carry flag to 1, indicating an error. The available characters are the ones from the starting index to the end of the string.

6. If the substring would exceed its specified maximum length, the program places only the specified maximum number of characters in the substring. It sets the Carry flag to 1, indicating an error.

```
;       Title           Copy a Substring from a String
;       Name:           COPY
;
;
;       Purpose:        Copy a substring from a string given a starting
;                       index and the number of bytes.
;
;       Entry:          TOP OF STACK
;                         Low byte of return address
;                         High byte of return address
;                         Number of bytes to copy
;                         Starting index to copy from
;                         Low byte of destination string address
;                         High byte of destination string address
;                         Low byte of source string address
;                         High byte of source string address
;                         Low byte of maximum length of destination string
;                         High byte of maximum length of destination string
;                           (always 0)
;
;                         Each string consists of a length byte
;                         followed by a maximum of 255 characters.
;
;       Exit:           Destination string := The substring from the
;                       string.
;                       If no errors then
;                         Carry := 0
;                       else
;                         begin
;                           the following conditions cause an
;                           error and the Carry flag = 1.
;                           if (index = 0) or (maxlen = 0) or
;                               (index > length(source)) then
;                             the destination string will have a zero
;                             length.
;                           if (index + count - 1) > length(source))
;                           then
;                             the destination string becomes everything
;                             from index to the end of source string.
;                         end
;
;       Registers Used: AX,BX,CX,DI,DX,F (clears D flag),SI
;
;
;       Time:           Approximately (20 X count) cycles plus
```

```
;                    196 cycles overhead
;
;       Size:        Program 75 bytes
;
;


COPY:
        ;
        ;OBTAIN PARAMETERS FROM STACK
        ;
        POP     DX          ;SAVE RETURN ADDRESS
        POP     BX          ;GET NUMBER OF BYTES TO COPY, STARTING
                            ;  INDEX
        POP     DI          ;GET BASE ADDRESS OF SUBSTRING
        POP     SI          ;GET BASE ADDRESS OF SOURCE STRING
        POP     AX          ;GET MAXIMUM LENGTH OF SUBSTRING
        PUSH    DX          ;PUT RETURN ADDRESS BACK IN STACK
        ;
        ;EXIT IF ZERO BYTES TO COPY, ZERO MAXIMUM SUBSTRING
        ;  LENGTH, OR ZERO STARTING INDEX
        ;LENGTH OF SUBSTRING IS ZERO IN ALL CASES
        ;
        MOV     BYTE PTR [DI],0 ;LENGTH OF SUBSTRING = 0
        TEST    BL,BL       ;CHECK NUMBER OF BYTES TO COPY
        JZ      OKEXIT      ;BRANCH IF ZERO BYTES TO COPY, NO ERROR
                            ; SUBSTRING WILL JUST HAVE ZERO LENGTH
                            ; TEST CLEARS CARRY
        TEST    AX,AX       ;CHECK MAXIMUM LENGTH OF SUBSTRING
        JZ      EREXIT      ;TAKE ERROR EXIT IF SUBSTRING HAS ZERO
                            ;  MAXIMUM LENGTH
        TEST    BH,BH       ;CHECK STARTING INDEX
        JZ      EREXIT      ;TAKE ERROR EXIT IF STARTING INDEX IS
                            ;  ZERO (LENGTH BYTE)
        ;
        ;CHECK IF SOURCE STRING REACHES STARTING INDEX
        ;TAKE ERROR EXIT IF IT DOESN'T
        ;
        MOV     DX,AX       ;SAVE MAXIMUM LENGTH OF SUBSTRING
        MOV     AH,[SI]     ;GET LENGTH OF SOURCE STRING
        CMP     BH,AH       ;COMPARE STARTING INDEX TO LENGTH OF
                            ; SOURCE STRING
        JA      EREXIT      ;TAKE ERROR EXIT IF STARTING INDEX IS
                            ; BEYOND END OF SOURCE STRING

        ;
        ;CHECK IF THERE ARE ENOUGH CHARACTERS IN SOURCE STRING
        ; TO SATISFY THE NEED
        ;THERE ARE IF STARTING INDEX + NUMBER OF BYTES TO COPY - 1
        ; IS LESS THAN OR EQUAL TO THE LENGTH OF THE SOURCE
        ; STRING
        ;
        SUB     AL,AL       ;INDICATE NO TRUNCATION NEEDED
        MOV     CL,BL       ;COUNT = NUMBER OF BYTES TO COPY
        SUB     CH,CH       ;EXTEND COUNT TO 16 BITS
        ADD     BL,BH       ;ADD COUNT TO STARTING INDEX
```

```
        JC          REDLEN      ;BRANCH IF SUM IS GREATER THAN 255
        DEC         BL          ;CALCULATE INDEX OF LAST BYTE IN AREA
                                ; SPECIFIED FOR COPYING
        CMP         BL,AH       ;COMPARE TO LENGTH OF SOURCE STRING
        JB          CHKMAX      ;BRANCH IF SOURCE STRING IS LONGER
        ;
        ;CALLER ASKED FOR TOO MANY CHARACTERS
        ;JUST RETURN EVERYTHING BETWEEN STARTING INDEX AND THE END OF
        ;  THE SOURCE STRING
        ;COUNT := LENGTH(SSTRG) - STARTING INDEX + 1
        ;INDICATE TRUNCATION OF COUNT
        ;
REDLEN:
        MOV         CL,AH       ;GET LENGTH OF SOURCE STRING
        SUB         CL,BH       ;COUNT = LENGTH - STARTING INDEX + 1
        INC         CX
        NOT         AL          ;INDICATE TRUNCATION OF COUNT BY
                                ; SETTING MARKER TO FF
        ;
        ;DETERMINE IF THERE IS ENOUGH ROOM IN THE SUBSTRING
        ;CHECK IF COUNT IS LESS THAN OR EQUAL TO MAXIMUM LENGTH
        ;  OF DESTINATION STRING.  IF NOT, SET COUNT TO
        ;  MAXIMUM LENGTH
        ;IF COUNT > MAXLEN THEN COUNT := MAXLEN
        ;
CHKMAX:
        CMP         CL,DL       ;COMPARE COUNT TO MAXIMUM SUBSTRING LENGTH
        JBE         MOVSTR      ;BRANCH (NO PROBLEM) IF COUNT IS LESS
                                ; THAN OR EQUAL TO MAXIMUM
        MOV         CL,DL       ;OTHERWISE, REPLACE COUNT WITH MAXIMUM
        ;
        ;SET LENGTH OF DESTINATION STRING
        ;SOURCE POINTER = BASE ADDRESS OF SOURCE STRING + STARTING
        ;  INDEX
        ;DESTINATION POINTER = BASE ADDRESS OF SUBSTRING + 1 (TO
        ;  ACCOUNT FOR LENGTH BYTE
        ;
MOVSTR:
        MOV         [DI],CL     ;LENGTH OF DESTINATION STRING = COUNT
        INC         DI          ;POINT TO FIRST ACTUAL CHARACTER IN
                                ;  DESTINATION STRING
        MOV         DL,BH       ;EXTEND STARTING INDEX TO 16 BITS
        SUB         DH,DH
        ADD         SI,DX       ;POINT TO FIRST CHARACTER IN AREA TO
                                ;  BE COPIED FROM SOURCE STRING
        ;
        ;MOVE SUBSTRING FROM COPY AREA TO DESTINATION STRING
        ;
        CLD                     ;SELECT AUTOINCREMENTING
  REP   MOVSB                   ;MOVE SUBSTRING TO DESTINATION
        SHR         AL,1        ;MAKE CARRY INDICATE WHETHER REQUEST WAS
                                ; FULLY SATISFIED (1 IF IT WAS, 0 IF NOT)
OKEXIT: RET
        ;
        ;ERROR EXIT - SET CARRY TO 1
        ;
```

```
EREXIT:  STC              ;SET CARRY, ERROR EXIT
         RET

;
;        SAMPLE EXECUTION:
;


SC5D:
         MOV      AX,[MXLEN]      ;GET MAXIMUM LENGTH OF SUBSTRING
         PUSH     AX
         MOV      BX,OFFSET SSTG  ;GET BASE ADDRESS OF SOURCE STRING
         PUSH     BX
         MOV      BX,OFFSET DSTG  ;GET BASE ADDRESS OF DEST. STRING
         PUSH     BX
         MOV      AL,[CNT]        ;GET NUMBER OF CHARACTERS TO COPY
         MOV      AH,[IDX]        ;GET STARTING INDEX FOR COPYING
         PUSH     AX
         CALL     COPY       ;COPY SUBSTRING
                             ;COPYING 3 CHARACTERS STARTING AT INDEX 4
                             ; FROM '12.345E+10' GIVES '345'
                             ;NOTE THAT VALID INDEXES START AT 1,
                             ; NOT 0
         JMP      SC5D       ;LOOP THROUGH TEST

;
;DATA SECTION
;
IDX      DB       4          ;STARTING INDEX FOR COPYING
CNT      DB       3          ;NUMBER OF CHARACTERS TO COPY
MXLEN    DW       20H        ;MAXIMUM LENGTH OF DESTINATION STRING
SSTG     DB       0AH        ;LENGTH OF STRING
         DB       '12.345E+10                      ' ;32 BYTE MAX
DSTG     DB       0          ;LENGTH OF SUBSTRING
         DB       '                                ' ;32 BYTE MAX

         END
```

5E Delete a substring from a string (DELETE)

Deletes a substring from a string, given a starting index and a length. The string consists of at most 256 bytes, including an initial byte containing the length. The Carry flag is cleared if the deletion can be performed as specified. The Carry flag is set if the starting index is 0 or beyond the length of the string; the string is left unchanged in either case. If the deletion extends beyond the end of the string, the Carry flag is set to 1 and only the characters from the starting index to the end of the string are deleted. The string is Pascal-style with a length byte, rather than C language-style with a terminating character.

Procedure The program exits immediately if either the starting index or the number of bytes to delete is 0. It also exits if the starting index is beyond the length of the string. If none of these conditions holds, the program checks whether the string extends beyond the area to be deleted. If it does not, the program simply truncates the string by setting the new length to the starting index minus 1. If it does, the program compacts the string by moving the bytes above the deleted area down. The program then determines the new string's length and exits with the Carry cleared if the specified number of bytes were deleted, and with the Carry set to 1 if any errors occurred.

Entry conditions

Order in stack (starting from the top)

Low byte of return address
High byte of return address

Number of bytes to delete
Starting index to delete from

Low byte of base address of string
High byte of base address of string

Exit conditions

Substring deleted from string. If no errors occur, the Carry flag is cleared. If the starting index is 0 or beyond the length of the string, the

Carry flag is set and the string is unchanged. If the number of bytes to delete would go beyond the end of the string, the Carry flag is set and the characters from the starting index to the end of the string are deleted.

Examples

1. Data: String = 26'SALES FOR MARCH AND APRIL OF THIS YEAR' ($26_{16} = 38_{10}$ is the length of the string)
   Number of bytes to delete = $0A_{16} = 10_{10}$
   Starting index to delete from = $10_{16} = 16_{10}$

   Result: String = 1C'SALES FOR MARCH OF THIS YEAR' ($1C_{16} = 28_{10}$ is the length of the string with 10 bytes deleted starting with the 16th character—the deleted material is 'AND APRIL ')
   Carry = 0, since no problems occurred in the deletion.

2. Data: String = 28'THE PRICE IS $3.00 ($2.00 BEFORE JUNE 1)' ($28_{16} = 40_{10}$ is the length of the string)
   Number of bytes to delete = $30_{16} = 48_{10}$
   Starting index to delete from = $13_{16} = 19_{10}$

   Result: String = 12'THE PRICE IS $3.00' ($12_{16} = 18_{10}$ is the length of the string with all remaining bytes deleted)
   Carry = 1, since there were not as many bytes left in the string as were supposed to be deleted

---

Registers used AX, BX, CX, DI, DX, F (clears D flag), SI

Execution time Approximately 20 × NUMBER OF BYTES MOVED DOWN + 155 cycles overhead if the string must be compacted. This is necessary if the deletion creates a 'hole' in the string that must be filled. NUMBER OF BYTES MOVED DOWN is equal to STRING LENGTH − STARTING INDEX − NUMBER OF BYTES TO DELETE.

125 cycles if the string can simply be truncated (i.e. the deletion continues all the way to the end).

Examples

1. STRING LENGTH = 20_{16} (32_{10})
STARTING INDEX = 19_{16} (25_{10})
NUMBER OF BYTES TO DELETE = 08

Since there are exactly 8 bytes left in the string starting at index 19_{16}, all the routine must do is truncate it (i.e. reduce its length). This takes 125 cycles.

2. STRING LENGTH = 40_{16} (64_{10})
STARTING INDEX = 19_{16} (25_{10})
NUMBER OF BYTES TO DELETE = 08

Since there are 20_{16} (32_{10}) bytes above the truncated area, the routine must move them down eight positions to fill the 'hole.' Thus NUMBER OF BYTES MOVED DOWN = 32_{10} and the execution time is

$$20 \times 32 + 155 = 640 + 155 = 795 \text{ cycles}$$

Program size 72 bytes

Data memory required None

Special cases

1. If the number of bytes to delete is 0, the program exits with the Carry flag cleared (no errors) and the string unchanged.

2. If the string does not even extend to the specified starting index, the program exits with the Carry flag set to 1 (indicating an error) and the string unchanged.

3. If the number of bytes to delete exceeds the number available, the program deletes all bytes from the starting index to the end of the string and exits with the Carry flag set to 1 (indicating an error).

```
;       Title           Delete a Substring from a String
;       Name:           DELETE
;
;       Purpose:        Delete a substring from a string given a
;                       starting index and a length.
;
;       Entry:          TOP OF STACK
;                         Low byte of return address
;                         High byte of return address
;                         Number of bytes to delete (count)
```

```
;                               Starting index to delete from (index)
;                               Low byte of string address
;                               High byte of string address
;
;                               The string consists of a length byte
;                               followed by a maximum of 255 characters.
;
;       Exit:                 Substring deleted.
;                             If no errors then
;                               Carry := 0
;                             else
;                               begin
;                                 the following conditions cause an
;                                 error with Carry flag = 1.
;                                 if (index = 0) or (index > length(string))
;                                   then do not change string
;                                 if count is too large then
;                                   delete only the characters from
;                                   index to end of string
;                               end
;
;       Registers Used: AX,BX,CX,DI,DX,F (clears D flag),SI
;
;       Time:           Approximately 20 X (LENGTH(STRG)-INDEX-COUNT+1)
;                       plus 155 cycles overhead
;
;       Size:           Program 72 bytes
;

DELETE:
        ;
        ;OBTAIN PARAMETERS FROM STACK
        ;
        POP     DX          ;SAVE RETURN ADDRESS
        POP     BX          ;GET NUMBER OF BYTES TO DELETE,
                            ;  STARTING INDEX TO DELETE FROM
        POP     SI          ;GET BASE ADDRESS OF STRING
        PUSH    DX          ;PUT RETURN ADDRESS BACK IN STACK
        ;
        ;EXIT IF COUNT IS ZERO, STARTING INDEX IS ZERO, OR
        ;  STARTING INDEX IS BEYOND THE END OF THE STRING
        ;
        TEST    BL,BL       ;TEST NUMBER OF BYTES TO DELETE
        JZ      OKEXIT      ;BRANCH (GOOD EXIT) IF NOTHING TO DELETE
        TEST    BH,BH       ;TEST STARTING INDEX
        JZ      EREXIT      ;BRANCH (ERROR EXIT) IF STARTING INDEX IS
                            ; ZERO - THAT IS, IN LENGTH BYTE
        MOV     CL,[SI]     ;GET LENGTH OF STRING
        CMP     BH,CL       ;CHECK IF STARTING INDEX IS WITHIN STRING
        JA      EREXIT      ;BRANCH (ERROR EXIT) IF STARTING INDEX
                            ;  IS BEYOND END OF STRING
        ;
        ;CHECK WHETHER NUMBER OF CHARACTERS REQUESTED TO BE
        ;  DELETED ARE PRESENT
        ;THEY ARE IF STARTING INDEX + NUMBER OF BYTES TO DELETE - 1
        ;  IS LESS THAN OR EQUAL TO STRING LENGTH
```

```
;IF NOT, THEN DELETE ONLY TO END OF STRING
;
        SUB     AL,AL       ;INDICATE NO TRUNCATION NECESSARY
        MOV     AH,BL       ;COMPUTE STARTING INDEX + COUNT
        ADD     AH,BH
        JC      TRUNC       ;TRUNCATE IF INDEX + COUNT > 255
        DEC     AH          ;END OF DELETED AREA IS AT INDEX GIVEN BY
                            ;  STARTING INDEX + COUNT - 1
        CMP     AH,CL       ;COMPARE TO LENGTH OF STRING
        JB      CNTOK       ;BRANCH IF MORE THAN ENOUGH CHARACTERS
        JE      TRUNC       ;TRUNCATE BUT NO ERROR (EXACTLY ENOUGH
                            ;  CHARACTERS)
        NOT     AL          ;INDICATE ERROR - NOT ENOUGH CHARACTERS
                            ;  TO DELETE
;
;TRUNCATE THE STRING - NO COMPACTING NECESSARY
;SIMPLY REDUCE ITS LENGTH TO STARTING INDEX - 1
;
TRUNC:
        DEC     BH          ;STRING LENGTH = STARTING INDEX - 1
        MOV     [SI],BH     ;SET LENGTH BYTE
;
;EXIT WITH ERROR INDICATOR IN CARRY
;
        SHR     AL,1        ;SET CARRY FROM TRUNCATION INDICATOR
        RET
;
;SET LENGTH OF STRING AFTER DELETION
;THIS IS ORIGINAL LENGTH MINUS NUMBER OF BYTES TO DELETE
;
CNTOK:
        MOV     CH,CL       ;GET ORIGINAL STRING LENGTH
        SUB     CH,BL       ;SUBTRACT NUMBER OF BYTES TO DELETE
        MOV     [SI],CH     ;SET LENGTH BYTE
;
;SET PARAMETERS FOR COMPACTING THE STRING
;SOURCE POINTER = FIRST BYTE ABOVE DELETED AREA.  THIS IS
; BASE ADDRESS OF STRING + STARTING INDEX
; + NUMBER OF BYTES TO DELETE + 1
;DESTINATION POINTER = FIRST BYTE IN DELETED AREA.  THIS IS
; BASE ADDRESS OF STRING + STARTING INDEX
;NUMBER OF BYTES TO MOVE = STRING LENGTH - INDEX OF LAST
; BYTE IN DELETED AREA

;
        MOV     DL,BH       ;EXTEND STARTING INDEX TO 16 BITS
        SUB     DH,DH
        ADD     SI,DX       ;CALCULATE BASE ADDRESS PLUS STARTING
                            ;  INDEX
        MOV     DI,SI
        MOV     DL,BL       ;EXTEND NUMBER OF BYTES TO DELETE
        ADD     SI,DX       ;CALCULATE ADDRESS AT END OF DELETED
                            ;  AREA
        SUB     CL,AH       ;NUMBER OF CHARACTERS TO MOVE = STRING
                            ;  LENGTH - INDEX AT END OF AREA
        SUB     CH,CH       ;EXTEND NUMBER TO 16-BIT COUNT
```

```
        CLD                     ;SELECT AUTOINCREMENTING
        ;
        ;COMPACT STRING BY MOVING ALL CHARACTERS ABOVE THE
        ;  DELETED AREA DOWN
        ;
   REP  MOVSB                   ;MOVE CHARACTERS DOWN INTO DELETED
                                ;  AREA, THUS COMPACTING STRING
        ;
        ;CLEAR CARRY, INDICATING NO ERRORS
        ;
OKEXIT:
        CLC                     ;CLEAR CARRY, NO ERRORS
        RET
        ;
        ;SET CARRY, INDICATING AN ERROR
        ;
EREXIT:
        STC                     ;SET CARRY, INDICATING ERROR
        RET

;
;       SAMPLE EXECUTION:
;

SC5E:
        MOV     BX,OFFSET SSTG   ;GET BASE ADDRESS OF STRING
        PUSH    BX
        MOV     AH,[IDX]  ;GET STARTING INDEX FOR DELETION
        MOV     AL,[CNT]  ;GET NUMBER OF CHARACTERS TO DELETE
        PUSH    AX
        CALL    DELETE    ;DELETE CHARACTERS
                    ;DELETING 4 CHARACTERS STARTING AT INDEX 1
                    ; FROM "JOE HANDOVER" LEAVES "HANDOVER"
        JMP     SC5E      ;LOOP THROUGH TEST

;
;DATA SECTION
;
IDX     DB      1         ;STARTING INDEX FOR DELETION
CNT     DB      4         ;NUMBER OF CHARACTERS TO DELETE
SSTG    DB      12        ;LENGTH OF STRING IN BYTES
        DB      'JOE HANDOVER' ;STRING
        END
```

5F Insert a substring into a string (INSERT)

Inserts a substring into a string, given a starting index. The string and substring each consist of at most 256 bytes, including an initial byte containing the length. The Carry flag is cleared if the insertion can be accomplished with no problems. The Carry flag is set if the starting index is 0 or beyond the length of the string. In the second case, the substring is concatenated to the end of the string. The Carry flag is also set if the insertion would make the string exceed a specified maximum length; in that case, the program inserts only enough of the substring to reach the maximum length. These are Pascal-style strings with a length byte, rather than C language-style strings with a terminating character.

Procedure The program exits immediately if the starting index or the length of the substring is 0. If neither is 0, the program checks whether the insertion would make the string longer than the specified maximum. If it would, the program truncates the substring. The program then checks whether the starting index is within the string. If not, the program simply concatenates the substring at the end of the string. If the starting index is within the string, the program must make room for the insertion by moving the remaining characters up in memory. This move must start at the highest address to avoid writing over any data. Finally, the program can move the substring into the open area. The program then determines the new string length. It exits with the Carry flag set to 0 if no problems occurred and to 1 if the starting index was 0, the substring had to be truncated, or the starting index was beyond the length of the string.

Entry conditions

Order in stack (starting from the top)

Low byte of base address
High byte of return address

Maximum length of string

Starting index at which to insert the substring

Low byte of base address of substring
High byte of base address of substring

Low byte of base address of string
High byte of base address of string

Exit conditions

Substring inserted into string. If no errors occur, the Carry flag is cleared. If the starting index or the length of the substring is 0, the Carry flag is set and the string is not changed. If the starting index is beyond the length of the string, the Carry flag is set and the substring is concatenated to the end of the string. If the insertion would make the string exceed its specified maximum length, the Carry flag is set and only enough of the substring is inserted to reach maximum length.

Examples

1. Data: String = 0A'JOHN SMITH' ($0A_{16} = 10_{10}$ is the length of the string)
   Substring = 08'WILLIAM ' (08 is the length of the substring)
   Maximum length of string = $14_{16} = 20_{10}$
   Starting index = 06

   Result: String = 12'JOHN WILLIAM SMITH' ($12_{16} = 18_{10}$ is the length of the string with the substring inserted)
   Carry = 0, since no problems occurred in the insertion

2. Data: String = 0A'JOHN SMITH' ($0A_{16} = 10_{10}$ is the length of the string)
   Substring = 0C'ROCKEFELLER' ($0C_{16} = 12_{10}$ is the length of the substring)
   Maximum length of string = $14_{16} = 20_{10}$
   Starting index = 06

   Result: String = 14'JOHN ROCKEFELLESMITH' ($14_{16} = 20_{10}$ is the length of the string with as much of the substring inserted as the maximum length would allow)
   Carry = 1, since some of the substring could not be inserted without exceeding the maximum length of the string.

Registers used AX, BX, CX, DI, DX, F (clears D flag), SI

Execution time Approximately

20 × NUMBER OF BYTES MOVED + 20 × NUMBER OF BYTES INSERTED + 226 cycles

NUMBER OF BYTES MOVED is the number of bytes that must be moved to make room for the insertion. If the starting index is beyond the end of the string, this is 0 since the substring is simply placed at the end. Otherwise, this is STRING LENGTH − STARTING INDEX + 1, since the bytes at or above the starting index must be moved.

NUMBER OF BYTES INSERTED is the length of the substring if no truncation occurs. It is the maximum length of the string minus its current length if inserting the substring would produce a string longer than the maximum.

Examples

1. STRING LENGTH = 20_{16} (32_{10})
STARTING INDEX = 19_{16} (25_{10})
MAXIMUM LENGTH = 30_{16} (48_{10})
SUBSTRING LENGTH = 06

That is, we want to insert a substring 6 bytes long, starting at the 25th character. Since 8 bytes must be moved up (NUMBER OF BYTES MOVED = 32 − 25 + 1) and 6 bytes must be inserted, the execution time is approximately

$$20 \times 8 + 20 \times 6 + 226 = 160 + 120 + 226 = 506 \text{ cycles.}$$

2. STRING LENGTH = 20_{16} (32_{10})
STARTING INDEX = 19_{16} (25_{10})
MAXIMUM LENGTH = 24_{16} (36_{10})
SUBSTRING LENGTH = 06

As opposed to Example 1, here we can insert only 4 bytes of the substring without exceeding the string's maximum length. Thus NUMBER OF BYTES MOVED = 8 and NUMBER OF BYTES INSERTED = 4. The execution time is approximately

$$20 \times 8 + 20 \times 4 + 226 = 160 + 80 + 226 = 466 \text{ cycles.}$$

Program size 93 bytes

Data memory required None

Special cases

1. If the length of the substring (the insertion) is 0, the program exits with the Carry flag cleared (no errors) and the string unchanged.

2. If the starting index for the insertion is 0 (i.e. the insertion would start in the length byte), the program exits with the Carry flag set to 1 (indicating an error) and the string unchanged.

3. If the insertion makes the string exceed the specified maximum length, the program inserts only enough characters to reach the maximum length. The Carry flag is set to 1 to indicate that the insertion has been truncated.

4. If the starting index of the insertion is beyond the end of the string, the program concatenates the insertion at the end of the string and indicates an error by setting the Carry flag to 1.

5. If the original length of the string exceeds its specified maximum length, the program exits with the Carry flag set to 1 (indicating an error) and the string unchanged.

```
;       Title           Insert a Substring into a String
;       Name:           INSERT
;
;
;       Purpose:        Insert a substring into a string given a
;                       starting index.
;
;       Entry:          TOP OF STACK
;                         Low byte of return address
;                         High byte of return address
;                         Maximum length of (source) string
;                         Starting index to insert the substring
;                         Low byte of substring address
;                         High byte of substring address
;                         Low byte of (source) string address
;                         High byte of (source) string address
;
;                         Each string consists of a length byte
;                         followed by a maximum of 255 characters.
;
;       Exit:           Substring inserted into string.
;                       If no errors then
;                         Carry = 0
;                        else
;                         begin
;                           the following conditions cause the
;                           Carry flag to be set.
;                           if index = 0 then
;                             do not insert the substring
;                           if length(string) > maximum length then
```

```
;                               do not insert the substring
;                             if index > length(string) then
;                               concatenate substring onto the end of the
;                               source string
;                             if length(string)+length(substring) > maxlen
;                               then insert only enough of the substring
;                               to reach maximum length
;                           end
;
;       Registers Used: AX,BX,CX,DI,DX,F (clears D flag),SI
;
;       Time:           Approximately
;                         20 X (LENGTH(STRING) - INDEX + 1) +
;                         20 X (LENGTH(SUBSTRING)) +
;                         226 cycles overhead
;
;       Size:           Program 93 bytes


INSERT:
        ;
        ;OBTAIN PARAMETERS FROM STACK
        ;
        POP     DX              ;SAVE RETURN ADDRESS
        POP     BX              ;GET MAXIMUM LENGTH OF SOURCE STRING,
                                ;  STARTING INDEX OF INSERTION
        POP     SI              ;GET BASE ADDRESS OF SUBSTRING
        POP     DI              ;GET BASE ADDRESS OF STRING
        PUSH    DX              ;PUT RETURN ADDRESS BACK IN STACK
        ;
        ;EXIT IF SUBSTRING LENGTH IS ZERO OR STARTING INDEX IS
        ; ZERO
        ;
        TEST    BH,BH           ;TEST STARTING INDEX
        STC                     ;INDICATE POSSIBLE ERROR
        JZ      EXITIN          ;EXIT, INDICATING ERROR, IF STARTING
                                ;  INDEX IS ZERO (LENGTH BYTE)
        MOV     AH,[SI]         ;GET LENGTH OF SUBSTRING (NUMBER OF
                                ;  CHARACTERS TO INSERT
        TEST    AH,AH           ;TEST SUBSTRING LENGTH
        JZ      EXITIN          ;EXIT IF NOTHING TO INSERT (NO ERROR)
        ;
        ;CHECK WHETHER THE STRING WITH THE INSERTION FITS IN THE
        ; SOURCE STRING (I.E., IF ITS LENGTH IS LESS THAN OR EQUAL
        ; TO THE MAXIMUM.
        ;IF NOT, TRUNCATE THE SUBSTRING AND SET THE TRUNCATION FLAG
        ;
        SUB     AL,AL           ;CLEAR ERROR FLAG, ASSUMING NO ERRORS
                                ; IN INSERTION PROCESS
        MOV     CL,AH           ;GET SUBSTRING LENGTH
        MOV     DH,[DI]         ;GET STRING LENGTH
        ADD     CL,DH           ;SUBSTRING LENGTH + STRING LENGTH
        JC      TRUNC           ;TRUNCATE SUBSTRING IF NEW LENGTH > 255
        CMP     CL,BL           ;COMPARE TO MAXIMUM STRING LENGTH
        JBE     SETLEN          ;BRANCH IF NEW LENGTH <= MAX LENGTH
        ;
```

```
        ;SUBSTRING DOES NOT FIT, SO TRUNCATE IT
        ;THAT IS, ONLY INSERT ENOUGH OF IT TO GIVE THE SOURCE
        ;  STRING ITS MAXIMUM LENGTH
        ;
TRUNC:
        NOT     AL          ;SET ERROR FLAG TO INDICATE SUBSTRING
                            ; WAS TRUNCATED
        MOV     CL,BL       ;NUMBER OF CHARACTERS TO INSERT =
        SUB     CL,DH       ; MAXIMUM LENGTH - STRING LENGTH
        JBE     EREXIT      ;EXIT, INDICATING ERROR FROM TRUNCATION
                            ; IF STRING LENGTH >= MAX LENGTH
        MOV     AH,CL       ;REPLACE SUBSTRING LENGTH WITH NUMBER
                            ; OF CHARACTERS TO INSERT
        MOV     CL,BL       ;NEW LENGTH = MAXIMUM LENGTH
        ;
        ;SET LENGTH AFTER INSERTION
        ;THIS IS OLD LENGTH PLUS NUMBER OF CHARACTERS TO INSERT
        ;THE VALUE IS EITHER SUBSTRING LENGTH PLUS STRING
        ;  LENGTH OR MAXIMUM LENGTH.
        ;
SETLEN: MOV     [DI],CL     ;SET NEW STRING LENGTH
        ;
        ;SET POINTERS FOR INSERTION
        ;SOURCE POINTER POINTS TO FIRST CHARACTER IN SUBSTRING
        ;DESTINATION POINTER POINTS TO CHARACTER AT STARTING
        ;  INDEX
        ;
        INC     SI          ;POINT TO FIRST CHARACTER IN SUBSTRING
                            ;  (SKIP OVER LENGTH BYTE)
        MOV     CL,BH       ;EXTEND STARTING INDEX TO 16 BITS
        SUB     CH,CH
        ADD     DI,CX       ;POINT TO POSITION AT WHICH FIRST
                            ;  CHARACTER WILL BE INSERTED
        ;
        ;CHECK WHETHER STARTING INDEX IS WITHIN THE STRING.  IF NOT,
        ;  CONCATENATE SUBSTRING ONTO THE END OF THE STRING
        ;
        CMP     BH,DH       ;COMPARE STARTING INDEX, STRING LENGTH
        JBE     LENOK       ;BRANCH IF STARTING INDEX IS WITHIN STRING
        INC     BH          ;ELSE SET STARTING INDEX TO END OF STRING
        MOV     AL,0FFH     ;INDICATE ERROR IN INSERT
        JMP     MVESUB      ;JUST PERFORM MOVE, NOTHING TO OPEN UP
        ;
        ;OPEN UP A SPACE IN SOURCE STRING FOR THE SUBSTRING BY MOVING
        ;  THE CHARACTERS FROM THE END OF THE SOURCE STRING DOWN TO
        ;  INDEX, UP BY NUMBER OF CHARACTERS TO INSERT
        ;
LENOK:
        ;
        ;CALCULATE NUMBER OF CHARACTERS TO MOVE
        ;  COUNT := STRING LENGTH - STARTING INDEX + 1
        ;
        MOV     CL,DH       ;GET STRING LENGTH
        SUB     CL,BH       ;SUBTRACT STARTING INDEX
        ;
        ;SET SOURCE AND DESTINATION POINTERS
```

```
        ;SOURCE POINTER POINTS TO LAST CHARACTER IN STRING
        ;DESTINATION POINTER POINTS FURTHER ON BY NUMBER OF
        ;  CHARACTERS TO INSERT
        ;
        PUSH    SI              ;SAVE ADDRESS OF FIRST CHARACTER IN
                                ;  SUBSTRING
        ADD     DI,CX           ;CALCULATE ADDRESS AT END OF STRING
        MOV     SI,DI
        MOV     DL,AH           ;MAKE NUMBER OF CHARACTERS TO INSERT
        SUB     DH,DH           ;  INTO 16 BIT OFFSET
        ADD     DI,DX           ;CALCULATE ADDRESS AT END OF STRING WITH
                                ;  INSERTION
        INC     CX              ;COUNT = STRING LENGTH - STARTING INDEX+1
        STD                     ;SELECT AUTODECREMENTING
        ;
        ;MOVE CHARACTERS UP IN MEMORY TO MAKE ROOM FOR SUBSTRING
        ;
   REP  MOVSB                   ;MOVE CHARACTERS UP IN MEMORY
                                ;THIS LEAVES ROOM FOR INSERTION OF
                                ; SUBSTRING
        MOV     DI,SI           ;MAKE DESTINATION POINTER POINT TO START
                                ;  OF INSERTION AREA
        INC     DI
        POP     SI              ;RESTORE SUBSTRING STARTING ADDRESS
        ;
        ;MOVE SUBSTRING INTO THE OPEN AREA
        ;
MVESUB:
        MOV     CL,AH           ;COUNT = SUBSTRING LENGTH
        CLD                     ;SELECT AUTOINCREMENTING
   REP  MOVSB                   ;MOVE SUBSTRING INTO OPEN AREA
        ;
        ;SET CARRY AS ERROR INDICATOR FROM ERROR FLAG
        ;
EREXIT: SHR     AL,1            ;SET CARRY FROM ERROR FLAG
EXITIN: RET                     ;EXIT

;
;       SAMPLE EXECUTION:
;


SC5F:
        MOV     BX,OFFSET STG  ;GET BASE ADDRESS OF STRING
        PUSH    BX
        MOV     BX,OFFSET SSTG ;GET BASE ADDRESS OF SUBSTRING
        PUSH    BX
        MOV     AH,[IDX]        ;GET STARTING INDEX
        MOV     AL,[MXLEN]      ;GET MAXIMUM LENGTH OF STRING
        PUSH    AX
        CALL    INSERT          ;INSERT SUBSTRING
                    ;RESULT OF INSERTING '-' INTO '123456' AT
                    ; INDEX 1 IS '-123456'
        JMP     SC5F        ;LOOP THROUGH TEST

;
```

```
;DATA SECTION
IDX       DB      1         ;STARTING INDEX FOR INSERTION
MXLEN     DB      20H             ;MAXIMUM LENGTH OF DESTINATION
STG       DB      6         ;LENGTH OF STRING
          DB      '123456                       ' ;32 BYTE MAX
SSTG      DB      1         ;LENGTH OF SUBSTRING
          DB      '-                            ' ;32 BYTE MAX

          END
```

5G Remove spaces from a string (SPACES)

Removes excess spaces from a string, including leading spaces, trailing spaces, and extra spaces within the string itself. The string consists of at most 256 bytes, including an initial byte containing the length. This is a Pascal-style string with a length byte, rather than a C language-style string with a terminating character.

Procedure The program exits immediately if the length of the string is 0. Otherwise, it first removes all leading spaces. It then sets a flag whenever it finds a space and deletes all subsequent spaces. If it reaches the end of the string with that flag set, it deletes the final trailing space as well. Finally, it adjusts the string's length.

Entry conditions

Base address of string in register BX

Exit conditions

Excess spaces removed from string. The string is left with no leading or trailing spaces and no groups of consecutive spaces inside it.

Examples

1. Data: String = 0F‘ JOHN SMITH ’ ($0F_{16} = 15_{10}$ is the length of the string)

   Result: String = 0A‘JOHN SMITH’ ($0A_{16} = 10_{10}$ is the length of the string with the extra spaces removed)

2. Data: String = 1B‘ PORTLAND, OREGON ’($1B_{16} = 27_{10}$ is the length of the string)

   Result: String = 10‘PORTLAND, OREGON’ ($10_{16} = 16_{10}$ is the length of the string with the extra spaces removed)

Registers used AX, CX, DI, DX, F (clears D flag), SI

Execution time Approximately

62 × LENGTH OF STRING IN BYTES + 102

If, for example, the string is 1C hex (28 decimal) bytes long, this is

$62 \times 28 + 102 = 1736 + 102 = 1838$ cycles

Program size 55 bytes

Data memory required None

```
;
;       Title               Remove Extra Spaces from a String
;       Name:               SPACES
;
;
;       Purpose:            Remove leading, trailing, and extra
;                           internal spaces from a string
;
;       Entry:              Register BX = Base address of string
;
;                             The string consists of a length byte
;                             followed by a maximum of 255 characters.
;
;       Exit:               Leading, trailing, and excess internal
;                           spaces removed
;
;       Registers Used: AX,CX,DI,F (clears D flag),SI
;
;       Time:               Approximately
;                            62 X (LENGTH(STRG)) + 102 cycles overhead
;
;       Size:               Program 55 bytes
;
;

SPACES:
        ;
        ;SAVE BASE ADDRESS OF STRING
        ;START COMPACTED STRING'S LENGTH AT ZERO
        ;INDICATE INITIALLY LAST CHARACTER WAS NOT A SPACE
        ;
        MOV     SI,BX       ;SAVE BASE ADDRESS OF STRING
        SUB     DX,DX       ;INDICATE LAST CHARACTER WAS NOT A SPACE
                            ;  (DL = 0)
                            ;COMPACTED STRING'S LENGTH (DH) = ZERO
        ;
        ;EXIT IF STRING LENGTH IS ZERO
        ;
        MOV     CL,[SI]     ;GET STRING LENGTH
        SUB     CH,CH       ;EXTEND STRING LENGTH TO 16 BITS
```

```
        TEST    CL,CL       ;TEST STRING LENGTH
        JZ      EXITRE      ;BRANCH (EXIT) IF STRING LENGTH IS ZERO
        ;
        ;REMOVE ALL LEADING SPACES
        ;
        INC     SI          ;POINT TO FIRST CHARACTER IN STRING
        MOV     DI,SI       ;START POINTERS TO BOTH ORIGINAL, COMPACTED
                            ;  STRINGS AT FIRST CHARACTER IN STRING
        CLD                 ;SELECT AUTOINCREMENTING
        MOV     AL,SPACE    ;GET SPACE FOR COMPARISON
  REPE  SCASB               ;KEEP EXAMINING CHARACTERS UNTIL EITHER
                            ;  COUNT REACHES ZERO OR NON-SPACE IS
                            ;  FOUND
                            ;NOTE THAT SCASB USES DI AND AL
        JE      SETLEN      ;BRANCH IF SCAN ENDED BECAUSE ALL
                            ;  CHARACTERS WERE EXAMINED - THIS MEANS
                            ;  ALL CHARACTERS WERE SPACES SO COMPACTED
                            ;  STRING IS EMPTY
        ;
        ;WORK THROUGH MAIN PART OF STRING, OMITTING SPACES
        ; THAT OCCUR IMMEDIATELY AFTER OTHER SPACES
        ;
        ;CHECK IF CURRENT CHARACTER IS A SPACE
        ;IF SO, CHECK IF PREVIOUS CHARACTER WAS A SPACE
        ;IF SO, OMIT CHARACTER FROM COMPACTED STRING
        ;IF NOT, MARK CHARACTER AS A SPACE
        ;
        XCHG    DI,SI       ;MAKE SOURCE POINTER POINT TO FIRST
                            ;  NON-BLANK CHARACTER, DESTINATION
                            ;  POINTER POINT TO FIRST CHARACTER
                            ;  IN SUBSTRING
        DEC     SI          ;NOTE FIRST NON-BLANK CHARACTER IS ONE
                            ;  BACK FROM CURRENT POINTER VALUE SINCE
                            ;  LOOP INCREMENTED POINTER AFTER MAKING
                            ;  FINAL COMPARISON
MVCHAR:
        LODSB               ;GET NEXT CHARACTER (AND INCREMENT
                            ;  SOURCE POINTER)
        CMP     AL,SPACE    ;IS IT A SPACE?
        JNE     MARKCH      ;BRANCH IF CHARACTER IS NOT A SPACE
        TEST    DL,DL       ;CHECK IF LAST CHARACTER WAS A SPACE
        JNZ     CNTCHR      ;BRANCH IF IT WAS, THUS DROPPING A SPACE
                            ;  THAT OCCURS AFTER ANOTHER SPACE
        NOT     DL          ;INDICATE CURRENT CHARACTER IS A SPACE
        JMP     SVCHR       ;GO SAVE FIRST SPACE
        ;
        ;INDICATE CURRENT CHARACTER IS NOT A SPACE
        ;
MARKCH:
        SUB     DL,DL       ;INDICATE CURRENT CHARACTER NOT A SPACE
        ;
        ;SAVE CURRENT CHARACTER IN COMPACTED STRING
        ;
SVCHR:
        STOSB               ;SAVE CHARACTER IN COMPACTED STRING (AND
                            ;  INCREMENT DESTINATION POINTER)
```

```
        INC     DH          ;ADD 1 TO LENGTH OF COMPACTED STRING
        ;
        ;COUNT CHARACTERS
        ;
CNTCHR: LOOP    MVCHAR      ;BRANCH IF ANY CHARACTERS LEFT
        ;
        ;OMIT LAST CHARACTER IF IT WAS A SPACE
        ;
        TEST    DL,DL       ;CHECK IF FINAL CHARACTER WAS A SPACE
        JZ      SETLEN      ;BRANCH IF IT WAS NOT
        DEC     DH          ;OMIT FINAL CHARACTER IF IT WAS A SPACE BY
                            ;  REDUCING LENGTH OF COMPACTED STRING
                            ;  BY 1
        ;
        ;SET LENGTH OF COMPACTED STRING
        ;
SETLEN:
        MOV     [BX],DH     ;SAVE LENGTH OF COMPACTED STRING
        ;
        ;EXIT
        ;
EXITRE: RET

;
;CHARACTER DEFINITION
;
SPACE   EQU     20H         ;ASCII SPACE CHARACTER


;
;       SAMPLE EXECUTION:
;


SC5G:
        MOV     BX,OFFSET STG    ;GET BASE ADDRESS OF STRING
        CALL    SPACES      ;REMOVE SPACES
                            ;RESULT OF REMOVING EXTRA SPACES FROM
                            ; ' JOHN  SMITH  ' IS 'JOHN SMITH'
;
;DATA SECTION
;
STG     DB      0EH         ;LENGTH OF STRING IN BYTES
        DB      ' JOHN  SMITH  '   ;STRING

        END
```

6 Array operations

6A 8-bit array summation (ASUM8)

Adds the elements of an array of byte-length elements, producing a 16-bit sum.

Procedure The program starts the sum at 0. It then adds elements one at a time to the sum's less significant byte. It also adds the carries to the sum's more significant byte.

Entry conditions

Base address of array in register BX
Size of array in bytes in register AX

Exit conditions

Sum in register AX

Example

Data: Size of array in bytes = [AX] = 0008

Array elements
$F7_{16} = 247_{10}$
$23_{16} = 35_{10}$
$31_{16} = 49_{10}$
$70_{16} = 112_{10}$
$5A_{16} = 90_{10}$
$16_{16} = 22_{10}$
$CB_{16} = 203_{10}$
$E1_{16} = 225_{10}$

Result: Sum = [AX] = $03D7_{16} = 983_{10}$

Registers used AX, BX, CX, F

Execution time Approximately 37 cycles per byte-length element plus 9 cycles overhead. If, for example, the array consists of $1C_{16}$ (28_{10}) elements, the execution time is approximately

$$37 \times 28 + 9 = 1036 + 9 = 1045 \text{ cycles}$$

Program size 15 bytes

Data memory required None

Special case An array size of 0 causes an immediate exit with a sum of 0.

```
;
;
;       Title            8-Bit Array Summation
;       Name:            ASUM8
;
;
;       Purpose:         Sum the elements of an array of byte-length
;                        elements, yielding a 16-bit result.
;
;       Entry:           Register BX = Base address of array
;                        Register AX = Size of array in bytes
;
;       Exit:            Register AX = Sum
;
;       Registers Used: AX,BX,CX,F
```

```
;
;       Time:           Approximately 37 cycles per element plus
;                       9 cycles overhead
;
;       Size:           Program 15 bytes
;

        ;
        ;TEST ARRAY LENGTH
        ;EXIT WITH SUM = 0 IF ARRAY HAS NO ELEMENTS
        ;
ASUM8:
        MOV     CX,AX           ;SAVE ARRAY LENGTH
        SUB     AX,AX           ;START SUM AT ZERO
        JCXZ    EXITAS          ;BRANCH (EXIT) IF ARRAY LENGTH IS
                                ; ZERO - SUM IS ZERO IN THIS CASE
        ;
        ;ADD BYTE-LENGTH ELEMENTS TO LOW BYTE OF SUM ONE AT A TIME
        ;ADD CARRIES TO HIGH BYTE OF SUM
        ;
SUMLP:
        ADD     AL,[BX]         ;ADD NEXT ELEMENT TO LOW BYTE OF
                                ; SUM
        ADC     AH,0            ;ADD CARRY TO HIGH BYTE OF SUM
        INC     BX
        LOOP    SUMLP           ;CONTINUE THROUGH ALL ELEMENTS
EXITAS:
        RET


;
;       SAMPLE EXECUTION
;
;
SC6A:
        MOV     BX,OFFSET BUF   ;GET BASE ADDRESS OF BUFFER
        MOV     AX,[BUFSZ]      ;GET BUFFER SIZE IN BYTES
        CALL    ASUM8           ;SUM ELEMENTS IN BUFFER
                                ;SUM OF TEST DATA IS 07F8 HEX,
                                ; REGISTER AX = 07F8H
        JMP     SC6A            ;LOOP FOR ANOTHER TEST

;TEST DATA, CHANGE FOR OTHER VALUES
BSIZE   EQU     10H             ;SIZE OF BUFFER IN BYTES
BUFSZ   DW      BSIZE           ;SIZE OF BUFFER IN BYTES

BUF     DB      0               ;BUFFER
        DB      11H             ;DECIMAL ELEMENTS ARE 0,17,34,51,68
        DB      22H             ;85,102,119,135,153,170
        DB      33H             ;187,204,221,238,255
        DB      44H
        DB      55H
        DB      66H
        DB      77H
        DB      88H
        DB      99H
        DB      0AAH
```

```
DB          0BBH
DB          0CCH
DB          0DDH
DB          0EEH
DB          0FFH                ;SUM = 07F8 (2040 DECIMAL)

END
```

6B 16-bit array summation (ASUM16)

Adds the elements of an array of word-length (16-bit) elements, producing a 32-bit sum. The elements are arranged in the usual 8086 format with the less significant byte first.

Procedure The program starts the sum at zero. It then adds elements to the sum's less significant word one at a time, beginning at the base address. Whenever an addition produces a carry, the program adds 1 to the sum's more significant word.

Entry conditions

Base address of array in BX
Size of array in 16-bit words in AX

Exit conditions

Low word of sum in AX
High word of sum in DX

The use of DX and AX for a 32-bit result is compatible with 8086 multiplication and division instructions.

Example

Data: Size of array (in 16-bit words) = [AX] = 0008
Array elements
$F7A1_{16} = 63{,}393_{10}$
$239B_{16} = 9{,}115_{10}$
$31D5_{16} = 12{,}757_{10}$
$70F2_{16} = 28{,}914_{10}$
$5A36_{16} = 23{,}094_{10}$
$166C_{16} = 5{,}740_{10}$
$CBF5_{16} = 52{,}213_{10}$
$E107_{16} = 57{,}607_{10}$

Result: Sum = $03DBA1_{16} = 252\,833_{10}$
[DX] = more significant word of sum = 0003_{16}
[AX] = less significant word of sum = $DBA1_{16}$

Registers used AX, BX, CX, DX, F

Execution time 39 cycles per 16-bit element plus 13 cycles overhead. If, for example, the array consists of 12_{16} (18_{10}) elements, the execution time is

$$39 \times 18 + 13 = 702 + 13 = 715 \text{ cycles}$$

Program size 18 bytes

Data memory required None

Special case An array size of 0 causes an immediate exit with a sum of 0.

```
;
;
;       Title                   16-Bit Array Summation
;       Name:                   ASUM16
;
;
;       Purpose:                Sum the elements of an array of word-length
;                               (16-bit) elements, yielding a 32-bit result.
;
;       Entry:                  Register BX = Base address of array
;                               Register AX = Size of array (in 16-bit words)
;
;       Exit:                   Register AX = Low word of sum
;                               Register DX = High word of sum
;
;       Registers Used: AX,BX,CX,DX,F
;
;       Time:                   Approximately 39 cycles per element plus
;                               13 cycles overhead
;
;       Size:                   Program 18 bytes
;
;

ASUM16:
        ;
        ;TEST ARRAY LENGTH
        ;EXIT WITH SUM = 0 IF ARRAY HAS NO ELEMENTS
        ;
        MOV     CX,AX           ;MOVE ARRAY LENGTH TO CX
        SUB     AX,AX           ;CLEAR 32-BIT SUM
        MOV     DX,AX
```

```
        JCXZ    EXITS1          ;BRANCH (EXIT) IF ARRAY LENGTH IS
                                ; ZERO - SUM IS ZERO IN THIS CASE

        ;
        ;ADD WORD-LENGTH ELEMENTS TO LOW WORD OF SUM ONE AT A TIME
        ;ADD CARRIES TO HIGH WORD OF SUM
        ;
SUMLP:  ADD     AX,[BX]         ;ADD ELEMENT TO LOW WORD OF SUM
        ADC     DX,0            ;ADD CARRY TO HIGH WORD OF SUM
        INC     BX              ;CONTINUE THROUGH ALL ELEMENTS
        INC     BX
        LOOP    SUMLP
        ;
        ;EXIT
        ;
EXITS1:
        RET

;
;       SAMPLE EXECUTION
;

;
SC6B:
        MOV     BX,OFFSET BUF   ;GET BASE ADDRESS OF BUFFER
        MOV     AX,[BUFSZ]      ;GET SIZE OF BUFFER IN WORDS
        CALL    ASUM16          ;SUM WORD-LENGTH ELEMENTS IN BUFFER
                                ; SUM OF TEST DATA IS 31FF8 HEX,
                                ; REGISTER AX = 1FF8H
                                ; REGISTER DX = 0003
        JMP     SC6B            ;LOOP FOR ANOTHER TEST

;TEST DATA, CHANGE FOR OTHER VALUES
BSIZE   EQU     10H             ;SIZE OF BUFFER IN WORDS
BUFSZ   DW      BSIZE           ;SIZE OF BUFFER IN WORDS

BUF     DW      0               ;BUFFER
        DW      111H            ;DECIMAL ELEMENTS ARE 0,273,546,819,1092
        DW      222H            ;1365,1638,1911,2184,2457,2730,3003,3276
        DW      333H            ;56797,61166,65535
        DW      444H
        DW      555H
        DW      666H
        DW      777H
        DW      888H
        DW      999H
        DW      0AAAH
        DW      0BBBH
        DW      0CCCH
        DW      0DDDDH
        DW      0EEEEH
        DW      0FFFFH          ;SUM = 31FF8 (204792 DECIMAL)

        END
```

6C Find maximum byte-length element (MAXELM)

Finds the maximum element in an array of unsigned byte-length elements.

Procedure The program exits immediately (setting Carry to 1) if the array has no elements. Otherwise, the program assumes that the element at the base address is the maximum. It then works through the array, comparing the supposed maximum with each element and retaining the larger value and its address. Finally, the program clears Carry to indicate a valid result.

Entry conditions

Base address of array in register BX
Size of array in bytes in register AX

Exit conditions

Largest unsigned element in register AL
Address of largest unsigned element in register BX

Carry = 0 if result is valid, 1 if size of array is 0 and result is meaningless

Example

Data: Size of array (in bytes) = [AX] = 0008

Array elements

$35_{16} = 53_{10}$ $44_{16} = 68_{10}$
$A6_{16} = 166_{10}$ $59_{16} = 89_{10}$
$D2_{16} = 210_{10}$ $7A_{16} = 122_{10}$
$1B_{16} = 27_{10}$ $CF_{16} = 207_{10}$

Result: The largest unsigned element is element #2 ($D2_{16} = 210_{10}$)
[AL] = largest element ($D2_{16}$)
[BX] = BASE + 2 (lowest address containing $D2_{16}$)
Carry = 0, indicating that array size is non-zero and the result is valid

Registers used AX, BX, CX, DI, F (clears D flag)

Execution time Approximately 39–60 cycles per element plus 26 cycles overhead. The larger number applies to each iteration in which the program replaces the presumed maximum value with the current element. If, on average, this occurs in half of the iterations, the execution time is approximately

$$(39 + 60) \times \text{ARRAY SIZE}/2 + 26 \text{ cycles}$$

If, for example, ARRAY SIZE $= 18_{16} = 24_{10}$ bytes, the approximate execution time is

$$99 \times 12 + 26 = 1188 + 26 = 1214 \text{ cycles}$$

Program size 24 bytes

Data memory required None

Special cases

1. An array size of 0 causes an immediate exit with Carry set to 1 to indicate an invalid result.

2. If the largest unsigned value occurs more than once, the program returns with the lowest possible address. That is, it returns with the address closest to the base address that contains the maximum value.

```
;
;
;       Title                   Find Maximum Byte-Length Element
;       Name:                   MAXELM
;
;
;       Purpose:                Given the base address and size of an array,
;                               find the largest element.
;
;       Entry:                  Register BX = Base address of array
;                               Register AX = Size of array in bytes
;
;       Exit:                   If size of array not zero then
;                                 Carry = 0
;                                 Register AL = Largest element
;                                 Register BX = Address of that element
;                                   If there are duplicate values of the largest
;                                   element, register BX contains the address
;
```

```
;                          nearest to the base address.
;                       else
;                         Carry = 1
;
;       Registers Used: AX,BX,CX,DI,F (clears D flag)
;
;       Time:           Approximately 39 to 60 cycles per byte
;                       plus 26 cycles overhead
;
;       Size:           Program 24 bytes
;
;

MAXELM:
        ;
        ;EXIT WITH CARRY SET IF NO ELEMENTS IN ARRAY
        ;
        STC                     ;SET CARRY IN CASE ARRAY HAS NO ELEMENTS
        MOV     CX,AX           ;SAVE NUMBER OF ELEMENTS
        JCXZ    EXITMX          ;BRANCH (EXIT) WITH CARRY SET IF NO
                                ; ELEMENTS - INDICATES INVALID RESULT
        ;
        ;EXAMINE ELEMENTS ONE AT A TIME, COMPARING EACH ONE'S VALUE
        ; WITH CURRENT MAXIMUM AND ALWAYS KEEPING LARGER VALUE AND
        ; ITS ADDRESS.  IN THE FIRST ITERATION, TAKE THE FIRST
        ; ELEMENT AS THE CURRENT MAXIMUM.
        ;
        CLD                     ;SELECT AUTOINCREMENTING
        MOV     DI,BX           ;SET POINTER AS IF PROGRAM HAD JUST
        INC     DI              ; EXAMINED THE FIRST ELEMENT AND FOUND
                                ; IT TO BE LARGER THAN PREVIOUS MAXIMUM
MAXLP:
        MOV     BX,DI           ;SAVE ADDRESS OF ELEMENT JUST EXAMINED
        DEC     BX              ; AS ADDRESS OF MAXIMUM
        MOV     AL,[BX]         ;SAVE ELEMENT JUST EXAMINED AS MAXIMUM
        ;
        ;COMPARE CURRENT ELEMENT TO MAXIMUM
        ;KEEP LOOKING UNLESS CURRENT ELEMENT IS LARGER
        ;
MAXLP1:
        DEC     CX              ;COUNT ELEMENTS
        JZ      EXITLP          ;BRANCH (EXIT) IF ALL ELEMENTS EXAMINED
        SCASB                   ;COMPARE CURRENT ELEMENT TO MAXIMUM
                                ; ALSO MOVE POINTER TO NEXT ELEMENT
        JAE     MAXLP1          ;CONTINUE UNLESS CURRENT ELEMENT LARGER
        JB      MAXLP           ;ELSE CHANGE MAXIMUM
                                ;TO RETURN LAST OCCURRENCE RATHER THAN
                                ; FIRST OCCURRENCE, CHANGE THE CONDITIONAL
                                ; BRANCHES TO JA AND JBE
        ;
        ;CLEAR CARRY TO INDICATE VALID RESULT - MAXIMUM FOUND
        ;
EXITLP:
        CLC                     ;CLEAR CARRY TO INDICATE VALID RESULT
EXITMX:
        RET
```

```
;
;       SAMPLE EXECUTION:
;

SC6C:
        MOV     BX,OFFSET ARY ;GET BASE ADDRESS OF ARRAY
        MOV     AX,SZARY  ;GET SIZE OF ARRAY IN BYTES
        CALL    MAXELM    ;FIND LARGEST UNSIGNED ELEMENT
                          ;RESULT FOR TEST DATA IS
                          ; AL = FF HEX (MAXIMUM), BX = ADDRESS OF
                          ; FF IN ARY.
        JMP     SC6C      ;LOOP FOR MORE TESTING

SZARY   EQU     10H       ;SIZE OF ARRAY IN BYTES
ARY     DB      8
        DB      7
        DB      6
        DB      5
        DB      4
        DB      3
        DB      2
        DB      1
        DB      0FFH
        DB      0FEH
        DB      0FDH
        DB      0FCH
        DB      0FBH
        DB      0FAH
        DB      0F9H
        DB      0F8H

        END
```

6D Find minimum byte-length element (MINELM)

Finds the minimum element in an array of unsigned byte-length elements.

Procedure The program exits immediately (setting Carry to 1) if the array has no elements. Otherwise, the program assumes that the element at the base address is the minimum. It then works through the array, comparing the current minimum to each element and retaining the smaller value and its address. Finally, the program clears Carry to indicate a valid result.

Entry conditions

Base address of array in register BX
Size of array in bytes in register AX

Exit conditions

Smallest unsigned element in register AL
Address of smallest unsigned element in register BX
Carry = 0 if result is valid, 1 if size of array is 0 and result is meaningless

Example

Data: Size of array (in bytes) = [AX] = 0008

Array elements

$35_{16} = 53_{10}$ $44_{16} = 68_{10}$
$A6_{16} = 166_{10}$ $59_{16} = 89_{10}$
$D2_{16} = 210_{10}$ $7A_{16} = 122_{10}$
$1B_{16} = 27_{10}$ $CF_{16} = 207_{10}$

Result: The smallest unsigned element is element #3 ($1B_{16} = 27_{10}$)
[AL] = smallest element ($1B_{16}$)
[BX] = BASE + 3 (lowest address containing $1B_{16}$)
Carry = 0, indicating that array size is non-zero and the result is valid

Registers used AX, BX, CX, DI, F (clears D flag)

Execution time Approximately 39 to 60 cycles per element plus 26 cycles overhead. The larger number of cycles applies to each iteration in which the program replaces the presumed minimum value with the current element. If, on the average, this occurs in half of the iterations, the execution time is approximately

$$(39 + 60) \times \text{ARRAY SIZE}/2 + 26 \text{ cycles}$$

If, for example, ARRAY SIZE $= 14_{16} = 20_{10}$, the approximate execution time is

$$99 \times 10 + 26 = 990 + 26 = 1016 \text{ cycles}$$

Program size 24 bytes

Data memory required None

Special cases

1. An array size of 0 causes an immediate exit with Carry set to 1 to indicate an invalid result.

2. If the smallest unsigned value occurs more than once, the program returns with the lowest possible address. That is, it returns with the address closest to the base address that contains the minimum value.

```
;
;
;       Title           Find Minimum Byte-Length Element
;       Name:           MINELM
;
;
;       Purpose:        Given the base address and size of an array,
;                       find the smallest element
;
;       Entry:          Register BX = Base address of array
;                       Register AX = Size of array in bytes
;
;       Exit:           If size of array not zero then
;                         Carry = 0
;                         Register AL = Smallest element
;                         Register BX = Address of that element
;                          If there are duplicate values of the smallest
```

```
;                       element, register BX contains the address
;                       nearest to the base address.
;                     else
;                       Carry = 1
;
;       Registers Used: AX,BX,CX,DI,F (clears D flag)
;
;       Time:           Approximately 39 to 60 cycles per byte
;                       plus 26 cycles overhead
;
;       Size:           Program 24 bytes
;
MINELM:
        ;
        ;EXIT WITH CARRY SET IF ARRAY CONTAINS NO ELEMENTS
        ;
        STC                     ;SET CARRY IN CASE ARRAY HAS NO ELEMENTS
        MOV     CX,AX           ;SAVE NUMBER OF ELEMENTS
        JCXZ    EXITMN          ;BRANCH (EXIT) WITH CARRY SET IF NO
                                ; ELEMENTS - INDICATES INVALID RESULT
        ;
        ;EXAMINE ELEMENTS ONE AT A TIME, COMPARING EACH VALUE WITH
        ; THE CURRENT MINIMUM AND ALWAYS KEEPING THE SMALLER VALUE
        ; AND ITS ADDRESS.  IN THE FIRST ITERATION, TAKE THE FIRST
        ; ELEMENT AS THE CURRENT MINIMUM.
        ;
        CLD                     ;SELECT AUTOINCREMENTING
        MOV     DI,BX           ;SET POINTER AS IF PROGRAM HAD JUST
        INC     DI              ; EXAMINED THE FIRST ELEMENT AND FOUND
                                ; IT TO BE SMALLER THAN PREVIOUS MINIMUM
MINLP:
        MOV     BX,DI           ;SAVE ADDRESS OF ELEMENT JUST EXAMINED
        DEC     BX              ; AS ADDRESS OF MINIMUM
        MOV     AL,[BX]         ;SAVE ELEMENT JUST EXAMINED AS MINIMUM
        ;
        ;COMPARE CURRENT ELEMENT TO SMALLEST
        ;KEEP LOOKING UNLESS CURRENT ELEMENT IS SMALLER
        ;
MINLP1:
        DEC     CX              ;COUNT ELEMENTS
        JZ      EXITLP          ;BRANCH (EXIT) IF ALL ELEMENTS EXAMINED
        SCASB                   ;COMPARE CURRENT ELEMENT TO MINIMUM
                                ; ALSO MOVE POINTER TO NEXT ELEMENT
        JBE     MINLP1          ;CONTINUE UNLESS CURRENT ELEMENT SMALLER
        JA      MINLP           ;ELSE CHANGE MINIMUM
                                ;TO RETURN LAST OCCURRENCE RATHER THAN
                                ; FIRST OCCURRENCE, CHANGE THE CONDITIONAL
                                ; BRANCHES TO JB AND JAE
        ;
        ;CLEAR CARRY TO INDICATE VALID RESULT - MINIMUM FOUND
        ;
EXITLP:
        CLC                     ;CLEAR CARRY TO INDICATE VALID RESULT
EXITMN:
        RET
```

```
;
;       SAMPLE EXECUTION:
;

SC6D:
        MOV     BX,OFFSET ARY ;GET BASE ADDRESS OF ARRAY
        MOV     AX,SZARY   ;GET SIZE OF ARRAY IN BYTES
        CALL    MINELM     ;FIND MINIMUM VALUE IN ARRAY
                           ;RESULT FOR TEST DATA IS
                           ; AL = 1 HEX (MINIMUM), BX = ADDRESS OF
                           ; 1 IN ARY.
        JMP     SC6D       ;LOOP FOR ANOTHER TEST

SZARY   EQU     10H        ;SIZE OF ARRAY IN BYTES
ARY     DB      8
        DB      7
        DB      6
        DB      5
        DB      4
        DB      3
        DB      2
        DB      1
        DB      0FFH
        DB      0FEH
        DB      0FDH
        DB      0FCH
        DB      0FBH
        DB      0FAH
        DB      0F9H
        DB      0F8H

        END
```

6E Binary search (BINSCH)

Searches an array of unsigned byte-length elements for a particular value. The elements are assumed to be arranged in increasing order. Clears Carry if it finds the value and sets Carry to 1 if it does not. Returns the address of the value if found.

Procedure The program does the search by repeatedly comparing the value with the middle remaining element. After each comparison, the program discards the part of the array that cannot contain the value (because of the ordering). The program retains upper and lower bounds for the part still being searched. If the value is larger than the middle element, the program discards that element and everything below it. The new lower bound is the address of the middle element plus 1. If the value is smaller than the middle element, the program discards that element and everything above it. The new upper bound is the address of the middle element minus 1. The program exits if it finds a match or if there is nothing left to search.

For example, assume that the array is

01_{16}, 02_{16}, 05_{16}, 07_{16}, 09_{16}, 09_{16}, $0D_{16}$, 10_{16}, $2E_{16}$, 37_{16}, $5D_{16}$, $7E_{16}$, $A1_{16}$, $B4_{16}$, $D7_{16}$, $E0_{16}$

and the value being sought is $0D_{16}$. The procedure works as follows.

In the first iteration, the lower bound is the base address and the upper bound is the address of the last element. So we have

LOWER BOUND = BASE
UPPER BOUND = BASE + LENGTH − 1 = BASE + $0F_{16}$
GUESS = (UPPER BOUND + LOWER BOUND)/2
= BASE + 7 (the result is truncated)
[GUESS] = ARRAY(7) = 10_{16} = 16_{10}

Since the value ($0D_{16}$) is less than ARRAY(7), we can discard the elements beyond #6. So we have

LOWER BOUND = BASE
UPPER BOUND = GUESS − 1 = BASE + 6
GUESS = (UPPER BOUND + LOWER BOUND)/2
= BASE + 3
[GUESS] = ARRAY(3) = 07

Since the value ($0D_{16}$) is greater than ARRAY(3), we can discard the elements below #4. So we have

LOWER BOUND = GUESS + 1 = BASE + 4
UPPER BOUND = BASE + 6
GUESS = (UPPER BOUND + LOWER BOUND)/2
= BASE + 5
[GUESS] = ARRAY(5) = 09

Since the value ($0D_{16}$) is greater than ARRAY(5), we can discard the elements below #6. So we have

LOWER BOUND = GUESS + 1 = BASE + 6
UPPER BOUND = BASE + 6
GUESS = (UPPER BOUND + LOWER BOUND)/2
= BASE + 6
[GUESS] = ARRAY(6) = $0D_{16}$

Since the value ($0D_{16}$) is equal to ARRAY(6), we have found the element. If, on the other hand, the value were $0E_{16}$, the new lower bound would be BASE + 7 and there would be nothing left to search.

Entry conditions

Order in stack (starting from the top)

Low byte of return address
High byte of return address

Value to find
Unused (wasted) byte

Low byte of size of array in bytes
High byte of size of array in bytes

Low byte of base address of array (address of smallest unsigned element)
High byte of base address of array (address of smallest unsigned element)

Exit conditions

Carry = 0 if the value is found, 1 if it is not found.
If the value is found, [BX] = its address.

Examples

Length of array = $10_{16} = 16_{10}$
Elements of array are: 01_{16}, 02_{16}, 05_{16}, 07_{16}, 09_{16}, 09_{16}, $0D_{16}$, 10_{16}, $2E_{16}$, 37_{16}, $5D_{16}$, $7E_{16}$, $A1_{16}$, $B4_{16}$, $D7_{16}$, $E0_{16}$

1. Data: Value to find = $0D_{16}$
   Result: Carry = 0, indicating value found
   [BX] = BASE + 6 (address containing $0D_{16}$)

2. Data: Value to find = $9B_{16}$
   Result: Carry = 1, indicating value not found

Registers used AX, BX, DI, F, SI

Execution time Approximately 70 cycles per iteration plus 75 cycles overhead. A binary search takes on the order of $\log_2 N$ iterations, where N is the number of elements in the array.

If, for example, $N = 32$, the binary search takes about $\log_2 32 = 5$ iterations. The execution time is then approximately

$$70 \times 5 + 75 = 350 + 75 = 425 \text{ cycles}$$

Program size 48 bytes

Data memory required None

Special case A size of 0 causes an immediate exit with Carry set to 1. That is, the array contains no elements and the value surely cannot be found.

```
;
;
;       Title               Binary Search
;       Name:               BINSCH
;
;
;       Purpose:            Search an ordered array of unsigned bytes,
;                           with a maximum size of 65,535 elements.
;
;       Entry:              TOP OF STACK
```

```
;                       Low byte of return address
;                       High byte of return address
;                       Value to find
;                       Unused byte
;                       Low byte of length (size) of array in bytes
;                       High byte of length (size) of array in bytes
;                       Low byte of base address of array
;                       High byte of base address of array
;
;       Exit:         If the value is found then
;                       Carry = 0
;                       Register BX = Address of value
;                     Else
;                       Carry = 1
;
;       Registers Used: AX,BX,DI,F,SI
;
;       Time:         Approximately 70 cycles per iteration of
;                     the search loop plus 75 cycles overhead
;
;                     A binary search takes on the order of log
;                     base 2 of N iterations, where N is the number of
;                     elements in the array.
;
;       Size:         Program 48 bytes
;

;
BINSCH:
        ;
        ;OBTAIN PARAMETERS FROM STACK
        ;
        POP     DI          ;GET RETURN ADDRESS
        POP     AX          ;GET VALUE TO FIND (IN AL)
        POP     BX          ;GET SIZE OF ARRAY IN BYTES
        POP     SI          ;GET BASE ADDRESS OF ARRAY
        PUSH    DI          ;PUT RETURN ADDRESS BACK IN STACK
        ;
        ;EXIT INDICATING VALUE NOT FOUND IF ARRAY CONTAINS NO ELEMENTS
        ;
        TEST    BX,BX       ;CHECK NUMBER OF ELEMENTS
        JZ      NOTFND      ;BRANCH (EXIT) IF NO ELEMENTS
                            ; VALUE SURELY CANNOT BE FOUND

        ;
        ;INITIALIZE POINTER TO UPPER BOUND
        ;LOWER BOUND = BASE ADDRESS
        ;UPPER BOUND = ADDRESS OF LAST ELEMENT =
        ; BASE ADDRESS + SIZE - 1
        ;
        LEA     DI,[BX+SI-1]    ;GET ADDRESS OF LAST ELEMENT
        ;
        ;ITERATION OF BINARY SEARCH
        ;1) COMPARE VALUE TO MIDDLE ELEMENT
        ;2) IF THEY ARE NOT EQUAL, DISCARD HALF THAT
        ;   CANNOT POSSIBLY CONTAIN VALUE (BECAUSE OF ORDERING)
        ;3) CONTINUE IF THERE IS ANYTHING LEFT TO SEARCH
```

```
        ;
SRLOOP:
        MOV     BX,DI       ;ADD LOWER AND UPPER BOUNDS
        ADD     BX,SI       ;NOTE THIS COULD PRODUCE A CARRY
        SHR     BX,1        ;DIVIDE SUM (INCLUDING CARRY) BY 2 TO
        ADC     BX,0        ; FIND ADDRESS OF MIDDLE ELEMENT, THEN
                            ; ROUND UPWARD BY ADDING CARRY TO
                            ; QUOTIENT
        ;
        ;IF ADDRESS OF MIDDLE ELEMENT IS GREATER THAN UPPER BOUND,
        ; THEN ELEMENT IS NOT IN ARRAY
        ;
        CMP     BX,DI       ;COMPARE ADDRESS OF MIDDLE ELEMENT TO
                            ; UPPER BOUND
        JA      NOTFND      ;BRANCH (NOT FOUND) IF INDEX GREATER
                            ; THAN UPPER BOUND
        ;
        ;IF ADDRESS OF MIDDLE ELEMENT IS LESS THAN LOWER BOUND, THEN
        ; ELEMENT IS NOT IN ARRAY
        ;
        CMP     BX,SI       ;COMPARE ADDRESS OF MIDDLE ELEMENT TO
                            ; LOWER BOUND
        JB      NOTFND      ;BRANCH (NOT FOUND) IF INDEX LESS
                            ; THAN LOWER BOUND
        ;
        ;CHECK IF MIDDLE ELEMENT IS THE VALUE BEING SOUGHT
        ;
        CMP     AL,[BX]     ;COMPARE ELEMENT WITH VALUE SOUGHT
        JA      RPLCLW      ;BRANCH IF VALUE LARGER THAN ELEMENT
        JE      FOUND       ;BRANCH IF VALUE FOUND
                            ;NOTE CARRY = 0 IN THIS CASE
        ;
        ;VALUE IS SMALLER THAN ELEMENT AT MIDDLE ADDRESS
        ;MAKE MIDDLE ADDRESS - 1 INTO NEW UPPER BOUND
        ;
        DEC     BX          ;SUBTRACT 1 SINCE VALUE CAN ONLY BE
                            ; FURTHER DOWN
        MOV     DI,BX       ;SAVE MIDDLE ADDRESS - 1 AS UPPER BOUND
        JMP     SRLOOP      ;CONTINUE SEARCHING
        ;
        ;VALUE IS LARGER THAN ELEMENT AT MIDDLE ADDRESS
        ;MAKE MIDDLE ADDRESS + 1 INTO NEW LOWER BOUND
        ;
RPLCLW:
        INC     BX          ;ADD 1 SINCE VALUE CAN ONLY BE FURTHER UP
        MOV     SI,BX       ;SAVE MIDDLE ADDRESS + 1 AS LOWER BOUND
        JMP     SRLOOP      ;CONTINUE SEARCHING
        ;
        ;EXIT WITH CARRY INDICATING SUCCESS OR FAILURE
        ;
NOTFND:
        STC                 ;SET CARRY, INDICATING VALUE NOT FOUND
FOUND:
        RET

;
```

```
;       SAMPLE EXECUTION
;
;
SC6E:
        ;SEARCH FOR A VALUE THAT IS IN THE ARRAY
        MOV     BX,OFFSET BUFFER ;GET BASE ADDRESS OF BUFFER
        PUSH    BX
        MOV     AX,[BUFSZ]  ;GET ARRAY SIZE IN BYTES
        PUSH    AX
        MOV     AL,7        ;GET VALUE TO FIND
        PUSH    AX          ;NOTE UNUSED HIGH BYTE HERE
        CALL    BINSCH      ;BINARY SEARCH
                            ;CARRY = 0 (VALUE FOUND)
                            ;BX = ADDRESS OF 7 IN ARRAY (BUFFER + 4)

        ;SEARCH FOR A VALUE THAT IS NOT IN THE ARRAY
        MOV     BX,OFFSET BUFFER ;GET BASE ADDRESS OF BUFFER
        PUSH    BX
        MOV     AX,[BUFSZ]  ;GET ARRAY SIZE IN BYTES
        PUSH    AX
        SUB     AL,AL       ;GET VALUE TO FIND (ZERO)
        PUSH    AX          ;NOTE UNUSED HIGH BYTE HERE
        CALL    BINSCH      ;BINARY SEARCH
                            ;CARRY = 1 (VALUE NOT FOUND)
        JMP     SC6E        ;LOOP FOR MORE TESTS
;
;DATA
;
BSIZE   EQU     10H         ;SIZE OF BUFFER IN BYTES
BUFSZ   DW      BSIZE       ;SIZE OF BUFFER IN BYTES
BUFFER  DB      1           ;BUFFER
        DB      2
        DB      4
        DB      5
        DB      7
        DB      9
        DB      10
        DB      11
        DB      23
        DB      50
        DB      81
        DB      123
        DB      191
        DB      199
        DB      250
        DB      255

        END
```

6F Shell sort (SSORT)

Arranges an array of unsigned word-length elements into ascending order using a Shell sort. Each iteration sorts a subset of the array consisting of elements separated by a gap or increment. A Shell sort is intermediate in efficiency between a crude insertion or bubble sort and a quicksort.

Procedure The program first deals with subsets of the array consisting of elements separated by a large gap. It then reduces the size of the gap between elements until it reaches 1. The idea here is that sorting subsets puts most elements in the proper order by the time the entire array must be handled. Shell's method is efficient because later sorts (with smaller gaps) never undo the ordering of earlier sorts (with larger gaps). This has been proved mathematically.

The program follows Shell's original suggestion of starting with a gap one-half the size of the array and dividing it in half (with truncation) after each iteration. Knuth (see the references) describes other methods of generating gaps; since none has been proved to be superior in all cases, we have chosen the simplest approach.

Entry conditions

Base address of array in BX
Number of elements in AX

Exit conditions

Array sorted into ascending order, considering the elements as unsigned words. Thus, the smallest unsigned word ends up stored starting at the base address.

Example

Data: Array size = $0C_{16} = 12_{10}$
Elements = $2B_{16}$, 57_{16}, $1D_{16}$, 26_{16}, 22_{16}, $2E_{16}$, $0C_{16}$, 44_{16}, 17_{16}, $4B_{16}$, 37_{16}, 27_{16}

Result: In the first iteration, the step is size/2 = 6
Ordering elements separated by 6 gives:
$0C_{16}, 44_{16}, 17_{16}, 26_{16},$
$22_{16}, 27_{16}, 2B_{16}, 57_{16},$
$1D_{16}, 4B_{16}, 37_{16}, 2E_{16}$
In the second iteration, the step is half the previous step (3)
Ordering elements separated by 3 gives:
$0C_{16}, 22_{16}, 17_{16}, 26_{16},$
$37_{16}, 1D_{16}, 2B_{16}, 44_{16},$
$27_{16}, 4B_{16}, 57_{16}, 2E_{16}$
In the third iteration, the step is half the previous step with truncation (1).
Finally, ordering elements separated by 1 gives:
$0C_{16}, 17_{16}, 1D_{16}, 22_{16},$
$26_{16}, 27_{16}, 2B_{16}, 2E_{16},$
$37_{16}, 44_{16}, 4B_{16}, 57_{16}$

References

D. E. Knuth, *The Art of Computer Programming. Vol. 3: Searching and Sorting*, Addison-Wesley, Reading, MA, 1973, pp. 84–95.

Y. Langsam *et al.*, *Data Structures for Personal Computers*, Prentice-Hall, Englewood Cliffs, NJ, 1985, pp. 459–462. The algorithms in this book are available as BASIC programs on disk for various computers. Other versions of the book are available for PL/I and Pascal.

Registers used AX, BX, CX, DI, DX, F, SI

Execution time Approximately 79 cycles per comparison. The number of comparisons has been proved to be proportional to $N \times (\log_2 N)^2$ where N is the number of elements. In practice, the program took the following amounts of time on a 4.77 MHz IBM PC (using an 8-bit 8088 chip):

5 s for 8K words
11 s for 16K words
17 s for 24K words

Program size 63 bytes

Data memory required 8 stack bytes

```
;       Title           Shell sort
;       Name:           SSORT
;
;       Purpose:        Arrange an array of unsigned words into
;                       ascending order using a Shell sort
;
;       Entry:          Base address of array in register BX
;                       Size of array in words in register AX
;
;       Exit:           Array sorted into ascending order.
;
;       Registers Used: AX,BX,CX,DI,DX,F,SI
;
;       Time:           Approximately 79 cycles per comparison.
;                       The number of comparisons is proportional to
;                       N X (log N)^2 where N is the size of the array.
;
;                       For example, sorting a 16,384-word array took
;                       about 11 s on an IBM PC with a 4.77 MHz 8088.
;
;       Size:           Program 63 bytes
;

;
;
SSORT:
        ;
        ;EXIT IF NO SORTING NECESSARY (LESS THAN 2 ELEMENTS
        ;  IN ARRAY)
        ;
        CMP     AX,2            ;EXIT IF LENGTH LESS THAN 2
        JB      SRTEND          ;  (NO SORTING NECESSARY)
        ;
        ;SAVE ARRAY LENGTH AT TOP OF STACK
        ;
        PUSH    BP              ;SAVE OLD BASE POINTER
        PUSH    AX              ;SAVE ARRAY LENGTH
        MOV     BP,SP           ;POINT TO ARRAY LENGTH
        ;
        ;START GAP AT ARRAY LENGTH
        ;NEXT GAP IS PREVIOUS GAP DIVIDED BY 2 WITH TRUNCATION
        ;
        MOV     DX,AX           ;INITIAL GAP = ARRAY LENGTH
NXTGAP: SHR     DX,1            ;NEXT GAP IS PREVIOUS GAP DIVIDED
                                ;  BY 2 WITH TRUNCATION
        JZ      REMLNG          ;DONE SORTING IF GAP IS ZERO
        ;
        ;SORT SUBSETS OF ELEMENTS SEPARATED BY CURRENT GAP
        ;USE SIMPLE INSERTION SORT ON EACH SUBSET
```

```
        ;SORT EACH SUBSET AS FAR AS TOP UPPER INDEX
        ;CONTINUE UNTIL TOP UPPER INDEX BEYOND END OF ARRAY
        ;
        MOV     CX,DX           ;START TOP UPPER INDEX AT GAP-1
        DEC     CX
NXTSUB:
        INC     CX              ;ADD 1 TO TOP UPPER INDEX FOR NEXT
                                ;  SUBSET
        CMP     CX,[BP]         ;CHECK IF TOP UPPER INDEX IN ARRAY
        JAE     NXTGAP          ;BRANCH IF TOP UPPER INDEX BEYOND
                                ;  END OF ARRAY
                                ;ALL SUBSETS WITH CURRENT GAP ARE
                                ;  SORTED WHEN THIS HAPPENS
        ;
        ;SORT SUBSET WITH GIVEN GAP UP TO TOP UPPER INDEX
        ;USE STANDARD INSERTION METHOD, EXCHANGING ELEMENTS
        ;  WHEN NECESSARY
        ;
        PUSH    BX              ;SAVE BASE ADDRESS OF ARRAY
        PUSH    CX              ;SAVE TOP UPPER INDEX
        MOV     DI,CX           ;POINT TO TOP ELEMENT IN SUBSET
        SHL     DI,1            ;  OF WORD-LENGTH ELEMENTS
        ADD     DI,BX
        MOV     BX,[DI]         ;GET TOP ELEMENT
NXTPR:
        SUB     CX,DX           ;CHECK IF THERE IS ANOTHER ELEMENT
                                ;  FURTHER DOWN IN SUBSET
        JB      ENDPRT          ;JUMP IF NO MORE ELEMENTS, HENCE
                                ;  SUBSET IS SORTED
        MOV     SI,DI           ;COMPARE NEXT PAIR OF ELEMENTS
                                ;  SEPARATED BY GAP
        SUB     DI,DX           ;STEP IS GAP X 2 SINCE ELEMENTS ARE
        SUB     DI,DX           ;  WORD-LENGTH
        MOV     AX,[DI]         ;COMPARE NEXT PAIR OF ELEMENTS
        CMP     AX,BX
        JBE     ENDPRT          ;DONE IF PAIR IN ORDER SINCE LATER
                                ;  PAIRS HAVE ALREADY BEEN SORTED
        MOV     [DI],BX         ;EXCHANGE PAIR IF OUT OF ORDER
        MOV     [SI],AX         ;TOP ELEMENT STAYS THE SAME FOR NEXT
                                ;  COMPARISON
        JMP     NXTPR           ;CONTINUE THROUGH PARTIAL SUBSET
ENDPRT:
        POP     CX              ;RESTORE TOP UPPER INDEX
        POP     BX              ;RESTORE BASE ADDRESS OF ARRAY
        JMP     NXTSUB          ;PROCEED TO NEXT PARTIAL SUBSET
        ;
        ;CLEAN STACK AND EXIT
        ;
REMLNG:
        POP     AX              ;REMOVE ARRAY LENGTH FROM STACK
        POP     BP              ;RESTORE BASE POINTER
SRTEND:
        RET                     ;EXIT

;
;
```

```
;         SAMPLE EXECUTION
;
;

SC6F:
          ;
          ;SORT AN ARRAY BETWEEN BEGBUF (FIRST ELEMENT)
          ; AND ENDBUF (LAST ELEMENT)
          ;
          MOV     BX,OFFSET BEGBUF ;GET BASE ADDRESS OF ARRAY
          MOV     AX,[SZARY]       ;GET SIZE OF ARRAY IN WORDS
          CALL    SSORT           ;SORT USING SHELL SORT
                                  ;RESULT FOR TEST DATA IS
                                  ; 0,1,2,3, ... ,14,15
          JMP     SC6F            ;LOOP TO REPEAT TEST

;
;DATA SECTION
;
BEGBUF    DW      15
          DW      14
          DW      13
          DW      12
          DW      11
          DW      10
          DW      9
          DW      8
          DW      7
          DW      6
          DW      5
          DW      4
          DW      3
          DW      2
          DW      1
          DW      0
SZARY     DW      16              ;SIZE OF ARRAY IN WORDS
          END
```

6G Quicksort (QSORT)

Arranges an array of unsigned word-length elements into ascending order using a quicksort algorithm. Each iteration selects an element and divides the array into two parts, one containing all elements larger than the selected element and the other containing all elements smaller than the selected element. Elements equal to the selected element may end up in either part. The parts are then sorted recursively in the same way. The algorithm continues until all parts contain either no elements or only one element. An alternative is to stop recursion when a part contains few enough elements (say, less than 20) to make a bubble sort practical.

The parameters are the array's base address, the address of its last element, and the lowest available stack address. The array can thus occupy all available memory, as long as there is room for the stack. Since the procedures that obtain the selected element, compare elements, move forward and backward in the array, and swap elements are all subroutines, they could be changed readily to handle other types of elements.

Ideally, quicksort should divide the array in half during each iteration. How closely the procedure approaches this ideal depends on how well the selected element is chosen. Since this element serves as a midpoint or pivot, the best choice woulld be the central value (or median). Of course, the true median is unknown. A simple but reasonable approximation is to select the median of the first, middle, and last elements.

Procedure The program first deals with the entire array. It selects the median of the current first, middle, and last elements as a central element. It moves that element to the first position and divides the array into two parts or partitions. It then operates recursively on the parts, dividing them into parts and stopping when a part contains no elements or only one element. Since each recursion places 6 bytes on the stack, the program must guard against overflow by checking whether the stack has reached to within a small buffer of its lowest available position.

Note that the selected element always ends up in the correct position after an iteration. Therefore, it need not be included in either partition.

Our rule for choosing the middle element is as follows, assuming that the first element is #1:

1. If the array has an odd number of elements, take the centre one. For example, if the array has 11 elements, take #6.

2. If the array has an even number of elements and its base address is even, take the element on the lower (base address) side of the centre. For example, if the array starts in 0300_{16} and has 12 elements, take #6.

3. If the array has an even number of elements and its base address is odd, take the element on the upper side of the center. For example, if the array starts in 0301_{16} and has 12 elements, take #7.

Entry conditions

Order in stack (starting from the top)

Low byte of return address
High byte of return address

Low byte of base address of array
High byte of base address of array

Low byte of address of last word in array
High byte of address of last word in array

Low byte of lowest possible stack address
High byte of lowest possible stack address

Exit conditions

Array sorted into ascending order, considering the elements as unsigned words. Thus, the smallest unsigned word ends up stored starting at the base address. Carry = 0 if the stack did not overflow and the result is proper. Carry = 1 if the stack overflowed and the final array is not sorted.

Example

Data: Length (size) of array = $0C_{16} = 12_{10}$
Elements = $2B_{16}$, 57_{16}, $1D_{16}$, 26_{16},
22_{16}, $2E_{16}$, $0C_{16}$, 44_{16},
17_{16}, $4B_{16}$, 37_{16}, 27_{16}

Result: In the first iteration, we have:
Selected element = median of the first (#1 = $2B_{16}$), middle (#6 = $2E_{16}$), and last (#12 = 27_{16}) elements. The selected element is therefore #1 ($2B_{16}$), and no swapping is necessary since it is already in the first position.

At the end of the iteration, the array is

27_{16}, 17_{16}, $1D_{16}$, 26_{16},
22_{16}, $0C_{16}$, $2B_{16}$, 44_{16},
$2E_{16}$, $4B_{16}$, 37_{16}, 57_{16}

The first partition, consisting of elements less than $2B_{16}$, is 27_{16}, 17_{16}, $1D_{16}$, 26_{16}, 22_{16}, and $0C_{16}$.

The second partition, consisting of elements greater than $2B_{16}$, is 44_{16}, $2E_{16}$, $4B_{16}$, 37_{16}, and 57_{16}.

Note that the selected element ($2B_{16}$) is now in the correct position and need not be included in either partition.

We may now sort the first partition recursively in the same way:

Selected element = median of the first (#1 = 27_{16}), middle (#3 = $1D_{16}$), and last (#6 = $0C_{16}$) elements. Here, #3 is the median and must be exchanged initially with #1.

The final order of the elements in the first partition is:

$0C_{16}$, 17_{16}, $1D_{16}$, 26_{16},
22_{16}, 27_{16}

The first partition of the first partition (consisting of elements less than $1D_{16}$) is $0C_{16}$, 17_{16}. We will call this the (1,1) partition for short.

The second partition of the first partition (consisting of elements greater than $1D_{16}$) is 26_{16}, 22_{16}, and 27_{16}.

As in the first iteration, the selected element ($1D_{16}$) is in the correct position and need not be considered further.

We may now sort the (1,1) partition recursively as follows:

Selected element = median of the first (#1 = $0C_{16}$), middle (#1 = $0C_{16}$), and last (#2 = 17_{16}) elements. Thus the selected element is the first element (#1 = $0C_{16}$), and no initial swap is necessary.

The final order is obviously the same as the initial order, and the two resulting partitions contain 0 and 1 element, respectively. Thus the next iteration concludes the recursion, and we then sort the other partitions by the same method. Obviously, quicksort's overhead becomes a major factor for arrays containing only a few elements. This is why one might use a bubble sort once quicksort has created small enough partitions.

Note that the example array does not contain any identical elements. During an iteration, elements that are the same as the selected element are never moved. Thus they may end up in either partition. Strictly speaking, then, the two partitions consist of elements 'less than or possibly equal to the selected element' and elements 'greater than or possibly equal to the selected element.'

References

N. Dale and S. C. Lilly, *Pascal Plus Data Structures*, D. C. Heath, Lexington, MA, 1985, pp. 300–307.

D. E. Knuth, *The Art of Computer Programming. Vol. 3: Searching and Sorting*, Addison-Wesley, Reading, MA, 1973, pp. 114–123.

Y. Langsam *et al.*, *Data Structures for Personal Computers*, Prentice-Hall, Englewood Cliffs, NJ, 1985, pp. 430–437. The algorithms in this book are available as BASIC programs for various computers. Other versions of the book are available for Pascal and PL/I.

Registers used AX, BX, DI, DX, F, SI

Execution time Approximately $N \times \log_2 N$ loops through PARTLP plus $2 \times N + 1$ overhead calls to SORT. Each iteration of PARTLP takes approximately 65 or 150 cycles (depending on whether an exchange is necessary), and each overhead call to SORT takes approximately 340 cycles. Thus the total execution time is on the order of

$$107 \times N \times \log_2 N + 340 \times (2 \times N + 1) \text{ cycles}$$

If, for example, $N = 16384$ (2^{14}), the total execution time should be around

$$107 \times 16384 \times 14 + 340 \times 32769 = 24500000 + 11100000 = \text{about } 35600000 \text{ cycles.}$$

This is about 7 s at a typical 8086 clock rate of 5 MHz.

Program size 179 bytes

Data memory required 8 bytes anywhere in RAM for pointers to the first and last element of a partition (2 bytes starting at addresses FIRST and LAST, respectively), a pointer to the bottom of the stack (2 bytes starting at address STKBTM), and the original value of the stack pointer (2 bytes starting at address OLDSP). Each recursion level requires 6 bytes of stack space, and the routines themselves require another 4 bytes.

Special case If the stack overflows (i.e. comes too close to its boundary), the program exits with Carry set to 1.

```
;       Title              Quicksort
;       Name:              QSORT
;
;
;       Purpose:           Arrange an array of unsigned words into
;                          ascending order using a quicksort, with a
;                          maximum size of 32767 words.
;
;       Entry:             TOP OF STACK
;                            Low byte of return address
;                            High byte of return address
;                            Low byte of address of first word in array
;                            High byte of address of first word in array
;                            Low byte of address of last word in array
;                            High byte of address of last word in array
;                            Low byte of lowest available stack address
;                            High byte of lowest available stack address
;
;       Exit:              If the stack did not overflow then
;                            The array is sorted into ascending order.
;                            Carry = 0
;                          Else
;                            Carry = 1
;
;       Registers Used: AX,BX,CX,DI,DX,F,SI
;
;       Time:              The timing is highly data-dependent but the
;                          quicksort algorithm takes approximately
;                          N X log (N) loops through PARTLP. There will be
;                                  2
;                          2 X N+1 calls to Sort. The number of recursions
;                          will probably be a fraction of N but if all
;                          data is the same, the recursion could be up to
;                          N. Therefore, the amount of stack space should
;                          be maximized. NOTE: Each recursion level takes
;                          6 bytes of stack space.
;
;                          In the above discussion, N is the number of
;                          array elements.
;
;       Size:              Program 179 bytes
;                          Data      8 bytes
;
;
QSORT:
        POP     DX              ;SAVE RETURN ADDRESS
        ;
        ;WATCH FOR STACK OVERFLOW
        ;CALCULATE A THRESHOLD TO WARN OF OVERFLOW
        ; (10 BYTES FROM THE END OF THE STACK)
        ;SAVE THIS THRESHOLD FOR LATER COMPARISONS
        ;ALSO SAVE THE POSITION OF THIS ROUTINE'S RETURN ADDRESS
```

```
        ; IN THE EVENT WE MUST ABORT BECAUSE OF STACK OVERFLOW
        ;
        POP     DI          ;GET ADDRESS OF LAST ELEMENT
        POP     SI          ;GET ADDRESS OF FIRST ELEMENT
        POP     BX          ;GET ADDRESS OF END OF STACK SPACE
        PUSH    DX          ;PUT RETURN ADDRESS BACK IN STACK
        MOV     [OLDSP],SP  ;SAVE CURRENT STACK POINTER IN CASE
                            ; WE MUST ABORT
        ADD     BX,10       ;ADD 10 BYTE BUFFER TO STACK END
        MOV     [STKBTM],BX ;SAVE STACK THRESHOLD FOR LATER
                            ; COMPARISONS
        ;
        ;WORK RECURSIVELY THROUGH THE QUICKSORT ALGORITHM AS
        ; FOLLOWS:
        ;  1. CHECK IF THE PARTITION CONTAINS 0 OR 1 ELEMENT.
        ;     MOVE UP A RECURSION LEVEL IF IT DOES.
        ;  2. USE MEDIAN TO OBTAIN A REASONABLE CENTRAL VALUE
        ;     FOR DIVIDING THE CURRENT PARTITION INTO TWO
        ;     PARTS.
        ;  3. MOVE THROUGH THE ARRAY SWAPPING ELEMENTS THAT
        ;     ARE OUT OF ORDER UNTIL ALL ELEMENTS BELOW THE
        ;     CENTRAL VALUE ARE AHEAD OF ALL ELEMENTS ABOVE
        ;     THE CENTRAL VALUE.  SUBROUTINE COMPARE
        ;     COMPARES ELEMENTS, SWAP EXCHANGES ELEMENTS,
        ;     PREV MOVES UPPER BOUNDARY DOWN ONE ELEMENT,
        ;     AND NEXT MOVES LOWER BOUNDARY UP ONE ELEMENT.
        ;  4. CHECK IF THE STACK IS ABOUT TO OVERFLOW.  IF IT
        ;     IS, ABORT AND EXIT.
        ;  5. ESTABLISH THE BOUNDARIES FOR THE FIRST PARTITION
        ;     (CONSISTING OF ELEMENTS LESS THAN THE CENTRAL VALUE)
        ;     AND SORT IT RECURSIVELY.
        ;  6. ESTABLISH THE BOUNDARIES FOR THE SECOND PARTITION
        ;     (CONSISTING OF ELEMENTS GREATER THAN THE CENTRAL
        ;     VALUE) AND SORT IT RECURSIVELY.
        ;
SORT:
        ;
        ;SAVE BASE ADDRESS AND ADDRESS OF LAST ELEMENT
        ; IN CURRENT PARTITION
        ;
        MOV     [FIRST],SI      ;SAVE BASE ADDRESS
        MOV     [LAST],DI       ;SAVE ADDRESS OF LAST ELEMENT
        ;
        ;CHECK IF PARTITION CONTAINS 0 OR 1 ELEMENTS
        ; IT DOES IF FIRST IS EITHER LARGER THAN (0)
        ; OR EQUAL TO (1) LAST.
        ;
        ;STOP WHEN FIRST >= LAST
        ;
        CMP     SI,[LAST]       ;COMPARE FIRST AND LAST
        JAE     EXITPR          ;RETURN IF FIRST >= LAST
                                ;THIS PART IS SORTED
        ;
        ;START ANOTHER ITERATION ON THIS PARTITION
        ;USE MEDIAN TO FIND A REASONABLE CENTRAL ELEMENT
        ;MOVE CENTRAL ELEMENT TO FIRST POSITION
```

```
        ;
        CALL    MEDIAN          ;SELECT CENTRAL ELEMENT, MOVE IT
                                ; TO FIRST POSITION
        MOV     BX,0            ;BIT 0 OF REGISTER BX = DIRECTION
                                ; IF IT IS 0 THEN DIRECTION IS UP
                                ; ELSE DIRECTION IS DOWN
        ;
        ;REORDER ARRAY BY COMPARING OTHER ELEMENTS WITH THE
        ; CENTRAL ELEMENT.  START BY COMPARING THAT ELEMENT WITH
        ; LAST ELEMENT.  EACH TIME WE FIND AN ELEMENT THAT
        ; BELONGS IN THE FIRST PART (THAT IS, IT IS LESS THAN
        ; THE CENTRAL ELEMENT), SWAP IT INTO THE FIRST PART IF IT
        ; IS NOT ALREADY THERE AND MOVE THE BOUNDARY OF THE
        ; FIRST PART DOWN ONE ELEMENT.  SIMILARLY, EACH TIME WE
        ; FIND  AN ELEMENT THAT BELONGS IN THE SECOND PART (THAT
        ; IS,  IT IS GREATER THAN THE CENTRAL ELEMENT),  SWAP IT
        ; INTO THE SECOND PART IF IT IS NOT ALREADY THERE AND MOVE
        ; THE BOUNDARY OF THE SECOND PART UP ONE ELEMENT.
        ;ULTIMATELY, THE BOUNDARIES COME TOGETHER
        ; AND THE DIVISION OF THE ARRAY IS THEN COMPLETE
        ;NOTE THAT ELEMENTS EQUAL TO THE CENTRAL ELEMENT ARE NEVER
        ; SWAPPED AND SO MAY END UP IN EITHER PART
        ;
PARTLP:
        ;
        ;LOOP SORTING UNEXAMINED PART OF PARTITION
        ; UNTIL THERE IS NOTHING LEFT IN IT
        ;
        CMP     SI,DI           ;COMPARE FIRST TO LAST
        JAE     DONE            ;EXIT WHEN EVERYTHING EXAMINED
        ;
        ;COMPARE NEXT 2 ELEMENTS.  IF OUT OF ORDER,  SWAP THEM
        ;AND CHANGE DIRECTION OF SEARCH
        ; IF FIRST > LAST THEN SWAP
        ;
        MOV     AX,[SI]         ;GET FIRST ELEMENT
        CMP     AX,[DI]         ;COMPARE FIRST TO LAST ELEMENT
        JBE     REDPRT          ;JUMP IF IN ORDER
        ;
        ;ELEMENTS OUT OF ORDER, SWAP THEM AND CHANGE DIRECTION
        ;
        NOT     BX              ;CHANGE DIRECTION
        CALL    SWAP            ;SWAP ELEMENTS
        ;
        ;REDUCE SIZE OF UNEXAMINED AREA
        ;IF NEW ELEMENT LESS THAN CENTRAL ELEMENT, MOVE
        ; TOP BOUNDARY DOWN
        ;IF NEW ELEMENT GREATER THAN CENTRAL ELEMENT, MOVE
        ; BOTTOM BOUNDARY UP
        ;IF ELEMENTS EQUAL, CONTINUE IN LATEST DIRECTION
        ;
REDPRT:
        TEST    BX,BX           ;CHECK DIRECTION
        JZ      UP              ;JUMP IF MOVING UP
        CALL    NEXT            ;MOVE TOP BOUNDARY DOWN ONE ELEMENT
        JMP     PARTLP          ;JUMP TO CHECK NEXT ELEMENT
```

```
UP:
        CALL    PREV            ;MOVE BOTTOM BOUNDARY UP ONE ELEMENT
        JMP     PARTLP
        ;
        ;THIS PARTITION HAS NOW BEEN SUBDIVIDED INTO TWO
        ; PARTITIONS. ONE STARTS AT THE TOP AND ENDS JUST
        ; ABOVE THE CENTRAL ELEMENT.  THE OTHER STARTS
        ; JUST BELOW THE CENTRAL ELEMENT AND CONTINUES
        ; TO THE BOTTOM.  THE CENTRAL ELEMENT IS NOW IN
        ; ITS PROPER SORTED POSITION AND NEED NOT BE
        ; INCLUDED IN EITHER PARTITION
        ;
DONE:
        ;
        ;FIRST CHECK WHETHER STACK MIGHT OVERFLOW
        ;IF IT IS GETTING TOO CLOSE TO THE BOTTOM, ABORT
        ; THE PROGRAM AND EXIT
        ;
        CMP     SP,[STKBTM]     ;COMPARE STACK POINTER TO THRESHOLD
        JB      ABORT           ;ABORT IF STACK IS TOO LARGE
        ;
        ;ESTABLISH BOUNDARIES FOR FIRST (LOWER) PARTITION
        ;LOWER BOUNDARY IS SAME AS BEFORE
        ;UPPER BOUNDARY IS ELEMENT JUST BELOW CENTRAL ELEMENT
        ;THEN RECURSIVELY QUICKSORT FIRST PARTITION
        ;
        MOV     DI,[LAST]       ;GET UPPER BOUNDARY
        PUSH    SI              ;SAVE CENTRAL AND LAST ADDRESS
        PUSH    DI
        TEST    SI,SI           ;CHECK IF CENTRAL ELEMENT IS AT
                                ;  LOWER BOUNDARY
        JZ      SKPDEC          ;DO NOT MOVE POINTER DOWN IF
                                ;  ALREADY AT ZERO
        MOV     DI,SI           ;CALCULATE LAST ELEMENT FOR FIRST
                                ;  PASS
        CALL    PREV            ;LAST = ELEMENT JUST BELOW CENTRAL
                                ;  ELEMENT
SKPDEC:
        MOV     SI,[FIRST]      ;LOWER BOUNDARY IS SAME AS BEFORE
        CALL    SORT            ;QUICKSORT FIRST PART
        ;
        ;ESTABLISH BOUNDARIES FOR SECOND (UPPER) PARTITION
        ;UPPER BOUNDARY IS SAME AS BEFORE
        ;LOWER BOUNDARY IS ELEMENT JUST ABOVE CENTRAL ELEMENT
        ;THEN RECURSIVELY QUICKSORT SECOND PARTITION
        ;
        POP     DI              ;GET FIRST AND LAST FOR SECOND PASS
        POP     SI
        CALL    NEXT            ;LOWER BOUNDARY = ELEMENT JUST ABOVE
                                ;  CENTRAL ELEMENT
        CALL    SORT            ;QUICKSORT SECOND PART
        CLC                     ;CLEAR CARRY, INDICATING NO ERRORS
EXITPR:
        RET                     ;GOOD EXIT
        ;
        ;ERROR EXIT, SET CARRY TO 1
```

```
        ;
ABORT:
        MOV     SP,[OLDSP]      ;GET ORIGINAL STACK POINTER
        STC                     ;INDICATE ERROR
        RET                     ;RETURN WITH ERROR INDICATOR TO
                                ; ORIGINAL CALLER

;***************************************************
;ROUTINE: MEDIAN
;PURPOSE: DETERMINE WHICH ELEMENT IN A PARTITION
;       SHOULD BE USED AS THE CENTRAL ELEMENT OR PIVOT
;ENTRY: ADDRESS OF FIRST ELEMENT IN REGISTER SI
;       ADDRESS OF LAST ELEMENT IN REGISTER DI
;EXIT:  CENTRAL ELEMENT IN FIRST POSITION
;       SI,DI UNCHANGED
;REGISTERS USED: AX,BX,F
;***************************************************

MEDIAN:
        ;
        ;DETERMINE ADDRESS OF MIDDLE ELEMENT
        ; MIDDLE := ALIGNED(FIRST + LAST) DIV 2
        ;
        MOV     DX,DI           ;SAVE ADDRESS OF LAST
        MOV     AX,DI           ;ADD FIRST TO LAST
        ADD     AX,SI           ;NOTE THIS COULD PRODUCE A CARRY
        RCR     AX,1            ;DIVIDE SUM (INCLUDING CARRY) BY 2
        AND     AX,0FFFEH       ;CLEAR LOWEST BIT TO ALIGN CENTRAL
        MOV     BX,AX           ;SAVE CENTRAL ADDRESS
        MOV     AX,SI           ;GET ADDRESS OF FIRST
        AND     AX,1            ;CLEAR ALL BUT LOWEST BIT
        ADD     BX,AX           ;ADD TO CENTRAL TO ALIGN ADDRESSES
        ;
        ;DETERMINE MEDIAN OF FIRST, MIDDLE, LAST ELEMENTS
        ;COMPARE FIRST AND MIDDLE
        ;
        MOV     AX,[SI]         ;GET FIRST ELEMENT
        CMP     AX,[BX]         ;COMPARE FIRST AND MIDDLE
        JAE     MIDD1           ;JUMP IF FIRST IS >= MIDDLE
        ;
        ;WE KNOW (MIDDLE > FIRST)
        ; SO COMPARE MIDDLE AND LAST
        ;
        MOV     AX,[DI]         ;GET LAST ELEMENT
        CMP     AX,[BX]         ;COMPARE LAST TO MIDDLE
        JAE     SWAPMF          ;JUMP IF LAST IS >= MIDDLE
        ;
        ;WE KNOW (MIDDLE > FIRST) AND (MIDDLE > LAST)
        ; SO COMPARE FIRST AND LAST (MEDIAN IS LARGER ONE)
        ;
        CMP     AX,[SI]         ;COMPARE LAST TO FIRST
        JA      SWAPLF          ;JUMP IF LAST > FIRST
        JMP     MEXIT           ;EXIT IF FIRST IS >= LAST
                                ;FIRST IS MEDIAN

        ;
        ;WE KNOW FIRST >= MIDDLE
```

```
        ;SO COMPARE FIRST AND LAST
        ;
MIDD1:
        MOV     AX,[DI]         ;COMPARE LAST TO FIRST
        CMP     AX,[SI]         ;EXIT IF LAST >= FIRST
        JAE     MEXIT           ;FIRST IS MEDIAN
        ;
        ;WE KNOW (FIRST >= MIDDLE) AND (FIRST > LAST)
        ; SO COMPARE MIDDLE AND LAST (MEDIAN IS LARGER ONE)
        ;
        CMP     AX,[BX]         ;COMPARE LAST TO MIDDLE
        JA      SWAPLF          ;JUMP IF LAST > MIDDLE
                                ; LAST IS MEDIAN
        ;
        ;MIDDLE IS MEDIAN, MOVE ITS POINTER TO LAST
        ;
SWAPMF:
        MOV     DI,BX           ;MOVE MIDDLE'S POINTER TO LAST
        ;
        ;LAST IS MEDIAN, SWAP IT WITH FIRST
        ;
SWAPLF:
        CALL    SWAP            ;SWAP LAST, FIRST
        ;
        ;RESTORE LAST AND EXIT
        ;
MEXIT:
        MOV     DI,DX           ;RESTORE ADDRESS OF LAST ELEMENT
        RET

;****************************************
;ROUTINE: SWAP
;PURPOSE: SWAP ELEMENTS POINTED TO BY SI,DI
;ENTRY: SI = ADDRESS OF ELEMENT 1
;       DI = ADDRESS OF ELEMENT 2
;EXIT:  ELEMENTS SWAPPED
;REGISTERS USED: AX
;****************************************

SWAP:
        MOV     AX,[SI]         ;GET FIRST ELEMENT
        XCHG    AX,[DI]         ;EXCHANGE WITH LAST ELEMENT
        MOV     [SI],AX         ;PUT LAST ELEMENT IN FIRST POSITION
        RET

;****************************************
;ROUTINE: NEXT
;PURPOSE: MAKE SI POINT TO NEXT ELEMENT
;ENTRY: SI = ADDRESS OF CURRENT ELEMENT
;EXIT:  SI = ADDRESS OF NEXT ELEMENT
;REGISTERS USED: F,SI
;****************************************

NEXT:
        INC     SI              ;MOVE POINTER TO NEXT ELEMENT
```

```
        INC         SI
        RET

;*******************************************
;ROUTINE: PREV
;PURPOSE: MAKE DI POINT TO PREVIOUS ELEMENT
;ENTRY: DI = ADDRESS OF CURRENT ELEMENT
;EXIT:  DI = ADDRESS OF PREVIOUS ELEMENT
;REGISTERS USED: DI,F
;*******************************************

PREV:
        DEC         DI                  ;MOVE POINTER TO PREVIOUS ELEMENT
        DEC         DI
        RET

;
;DATA SECTION
;
FIRST   DW          0                   ;POINTER TO FIRST ELEMENT OF PART
LAST    DW          0                   ;POINTER TO LAST ELEMENT OF PART
OLDSP   DW          0                   ;POINTER TO ORIGINAL RETURN ADDRESS
                                        ;  (INITIAL STACK POINTER)
STKBTM  DW          0                   ;THRESHOLD FOR STACK OVERFLOW

;
;       SAMPLE EXECUTION
;

;
;PROGRAM SECTION
SC6G:
        ;
        ;SORT AN ARRAY BETWEEN BEGBUF (FIRST ELEMENT)
        ; AND ENDBUF (LAST ELEMENT)
        ;LET STACK EXPAND 1000 HEX BYTES
        ;
        MOV         BX,SP               ;GET CURRENT STACK ADDRESS
        SUB         BX,1000H            ;SUBTRACT 1000 HEX TO SPECIFY END OF
        PUSH        BX                  ;  STACK ADDRESS
        MOV         BX,OFFSET BEGBUF  ;ADDRESS OF FIRST ELEMENT
        PUSH        BX
        MOV         BX,OFFSET ENDBUF  ;ADDRESS OF LAST ELEMENT
        PUSH        BX
        CALL        QSORT               ;SORT USING QUICKSORT
                                        ;RESULT FOR TEST DATA IS
                                        ; 0,1,2,3, ... ,14,15
        JMP         SC6G                ;LOOP TO REPEAT TEST

;
;DATA SECTION
;
BEGBUF  DW          15
        DW          14
        DW          13
        DW          12
```

```
        DW      11
        DW      10
        DW      9
        DW      8
        DW      7
        DW      6
        DW      5
        DW      4
        DW      3
        DW      2
        DW      1
ENDBUF  DW      0

        END
```

6H Merge sort (MSORT)

Merges two lists of unsigned word-length elements into ascending order. Both original lists are assumed to be already arranged in ascending order. The merged list replaces list 1, the list with the base address higher in the stack.

Procedure The program starts at the end of the expanded list (i.e. the extension of list 1 to include the elements of list 2). It repeatedly compares the next remaining elements of the two lists, moves the larger element into the merged list, and updates the counters and pointers appropriately. If there are elements left from the second list when the program finishes with the first list, they are moved to the front of the expanded list.

Entry conditions

Order in stack (starting from the top)

Low byte of return address
High byte of return address

Low byte of base address of list 1
High byte of base address of list 1

Low byte of size of list 1 in words
High byte of size of list 1 in words

Low byte of base address of list 2
High byte of base address of list 2

Low byte of size of list 2 in words
High byte of size of list 2 in words

Exit conditions

List 1 replaced by list 1 merged with list 2. List 1 is sorted into ascending order, considering the elements as unsigned words. Thus, the smallest unsigned word ends up stored starting at the base address of list 1.

Example

Data: Length (size) of list 1 = $0C_{16} = 12_{10}$
Elements = $0D_{16}$, 17_{16}, $1D_{16}$, 22_{16}, 26_{16}, 27_{16}, $2B_{16}$, $2E_{16}$, 37_{16}, 44_{16}, $4B_{16}$, 57_{16}
Length (size) of list 2 = 08
Elements = $0B_{16}$, 12_{16}, 13_{16}, 17_{16}, 25_{16}, $2D_{16}$, 41_{16}, 62_{16}

Result: Length (size) of list 1 = $14_{16} = 20_{10}$
Elements = $0B_{16}$, $0D_{16}$, 12_{16}, 13_{16}, 17_{16}, 17_{16}, $1D_{16}$, 22_{16}, 25_{16}, 26_{16}, 27_{16}, $2B_{16}$, $2D_{16}$, $2E_{16}$, 37_{16}, 41_{16}, 44_{16}, $4B_{16}$, 57_{16}, 62_{16}

References

D. E. Knuth, *The Art of Computer Programming. Vol. 3: Searching and Sorting*, Addison-Wesley, Reading, MA, 1973, pp. 159–170, 198–209.

Y. Langsam *et al.*, *Data Structures for Personal Computers*, Prentice-Hall, Englewood Cliffs, NJ, 1985, pp. 467–470, 474–476. The algorithms in this book are available as BASIC programs for various computers. Other versions of the book are available for Pascal and PL/I.

Registers used AX, BX, CX, DI, DX, F (sets D flag), SI

Execution time Approximately 72 cycles per element plus 120 cycles overhead. If, for example, the two lists have 1000 and 250 elements, respectively, the execution time is approximately

$$72 \times (1000 + 250) + 120 = 90\,120 \text{ cycles}$$

Program size 56 bytes

Data memory required None

Special cases

1. If list 1 has zero length, the program simply moves list 2 to list 1.
2. If list 2 has zero length, the program returns list 1 unchanged.

```
;       Title           Merge sort
;       Name:           MSORT
;
;
;       Purpose:        Merges two lists into one.  Both original
;                       lists and the merged list are arranged
;                       in ascending order.
;
;       Entry:          TOP OF STACK
;                         Low byte of return address
;                         High byte of return address
;                         Low byte of base address of list 1
;                         High byte of base address of list 1
;                         Low byte of size of list 1 in words
;                         High byte of size of list 1 in words
;                         Low byte of base address of list 2
;                         High byte of base address of list 2
;                         Low byte of size of list 2 in words
;                         High byte of size of list 2 in words
;
;       Exit:           List 1 combines its original contents with
;                         list 2. Combined list is sorted into ascending
;                         order.
;
;       Registers Used: AX,BX,CX,DI,DX,F (sets D flag),SI
;
;       Time:           Approximately 72 cycles per element plus
;                       120 cycles overhead
;
;       Size:           Program 56 bytes
;
;
MSORT:
        ;
        ;REMOVE PARAMETERS FROM STACK
        ;EXIT (DONE) IF LIST 2 HAS NO ELEMENTS
        ;
        POP     BX              ;SAVE RETURN ADDRESS
        POP     DI              ;GET BASE ADDRESS OF LIST 1
        POP     AX              ;GET SIZE OF LIST 1 IN WORDS
        POP     SI              ;GET BASE ADDRESS OF LIST 2
        POP     CX              ;GET SIZE OF LIST 2 IN WORDS
        PUSH    BX              ;PUT RETURN ADDRESS BACK ON STACK
        JCXZ    EXITMS          ;NO MERGE NECESSARY IF LIST 2 HAS
                                ;  NO ELEMENTS
        ;
        ;SET POINTERS TO LAST ELEMENTS IN LISTS
        ;POINTER = BASE ADDRESS OF LIST + 2 X (SIZE OF LIST - 1)
        ;
        STD                     ;SELECT AUTODECREMENTING
```

```
        MOV     BX,CX       ;POINT TO LAST ELEMENT IN LIST 2
        DEC     BX          ;POINTER = BASE L2 + 2 X (SIZE L2 - 1)
        SHL     BX,1
        ADD     SI,BX
        MOV     DX,AX       ;POINT TO LAST ELEMENT IN MERGED LIST
        SHL     DX,1        ;POINTER = BASE L1 + 2 X (SIZE L1 +
                            ;  SIZE L2 - 1)
        ADD     BX,DX
        ADD     BX,DI
        XCHG    BX,DI
        TEST    AX,AX       ;TEST LENGTH OF LIST 1
        JZ      MVREM       ;SIMPLY MOVE LIST 2 TO LIST 1 IF LIST 1
                            ;  HAS NO ELEMENTS
        DEC     DX          ;POINT TO LAST ELEMENT IN LIST 1
        DEC     DX          ;POINTER = BASE L1 + 2 X (SIZE L1 - 1)
        ADD     BX,DX
        MOV     DX,AX       ;SAVE SIZE OF LIST 1
        ;
        ;MERGE LISTS BY COMPARING NEXT ELEMENTS AND MOVING LARGER
        ;  ELEMENT TO COMBINED LIST
        ;
CMPNXT:
        MOV     AX,[BX]     ;GET NEXT ELEMENT FROM LIST 1
        CMP     AX,[SI]     ;COMPARE TO ELEMENT FROM LIST 2
        JA      MVLST1      ;JUMP IF LIST 1 ELEMENT IS LARGER
        ;
        ;LIST 2 ELEMENT IS LARGER
        ;MOVE IT TO COMBINED LIST AND PROCEED TO NEXT ELEMENT
        ;  IN LIST 2
        ;
        MOVSW               ;MOVE LIST 2 ELEMENT INTO MERGED LIST
        LOOP    CMPNXT      ;COUNTDOWN ON LIST 2
        JMP     EXITPR      ;DONE IF ALL LIST 2 ELEMENTS MERGED SINCE
                            ;  REMAINING LIST 1 ELEMENTS ARE ALREADY
                            ;  WHERE THEY BELONG
        ;
        ;LIST 1 ELEMENT IS LARGER
        ;MOVE IT TO COMBINED LIST AND PROCEED TO NEXT ELEMENT
        ;  IN LIST 1
        ;
MVLST1:
        STOSW               ;MOVE LIST 1 ELEMENT INTO MERGED LIST
        DEC     BX          ;POINT TO NEXT LIST 1 ELEMENT
        DEC     BX
        DEC     DX          ;COUNTDOWN ON LIST 1
        JNZ     CMPNXT      ;KEEP COMPARING IF ELEMENTS STILL
                            ;  LEFT IN LIST 1
        ;
        ;LIST 1 IS MERGED COMPLETELY INTO COMBINED LIST
        ;MOVE REMAINING ELEMENTS FROM LIST 2 TO FRONT OF COMBINED
        ;  LIST
        ;
MVREM:
    REP MOVSW               ;MOVE REST OF LIST 2 INTO MERGED LIST
EXITMS:
        RET                 ;EXIT
```

```
;

;
;       SAMPLE EXECUTION
;

;
SC6H:
        ;
        ;MERGE AN ARRAY BETWEEN BEGBF1 (FIRST ELEMENT)
        ; AND ENDBF1 (LAST ELEMENT) WITH AN ARRAY BETWEEN
        ; BEGBF2 (FIRST ELEMENT) AND ENDBF2 (LAST ELEMENT)
        ;
        MOV     AX,[SIZE2]      ;GET SIZE OF LIST 2
        PUSH    AX
        MOV     BX,OFFSET BEGBF2 ;GET BASE ADDRESS OF LIST 2
        PUSH    BX
        MOV     AX,[SIZE1]      ;GET SIZE OF LIST 1
        PUSH    AX
        MOV     BX,OFFSET BEGBF1 ;GET BASE ADDRESS OF LIST 1
        PUSH    BX
        CALL    MSORT           ;MERGE LISTS
                                ;RESULT FOR TEST DATA IS
                                ; 0,1,2,3, ... ,14,15
        JMP     SC6H            ;LOOP TO REPEAT TEST

;
;DATA SECTION
;
SIZE1   DW      8               ;SIZE OF LIST 1
BEGBF1  DW      1               ;LIST 1
        DW      3
        DW      5
        DW      7
        DW      9
        DW      11
        DW      13
        DW      15
        DW      8 DUP(?)        ;EXTRA SPACE REQUIRED TO MERGE
                                ; ELEMENTS FROM LIST 2
SIZE2   DW      8               ;SIZE OF LIST 2
BEGBF2  DW      0               ;LIST 2
        DW      2
        DW      4
        DW      6
        DW      8
        DW      10
        DW      12
        DW      14

        END
```

6I RAM test (RAMTST)

Tests a RAM area specified by a 20-bit even base address and a 20-bit even length in bytes. Writes the values 0, $FFFF_{16}$, 1010101010101010_2 ($AAAA_{16}$), and 0101010101010101_2 (5555_{16}) into each word and checks whether they can be read back correctly. Places 1 in each bit position of each word and checks whether it can be read back correctly with all other bits cleared. Clears Carry if all tests run correctly; if it finds an error, it exits immediately, setting Carry, clearing the Zero flag, and returning the test value and the address at which the error occurred. If either the base address or the length in bytes is odd, the program exits without testing any memory and returns both the Carry and Zero flags set to 1.

Procedure The program performs the single value tests (with 0, $FFFF_{16}$, $AAAA_{16}$, and 5555_{16}) by first filling the memory area and then comparing each word with the specified value. Filling the entire area first should provide enough delay between writing and reading to detect a failure to retain data (perhaps caused by improperly designed refresh circuitry). The program then performs the walking bit test, starting with bit 15; here it writes the data into memory and reads it back immediately for a comparison.

Entry conditions

Low word of area size in bytes in register AX
High byte of area size in bytes in register DL (must be less than 16)
Segmented base address of test area in registers DS and SI

Exit conditions

1. If a memory error is found:
   Carry = 1
   Zero = 1
   Address containing error in registers ES and BX
   Byte-length test value in AL
2. If a specification error (odd area size in bytes or odd base address) is found:

Carry = 1
Zero = 1
0 in registers ES and BX

3. If no error is found:
Carry = 0
All bytes in test area contain 0

Example

Data: Base address = 00380_{16} (offset 0380_{16} in segment 0)
Length (size) of area = 30200_{16}

Result: Area tested is the 30200_{16} bytes starting at address 00380_{16}, that is, addresses 00380_{16} through $3057F_{16}$. The order of the tests is:

1. Write and read 0

2. Write and read FF_{16}

3. Write and read AA_{16} (10101010_2)

4. Write and read 55_{16} (01010101_2)

5. Walking bit test, starting with 1 in bit 7. That is, start with 10000000_2 (80_{16}) and move the 1 one position right for each subsequent test of a byte.

Registers used AX, BX, CX, DI, DX, ES, F, SI

Execution time Approximately 1048 cycles per word tested plus 519 cycles overhead plus 200 cycles for each crossover into a new segment. Thus, for example, to test an area of size $20400_{16} = 132\,096_{10}$ would take

$$1048 \times 66\,048 + 519 + 400 = 69\,200\,000$$

This is about 14 s at a standard 8086 clock rate of 5 MHz.

Program size 190 bytes

Data memory required None

Special cases

1. An area size of 00000_{16} causes an immediate exit with no memory tested. Carry is cleared to indicate no errors.

2. Since the routine changes all bytes in the tested area, using it to test an area that includes itself will yield unpredictable results.

Note that Case 1 means you cannot ask this routine to test the entire memory, but such a request would be meaningless anyway since it would require the routine to test itself.

3. Testing a ROM causes a return with an error indication after the first occasion on which the test value differs from the memory's contents.

4. If either the area size in bytes or the base address is odd, the program exits immediately, setting both the Carry and the Zero flags to 1 to indicate an invalid condition. It also returns 0 in both registers ES and BX.

```
;
;
;       Title              RAM Test
;       Name:              RAMTST
;
;
;       Purpose:           Test a RAM (read/write memory) area as follows:
;                            1) Write all 0 and test
;                            2) Write all 11111111 binary and test
;                            3) Write all 10101010 binary and test
;                            4) Write all 01010101 binary and test
;                            5) Shift a single 1 through each bit,
;                               while clearing all other bits
;
;                            If the program finds an error, it exits
;                            immediately with the Carry flag set and
;                            indicates the test value and where the
;                            error occurred.
;
;       Entry:             Low word of area size in bytes in BX
;                          High byte of area size in bytes in DL (must
;                            be less than 16)
;
;                          Offset of base address of area in SI
;                          Segment number of base address of area in DS
;
;       Exit:              If there are no errors then
;                            Carry = 0
;                            test area contains 0 in all bytes
;                          else if memory error found then
;                            Carry = 1
;                            Zero = 0
```

```
;                       Registers ES and BX = Segmented address of
;                         error
;                       Register AL = Byte-length test value
;                     else if specification error then
;                       Carry = 1
;                       Zero = 1
;                       Registers ES and BX = 0
;
;       Registers Used: AX,BX,CX,DI,DX,ES,F,SI
;
;       Time:           Approximately 1048 cycles per word plus
;                       519 cycles overhead plus 200 cycles for
;                       each segment crossing
;
;       Size:           Program 190 bytes

;
RAMTST:
        ;
        ;EXIT INDICATING NO ERROR IF AREA SIZE IS ZERO
        ;
        TEST    DL,DL           ;TEST HIGH BYTE OF AREA SIZE
        JNZ     NXTEST          ;JUMP IF AREA SIZE NONZERO
        TEST    BX,BX           ;TEST LOW WORD OF AREA SIZE
        JZ      EXITRT          ;BRANCH (EXIT) IF AREA SIZE IS ZERO
                                ; CARRY = 0 (NO ERROR) IN THIS CASE
                                ; BECAUSE OF TEST
        ;
        ;COMPUTE COUNT IN WORDS
        ;EXIT, INDICATING SPECIFICATION ERROR, IF BYTE COUNT IS
        ; ODD OR IF BASE ADDRESS IS ODD
        ;SPECIFICATION ERROR IS INDICATED BY THE CONDITION C=1,Z=1
        ;
NXTEST:
        SHR     DL,1            ;WORD COUNT = AREA SIZE DIVIDED BY 2
        RCR     BX,1
        JC      EXITSP          ;SPECIFICATION ERROR IF AREA SIZE IS ODD
        AND     BX,BX           ;TEST LOW WORD OF WORD COUNT
        JNZ     TESTBS          ;JUMP IF LOW WORD IS NONZERO
        DEC     DL              ;REDUCE UPPER BYTE BY 1 IF LOW WORD = 0
                                ; TO MAKE COUNT WORK PROPERLY.  THAT IS,
                                ; COUNTING MECHANISM TREATS A 0 LOW WORD
                                ; AS 10000
 TESTBS:
        TEST    SI,1            ;TEST IF BASE ADDRESS ON A WORD BOUNDARY
        JNZ     EXITSP          ;SPECIFICATION ERROR IF BASE ADDRESS ODD
        ;
        ;FILL MEMORY WITH 0 AND TEST
        ;
        SUB     AX,AX           ;GET ZERO VALUE
        CALL    FILCMP          ;FILL AND TEST MEMORY
        JC      EXITRT          ;BRANCH (EXIT) IF ERROR FOUND
        ;
        ;FILL MEMORY WITH FF HEX (ALL 1'S) AND TEST
        ;
        MOV     AX,0FFFFH ;GET ALL 1'S VALUE
```

```
        CALL    FILCMP  ;FILL AND TEST MEMORY
        JC      EXITRT  ;BRANCH (EXIT) IF ERROR FOUND
        ;
        ;FILL MEMORY WITH ALTERNATING 1'S AND 0'S AND TEST
        ;
        MOV     AX,0AAAAH ;GET ALTERNATING 1'S AND 0'S PATTERN
        CALL    FILCMP  ;FILL AND TEST MEMORY
        JC      EXITRT  ;BRANCH (EXIT) IF ERROR FOUND
        ;
        ;FILL MEMORY WITH ALTERNATING 0'S AND 1'S AND TEST
        ;
        MOV     AX,5555H ;GET ALTERNATING 0'S AND 1'S PATTERN
        CALL    FILCMP  ;FILL AND TEST MEMORY
        JC      EXITRT  ;BRANCH (EXIT) IF ERROR FOUND
        ;
        ;PERFORM WALKING BIT TEST. PLACE A 1 IN BIT 15 AND
        ; SEE IF IT CAN BE READ BACK.  THEN MOVE THE 1 TO
        ; BITS 14, 13, 12,...,2, 1, 0 AND SEE IF IT CAN
        ; BE READ BACK
        ;
        MOV     DI,SI   ;GET BASE ADDRESS OF TEST AREA
        MOV     CX,DS   ;START IN CURRENT DATA SEGMENT
        MOV     ES,CX
        MOV     CX,BX   ;GET LOWER WORD OF WORD COUNT
        MOV     DH,DL   ;GET UPPER BYTE OF WORD COUNT
WLKLP:
        MOV     AX,8000H ;MAKE BIT 15 1, ALL OTHER BITS 0
WLKLP1:
        MOV     [DI],AX ;STORE TEST PATTERN IN MEMORY
        CMP     AX,[DI] ;TRY TO READ IT BACK
        JNE     EXITCS  ;BRANCH (EXIT) IF ERROR FOUND
        SHR     AX,1    ;SHIFT PATTERN TO MOVE 1 BIT RIGHT
        JNZ     WLKLP1  ;CONTINUE UNTIL PATTERN BECOMES ZERO
                        ; THAT IS, UNTIL 1 BIT MOVES ALL THE
                        ; WAY ACROSS THE WORD
        MOV     [DI],AX ;CLEAR BYTE JUST CHECKED
                        ; NOTE AX MUST CONTAIN 0 OR JNZ
                        ; WOULD HAVE BRANCHED
        INC     DI      ;POINT TO NEXT WORD
        INC     DI      ;NOTE: CANNOT USE STOSW HERE SINCE
                        ; WE MUST RECOGNIZE SEGMENT CROSSINGS
        LOOPNZ  WLKLP   ;CONTINUE UNTIL SEGMENT BOUNDARY REACHED
                        ; OR LOW WORD OF WORD COUNT REDUCED TO 0
        JCXZ    CHKHI   ;IF LOW WORD OF WORD COUNT REDUCED TO 0,
                        ; JUMP TO CHECK HIGH BYTE
        ;
        ;CROSSED BOUNDARY OF CURRENT SEGMENT
        ;MOVE ON TO NEXT 64K SEGMENT BY INCREASING SEGMENT REGISTER
        ; BY 1000 HEX
        ;
        MOV     DI,ES   ;GET CURRENT SEGMENT NUMBER
        ADD     DI,1000H ;MOVE ON TO NEXT 64K BYTE SEGMENT
        MOV     ES,DI
        SUB     DI,DI   ;START AT OFFSET 0 IN NEXT SEGMENT
        JMP     WLKLP   ;CONTINUE TEST
        ;
```

```
        ;CHECK IF ENTIRE WORD COUNT EXHAUSTED BY REDUCING AND
        ; TESTING HIGH DIGIT
        ;
CHKHI:
        DEC     DH          ;DECREMENT HIGH BYTE OF WORD COUNT
        JNS     WLKLP       ;CONTINUE TEST IF MORE WORDS LEFT
        CLC                 ;ALL WORDS TESTED WITH NO ERRORS SO
                            ; CLEAR CARRY TO INDICATE SUCCESS
EXITRT: RET
        ;
        ;SPECIFICATION ERROR - SET ZERO FLAG BEFORE SETTING CARRY
        ;
EXITSP:
        SUB     DI,DI       ;SET ZERO FLAG, SET ENTIRE ADDRESS
        MOV     ES,DI       ; OF SUPPOSED ERROR TO ZERO
        ;
        ;FOUND AN ERROR - SET CARRY TO INDICATE IT
        ;
EXITCS:
        MOV     BX,DI       ;GET OFFSET IN WHICH ERROR OCCURRED
                            ; NOTE: SEGMENT NUMBER IS IS IN ES
        STC                 ;SET CARRY TO INDICATE ERROR
        RET

;****************************************
;ROUTINE: FILCMP
;PURPOSE: FILL MEMORY WITH A VALUE AND TEST
;         THAT IT CAN BE READ BACK
;ENTRY:   AX = TEST VALUE
;         DL = HIGH BYTE OF WORD COUNT
;         BX = LOW WORD OF WORD COUNT
;         DS = SEGMENT NUMBER OF BASE ADDRESS OF TEST AREA
;         SI = OFFSET OF BASE ADDRESS OF TEST AREA
;EXIT:    IF NO ERRORS THEN
;           CARRY = 0
;         ELSE
;           CARRY = 1
;           BX = OFFSET OF ERROR
;           ES = SEGMENT NUMBER OF ERROR
;           AX = TEST VALUE
;REGISTERS USED: AX,BX,CX,DI,DH,ES,F
;****************************************

FILCMP:
        ;
        ;FILL MEMORY WITH TEST VALUE
        ;
        MOV     DI,SI           ;GET OFFSET OF BASE ADDRESS OF AREA
        MOV     CX,DS           ;STARTING SEGMENT NUMBER = CURRENT
        MOV     ES,CX           ; DATA SEGMENT
        MOV     CX,BX           ;GET LOW WORD OF WORD COUNT
        MOV     DH,DL           ;GET HIGH BYTE OF WORD COUNT
FILWRD:
        MOV     [DI],AX         ;FILL MEMORY WITH TEST VALUE
        INC     DI              ;POINT TO NEXT WORD
        INC     DI              ;NOTE: CANNOT USE STOSW HERE BECAUSE
```

```
                                        ; WE MUST RECOGNIZE SEGMENT CROSSINGS
        LOOPNZ      FILWRD              ;LOOP UNTIL SEGMENT BOUNDARY REACHED
                                        ; OR LOW WORD OF WORD COUNT IS 0
        JCXZ        FDECHI              ;BRANCH IF LOW WORD OF COUNT IS 0 -
                                        ; GO CHECK HIGH BYTE
        MOV         DI,ES               ;SEGMENT BOUNDARY REACHED SO PROCEED
                                        ; TO NEXT 64KB SEGMENT
        ADD         DI,1000H
        MOV         ES,DI
        SUB         DI,DI               ;START AT OFFSET 0 IN NEXT SEGMENT
        JMP         FILWRD              ;CONTINUE FILL
FDECHI:
        DEC         DH                  ;DECREMENT HIGH BYTE OF WORD COUNT
        JNS         FILWRD              ;CONTINUE IF MORE WORDS TO FILL
        ;
        ;COMPARE MEMORY AND TEST VALUE
        ;
        MOV         DI,SI               ;GET OFFSET OF BASE ADDRESS OF AREA
        MOV         CX,DS               ;STARTING SEGMENT NUMBER = CURRENT
        MOV         ES,CX               ; DATA SEGMENT
        MOV         CX,BX               ;GET LOW WORD OF WORD COUNT
        MOV         DH,DL               ;GET HIGH BYTE OF WORD COUNT
CMPWRD:
        CMP         AX,[DI]             ;COMPARE TEST VALUE AND MEMORY WORD
        JNE         EREXIT              ;BRANCH (ERROR EXIT) IF NO EQUAL
        INC         DI                  ;POINT TO NEXT WORD
        INC         DI                  ;NOTE: CANNOT USE SCASW HERE BECAUSE
                                        ; WE MUST RECOGNIZE SEGMENT CROSSINGS
        LOOPNZ      CMPWRD              ;LOOP UNTIL SEGMENT BOUNDARY REACHED
                                        ; OR LOW WORD OF WORD COUNT IS 0
        JCXZ        CDECHI              ;BRANCH IF LOW WORD OF COUNT IS 0 -
                                        ; GO CHECK HIGH BYTE
        MOV         DI,ES               ;SEGMENT BOUNDARY REACHED SO PROCEED
                                        ; TO NEXT 64KB SEGMENT
        ADD         DI,1000H
        MOV         ES,DI
        SUB         DI,DI               ;START AT OFFSET 0 IN NEXT SEGMENT
        JMP         CMPWRD              ;CONTINUE COMPARISON
CDECHI:
        DEC         DH                  ;DECREMENT HIGH BYTE OF WORD COUNT
        JNS         CMPWRD              ;CONTINUE IF MORE WORDS TO COMPARE
        ;
        ;NO ERRORS FOUND, CLEAR CARRY AND EXIT
        ;
        CLC                             ;INDICATE NO ERRORS
        RET
        ;
        ;ERROR FOUND, SET CARRY, POINT TO ERROR, AND EXIT
        ;
EREXIT:
        MOV         BX,DI               ;GET ADDRESS OF ERROR
        STC                             ;INDICATE AN ERROR
        RET

;
;       SAMPLE EXECUTION
```

```
;

;
SC6I:
        ;
        ;TEST RAM FROM 02000 HEX THROUGH 3300F HEX
        ;  SIZE OF AREA = 31010 HEX BYTES
        ;
        MOV     BX,1010H        ;GET LOW WORD OF AREA SIZE IN BYTES
        MOV     DL,3            ;GET HIGH BYTE OF AREA SIZE IN BYTES
        MOV     SI,2000H        ;GET OFFSET OF BASE ADDRESS OF TEST
                                ; AREA
        SUB     DI,DI           ;GET SEGMENT NUMBER OF BASE ADDRESS
        MOV     DS,DI           ; OF TEST AREA (0)
        CALL    RAMTST          ;TEST MEMORY
                                ;CARRY WILL BE 0 IF NO MEMORY ERRORS
                                ; ARE FOUND IN THIS AREA

        END
```

6J Jump table (JTAB)

Transfers control to a 32-bit segmented address selected from a table according to an index. The segmented addresses are stored in the usual 8086 format (instruction pointer value first, then code segment register value, with both arranged less significant byte first), starting at address JMPTBL. The size of the table (number of addresses) is a constant LENSUB. If the index is greater than or equal to LENSUB, the program returns control immediately with Carry set to 1.

Procedure The program first checks if the index is greater than or equal to the size of the table (LENSUB). If it is, the program returns control with the Carry flag set. If it is not, the program obtains the starting address of the appropriate subroutine from the table and jumps to it. The result is like an indexed CALL instruction with range checking and automatic accounting for the 32-bit length of segmented addresses (instruction pointer value and code segment register value).

Entry conditions

Index in AX

Exit conditions

If [AX] is greater than LENSUB, an immediate return with Carry = 1. Otherwise, control is transferred to appropriate subroutine as if an indexed call had been performed. The return address (presumably 32 bits long) remains at the top of the stack.

Example

Data: LENSUB (size of subroutine table) = 03
Table consists of addresses CS0:SUB0, CS1:SUB1, and CS2:SUB2.
Index = [AX] = 2

Result: Control transferred to address CS2:SUB2 (i.e. code segment register = CS2, instruction pointer = SUB2)

Registers used AX, BX, F

Execution time 48 cycles besides the time required to execute the actual subroutine.

Program size 17 bytes plus 4 × LENSUB bytes for the table of starting addresses, where LENSUB is the number of subroutines.

Data memory required None

Special case Entry with an index greater than or equal to LENSUB causes an immediate exit with Carry set to 1.

```
;       Title               Jump Table
;       Name:               JTAB
;
;       Purpose:            Given an index, jump to the subroutine with
;                           that index in a table
;       Entry:              Subroutine number (0 to LENSUB-1, the number of
;                             subroutines) in AX. LENSUB must be less than
;                             or equal to 16,383.
;       Exit:               If the routine number is valid then
;                             execute the routine
;                           else
;                             Carry = 1
;
;       Registers Used: AX,BX,F
;
;       Time:               48 cycles plus execution time of subroutine
;
;       Size:               Program 17 bytes plus size of table (4 X LENSUB)
;


;
;       EXIT WITH CARRY SET IF ROUTINE NUMBER IS INVALID
;       THAT IS, IF IT IS TOO LARGE FOR TABLE (>LENSUB - 1)
;
JTAB:
        CMP     AX,LENSUB       ;COMPARE ROUTINE NUMBER, TABLE LENGTH
        JAE     EREXIT          ;BRANCH (EXIT) IF ROUTINE NUMBER TOO
                                ; LARGE
;
;       INDEX INTO TABLE OF DOUBLE-WORD-LENGTH ADDRESSES
```

```
;           OBTAIN ROUTINE ADDRESS FROM TABLE AND TRANSFER CONTROL
;             TO IT
;
            SHL         AX,1            ;MULTIPLY INDEX BY 4 TO ACCOUNT FOR
            SHL         AX,1            ; DOUBLE-WORD-LENGTH ENTRIES
            MOV         BX,AX
            JMP         DWORD PTR [BX+JMPTBL] ;JUMP INDIRECTLY TO SUBROUTINE
;
;           ERROR EXIT - EXIT WITH CARRY SET
;
EREXIT:
            STC                         ;INDICATE BAD ROUTINE NUMBER
            RET

CSEG        EQU         0               ;ARBITRARY CODE SEGMENT NUMBER
LENSUB      EQU         3               ;NUMBER OF SUBROUTINES IN TABLE

;
;JUMP TABLE
;
JMPTBL:
            DW          SUB0            ;INSTRUCTION POINTER VALUE FOR
                                        ;  ROUTINE 0
            DW          CSEG            ;CODE SEGMENT REGISTER VALUE FOR
                                        ;  ROUTINE 0
            DW          SUB1            ;INSTRUCTION POINTER VALUE FOR
                                        ;  ROUTINE 1
            DW          CSEG            ;CODE SEGMENT REGISTER VALUE FOR
                                        ;  ROUTINE 1
            DW          SUB2            ;INSTRUCTION POINTER VALUE FOR
                                        ;  ROUTINE 2
            DW          CSEG            ;CODE SEGMENT REGISTER VALUE FOR
                                        ;  ROUTINE 2

;
;THREE TEST SUBROUTINES FOR JUMP TABLE
;
SUB0:
            MOV         AX,1            ;TEST ROUTINE 0 SETS [AX] = 1
            RET

SUB1:
            MOV         AX,2            ;TEST ROUTINE 1 SETS [AX] = 2
            RET

SUB2:
            MOV         AX,3            ;TEST ROUTINE 2 SETS [AX] = 3
            RET

;
;           SAMPLE EXECUTION
;

;
;PROGRAM SECTION
SC6J:
```

```
SUB     AX,AX       ;EXECUTE ROUTINE 0
CALL    JTAB        ;AFTER EXECUTION, [AX] = 1
MOV     AX,1        ;EXECUTE ROUTINE 1
CALL    JTAB        ;AFTER EXECUTION, [AX] = 2
MOV     AX,2        ;EXECUTE ROUTINE 2
CALL    JTAB        ;AFTER EXECUTION, [AX] = 3
MOV     AX,3        ;EXECUTE ROUTINE 3
CALL    JTAB        ;AFTER EXECUTION, CARRY = 1
                    ;  INDICATING BAD ROUTINE NUMBER
JMP     SC6J        ;LOOP FOR MORE TESTS
END
```

6K Matrix multiplication (MATMUL)

Multiplies two square matrixes and saves the result in a third matrix. The matrixes consist of unsigned byte-length elements.

Procedure The program starts by clearing the entire result area. It then multiplies each row of matrix 1 by each column of matrix 2 to obtain the elements of the result matrix. Matrix 1 is the matrix with the base address lower in the stack.

Entry conditions

Order in stack (starting from the top)

Low byte of return address
High byte of return address

Low byte of base address of result matrix
High byte of base address of result matrix

Low byte of base address of matrix 2
High byte of base address of matrix 2

Low byte of base address of matrix 1
High byte of base address of matrix 1

Low byte of size of matrixes in bytes
High byte of size of matrixes in bytes

Exit conditions

Result matrix = matrix 1 × matrix 2

Example

Data: Size of matrixes = 3 by 3

$$\text{Matrix 1} = \begin{matrix} 1 & 2 & 3 \\ 4 & 3 & 2 \\ 3 & 1 & 2 \end{matrix}$$

$$\text{Matrix 2} = \begin{matrix} 1 & 2 & 3 \\ 2 & 3 & 1 \\ 4 & 1 & 2 \end{matrix}$$

Result:

$$\text{Result matrix} = \begin{matrix} 11 & 0B & 0B \\ 12 & 13 & 13 \\ 0D & 0B & 0E \end{matrix}$$

The elements are hexadecimal numbers.

Registers used AX, BX, CX, DI, DX, F (clears D flag), SI

Execution time Approximately 500 × SIZE³ + 28 × SIZE + 177 cycles, where SIZE is the number of rows or columns in the square matrixes. If, for example, the matrixes are 4 by 4, the execution time is

$$500 \times 4^3 + 28 \times 4 + 177 = 32\,000 + 289 = 32\,289 \text{ cycles}$$

Program size 116 bytes

Data memory required None

Special case If the size of the matrixes is 0, the program returns immediately with no memory locations changed. Carry is set to 1 to indicate an error.

```
;       Title           Matrix Multiplication
;       Name:           MATMUL
;
;
;       Purpose:        Multiplies two square matrixes of
;                       byte-length elements
;
;       Entry:          TOP OF STACK
;                         Low byte of return address
;                         High byte of return address
;                         Low byte of base address of result matrix
;                         High byte of base address of result matrix
;                         Low byte of base address of matrix 2
;                         High byte of base address of matrix 2
;                         Low byte of base address of matrix 1
;                         High byte of base address of matrix 1
;                         Low byte of size of matrixes in bytes
;                         High byte of size of matrixes in bytes
```

```
;       Exit:               Result matrix = matrix 1 X matrix 2
;
;       Registers Used: AX,BX,CX,DI,DX,F (clears D flag),SI
;
;       Time:               Approximately 500 X size^3 + 28 X size +
;                             177 cycles where size is the number of
;                             rows or columns in the square matrixes
;
;       Size:               Program 116 bytes
;

MATMUL:
        ;
        ;CLEAR ENTIRE RESULT AREA
        ;
        PUSH    BP              ;SAVE OLD BASE POINTER
        MOV     BP,SP           ;POINT TO PARAMETERS
        MOV     DI,[BP+4]       ;GET BASE ADDRESS OF RESULT MATRIX
        MOV     BX,[BP+10]      ;GET SIZE OF MATRIXES
        MOV     AL,BL           ;SQUARE SIZE TO GET TOTAL NUMBER
        MUL     BL              ;  OF MATRIX ELEMENTS
        MOV     CX,AX           ;SAVE TOTAL NUMBER OF ELEMENTS
        STC                     ;INDICATE POSSIBLE ERROR
        JCXZ    MEXIT           ;EXIT WITH ERROR INDICATOR IF
                                ;  SIZE = 0
        SUB     AX,AX           ;GET ZERO FOR CLEARING
        CLD                     ;SELECT AUTOINCREMENTING
   REP  STOSB                   ;CLEAR ENTIRE RESULT MATRIX
        ;
        ;MULTIPLY MATRIXES AS FOLLOWS:
        ;FOR I = 0 TO SIZE - 1
        ;FOR J = 0 TO SIZE - 1
        ;FOR K = 0 TO SIZE - 1
        ;  DO MR (I,J) = M1(I,K) X M2(K,J) + MR(I,J)
        ;
        ;THAT IS, EACH ELEMENT OF RESULT MATRIX CONSISTS OF A ROW
        ;  OF MATRIX 1 TIMES A COLUMN OF MATRIX 2
        ;
        MOV     CX,BX           ;GET MATRIX SIZE
        SUB     BX,BX           ;CLEAR INDEXES I (BL) AND J (BH)
        SUB     DX,DX           ;CLEAR INDEX K (DL)
        ;
        ;COMPUTE PRODUCT ELEMENT-BY-ELEMENT
        ;
COMPEL:
        ;
        ;ADDRESS OF ELEMENT IN MATRIX 1 = INDEX I X SIZE + INDEX K
        ;  + BASE ADDRESS OF MATRIX 1
        ;
        MOV     AX,[BP+10]      ;GET SIZE OF MATRIXES
        MUL     BL              ;INDEX I X SIZE
        MOV     DI,[BP+8]       ;GET BASE ADDRESS OF MATRIX 1
        ADD     DI,AX           ;COMPUTE ADDRESS OF M1(I,0)
        MOV     AL,DL           ;GET INDEX K
        CBW                     ;EXTEND TO 16 BITS
        ADD     DI,AX           ;COMPUTE ADDRESS OF M1(I,K)
```

```
;
;ADDRESS OF ELEMENT IN MATRIX 2 = INDEX K X SIZE + INDEX J
;  + BASE ADDRESS OF MATRIX 2
;
MOV      AX,[BP+10]       ;GET SIZE OF MATRIXES
MUL      DL               ;INDEX K X SIZE
MOV      SI,[BP+6]        ;GET BASE ADDRESS OF MATRIX 2
ADD      SI,AX            ;COMPUTE ADDRESS OF M2(K,0)
MOV      AL,BH            ;GET INDEX J
CBW                       ;EXTEND TO 16 BITS
ADD      SI,AX            ;COMPUTE ADDRESS OF M2(K,J)
;
;MULTIPLY M1(I,K) TIMES M2(K,J)
;
MOV      AL,[SI]          ;GET M1(I,K)
MOV      AH,[DI]          ;GET M2(K,J)
MUL      AH               ;MULTIPLY M1(I,K) X M2(K,J)
MOV      DH,AL            ;SAVE PRODUCT
;
;ADDRESS OF ELEMENT IN RESULT MATRIX = INDEX I X SIZE +
;  INDEX J + BASE ADDRESS OF RESULT MATRIX
;
MOV      AX,[BP+10]       ;GET SIZE OF MATRIXES
MUL      BL               ;INDEX I X SIZE
MOV      SI,[BP+4]        ;GET BASE ADDRESS OF RESULT MATRIX
ADD      SI,AX            ;COMPUTE ADDRESS OF MR(I,0)
MOV      AL,BH            ;GET INDEX J
CBW                       ;EXTEND TO 16 BITS
ADD      SI,AX            ;COMPUTE ADDRESS OF MR(I,J)
;
;ADD PRODUCT OF M1(I,K) AND M2(K,J) TO MR(I,J)
;
ADD      [SI],DH
;
;CONTINUE COMPUTING ROW OF MATRIX 1 X COLUMN OF MATRIX 2
;
INC      DL               ;INDEX K = K + 1
LOOP     COMPEL           ;CONTINUE THROUGH ROW X COLUMN
;
;PROCEED TO NEXT ELEMENT IN RESULT MATRIX
;
SUB      DL,DL            ;INDEX K = 0
INC      BH               ;INDEX J = J + 1
MOV      CX,[BP+10]       ;GET SIZE OF MATRIXES
CMP      BH,CL            ;CHECK IF J EXCEEDS BOUNDS
JNE      COMPEL           ;JUMP IF NOT - START NEXT ELEMENT
                          ;ELSE PROCEED TO NEXT ROW
SUB      BH,BH            ;INDEX J = 0
INC      BL               ;INDEX I = I + 1
CMP      BL,CL            ;CHECK IF FINISHED (BL = SIZE)
JNE      COMPEL           ;JUMP IF NOT - START NEXT ELEMENT
                          ;ELSE DONE, NOTE CARRY IS SURELY
                          ;  ZERO INDICATING GOOD EXIT
;
;REMOVE PARAMETERS FROM STACK AND EXIT
;
```

```
MEXIT:
          POP       BP                  ;RESTORE BASE POINTER
          POP       DX                  ;SAVE RETURN ADDRESS
          ADD       SP,8                ;REMOVE PARAMETERS FROM STACK
          JMP       DX                  ;EXIT TO RETURN ADDRESS


;
;PROGRAM SECTION
SC6K:
          MOV       AX,MSIZE            ;GET MATRIX SIZE
          PUSH      AX
          MOV       AX,OFFSET MAT1 ;GET BASE ADDRESS OF MATRIX 1
          PUSH      AX
          MOV       AX,OFFSET MAT2 ;GET BASE ADDRESS OF MATRIX 2
          PUSH      AX
          MOV       AX,OFFSET MATR ;GET BASE ADDRESS OF RESULT MATRIX
          PUSH      AX
          CALL      MATMUL              ;DO MATRIX MULTIPLICATION
                                        ;RESULT IN MATR =
                                        ;  33H, 2FH, 2BH, 27H
                                        ;  27H, 2BH, 2FH, 33H
                                        ;  7BH, 77H, 73H, 6FH
                                        ;  6FH, 73H, 77H, 7BH
          JMP       SC6K                ;LOOP FOR MORE TESTS
;
;DATA SECTION
;
MSIZE     EQU       4                   ;SIZE OF MATRIXES
MAT1      DB        1,2,3,4             ;MATRIX 1
          DB        4,3,2,1
          DB        5,6,7,8
          DB        8,7,6,5
MAT2      DB        1,2,3,4             ;MATRIX 2
          DB        5,6,7,8
          DB        8,7,6,5
          DB        4,3,2,1
MATR      DB        MSIZE*MSIZE DUP(0)  ;RESULT MATRIX

          END
```

7 Data structure manipulation

7A Queue manager (INITQ, INSRTQ, REMOVQ)

Manages a queue of 16-bit words on a first-in, first-out basis. The queue may contain up to 32763 word-length elements plus an 8-byte header and an overflow word. The overflow word allows the manager to distinguish a full queue from an empty queue. The manager consists of the following routines:

1. INITQ starts the queue's head and tail pointers at the base address of its data area, sets the queue's length to 0, and sets its end pointer to just beyond the end of the data area.

2. INSRTQ inserts an element at the tail of the queue if there is room for it.

3. REMOVQ removes an element from the head of the queue if one is available.

These routines assume a data area of fixed length. The actual queue may occupy any part of it. If either the head or the tail reaches the end pointer, the routine simply sets it back to the base address, thus providing wraparound.

The queue header contains the following information:

1. Queue length (number of elements currently in it)

2. Head pointer (address of oldest element in queue)

3. Tail pointer (address at which next entry will be placed)

4. End pointer (address just beyond the end of the data area).

Note that the queue never occupies the entire data area. The queue is full when its tail pointer is one element behind its head pointer. This leaves one word (an overflow word) unoccupied. The queue is empty when its tail pointer and head pointer are equal. An alternate approach is to keep the size of the data area in the header. This makes the header larger (and the routines somewhat longer) but eliminates the need for an overflow word.

Procedure

1. INITQ sets the head and tail pointers to the base address of the data area, sets the queue's length to 0, and sets the end pointer to the address just beyond the end of the data area.

2. INSRTQ stores the element at the tail and increases the tail pointer. If this moves the tail pointer beyond the end of the data area, INSRTQ sets it back to the base address. It then checks whether the queue was already full (i.e. whether increasing the tail pointer made it equal to the head pointer). If so, it discards the incremented tail pointer and sets Carry to indicate an overflow. If not, it saves the incremented tail pointer and clears Carry.

3. REMOVQ checks whether the queue is empty. If so, it sets the Carry flag to indicate an underflow. If not, it removes the element from the head and increases the head pointer. If this moves the head pointer beyond the end of the data area, REMOVQ sets it back to the base address.

A sequence of INSRTQs and REMOVQs makes the head 'chase' the tail across the data area. The occupied part of the area starts at the head and ends just before the tail. Note that INSRTQ will put an element in the overflow word if the queue is full, but this word is not actually part of the queue and the element cannot be retrieved.

Entry conditions

1. INITQ
Base address of queue in register BX
Capacity of queue in words in register AX

2. INSRTQ
Base address of queue in register BX
Element to be inserted in register AX

3. REMOVQ
Base address of queue in register BX

Exit conditions

1. INITQ
Head pointer and tail pointer both set to base address of data area, queue length set to 0, and end pointer set to address just beyond the end of the data area.

2. INSRTQ
Element inserted into queue, queue length increased by 1, and tail pointer adjusted if queue is not full; otherwise, Carry = 1.

3. REMOVQ
Element removed from queue in register AX, queue length reduced by 1, and head pointer adjusted if queue is not empty; otherwise, Carry = 1.

Example

A typical sequence of queue operations proceeds as follows:

1. Initialize the queue. Call INITQ to set the head and tail pointers to the data area's base address, the queue length to 0, and the end pointer to the address just beyond the end of the data area.

2. Insert an element into the queue. Call INSRTQ to insert the element, increase the tail pointer by 2, and increase the queue length by 1.

3. Insert another element into the queue. Call INSRTQ again to insert the element, increase the tail pointer by 2, and increase the queue length by 1.

4. Remove an element from the queue. Call REMOVQ to remove an element, increase the head pointer by 2, and decrease the queue length by 1. Since the queue is organized on a first-in, first-out basis, the element removed is the first one inserted.

Reference

Y. Langsam, *et al.*, *Data Structures for Personal Computers*, Prentice-Hall, Englewood Cliffs, NJ, 1985, pp. 154–164.

Registers used

1. INITQ: AX, BX, DI, DX, F (clears D flag)
2. INSRTQ: AX, DI, DX, F (clears D flag)
3. REMOVQ: AX, DX, F (clears D flag), SI

Execution time

1. INITQ: 72 cycles
2. INSRTQ: 135 cycles
3. REMOVQ: 117 cycles

Program size

1. INITQ: 23 bytes
2. INSRTQ: 28 bytes
3. REMOVQ: 28 bytes

Data memory required None

```
;       Title           Queue Manager
;       Name:           INITQ, INSRTQ, REMOVQ
;

;       Purpose:        This program consists of three
;                       subroutines that manage a queue.
;                       INITQ initializes an empty queue.
;                       INSRTQ inserts a 16-bit element into
;                         the queue.
;                       REMOVQ removes a 16-bit element from
;                         the queue.
;
;       Entry:          INITQ
;                         Base address of queue in BX
;                         Queue capacity in 16-bit elements in AX
;
;                       INSRTQ
```

```
;                         Base address of queue in BX
;                         Element to be inserted in AX
;
;                       REMOVQ
;                         Base address of queue in BX
;
;       Exit:           INITQ
;                         Head pointer = Base address of data area
;                         Tail pointer = Base address of data area
;                         Queue length = 0
;                         End pointer = Base address of data area +
;                           2 X Queue capacity in 16-bit elements + 2
;
;                       INSRTQ
;                         If queue is not full,
;                             Element added to queue
;                             Tail pointer = Tail pointer + 2
;                             Queue length = Queue length + 1
;                             Carry = 0
;                         else Carry = 1
;
;                       REMOVQ
;                         If queue is not empty,
;                             Element removed from queue in AX
;                             Head pointer = Head pointer + 2
;                             Queue length = Queue length - 1
;                             Carry = 0
;                         else Carry = 1
;
;       Registers Used: INITQ
;                         AX,BX,DI,DX,F (clears D flag)
;                       INSRTQ
;                         AX,DI,DX,F (clears D flag)
;                       REMOVQ
;                         AX,DX,F (clears D flag),SI
;
;       Time:           INITQ
;                         72 cycles
;                       INSRTQ
;                         135 cycles
;                       REMOVQ
;                         117 cycles
;
;       Size:           Program 79 bytes
;


;
;INITIALIZE AN EMPTY QUEUE
;HEADER CONTAINS:
;    1) QUEUE LENGTH IN WORDS
;    2) HEAD POINTER (ADDRESS OF OLDEST ELEMENT)
;    3) TAIL POINTER (NEXT AVAILABLE ADDRESS)
;    4) END POINTER (ADDRESS JUST BEYOND END OF DATA AREA)
;
INITQ:
        ;
```

```
        ;SET QUEUE LENGTH IN HEADER TO ZERO
        ;
        MOV     DI,BX           ;SAVE BASE ADDRESS OF QUEUE
        ADD     BX,8            ;POINT TO START OF DATA AREA
        CLD                     ;SELECT AUTOINCREMENTING
        MOV     DX,AX           ;SAVE QUEUE CAPACITY
        SUB     AX,AX           ;QUEUE LENGTH = ZERO
        STOSW                   ;SET QUEUE LENGTH IN HEADER
        ;
        ;INITIALIZE HEAD AND TAIL POINTERS TO START OF DATA AREA
        ;
        MOV     AX,BX           ;GET POINTER TO DATA AREA
        STOSW                   ;HEAD POINTER = START OF DATA AREA
        STOSW                   ;TAIL POINTER = START OF DATA AREA
        ;
        ;INITIALIZE END POINTER TO ADDRESS JUST BEYOND DATA AREA
        ;
        SHL     DX,1            ;MULTIPLY QUEUE CAPACITY TIMES 2
                                ;  SINCE CAPACITY IS IN WORDS
        ADD     AX,DX           ;ADD DOUBLED CAPACITY TO BASE ADDRESS
        INC     AX              ;ADD 2 EXTRA BYTES (OVERFLOW WORD)
        INC     AX              ;  TO DISTINGUISH EMPTY QUEUE FROM
                                ;  FULL QUEUE
        STOSW                   ;END POINTER = ADDRESS JUST BEYOND
                                ;  END OF DATA AREA
        RET

;
;INSERT AN ELEMENT INTO A QUEUE
;
INSRTQ:
        ;
        ;STORE ELEMENT AT TAIL, THEN CHECK IF QUEUE WAS FULL
        ;
        MOV     DI,[BX+4]       ;GET TAIL POINTER
        CLD                     ;SELECT AUTOINCREMENTING
        STOSW                   ;INSERT ELEMENT AT TAIL AND INCREASE
                                ;  TAIL POINTER BY 2
                                ;IF QUEUE WAS ALREADY FULL, THIS
                                ;  STORES ELEMENT IN OVERFLOW WORD
                                ;  WHICH IS NOT ACTUALLY PART OF THE
                                ;  QUEUE
        ;
        ;IF TAIL POINTER HAS REACHED END OF DATA AREA, SET IT
        ;  BACK TO BASE ADDRESS
        ;
        CMP     DI,[BX+6]       ;COMPARE TAIL POINTER TO END POINTER
        JNE     STORTP          ;BRANCH IF TAIL NOT AT END OF DATA
                                ; AREA
        MOV     DI,BX           ;OTHERWISE, MOVE TAIL POINTER BACK TO
                                ;  BASE ADDRESS OF DATA AREA
        ADD     DI,8
        ;
        ;
        ;CHECK IF QUEUE WAS ALREADY FULL
        ;IT WAS IF INCREMENTED TAIL POINTER IS EQUAL TO HEAD POINTER
```

```
        ;IF SO, EXIT WITHOUT UPDATING TAIL POINTER
        ;IT THEN RETAINS ITS OLD VALUE AND THE ELEMENT IS NOT
        ;  ACTUALLY ENTERED INTO THE QUEUE
        ;IF NOT, UPDATE TAIL POINTER AND ADD 1 TO QUEUE LENGTH
        ;CARRY INDICATES WHETHER INSERT SUCCEEDED (0 IF IT DID, 1
        ;  IF NOT)
        ;
        CMP     DI,[BX+2]       ;COMPARE TAIL POINTER TO HEAD POINTER
        STC                     ;INDICATE QUEUE FULL (OVERFLOW)
        JE      EXITIS          ;BRANCH (EXIT) IF QUEUE WAS FULL
        MOV     [BX+4],DI       ;SAVE UPDATED TAIL POINTER
        INC     WORD PTR [BX]   ;ADD 1 TO QUEUE LENGTH
        CLC                     ;CLEAR CARRY TO INDICATE ELEMENT WAS
                                ;  INSERTED INTO QUEUE SUCCESSFULLY
EXITIS:
        RET

;
;REMOVE AN ELEMENT FROM A QUEUE
;
REMOVQ:
        ;
        ;CHECK IF QUEUE IS EMPTY BY COMPARING HEAD AND TAIL POINTERS
        ;EQUAL POINTERS INDICATE AN EMPTY QUEUE
        ;EXIT WITH CARRY SET IF QUEUE IS EMPTY
        ;
        MOV     SI,[BX+2]       ;GET HEAD POINTER
        CMP     SI,[BX+4]       ;COMPARE TO TAIL POINTER
        STC                     ;INDICATE QUEUE EMPTY (UNDERFLOW)
        JE      EXITRQ          ;BRANCH (EXIT) IF QUEUE IS EMPTY
        ;
        ;QUEUE NOT EMPTY, SO REMOVE ELEMENT FROM HEAD
        ;SUBTRACT 1 FROM QUEUE LENGTH
        ;
        CLD                     ;SELECT AUTOINCREMENTING
        LODSW                   ;GET ELEMENT FROM HEAD OF QUEUE AND
                                ;  MOVE HEAD POINTER UP ONE ELEMENT
        DEC     WORD PTR [BX]   ;SUBTRACT 1 FROM QUEUE LENGTH
        ;
        ;IF HEAD POINTER HAS REACHED END OF DATA AREA, SET IT BACK
        ;  TO BASE ADDRESS OF DATA AREA
        ;
        CMP     SI,[BX+6]       ;COMPARE HEAD POINTER TO END POINTER
        JNE     STORHP          ;BRANCH IF NOT AT END OF DATA AREA
        MOV     SI,BX           ;OTHERWISE, MOVE HEAD POINTER BACK
        ADD     SI,8            ;  TO BASE ADDRESS OF DATA AREA
STORHP:
        MOV     [BX+4],SI       ;SAVE UPDATED HEAD POINTER
        CLC                     ;INDICATE QUEUE NON-EMPTY,
                                ;  ELEMENT FOUND
EXITRQ:
        RET                     ;EXIT, CARRY INDICATES WHETHER
                                ;  ELEMENT WAS FOUND (0 IF SO,
                                ;  1 IF NOT)

;
```

```
;       SAMPLE EXECUTION
;
;
SC7A:
        ;
        ;INITIALIZE EMPTY QUEUE
        ;
        MOV     AX,5            ;DATA AREA HAS ROOM FOR 5 WORD-LENGTH
                                ;  ELEMENTS
        MOV     BX,OFFSET QUEUE ;GET BASE ADDRESS OF QUEUE BUFFER
        CALL    INITQ           ;INITIALIZE QUEUE
        ;
        ;INSERT ELEMENTS INTO QUEUE
        ;
        MOV     AX,0AAAAH       ;ELEMENT TO BE INSERTED IS AAAA
        MOV     BX,OFFSET QUEUE ;GET BASE ADDRESS OF QUEUE
        CALL    INSRTQ          ;INSERT ELEMENT INTO QUEUE
        MOV     AX,0BBBBH       ;ELEMENT TO BE INSERTED IS BBBB
        MOV     BX,OFFSET QUEUE ;GET BASE ADDRESS OF QUEUE
                                ;NOT ACTUALLY NECESSARY IN THIS
                                ;  SEQUENCE SINCE INSRTQ DOES NOT
                                ;  CHANGE BX
        CALL    INSRTQ          ;INSERT ELEMENT INTO QUEUE
        ;
        ;REMOVE ELEMENT FROM QUEUE
        ;
        MOV     BX,OFFSET QUEUE ;GET BASE ADDRESS OF QUEUE
        CALL    REMOVQ          ;REMOVE ELEMENT FROM QUEUE
                                ; [AX] = 0AAAAH (FIRST ELEMENT
                                ; INSERTED)
        JMP     SC7A            ;REPEAT TEST

;
;DATA
;
QUEUE   DW      10 DUP (?)      ;QUEUE BUFFER CONSISTS OF AN 8 BYTE
                                ; HEADER FOLLOWED BY 12 BYTES FOR
                                ; DATA. THIS IS ENOUGH ROOM FOR FIVE
                                ; WORD-LENGTH ELEMENTS PLUS AN
                                ; OVERFLOW WORD.

        END
```

7B Stack manager (INITST, PUSHS, POPS, STKTOP)

Manages a stack of 16-bit words on a first-in, last-out basis. The stack can contain up to 32 765 elements. Consists of the following routines:

1. INITST initializes the stack header, consisting of the stack pointer and its upper and lower bounds.

2. PUSHS inserts an element into the stack if there is room for it.

3. POPS removes an element from the stack if one is available.

4. STKTOP returns the top element and its address.

Procedures

1. INITST sets the stack pointer and its lower bound to the base address of the stack's data area. It sets the upper bound to the address of the last word in the data area.

2. PUSHS checks whether the stack pointer exceeds its upper bound. If so, it sets the Carry flag to indicate overflow. If not, it inserts the element at the stack pointer, increases the stack pointer by 2, and clears the Carry flag.

3. POPS checks whether decreasing the stack pointer by 2 will make it less than its lower bound. If so, it sets the Carry flag to indicate underflow. If not, it decreases the stack pointer by 2, removes the element, and clears the Carry flag.

4. STKTOP checks whether decreasing the stack pointer by 2 will make it less than its lower bound. If so, it sets the Carry flag to indicate an empty stack. If not, it returns the top element and its address and clears the Carry flag. Note that the top element's address is not the stack pointer, but rather the location immediately below it.

The software stack differs from the 8086's hardware stack in the following regards:

1. It grows up in memory (i.e. toward higher addresses), whereas the hardware stack grows down (i.e. toward lower addresses).

2. Its pointer contains the next available memory address, whereas the hardware pointer contains the last occupied address.

Entry conditions

1. INITST
Base address of stack in register BX
Size of stack data area in words in register AX

2. PUSHS
Base address of stack in register BX
Element in register AX

3. POPS
Base address of stack in register BX

4. STKTOP
Base address of stack in register BX

Exit conditions

1. INITST
Stack header set up with:

Stack pointer = Base address of stack's data area
Lower bound = Base address of stack's data area
Upper bound = Address of last word in stack's data area

2. PUSHS
Element inserted into stack and stack pointer increased if there is room in the data area; otherwise, Carry = 1, indicating an overflow.

3. POPS
Element removed from stack in register AX and stack pointer decreased if stack was not empty; otherwise, Carry = 1, indicating an underflow.

4. STKTOP
Top element in register AX and its address in register BX if stack is not empty; otherwise, Carry = 1, indicating an empty stack.

Example

A typical sequence of stack operations proceeds as follows:

1. Initialize the empty stack with INITST. This sets the stack pointer and the lower bound to the base address of the stack's data area, and the upper bound to the address of the last word in the data area.

2. Insert an element into the stack. Call PUSHS to store an element at the top of the stack and increase the stack pointer by 2.

3. Insert another element into the stack. Call PUSHS to store a second element at the top of the stack and increase the stack pointer by 2.

4. Remove an element from the stack. Call POPS to decrease the stack pointer by 2 and remove an element from the top of the stack. Since the stack is organized on a last-in, first-out basis, the element removed is the latest one inserted.

You can use STKTOP at any time to obtain the top element and its address without popping the stack. This allows you to use the top of the stack as an extra register. You can examine its contents, replace them, or exchange them with a hardware register. You can also determine the stack's current position if you need to save it or index from it. The wide range of uses is why we include STKTOP here, even though it is not an elementary operation (it is equivalent to POPS followed immediately by PUSHS).

Reference

Y. Langsam *et al.*, *Data Structures for Personal Computers*, Prentice-Hall, Englewood Cliffs, NJ, 1985, pp. 108–118.

Registers used

1. INITST: AX,DI,F
2. PUSHS: DI,F (clears D flag)
3. POPS: AX,DI,F
4. STKTOP: AX,BX,DI,F

Execution time

1. INITST: 71 cycles
2. PUSHS: 70 cycles
3. POPS: 74 cycles
4. STKTOP: 62 cycles

Program size

1. INITST: 19 bytes
2. PUSHS: 12 bytes
3. POPS: 14 bytes
4. STKTOP: 14 bytes

Data memory required None

```
;       Title                   Stack Manager
;       Name:                   INITST, PUSHS, POPS, STKTOP
;
;       Purpose:                This program consists of four
;                               subroutines that manage a stack.
;
;                               INITST initializes the stack pointer and
;                                 the stack's upper and lower bounds
;                               PUSHS inserts a 16-bit element into
;                                 the stack.
;                               POPS removes a 16-bit element from
;                                 the stack.
;                               STKTOP returns the top element and its
;                                 address without changing the stack
;
;       Entry:                  INITST
;                                 Base address of stack in BX
;                                 Size of stack data area in words in AX
;                               PUSHS
;                                 Base address of stack in BX
;                                 Element in AX
;                               POPS
;                                 Base address of stack in BX
;                               STKTOP
;                                 Base address of stack in BX
;
;       Exit:                   INITST
;                                 Stack header set up with:
;                                   Stack pointer = Base address of stack
;                                     data area
;                                   Lower bound = Base address of stack
;                                     data area
;                                   Upper bound = Address of last word
;                                     in stack data area
;
;                               PUSHS
;                                 If stack pointer is at or below upper
;                                 bound,
;                                    Element inserted into stack
;                                    Stack pointer = Stack pointer + 2
;                                    Carry = 0
```

```
;                          else Carry = 1
;
;                       POPS
;                         If stack pointer - 2 is at or above lower
;                         bound,
;                            Element removed from stack in AX
;                            Stack pointer = Stack pointer - 2
;                            Carry = 0
;                         else Carry = 1
;
;                       STKTOP
;                         If stack pointer - 2 is at or above lower
;                         bound,
;                            Top element in AX
;                            Top element's address (stack pointer - 2)
;                              in BX
;                            Carry = 0
;                          else Carry = 1
;
;       Registers Used: INITST
;                         AX,DI,F
;                       PUSHS
;                         DI,F (clears D flag)
;                       POPS
;                         AX,DI,F
;                       STKTOP
;                         AX,BX,DI,F
;
;       Time:           INITST
;                         71 cycles
;                       PUSHS
;                         70 cycles
;                       POPS
;                         74 cycles
;                       STKTOP
;                         62 cycles
;
;       Size:           Program 59 bytes                  ;
;                                                         ;


;
;INITIALIZE AN EMPTY STACK
;HEADER CONTAINS:
;     1) STACK POINTER (2 BYTES)
;     2) LOWER BOUND (2 BYTES)
;     3) UPPER BOUND (2 BYTES)
;
        ;
        ;STACK POINTER = BASE ADDRESS OF STACK DATA AREA
        ;LOWER BOUND = BASE ADDRESS OF STACK DATA AREA
        ;
INITST:
        MOV     DI,BX           ;COMPUTE BASE ADDRESS OF STACK DATA
        ADD     DI,6            ;  AREA (BASE OF STACK + HEADER SIZE)
        MOV     [BX],DI         ;STORE IT AS INITIAL STACK POINTER
        MOV     [BX+2],DI       ;STORE IT AS LOWER BOUND ALSO
```

```
        ;
        ;UPPER BOUND = ADDRESS OF LAST WORD IN STACK DATA AREA
        ;
        DEC     AX              ;INDEX OF LAST WORD = STACK SIZE - 1
        SHL     AX,1            ;MULTIPLY INDEX TIMES 2 SINCE
                                ;  ELEMENTS ARE WORD-LENGTH
        ADD     DI,AX           ;ADD DOUBLED INDEX TO BASE ADDRESS OF
                                ; STACK DATA AREA
        MOV     [BX+4],DI       ;STORE SUM AS UPPER BOUND OF STACK
        RET

;
;INSERT A 16-BIT ELEMENT INTO A STACK
;
PUSHS:
        ;
        ;EXIT INDICATING OVERFLOW (CARRY SET) IF STACK IS FULL
        ;
        MOV     DI,[BX]         ;GET STACK POINTER
        CMP     [BX+4],DI       ;COMPARE TO UPPER BOUND
        JB      PSEXIT          ;BRANCH IF STACK POINTER IS
                                ; ABOVE UPPER BOUND
                                ; NOTE: THIS COMPARISON HANDLES
                                ; SITUATIONS IN WHICH THE STACK
                                ; POINTER HAS BECOME MISALIGNED OR
                                ; HAS GONE OUTSIDE ITS NORMAL RANGE.
                                ;CARRY = 1 IF A BRANCH OCCURS, 0 IF
                                ; NOT
        ;
        ;NO OVERFLOW - INSERT ELEMENT INTO STACK
        ;UPDATE STACK POINTER
        ;
        CLD                     ;SELECT AUTOINCREMENTING
        STOSW                   ;INSERT ELEMENT INTO STACK AND
                                ;  INCREASE STACK POINTER
        MOV     [BX],DI         ;SAVE UPDATED STACK POINTER
                                ;CARRY IS CLEARED, INDICATING
                                ;  SUCCESSFUL PUSH, BY BOUNDARY
                                ;  CHECK ABOVE
PSEXIT:
        RET                     ;EXIT, CARRY INDICATES WHETHER
                                ;  PUSH WORKED (0) OR STACK WAS
                                ;  FULL (1)

;
;REMOVE A 16-BIT ELEMENT FROM A STACK
;
POPS:
        ;
        ;EXIT INDICATING UNDERFLOW (CARRY = 1) IF STACK IS EMPTY
        ;
        MOV     DI,[BX]         ;GET STACK POINTER
        DEC     DI              ;DECREASE STACK POINTER BY 2
        DEC     DI
        CMP     DI,[BX+2]       ;COMPARE TO LOWER BOUND
```

```
        JB      EXITPOP          ;BRANCH (EXIT) IF BELOW LOWER BOUND
                                 ; NOTE: THIS COMPARISON HANDLES
                                 ; SITUATIONS IN WHICH THE STACK
                                 ; POINTER HAS BECOME MISALIGNED OR
                                 ; GONE OUTSIDE ITS NORMAL RANGE.
                                 ; NOTE: JB IS THE SAME AS JC SO
                                 ; CARRY IS SET IF A BRANCH OCCURS,
                                 ; CLEARED IF NOT.

        ;
        ;NO UNDERFLOW - REMOVE ELEMENT AND DECREASE STACK POINTER
        ;
        MOV     [BX],DI          ;SAVE UPDATED STACK POINTER
        MOV     AX,[DI]          ;REMOVE ELEMENT FROM STACK
EXITPOP:
        RET                      ;EXIT - CARRY INDICATES WHETHER
                                 ;  POP WORKED (0) OR STACK WAS
                                 ;  EMPTY (1)

;
;RETURN TOP ELEMENT AND ITS ADDRESS
;
STKTOP:
        ;
        ;EXIT INDICATING ERROR (CARRY = 1) IF STACK IS EMPTY
        ;
        MOV     DI,[BX]          ;GET STACK POINTER
        DEC     DI               ;DECREASE STACK POINTER BY 2
        DEC     DI
        CMP     DI,[BX+2]        ;COMPARE TO LOWER BOUND
        JB      EXITTOP          ;BRANCH (EXIT) IF BELOW LOWER BOUND
                                 ; NOTE: THIS COMPARISON HANDLES
                                 ; SITUATIONS IN WHICH THE STACK
                                 ; POINTER HAS BECOME MISALIGNED OR
                                 ; GONE OUTSIDE ITS NORMAL RANGE.
                                 ; NOTE: JB IS THE SAME AS JC SO
                                 ; CARRY IS SET IF A BRANCH OCCURS,
                                 ; CLEARED IF NOT.

        ;
        ;NO ERROR - RETURN TOP ELEMENT AND ITS ADDRESS
        ;
        MOV     BX,DI            ;RETURN TOP ELEMENT'S ADDRESS IN BX
        MOV     AX,[DI]          ;RETURN TOP ELEMENT IN AX
                                 ;NOTE STACK POINTER DOES NOT CHANGE
EXITTOP:
        RET                      ;EXIT - CARRY INDICATES WHETHER
                                 ; ELEMENT VALID (0) OR STACK WAS
                                 ; EMPTY (1)


;
;       SAMPLE EXECUTION
;
;
SC7B:
        ;
        ;INITIALIZE EMPTY STACK
        ;
        MOV     BX,OFFSET STACK  ;GET BASE ADDRESS OF STACK
```

```
        MOV     AX,STKSZ        ;GET SIZE OF STACK DATA AREA IN WORDS
        CALL    INITST          ;INITIALIZE STACK HEADER
        ;
        ;PUT ELEMENT 1 IN STACK
        ;
        MOV     AX,[ELEM1]      ;GET ELEMENT 1
                                ;NOTE THAT THE STACK ADDRESS STAYS
                                ; IN BX SINCE ONLY STKTOP CHANGES
                                ; THAT REGISTER
        CALL    PUSHS           ;PUT ELEMENT 1 IN STACK
        ;
        ;PUT ELEMENT 2 IN STACK
        ;
        MOV     AX,[ELEM2]      ;GET ELEMENT 2
        MOV     BX,OFFSET STACK ;GET BASE ADDRESS OF STACK AREA
        CALL    PUSHS           ;PUT ELEMENT 2 IN STACK
        ;
        ;REMOVE ELEMENT FROM STACK
        ;
        MOV     BX,OFFSET STACK ;GET BASE ADDRESS OF STACK AREA
        CALL    POPS            ;REMOVE ELEMENT FROM STACK TO AX
                                ; AX NOW CONTAINS ELEMENT 2
                                ; SINCE STACK IS ORGANIZED ON A
                                ; LAST-IN, FIRST-OUT BASIS

        ;
        ;OBTAIN TOP ELEMENT AND ITS ADDRESS
        ;
        MOV     BX,OFFSET STACK ;GET BASE ADDRESS OF STACK AREA
        CALL    STKTOP          ;GET TOP ELEMENT AND ITS ADDRESS
                                ; AX NOW CONTAINS ELEMENT 1
                                ; BX CONTAINS ADDRESS STACK, THE
                                ;  TOP OCCUPIED ADDRESS
                                ;NOTE THAT STKTOP DOES NOT CHANGE
                                ; THE STACK OR ITS POINTER
        JMP     SC7B            ;LOOP FOR MORE TESTS

;
;DATA
;
STACK   DB      16 DUP(?)       ;STACK HAS ROOM FOR 6-BYTE HEADER
                                ; AND 10 BYTES OF DATA (5 WORD-
                                ; LENGTH ELEMENTS)
ELEM1   DW      1111H           ;2-BYTE ELEMENT
ELEM2   DW      2222H           ;2-BYTE ELEMENT
STKSZ   EQU     5               ;SIZE OF STACK DATA AREA IN WORDS

        END
```

7C Singly linked list manager (INLST, RMLST, NFOLLO)

Manages a linked list of elements, each of which has the address of its successor (or 0 if it has no successor) in its first two bytes. Consists of the following routines:

1. INLST inserts an element into the list, given its predecessor.

2. RMLST removes an element from the list (if one exists), given its predecessor.

3. NFOLLO determines the number of successors to a given element.

Note that you can add or remove elements anywhere in the linked list. All you need is the address of the predecessor to provide the linkage.

Procedures

1. INLST obtains the link from the predecessor, changes that link to the new element, and sets the new element's link to the one from the predecessor.

2. RMLST first determines if a successor exists. If not, it sets the Carry flag. If so, it obtains that element's link and puts it in the current element. This unlinks the element and removes it from the list.

3. NFOLLO starts the element count at −1. It then repeatedly adds 1 to the element count and replaces the current element with its link until it finds a zero link (indicating no successor).

Entry conditions

1. INLST
Base address of predecessor in BX
Base address of new element in AX

2. RMLST
Base address of predecessor in BX

3. NFOLLO
Base address of given element in BX

Exit conditions

1. INLST
Element inserted into list with predecessor linked to it. It is linked to the element that had been linked to the predecessor.

2. RMLST
If a successor exists, it is removed from the list, its base address is placed in register AX, and Carry is cleared.
Otherwise, register AX = 0 and Carry = 1.

3. NFOLLO
Number of elements after given element in AX

Example

A typical sequence of operations on a linked list is:

1. Initialize the empty list by setting the link in the header to 0.

2. Insert an element into the list by using the base address of the header as the predecessor.

3. Insert another element into the list by using the base address of the element just inserted as the predecessor.

4. Remove the first element from the linked list by using the base address of the header as the predecessor. Note that we can remove either element from the list by supplying the appropriate predecessor.

These routines require the user to keep track of the list's length separately. An alternative approach is to put the length in the header and update it during each insertion or removal. While NFOLLO can determine the list's length at any time, it is slow for long lists since it must examine each element.

Reference

Y. Langsam *et al.*, *Data Structures for Personal Computers*, Prentice-Hall, Englewood Cliffs, NJ, 1985, pp. 164–189.

Registers used

1. INLST: AX, DI
2. RMLST: AX, DI, F
3. NFOLLO: AX, BX, F

Execution time

1. INLST: 51 cycles
2. RMLST: 61 cycles
3. NFOLLO: 34 cycles per element plus 12 cycles overhead

Program size

1. INLST: 9 bytes
2. RMLST: 15 bytes
3. NFOLLO: 11 bytes

Data memory required None

```
;       Title           Singly Linked List Manager
;       Name:           INLST, RMLST, NFOLLO
;
;
;       Purpose:        This program consists of three subroutines
;                       that manage a singly linked list.
;
;                       INLST inserts an element into the linked
;                         list.
;                       RMLST removes an element from the linked
;                         list.
;                       NFOLLO determines the number of elements
;                         following a given element.
;
;       Entry:          INLST
;                          Predecessor's address in register BX
;                          Entry's address in register AX
;                       RMLST
;                          Predecessor's address in register BX
;                       NFOLLO
;                          Given element's address in register BX
;
;       Exit:           INLST
;                         Element added to list
;                       RMLST
```

```
;                             If successor exists,
;                               its address is in register AX
;                               Carry = 0
;                             else
;                               register AX = 0
;                               Carry = 1
;                           NFOLLO
;                             Number of elements in register AX
;
;         Registers Used:   INLST
;                             AX,DI,DX
;                           RMLST
;                             AX,DI,F
;                           NFOLLO
;                             AX,BX,F
;
;         Time:             INLST
;                             51 cycles
;                           RMLST
;                             61 cycles
;                           NFOLLO
;                             34 cycles per element plus 12 cycles
;                               overhead
;
;         Size:             Program 35 bytes
;
;
;           INSERT AN ELEMENT INTO A SINGLY LINKED LIST
;
INLST:
          ;
          ;UPDATE LINKS TO INCLUDE NEW ELEMENT
          ;LINK PREDECESSOR TO NEW ELEMENT
          ;LINK NEW ELEMENT TO ELEMENT FORMERLY LINKED TO
          ;  PREDECESSOR
          ;
          MOV      DI,AX           ;SAVE NEW ELEMENT
          MOV      AX,[BX]         ;GET LINK FROM PREDECESSOR
          MOV      [DI],AX         ;STORE LINK IN NEW ELEMENT
          MOV      [BX],DI         ;STORE NEW ELEMENT AS LINK IN
                                   ; PREDECESSOR
          ;
          ;NOTE: IF LINKS ARE NOT IN FIRST TWO BYTES OF ELEMENTS, PUT
          ;  LINK OFFSET IN LAST 3 INSTRUCTIONS
          ;
          ;EXIT
          ;
          RET

;
;         REMOVE AN ELEMENT FROM A SINGLY LINKED LIST
;
RMLST:
          ;
          ;EXIT INDICATING FAILURE (CARRY SET) IF NO SUCCESSOR
          ;
```

```
        MOV     DI,[BX]         ;GET LINK TO POSSIBLE SUCCESSOR
        TEST    DI,DI           ;CHECK IF SUCCESSOR IS NULL (LINK=0)
        STC                     ;INDICATE SUCCESSOR IS NULL
        JE      RMEXIT          ;BRANCH IF SUCCESSOR IS NULL
        ;
        ;UNLINK REMOVED ELEMENT BY TRANSFERRING ITS LINK TO
        ;  PREDECESSOR
        ;NOTE: IF LINKS NOT IN FIRST TWO BYTES OF ELEMENTS, PUT
        ;  LINK OFFSET IN STATEMENTS
        ;
        MOV     AX,[DI]         ;GET LINK FROM REMOVED ELEMENT
        MOV     [BX],AX         ;MOVE LINK TO PREDECESSOR
        CLC                     ;INDICATE ELEMENT FOUND
        ;
        ;EXIT
        ;
RMEXIT:
        MOV     AX,DI           ;EXIT WITH BASE ADDRESS OF REMOVED
                                ; ELEMENT OR 0 IN AX
        RET                     ;CARRY = 0 IF ELEMENT FOUND, 1
                                ; IF NOT
;
;       DETERMINE NUMBER OF SUCCESSORS TO A GIVEN ELEMENT
;
NFOLLO:
        ;
        ;COUNT ELEMENTS UNTIL ENCOUNTERING ONE WITH A ZERO LINK
        ;  (NO SUCCESSOR)
        ;
        MOV     AX,-1           ;START ELEMENT COUNT AT -1
CHKNXT: INC     AX              ;ADD 1 TO ELEMENT COUNT
        MOV     BX,[BX]         ;REPLACE ELEMENT WITH SUCCESSOR
        TEST    BX,BX           ;TEST IF SUCCESSOR EXISTS
        JNZ     CHKNXT          ;BRANCH (CONTINUE) IF SUCCESSOR
                                ;  EXISTS
        RET                     ;EXIT

;                                                               ;
;       SAMPLE EXECUTION                                        ;
;                                                               ;
;
SC7C:
        ;
        ;INITIALIZE EMPTY LINKED LIST
        ;
        MOV     WORD PTR [LLHDR],0  ;CLEAR LINKED LIST HEADER
                                ;  0 INDICATES NO SUCCESSOR
        ;
        ;INSERT AN ELEMENT INTO LINKED LIST
        ;
        MOV     AX,OFFSET ELEM1 ;GET BASE ADDRESS OF ELEMENT 1
        MOV     BX,OFFSET LLHDR ;GET PREDECESSOR (HEADER)
        CALL    INLST           ;INSERT ELEMENT INTO LIST
        ;
        ;INSERT ANOTHER ELEMENT INTO LINKED LIST
        ;
```

```
        MOV     AX,OFFSET ELEM2 ;GET BASE ADDRESS OF ELEMENT 2
        MOV     BX,OFFSET ELEM1 ;GET PREDECESSOR (ELEMENT 1)
        CALL    INLST           ;INSERT ELEMENT INTO LIST
        ;
        ;DETERMINE LENGTH OF LIST
        ;
        MOV     BX,OFFSET LLHDR ;GET ADDRESS OF HEADER
        CALL    NFOLLO          ;DETERMINE NUMBER OF ELEMENTS
                                ;  FOLLOWING HEADER.  RESULT
                                ;  SHOULD BE [AX] = 2
        ;
        ;REMOVE FIRST ELEMENT FROM LINKED LIST
        ;
        MOV     BX,OFFSET LLHDR ;GET PREDECESSOR
        CALL    RMLST           ;REMOVE ELEMENT FROM LIST
                                ;END UP WITH HEADER LINKED TO
                                ;  SECOND ELEMENT
                                ;AX CONTAINS ADDRESS OF
                                ;  FIRST ELEMENT
        JMP     SC7C            ;REPEAT TEST

;
;DATA
;
LLHDR   DW      ?               ;LINKED LIST HEADER
ELEM1   DW      ?               ;ELEMENT 1 - HEADER (LINK) ONLY
ELEM2   DW      ?               ;ELEMENT 2 - HEADER (LINK) ONLY
        END
```

7D Doubly linked list manager (INSRDL, INSLDL, DELDL)

Manages a doubly linked list of elements. Each element contains the address of its successor (or 0 if it has no successor) in its first two bytes. It contains the address of its predecessor (or 0 if it has no predecessor) in its next two bytes. The manager consists of the following routines:

1. INSRDL inserts an element into the list, given its predecessor. That is, it inserts to the right.

2. INSLDL inserts an element into the list, given its successor. That is, it inserts to the left.

3. DELDL deletes an element from the list by linking its successor (if it has one) directly to its predecessor (if it has one) and vice versa.

As with a singly linked list, you can add or remove elements anywhere. All you need is the address of the predecessor (for INSRDL) or successor (for INSLDL) to insert an element. No parameters are needed to delete an element, since each one contains links to both its successor and its predecessor.

Procedures

1. INSRDL first obtains the forward link from the predecessor. It then changes the links as follows:

(a) The new element becomes the forward link of the predecessor.
(b) The predecessor becomes the backward link of the new element.
(c) The old forward link from the predecessor becomes the forward link of the new element.
(d) The new element becomes the backward link of the predecessor's successor if the old forward link was non-null.

2. INSLDL works just like INSRDL except that it first obtains the backward link from the successor. Here, of course, the successor is known to exist, whereas the backward link could be null (i.e. the successor might not have a predecessor).

3. DELDL first obtains the element's forward and backward links. If a successor exists, it sets that element's backward link to the deleted element's backward link. If a predecessor exists, it sets that element's forward link to the deleted element's forward link. This unlinks the element, removing it from the list. An optional extension would be to clear the element's links so that no vestiges remain of its previous state.

Entry conditions

1. INSRDL
Address of predecessor in register BX
Address of new element in register AX

2. INSLDL
Address of successor in register BX
Address of new element in register AX

3. DELDL
Address of element to be deleted in register BX

Exit conditions

1. INSRDL
Element added to list after its predecessor. The new links make it the successor of its predecessor and the predecessor of its predecessor's successor if such an element exists.

2. INSLDL
Element added to list before its successor. The new links make it the predecessor of its successor and the successor of its successor's predecessor if such an element exists.

3. DELDL
Element removed from the list. The new links make its successor the successor of its predecessor, and its predecessor the predecessor of its successor, assuming that these elements exist.

Example

A typical sequence of operations on a doubly linked list is:

1. Initialize the empty list by setting both links in the header to 0.

2. Insert an element into the list (with INSRDL) using the address of the header as its predecessor.

3. Insert another element into the list (with INSRDL) by using the address of the element just added as the predecessor. An alternative would be to insert the new element between the header and the previous element (with INSLDL).

4. Delete the first element from the list with DELDL, leaving only the header and the second element.

Note that we can delete either element from the list and can insert elements on either side of existing elements.

Reference

Y. Langsam *et al.*, *Data Structures for Personal Computers*, Prentice-Hall, Englewood Cliffs, NJ, 1985, pp. 210–217.

Registers used

1. INSRDL: DI, F, SI
2. INSLDL: DI, F, SI
3. DELDL: BX, DI, F

Execution time

1. INSRDL: 96 cycles
2. INSLDL: 96 cycles
3. DELDL: 84 cycles

Program size

1. INDLST: 19 bytes
2. INSLDL: 19 bytes
3. DELDL: 19 bytes

Data memory required None

```
;       Title               Doubly Linked List Manager
;       Name:               INSRDL, INSLDL, DELDL
;
;       Purpose:            This program consists of three subroutines
;                           that manage a doubly linked list.
;
;                           INSRDL inserts an element into the doubly
;                             linked list as the successor of a given
;                             element.
;                           INSLDL inserts an element into the doubly
;                             linked list as the predecessor of a given
;                             element.
;                           DELDL removes an element from the
;                             doubly linked list.
;
;       Entry:              INSRDL
;                             Predecessor in register BX
;                             New element in register AX
;                           INSLDL
;                             Successor in register BX
;                             New element in register AX
;                           DELDL
;                             Element in register BX
;
;       Exit:               INSRDL
;                             Element inserted into list after predecessor
;                           INSLDL
;                             Element inserted into list before successor
;                           DELDL
;                             Element removed from list
;
;       Registers Used:     INSRDL
;                             DI,F,SI
;                           INSLDL
;                             DI,F,SI
;                           DELDL
;                             DI,F
;
;       Time:               INSRDL
;                             96 cycles
;                           INSLDL
;                             96 cycles
;                           DELDL
;                             84 cycles
;
;       Size:               Program 57 bytes                          ;
;                                                                     ;


;
;         INSERT AN ELEMENT INTO A DOUBLY LINKED LIST, GIVEN ITS
;           PREDECESSOR
;         THAT IS, INSERT AN ELEMENT TO THE RIGHT OF A GIVEN ELEMENT
;
INSRDL:
        ;
```

```
        ;UPDATE LINKS TO INCLUDE NEW ELEMENT
        ;MAKE NEW ELEMENT PREDECESSOR'S FORWARD LINK
        ;MAKE PREDECESSOR NEW ELEMENT'S BACKWARD LINK
        ;MOVE PREDECESSOR'S PREVIOUS FORWARD LINK TO NEW ELEMENT
        ;
        MOV     DI,AX           ;SAVE NEW ELEMENT
        MOV     SI,[BX]         ;GET FORWARD LINK FROM PREDECESSOR
        MOV     [BX],DI         ;MAKE NEW ELEMENT INTO PREDECESSOR'S
                                ;  FORWARD LINK
        MOV     [DI+2],BX       ;MAKE PREDECESSOR NEW ELEMENT'S
                                ;  BACKWARD LINK
        MOV     [DI],SI         ;MOVE PREDECESSOR'S PREVIOUS FORWARD
                                ;  LINK TO NEW ELEMENT
        ;
        ;IF PREDECESSOR HAS A SUCCESSOR, LINK IT TO NEW ELEMENT
        ;THAT IS, MAKE NEW ELEMENT SUCCESSOR'S BACKWARD LINK
        ;
        TEST    SI,SI           ;CHECK IF SUCCESSOR EXISTS
        JZ      INREXT          ;BRANCH (EXIT) IF SUCCESSOR IS NULL
        MOV     [SI+2],DI       ;MAKE NEW ELEMENT SUCCESSOR'S
                                ;  BACKWARD LINK
        ;
        ;NOTE: IF LINKS ARE NOT IN FIRST FOUR BYTES OF ELEMENTS,
        ;  PUT LINK OFFSETS IN ALL TRANSFERS
        ;
        ;
        ;EXIT
        ;
INREXT:
        RET                     ;EXIT
;
;       INSERT AN ELEMENT INTO A DOUBLY LINKED LIST, GIVEN ITS
;         SUCCESSOR
;       THAT IS, INSERT AN ELEMENT TO THE LEFT OF A GIVEN ELEMENT
;
INSLDL:
        ;
        ;UPDATE LINKS TO INCLUDE NEW ELEMENT
        ;MAKE NEW ELEMENT SUCCESSOR'S BACKWARD LINK
        ;MAKE SUCCESSOR NEW ELEMENT'S FORWARD LINK
        ;MOVE PREDECESSOR'S PREVIOUS BACKWARD LINK TO NEW ELEMENT
        ;
        MOV     DI,AX           ;SAVE NEW ELEMENT
        MOV     SI,[BX+2]       ;GET BACKWARD LINK FROM SUCCESSOR
        MOV     [BX+2],DI       ;MAKE NEW ELEMENT INTO SUCCESSOR'S
                                ;  BACKWARD LINK
        MOV     [DI],BX         ;MAKE SUCCESSOR NEW ELEMENT'S
                                ;  FORWARD LINK
        MOV     [DI+2],SI       ;MOVE SUCCESSOR'S PREVIOUS BACKWARD
                                ;  LINK TO NEW ELEMENT
        ;
        ;IF SUCCESSOR HAS A PREDECESSOR, LINK IT TO NEW ELEMENT
        ;THAT IS, MAKE NEW ELEMENT PREDECESSOR'S FORWARD LINK
        ;
        TEST    SI,SI           ;CHECK IF PREDECESSOR EXISTS
        JZ      INLEXT          ;BRANCH IF PREDECESSOR IS NULL
```

```
        MOV     [SI],DI         ;MAKE NEW ELEMENT PREDECESSOR'S
                                ;  FORWARD LINK
        ;
        ;NOTE: IF LINKS ARE NOT IN FIRST FOUR BYTES OF ELEMENTS,
        ;  PUT LINK OFFSETS IN ALL TRANSFERS
        ;
        ;
        ;EXIT
        ;
        RET                     ;EXIT
INLEXT:
;
;       REMOVE AN ELEMENT FROM A DOUBLY LINKED LIST
;
DELDL:
        ;
        ;GET ELEMENT'S FORWARD AND BACKWARD LINKS
        ;
        MOV     DI,[BX]         ;GET ELEMENT'S FORWARD LINK
        MOV     BX,[BX+2]       ;GET ELEMENT'S BACKWARD LINK
        ;
        ;IF ELEMENT HAS A SUCCESSOR, MOVE ELEMENT'S BACKWARD
        ;  LINK TO SUCCESSOR
        ;
        TEST    DI,DI           ;CHECK IF SUCCESSOR EXISTS
        JZ      CHKPR           ;BRANCH IF SUCCESSOR IS NULL
        MOV     [DI+2],BX       ;MOVE ELEMENT'S BACKWARD LINK
                                ;  TO SUCCESSOR
        ;
        ;IF ELEMENT HAS A PREDECESSOR, MOVE ELEMENT'S FORWARD
        ;  LINK TO PREDECESSOR
        ;
CHKPR:
        TEST    BX,BX           ;CHECK IF PREDECESSOR EXISTS
        JZ      DELEXT          ;BRANCH IF PREDECESSOR IS NULL
        MOV     [BX],DI         ;MOVE ELEMENT'S FORWARD LINK
                                ;  TO PREDECESSOR
        ;
        ;NOTE: IF LINKS ARE NOT IN FIRST FOUR BYTES OF ELEMENTS,
        ;  PUT LINK OFFSETS IN ALL TRANSFERS
        ;
DELEXT:
        RET                     ;EXIT

;                                                               ;
;       SAMPLE EXECUTION                                        ;
;                                                               ;
;
SC7D:
        ;
        ;INITIALIZE EMPTY DOUBLY LINKED LIST
        ;
        SUB     AX,AX           ;CLEAR LINKED LIST HEADER
        MOV     [HDRFWD],AX     ;FORWARD LINK
        MOV     [HDRBCK],AX     ;BACKWARD LINK
                                ;0 INDICATES NO LINK IN THAT
```

```
                                          ; DIRECTION
        ;
        ;INSERT ELEMENT INTO DOUBLY LINKED LIST
        ;
        MOV     AX,OFFSET ELEM1   ;GET ELEMENT 1
        MOV     BX,OFFSET HDRFWD ;GET PREDECESSOR (HEADER)
        CALL    INSRDL           ;INSERT ELEMENT 1 INTO LIST AFTER
                                 ;  HEADER
        ;
        ;INSERT ANOTHER ELEMENT INTO DOUBLY LINKED LIST
        ;
        MOV     AX,OFFSET ELEM2  ;GET ELEMENT 2
        MOV     BX,OFFSET ELEM1  ;GET SUCCESSOR
        CALL    INSLDL           ;INSERT ELEMENT 2 INTO LIST BEFORE
                                 ;  ELEMENT 1
        ;
        ;REMOVE FIRST ELEMENT FROM DOUBLY LINKED LIST
        ;
        MOV     BX,OFFSET ELEM1   ;GET ELEMENT
        CALL    DELDL            ;REMOVE ELEMENT 1 FROM LIST
                                 ;END UP WITH HEADER LINKED TO
                                 ;  ELEMENT 2

        JMP     SC7D             ;REPEAT TEST

;
;DATA
;
HDRFWD  DW      ?                ;HEADER - FORWARD LINK
HDRBCK  DW      ?                ;HEADER - BACKWARD LINK
ELEM1   DD      ?                ;ELEMENT 1 - HEADER (LINKS) ONLY
ELEM2   DD      ?                ;ELEMENT 2 - HEADER (LINKS) ONLY
        END
```

7E Dynamic memory allocation (INITFS, ALLOCM, DALLOC)

Allocates memory dynamically in blocks of arbitrary size. The free space is organized as a linked list; each element has a header containing its size and a link to the next element. Consists of the following routines:

1. INITFS initializes the free space as a single block with a null link.
2. ALLOCM obtains a block of given size from the list.
3. DALLOC releases a block of given size to the list.

These routines allow you to obtain and release memory blocks of any size.

Procedures

1. INITFS first determines if there is enough free memory for a header and some data. If not, it sets Carry. If so, it clears the link to the next element, sets the size of the free area to the given size minus the header's size (4 bytes), and clears Carry.

2. ALLOCM searches the list for elements large enough to satisfy the request. It accepts either the element closest in size to the request or the first element within a threshold of the request size. If it finds such an element, it reduces its size by the request and returns a pointer to the allocated memory. The pointer is set to the furthest available part of the block to maintain the header. The Carry is cleared if the request can be satisfied and set otherwise.

3. DALLOC first determines if enough memory has been released to hold a header and some data. If not, it sets Carry. If so, it links the released area to the initial element, forms its header, and clears Carry. This links the released area to the element to which the initial element had been linked; its size is the amount of memory released minus the size of the header.

Entry conditions

1. INITFS
Base address of free area in BX
Size of free area in bytes in AX

2. ALLOCM

Base address of free area in BX
Size of request in bytes in AX

3. DALLOC
Base address of free area in BX
Base address of released area in DI
Size of released area in AX

Exit conditions

1. INITFS
Free area established as a single block with a header containing a null link. Its size is the number of bytes allocated minus the header's size. Carry = 0 if enough space was allocated for the header and some data, and 1 if not.

2. ALLOCM
If there is a block large enough to satisfy the request, the base address of the selected block is returned in BX and Carry = 0. The selected block is either the one closest in size to the request or the first one that has a size within a threshold of the request. Otherwise, Carry = 1.

3. DALLOC
If enough memory was released to hold a header and some data, it is linked to the list and Carry = 0. Otherwise, Carry = 1.

Example

A typical sequence of memory allocations and releases is:

1. Make the free space into a single list element by calling INITFS.

2. Obtain memory for an overall program's temporary storage by calling ALLOCM.

3. Obtain memory for a subprogram's temporary storage by calling ALLOCM.

4. Free the memory used by the subprogram by calling DALLOC when it finishes running.

5. Obtain memory for a second subprogram's temporary storage by calling ALLOCM.

6. Obtain memory for a subsubprogram's temporary storage by calling ALLOCM.

7. Free the memory used by the subsubprogram by calling DALLOC when it finishes running.

8. Free the memory used by the second subprogram by calling DALLOC when it finishes running.

9. Free the memory used by the overall program by calling DALLOC when it finishes running.

Note that, even if the sequence allocates and releases equal amounts of memory, the system will not return to its initial state. Released blocks will become additional elements with their own headers rather than being combined into a single element. Obviously, this fragments the free memory, as well as resulting in a large number of headers. Eventually, the system is unable to grant any sizeable request for memory. In real applications, this usually forces the running of a compaction or 'garbage collection' routine that combines small blocks or returns the system to its initialized state as a single large block of free memory.

There are many methods for efficient allocation and deallocation of memory (see the references). The one we have implemented here is to search for the block that is closest in size to the request or has a size within a threshold of the request. This approach avoids breaking up large blocks to satisfy small requests. The threshold prevents the allocation routine from wasting time searching for a closer fit that results in only a marginal improvement.

References

M. Augenstein and A. Tenenbaum, *Data Structures and PL/I Programming*, Prentice-Hall, Englewood Cliffs, NJ, 1979, Chapter 10. There is also a Pascal version of this book from the same publisher.

D. E. Knuth, *The Art of Computer Programming, 2nd Ed. Volume 1: Fundamental Algorithms*, Addison-Wesley, Reading, MA, 1973, pp. 435–455.

Registers used

1. INITFS: AX, F

2. ALLOCM: BX, DI, DX, F, SI

3. DALLOC: AX, F

Execution time

1. INITFS: 51 cycles

2. ALLOCM: 68–86 cycles per block that must be examined plus 54 cycles overhead

3. DALLOC: 77 cycles

Program size

1. INITFS: 15 bytes

2. ALLOCM: 51 bytes

3. DALLOC: 18 bytes

Data memory required None

Special case An attempt to initialize or release an amount of memory that is less than or equal to the size of the header will result in an immediate return with the Carry set to 1.

```
;       Title           Dynamic Memory Allocation
;       Name:           INITFS, ALLOCM, DALLOC
;
;
;       Purpose:        This program consists of three subroutines
;                       that allocate memory dynamically, that is, on
;                       a demand basis in units of variable size.
;
;                       INITFS initializes the free memory area as
;                         a linked list with a single element.
;                       ALLOCM allocates a block of memory of specified
;                         size. It searches the list for an element
;                         whose size most closely matches the request.
;                       DALLOC releases a block of memory of specified
;                         size
;
;       Entry:          INITFS
;                         Base address of free area in BX
```

```
;                          Size of free area in bytes in AX
;                        ALLOCM
;                          Base address of free area in BX
;                          Size of request in bytes in AX
;                        DALLOC
;                          Base address of free memory in BX
;                          Base address of released area in DI
;                          Size of released area in AX
;
;        Exit:           INITFS
;                          Free area set up as a linked list consisting
;                            of a single element
;                        ALLOCM
;                          If a block of sufficient size exists,
;                            base address of selected block is in
;                              register BX
;                            Carry = 0
;                          else
;                            Carry = 1
;                          If more than one such block exists, the
;                            one closest in size to the request or the
;                            first one encountered within a threshold of
;                            the size of the request is allocated.
;                        DALLOC
;                          If the released block is large enough, it is
;                            placed in the linked list
;                            Carry = 0
;                          else
;                            Carry = 1
;
;        Registers Used: INITFS
;                          AX,F
;                        ALLOCM
;                          BX,DI,DX,F,SI
;                        DALLOC
;                          AX,F
;
;        Time:           INITFS
;                          51 cycles
;                        ALLOCM
;                          68-86 cycles per block that must be examined
;                          plus 54 cycles overhead
;                        DALLOC
;                          77 cycles
;
;        Size:           Program 84 bytes                                ;
;                                                                        ;


;
;DECLARATIONS
;
HEADLN    EQU      4              ;LENGTH OF HEADER IN BYTES
DIFLMT    EQU      20H            ;BLOCK SIZE DIFFERENCE LIMIT
                                  ;SIZE DIFFERENCES LESS THAN THIS
                                  ; LIMIT ARE CONSIDERED SMALL ENOUGH
                                  ; TO HALT THE BLOCK SEARCH.  THIS
```

```
                                    ; LIMIT HELPS AVOID WASTING TIME
                                    ; WHEN NLY A MINOR IMPROVEMENT IS
                                    ; POSSIBLE.  IF THE LIMIT IS 0, THE
                                    ; BLOCK WITH THE SMALLEST SIZE
                                    ; DIFFERENCE IS CHOSEN.
;
;       INITIALIZE FREE SPACE AS A LINKED LIST WITH A SINGLE ELEMENT
;
INITFS:
        ;
        ;CHECK IF ENOUGH SPACE AVAILABLE FOR HEADER
        ;IF NOT (OR JUST ENOUGH), EXIT WITH CARRY SET
        ;
        SUB     AX,HEADLN          ;IS THERE ENOUGH ROOM FOR HEADER?
        JBE     EREXIT             ;BRANCH TO ERROR EXIT IF NOT
        ;
        ;SET UP HEADER FOR SINGLE BLOCK OF FREE MEMORY:
        ;  LINK TO NEXT ELEMENT = NULL (0) IN FIRST TWO BYTES
        ;  SIZE OF AREA = ALLOCATED AREA MINUS HEADER SIZE IN
        ;    NEXT TWO BYTES
        ;
        MOV     [BX+2],AX          ;SET AREA SIZE IN HEADER
        SUB     AX,AX              ;CLEAR LINK (MAKE IT NULL)
                                   ;THIS ALSO CLEARS CARRY, INDICATING
                                   ;  NO ERRORS
        MOV     [BX],AX
        RET
        ;
        ;ERROR EXIT WITH CARRY SET
        ;
EREXIT:
        STC                        ;ERROR - BLOCK TOO SMALL
        RET
;
;       ALLOCATE A BLOCK OF MEMORY
;
ALLOCM:
        ;
        ;INITIALIZE VARIABLES FOR BLOCK SIZE SEARCH
        ;
        MOV     DX,OFFFFH          ;INITIALIZE SMALLEST DIFFERENCE
                                   ;  REGISTER TO MAXIMUM DIFFERENCE
        SUB     DI,DI              ;INITIALIZE BLOCK ADDRESS TO NULL
        ;
        ;CHECK NEXT ELEMENT TO SEE IF IT CAN SATISFY REQUEST
        ;
GETBSZ:
        MOV     SI,[BX+2]          ;GET BLOCK SIZE
        CMP     SI,AX              ;IS NEXT ELEMENT LARGE ENOUGH?
        JB      CHKNXT             ;BRANCH IF IT IS TOO SMALL
        SUB     SI,AX              ;CALCULATE SIZE DIFFERENCE
        CMP     SI,DIFLMT          ;COMPARE DIFFERENCE TO THRESHOLD
        JBE     GETSP              ;JUMP IF DIFFERENCE <= THRESHOLD
        CMP     SI,DX              ;COMPARE TO SMALLEST FOUND DIFFERENCE
        JAE     CHKNXT             ;JUMP IF NEW DIFFERENCE >= OLD
                                   ;  DIFFERENCE SO NOT WORTH KEEPING
```

```
        MOV     DX,SI           ;SAVE NEW DIFFERENCE AS SMALLEST
        MOV     DI,BX           ;SAVE BASE ADDRESS OF BLOCK WITH
                                ; SMALLEST SIZE DIFFERENCE
        ;
        ;CHECK IF THERE ARE MORE BLOCKS IN LIST
        ;
CHKNXT:
        MOV     BX,[BX]         ;GET LINK TO NEXT ELEMENT
        TEST    BX,BX           ;IS THERE A NEXT ELEMENT?
        JNZ     GETBSZ          ;BRANCH IF THERE IS (LINK NONZERO)
        ;
        ;NO MORE ELEMENTS - CHECK IF A BLOCK WAS FOUND
        ;
        TEST    DI,DI           ;CHECK IF BLOCK FOUND
        JZ      AERXIT          ;JUMP IF NO BLOCK FOUND
        MOV     BX,DI           ;GET BLOCK ADDRESS
        ;
        ;BLOCK WITH SMALLEST SIZE DIFFERENCE FOUND
        ;ALLOCATE THAT BLOCK'S LAST BYTES
        ;REDUCE BLOCK'S SIZE BY THE NUMBER OF BYTES ALLOCATED
        ;
GETSP:
        MOV     [BX+2],SI       ;NEW SIZE IS OLD SIZE MINUS SIZE
                                ; OF REQUEST
        ADD     BX,SI           ;BASE ADDRESS OF ALLOCATED AREA =
        ADD     BX,HEADLN       ; BASE ADDRESS OF ELEMENT +
                                ; DIFFERENCE + HEADER LENGTH
                                ;THIS ALLOCATES THE END OF THE DATA
                                ; AREA, LEAVING THE FIRST PART
                                ; (INCLUDING THE HEADER) AVAILABLE
                                ; FOR LATER REQUESTS
        ;
        ;CLEAR CARRY TO INDICATE SUCCESS AND EXIT
        ;
        CLC                     ;CLEAR CARRY
        RET
        ;
        ;SET CARRY TO INDICATE FAILURE AND EXIT
        ;
AERXIT:
        STC                     ;NO BLOCK FOUND, SO SET CARRY
        RET


;
;DEALLOCATE A BLOCK OF MEMORY
;
DALLOC:
        ;
        ;ERROR EXIT IF RELEASED BLOCK TOO SMALL TO HOLD HEADER
        ; OR JUST LARGE ENOUGH FOR IT
        ;
        SUB     AX,HEADLN       ;IS BLOCK LARGE ENOUGH FOR HEADER?
        JBE     EREXIT          ;BRANCH IF NOT LARGE ENOUGH
        ;
        ;PUT RELEASED BLOCK IN LINKED LIST - LINK IT TO BLOCK AT
```

```
        ;  BOTTOM OF FREE AREA AND ESTABLISH ITS SIZE
        ;
        MOV     [DI+2],AX       ;BLOCK SIZE = RELEASED AREA - SIZE
                                ;  OF HEADER
        MOV     AX,[BX]         ;GET LINK FROM BLOCK AT BOTTOM OF
                                ;  FREE AREA
        MOV     [BX],DI         ;LINK RELEASED BLOCK TO BLOCK AT
                                ;  BOTTOM
        MOV     [DI],AX         ;LINK RELEASED BLOCK TO BLOCK THAT
                                ;  WAS LINKED TO BOTTOM
        ;
        ;CLEAR CARRY TO INDICATE SUCCESS AND EXIT
        ;
        CLC
        RET
        ;
        ;ERROR EXIT - SET CARRY - BLOCK TOO SMALL
EREXIT:
        STC                     ;ERROR - BLOCK TOO SMALL
        RET

;                                                                 ;
;       SAMPLE EXECUTION                                          ;
;                                                                 ;
;
SC7E:
        ;
        ;INITIALIZE FREE MEMORY AREA
        ;
        MOV     BX,OFFSET FREEM ;GET BASE ADDRESS OF FREE AREA
        MOV     AX,FSIZE        ;GET SIZE OF FREE AREA (100 HEX BYTES)
        CALL    INITFS          ;INITIALIZE FREE AREA AS LINKED LIST
        MOV     AX,20H          ;REQUEST 20 HEX BYTES
        CALL    ALLOCM          ;THIS WILL ALLOCATE BYTES E0-FF HEX
                                ;  ADDRESS FREEM+E0H RETURNED IN BX
        MOV     BX,OFFSET FREEM ;GET BASE ADDRESS OF FREE AREA
        MOV     AX,30H          ;REQUEST 30 HEX BYTES
        CALL    ALLOCM          ;THIS WILL ALLOCATE BYTES B0-DF HEX
                                ;  ADDRESS FREEM+B0H RETURNED IN BX
        MOV     BX,OFFSET FREEM ;GET BASE ADDRESS OF FREE AREA
        MOV     DI,OFFSET FREEM+0E0H ;RELEASE 20 HEX BYTES STARTING
                                ;  AT FREEM+E0H
        MOV     AX,20H
        CALL    DALLOC          ;THE RESULT HERE WILL BE AN
                                ;  AREA OF B0 HEX BYTES STARTING
                                ;  AT ADDRESS FREEM. ONLY AC OF
                                ;  THESE BYTES WILL BE AVAILABLE
                                ;  SINCE THE FIRST 4 ARE USED AS
                                ;  A HEADER.  THIS AREA WILL BE
                                ;  LINKED TO AN AREA OF 20 HEX
                                ;  BYTES (1C AVAILABLE) STARTING
                                ;  AT ADDRESS FREEM+0E0H
                                ;

        MOV     BX,OFFSET FREEM  ;GET BASE ADDRESS OF FREE AREA
        MOV     AX,10H          ;REQUEST 10H BYTES
```

```
        CALL    ALLOCM          ;THIS WILL ALLOCATE BYTES F0-FFH
                                ;ADDRESS FREEM+F0H RETURNED IN BX
                                ;
        JMP     SC7E            ;REPEAT TEST

;
;DATA
;
FSIZE   EQU     100H            ;SIZE OF FREE AREA IN BYTES
FREEM   DB      100H DUP (?)    ;FREE AREA
        END
```

8 Input/output

8A Read a line from a terminal (RDLINE)

Reads a line of ASCII characters ending with a carriage return and saves it in a buffer. Defines the control characters Control H (08 hex), which deletes the latest character, and Control X (18 hex), which deletes the entire line. Sends a bell character (07 hex) to the terminal if the buffer overflows. Echoes each character placed in the buffer. Echoes non-printable characters as an up-arrow or caret (^) followed by the printable equivalent (see Table 8-1). Sends a new line sequence (typically carriage return, line feed) to the terminal before exiting.

RDLINE assumes the following system-dependent subroutines:

1. RDCHAR reads a character from the terminal and puts it in register AL.

2. WRCHAR sends the character in register AL to the terminal.

3. WRNEWL sends a new line sequence to the terminal.

These subroutines are assumed to change all user registers except BP, SS, and DS (in accordance with Intel's PL/M-86 interface as described in *An Introduction to ASM86*, Intel Corporation, Santa Clara, CA, 1981).

RDLINE is an example of a terminal input handler. The control characters and I/O subroutines in an actual system will, of course, be computer-dependent. A specific example in the listing is for an IBM PC running MS-DOS. The example works for any version of DOS, but the comments assume Version 2.0 or later in which I/O functions refer to standard input and output devices (which can be redirected) rather than to the keyboard and video display specifically. Table 8-2 lists common MS-DOS function calls using interrupt 21 hex. For more information on IBM PC and MS-DOS functions, see P. Norton and R. Wilton, *Programmer's Guide to the IBM PC and PS/2*, Microsoft Press, Redmond, WA, 1989.

Table 8-1: ASCII control characters and printable equivalents

Name	Hex value	Printable equivalent
NUL	00	Control @
SOH	01	Control A
STX	02	Control B
ETX	03	Control C
EOT	04	Control D
ENQ	05	Control E
ACK	06	Control F
BEL	07	Control G
BS	08	Control H
HT	09	Control I
LF	0A	Control J
VT	0B	Control K
FF	0C	Control L
CR	0D	Control M
SO	0E	Control N
SI	0F	Control O
DLE	10	Control P
DC1	11	Control Q
DC2	12	Control R
DC3	13	Control S
DC4	14	Control T
NAK	15	Control U
SYN	16	Control V
ETB	17	Control W
CAN	18	Control X
EM	19	Control Y
SUB	1A	Control Z
ESC	1B	Control [
FS	1C	Control \
GS	1D	Control]
RS	1E	Control ^
VS	1F	Control _

Table 8-2: Common DOS functions for MS-DOS 2.0 (invoked with INT 21H)

Function number (hex in Reg AH)	Function name	Input parameters	Output parameters
0	Terminate program	None	None
1	Keyboard input with echo	None	AL = ASCII character
2	Display output	DL = ASCII character	None
3	Serial input	None	AL = ASCII character
4	Serial output	DL = ASCII character	None
5	Printer output	DL = ASCII character	None
6	Direct console input	DL = FF_{16}	AL = ASCII character if ready and ZF = 1; if no char is available, AL = 0 and ZF = 0
6	Direct console output	DL = ASCII character	None
7	Keyboard input without echo	None	AL = ASCII character
9	Print string	DX = String address	None
A	Read keyboard buffer	DX = Buffer address	None
B	Get keyboard status	None	AL = 00 (no character) or AL = FF (char ready)

Procedure The program starts the loop by reading a character. If it is a carriage return, the program sends a new line sequence to the terminal and exits. Otherwise, it checks for the special characters Control H and Control X. If the buffer is not empty, Control H makes the program reduce the buffer pointer and character count by 1 and send a backspace string (cursor left, space, cursor left) to the terminal. Control X makes the program delete characters until it empties the buffer.

If the character is not special, the program determines whether the buffer is full. If so, the program sends a bell character to the console. If not, the program stores the character in the buffer, echoes it to the display, and increments the character count and buffer pointer.

Before echoing a character or deleting one from the display, the program must determine whether it is printable. If not (i.e. it is a non-printable ASCII control character), the program must display or delete two characters, the control indicator (up-arrow or caret) and the printable equivalent (see Table 8-1). Note, however, that the character is stored in its non-printable form.

Entry conditions

Base address of buffer in register BX
Length (size) of buffer in bytes in register AL

Exit conditions

Number of characters in the buffer in register AL

Examples

1. Data: Line from keyboard is 'ENTERcr'
   Result: Character count = 5 (line length)
   Buffer contains 'ENTER'
   'ENTER' echoed to terminal, followed by the new line sequence (carriage return, line feed)
   Note that the 'cr' (carriage return) character does not appear in the buffer.
2. Data: Line from keyboard is 'DMcontrolHNcontrolXENTET-controlHRcr'
   Result: Character count = 5 (length of final line after deletions)
   Buffer contains 'ENTER'
   'DMBackspaceStringNBackspaceStringBackspaceS-tringENTETBackspaceStringR' sent to screen, followed by a new line sequence. The backspace string deletes a character from the screen and moves the cursor left one column.
   The sequence of operations is as follows:

Character typed	Initial buffer	Final buffer	Sent to terminal
D	empty	'D'	D
M	'D'	'DM'	M
Control H	'DM'	'D'	backspace string
N	'D'	'DN'	N
Control X	'DN'	empty	2 backspace strings
E	empty	'E'	E
N	'E'	'EN'	N
T	'EN'	'ENT'	T
E	'ENT'	'ENTE'	E
T	'ENTE'	'ENTET'	T

Control H	'ENTET'	'ENTE'	backspace string
R	'ENTE'	'ENTER'	R
cr	'ENTER'	'ENTER'	New line string

What happened is the following:

(a) The operator types 'D', 'M'.
(b) The operator sees that 'M' is wrong (it should be 'N'), presses control H to delete it, and types 'N'.
(c) The operator then sees that the initial 'D' is also wrong (it should be 'E'). Since the error is not the latest character, the operator presses Control X to delete the entire line, and then types 'ENTET'.
(d) The operator notes that the second 'T' is wrong (it should be 'R'), presses Control H to delete it, and types 'R'.
(e) The operator types a carriage return to end the line.

Registers used AX, BX, CX, DI, DX, F, SI

Execution time Approximately 152 cycles to put an ordinary character in the buffer, not considering the execution time of either RDCHAR or WRCHAR.

Program size 72 bytes

Data memory required None

Special cases

1. If the buffer is empty, typing Control H (delete one character) or Control X (delete the entire line) has no effect.

2. If the program receives an ordinary character when the buffer is full, it discards the character and sends a bell character to the terminal (ringing the bell).

```
;       Title           Read Line
;       Name:           RDLINE
;
;
;       Purpose:        Read characters from an input device until
```

```
;                       a carriage return is found. Defines the
;                       control characters
;                         Control H -- Delete latest character.
;                         Control X -- Delete all characters.
;                       Any other control character is placed in
;                       the buffer and displayed as the equivalent
;                       printable ASCII character preceded by an
;                       up-arrow or caret.
;
;       Entry:          Register BX = Base address of buffer
;                       Register AL = Length of buffer in bytes
;
;       Exit:           Register AL = Number of characters in buffer
;
;       Registers Used: AX,BX,CX,DI,DX,F,SI
;
;       Time:           Not applicable.
;
;       Size:           Program 72 bytes
;

;EQUATES
BELL    EQU     07H             ;BELL CHARACTER (MAKES IBM PC BEEP)
BSKEY   EQU     08H             ;BACKSPACE KEYBOARD CHARACTER
CR      EQU     0DH             ;CARRIAGE RETURN FOR CONSOLE
CRKEY   EQU     0DH             ;CARRIAGE RETURN KEYBOARD CHARACTER
                                ;  (ENTER KEY ON PC)
CSRLFT  EQU     08H             ;MOVE CURSOR LEFT FOR CONSOLE
CTLOFF  EQU     40H             ;OFFSET FROM CONTROL CHARACTER TO PRINTED
                                ;  FORM (E.G., CONTROL-X TO X)
DELKEY  EQU     18H             ;DELETE LINE KEYBOARD CHARACTER
LF      EQU     0AH             ;LINE FEED FOR CONSOLE
SPACE   EQU     20H             ;SPACE CHARACTER (ALSO MARKS END OF CONTROL
                                ;  CHARACTERS IN ASCII SEQUENCE)
STERM   EQU     24H             ;MS-DOS STRING TERMINATOR (DOLLAR SIGN)
UPARRW  EQU     5EH             ;UP-ARROW OR CARET USED AS CONTROL INDICATOR

DIRIO   EQU     6               ;MS-DOS DIRECT I/O FUNCTION
INPUT   EQU     0FFH            ;INPUT CODE FOR MS-DOS DIRECT I/O FUNCTION
PSTRG   EQU     9               ;MS-DOS PRINT (DISPLAY) STRING FUNCTION
                                ;THIS FUNCTION PRINTS A STRING ENDING IN $
                                ;  ON THE STANDARD OUTPUT DEVICE, NOT ON
                                ;  THE PRINTER
RDLINE:
        ;
        ;INITIALIZE CHARACTER COUNT TO ZERO, SAVE BUFFER LENGTH
        ;  AND BUFFER POINTER
        ;
        SUB     CL,CL           ;CHARACTER COUNT = 0
        MOV     CH,AL           ;SAVE BUFFER LENGTH
        MOV     DI,BX           ;SAVE BUFFER POINTER
        CLD                     ;SELECT AUTOINCREMENTING
        ;
        ;READ LOOP
        ;READ CHARACTERS UNTIL A CARRIAGE RETURN IS TYPED
        ;
```

```
RDLOOP:
        CALL    RDCHAR          ;READ CHARACTER FROM KEYBOARD
                                ;DOES NOT ECHO CHARACTER
        ;
        ;CHECK FOR CARRIAGE RETURN, EXIT IF FOUND
        ;
        CMP     AL,CR           ;CHECK FOR CARRIAGE RETURN
        JE      EXITRD          ;END OF LINE IF CARRIAGE RETURN
        ;
        ;CHECK FOR BACKSPACE AND DELETE CHARACTER IF FOUND
        ;
        CMP     AL,BSKEY        ;CHECK FOR BACKSPACE KEY
        JNE     RDLP1           ;BRANCH IF NOT BACKSPACE
        CALL    BACKSP          ;IF BACKSPACE, DELETE ONE CHARACTER
        JMP     RDLOOP          ;THEN START READ LOOP AGAIN
        ;
        ;CHECK FOR DELETE LINE CHARACTER AND EMPTY BUFFER IF FOUND
        ;
RDLP1:
        CMP     AL,DELKEY       ;CHECK FOR DELETE LINE KEY
        JNE     RDLP2           ;BRANCH IF NOT DELETE LINE
DEL1:
        CALL    BACKSP          ;DELETE A CHARACTER
        JNZ     DEL1            ;CONTINUE UNTIL BUFFER EMPTY
                                ;THIS ACTUALLY BACKS UP OVER EACH
                                ; CHARACTER RATHER THAN JUST MOVING
                                ; UP A LINE
        JMP     RDLOOP
        ;
        ;KEYBOARD ENTRY IS NOT A SPECIAL CHARACTER
        ;CHECK IF BUFFER IS FULL
        ;IF FULL, RING BELL (BEEP ON IBM PC) AND CONTINUE
        ;IF NOT FULL, STORE CHARACTER AND ECHO
        ;
RDLP2:
        CMP     CL,CH           ;COMPARE COUNT AND BUFFER LENGTH
        JB      STRCH           ;JUMP IF BUFFER NOT FULL
        MOV     AL,BELL         ;BUFFER FULL, RING BELL
        CALL    WRCHAR
        JMP     RDLOOP          ;THEN CONTINUE THE READ LOOP
        ;
        ;BUFFER NOT FULL, STORE CHARACTER
        ;
STRCH:
        STOSB                   ;STORE CHARACTER IN BUFFER
                                ;  AND ADD 1 TO BUFFER POINTER
        INC     CL              ;ADD 1 TO CHARACTER COUNT
        ;
        ;IF CHARACTER IS CONTROL, THEN OUTPUT
        ; UP-ARROW FOLLOWED BY PRINTABLE EQUIVALENT
        ;
        CMP     AL,SPACE        ;CONTROL CHARACTER IF CODE IS
                                ;  BELOW SPACE (20 HEX) IN ASCII
                                ;  SEQUENCE
        JAE     PRCH            ;JUMP IF A PRINTABLE CHARACTER
        PUSH    AX              ;SAVE NONPRINTABLE CHARACTER
```

```
        MOV     AL,UPARRW       ;WRITE UP-ARROW OR CARET
        CALL    WRCHAR
        POP     AX              ;RECOVER NONPRINTABLE CHARACTER
        ADD     AL,CTLOFF       ;CHANGE TO PRINTABLE FORM
PRCH:
        CALL    WRCHAR          ;ECHO CHARACTER TO TERMINAL
        JMP     RDLOOP          ;THEN CONTINUE READ LOOP
        ;
        ;EXIT
        ;SEND NEW LINE SEQUENCE (USUALLY CR,LF) TO TERMINAL
        ;LINE LENGTH = CHARACTER COUNT
        ;
EXITRD:
        CALL    WRNEWL          ;ECHO NEW LINE SEQUENCE
        MOV     AL,CL           ;LINE LENGTH = CHARACTER COUNT
        RET


;***********************************************************
;
; THE FOLLOWING SUBROUTINES ARE TYPICAL EXAMPLES FOR AN
; IBM PC RUNNING MS-DOS (ANY VERSION)
;
;***********************************************************


;***********************************************************
;ROUTINE: RDCHAR
;PURPOSE: READ A CHARACTER FROM STANDARD INPUT BUT DO NOT
;         ECHO TO STANDARD OUTPUT
;ENTRY: NONE
;EXIT:  REGISTER AL = CHARACTER
;REGISTERS USED: AX,DL,F
;***********************************************************

RDCHAR:
        ;
        ;WAIT FOR CHARACTER FROM KEYBOARD
        ;RETURN WITH IT IN REGISTER AL
        ;
RDWAIT:
        MOV     AH,DIRIO        ;DIRECT KEYBOARD/DISPLAY I/O
        MOV     DL,INPUT        ;INDICATE INPUT
        INT     21H             ;READ CHARACTER FROM KEYBOARD
        TEST    AL,AL           ;CHECK IF A CHARACTER (AL = 0 IF NOT)
        JZ      RDWAIT          ;BRANCH (LOOP) IF NO CHARACTER
        RET                     ;RETURN WITH CHARACTER IN REGISTER AL

;***********************************************************
;ROUTINE: WRCHAR
;PURPOSE: WRITE CHARACTER TO STANDARD OUTPUT DEVICE
;ENTRY: REGISTER AL = CHARACTER
;EXIT:  NONE
;REGISTERS USED: AX,DL,F
;***********************************************************
```

```
WRCHAR:
        ;
        ;WRITE A CHARACTER TO STANDARD OUTPUT DEVICE
        ;
        MOV     AH,DIRIO        ;DIRECT KEYBOARD/DISPLAY I/O
        MOV     DL,AL           ;INDICATE OUTPUT - CHARACTER IN DL
        INT     21H             ;WRITE CHARACTER ON STANDARD OUTPUT
        RET

;***********************************************************
;ROUTINE: WRNEWL
;PURPOSE: ISSUE NEW LINE SEQUENCE TO VIDEO DISPLAY (STANDARD OUTPUT)
;         NORMALLY, THIS SEQUENCE IS A CARRIAGE RETURN AND
;         LINE FEED, BUT SOME OUTPUT DEVICES REQUIRE ONLY
;         A CARRIAGE RETURN.
;ENTRY: NONE
;EXIT:  NONE
;REGISTERS USED: DX,F
;***********************************************************

WRNEWL:
        ;
        ;SEND NEW LINE STRING TO STANDARD OUTPUT
        ;
        CALL    WRSTRG          ;SEND STRING TO STANDARD OUTPUT
        RET
NLSTRG  DB      CR,LF,STERM     ;NEW LINE STRING WITH $ TERMINATOR

;***********************************************************
;ROUTINE: BACKSP
;PURPOSE: PERFORM A DESTRUCTIVE BACKSPACE
;ENTRY: CL = NUMBER OF CHARACTERS IN BUFFER
;       DI = NEXT AVAILABLE BUFFER ADDRESS
;EXIT:  IF NO CHARACTERS IN BUFFER
;         Z = 1
;       ELSE
;         Z = 0
;         CHARACTER REMOVED FROM BUFFER
;REGISTERS USED: AX,CL,DI,DX,F
;***********************************************************

BACKSP:
        ;
        ;CHECK FOR EMPTY BUFFER
        ;
        TEST    CL,CL           ;TEST NUMBER OF CHARACTERS
        JZ      EXITBS          ;BRANCH (EXIT) IF BUFFER EMPTY
        ;
        ;OUTPUT BACKSPACE STRING
        ; TO REMOVE CHARACTER FROM DISPLAY
        ;
        DEC     DI              ;DECREMENT BUFFER POINTER
        MOV     AL,[DI]         ;GET CHARACTER
        CMP     AL,SPACE        ;IS IT A CONTROL CHARACTER?
        JAE     BS1             ;NO, BRANCH, DELETE ONLY ONE CHARACTER
```

```
        MOV     DX,OFFSET BSSTRG ;YES, DELETE 2 CHARACTERS
                                 ; (UP-ARROW AND PRINTABLE EQUIVALENT)
        CALL    WRSTRG           ;WRITE BACKSPACE STRING
BS1:    MOV     DX,OFFSET BSSTRG
        CALL    WRSTRG           ;WRITE BACKSPACE STRING
        ;
        ;SUBTRACT 1 FROM CHARACTER COUNT
        ;
        DEC     CL               ;ONE LESS CHARACTER IN BUFFER
EXITBS:
        RET
;
;DESTRUCTIVE BACKSPACE STRING FOR VIDEO DISPLAY
;MOVES CURSOR LEFT, PRINTS SPACE OVER CHARACTER, MOVES
;  CURSOR LEFT
;NOTE: STERM ($) IS MS-DOS STRING TERMINATOR
;
BSSTRG  DB      CSRLFT,SPACE,CSRLFT,STERM

;***********************************************************
;ROUTINE: WRSTRG
;PURPOSE: OUTPUT STRING TO VIDEO DISPLAY (STANDARD OUTPUT)
;ENTRY: DX = BASE ADDRESS OF STRING
;EXIT:  NONE
;REGISTERS USED: AX,DX,F
;***********************************************************

WRSTRG:
        MOV     AH,PSTRG         ;FUNCTION IS PRINT (DISPLAY) STRING
        INT     21H              ;OUTPUT STRING TERMINATED WITH $
        RET
;       SAMPLE EXECUTION:
;
;EQUATES
PROMPT  EQU     '?'              ;OPERATOR PROMPT = QUESTION MARK

SC8A:
        ;
        ;READ LINE FROM STANDARD INPUT DEVICE (KEYBOARD)
        ;
        MOV     AL,PROMPT        ;WRITE PROMPT (?)
        CALL    WRCHAR
        MOV     BX,OFFSET INBUFF ;GET INPUT BUFFER ADDRESS
        MOV     AL,LENBUF        ;GET LENGTH OF BUFFER
        CALL    RDLINE           ;READ LINE
        TEST    AL,AL            ;CHECK LINE LENGTH
        JZ      SC8A             ;READ NEXT LINE IF LENGTH IS 0
        ;
        ;ECHO LINE TO CONSOLE
        ;
        MOV     CL,AL            ;SAVE NUMBER OF CHARACTERS IN BUFFER
        MOV     DI,OFFSET INBUFF ;POINT TO START OF BUFFER
WRBUFF:
        MOV     AL,[DI]          ;WRITE NEXT CHARACTER
        CALL    WRCHAR
        INC     DI               ;INCREMENT BUFFER POINTER
```

```
        DEC     CL                      ;DECREMENT CHARACTER COUNT
        JNZ     WRBUFF                  ;CONTINUE UNTIL ALL CHARACTERS SENT
        CALL    WRNEWL                  ;THEN END WITH CR,LF
        JMP     SC8A                    ;READ NEXT LINE

;DATA SECTION
LENBUF  EQU     16                      ;LENGTH OF INPUT BUFFER
INBUFF  DW      LENBUF DUP(?)           ;INPUT BUFFER

        END
```

8B Write a line to an output device (WRLINE)

Writes characters until it empties a buffer with given length and base address. Assumes the system-dependent subroutine WRCHAR, which sends the character in register AL to an output device.

WRLINE is an example of an output driver. The actual I/O subroutines will, of course, be computer-dependent. A specific example in the listing is for an IBM PC running MS-DOS (see Table 8-2 for a list of DOS routines).

Procedure The program exits immediately if the buffer is empty. Otherwise, it sends characters to the output device one at a time until it empties the buffer. The program saves all temporary data in memory rather than in registers to avoid dependence on WRCHAR.

Entry conditions

Base address of buffer in register BX
Number of characters in the buffer in register AL

Exit conditions

None

Example

Data: Number of characters = 5
Buffer contains 'ENTER'
Result: 'ENTER' sent to the output device.

Registers used AL, CX, F, SI

Execution time 26 cycles overhead plus 48 cycles per byte. This does not, of course, include the execution time of WRCHAR.

Program size 18 bytes

Data memory required None

Special case An empty buffer results in an immediate exit with nothing sent to the output device.

```
;       Title                Write a Line to an Output Device
;       Name:                WRLINE
;
;
;       Purpose:             Write characters to MS-DOS standard
;                              output device
;
;       Entry:               Register BX = Base address of buffer
;                            Register AL = Number of characters in buffer
;
;       Exit:                None
;
;       Registers Used: AL,CX,F,SI
;
;       Time:                Indeterminate, depends on the speed of the
;                            WRCHAR routine.
;
;       Size:                Program 18 bytes
;

        ;EQUATES
DIRIO   EQU     6                    ;MS-DOS DIRECT I/O FUNCTION

WRLINE:
        ;
        ;EXIT IMMEDIATELY IF BUFFER IS EMPTY
        ;
        TEST    AL,AL                ;TEST NUMBER OF CHARACTERS IN BUFFER
        JZ      EXITWL               ;BRANCH (EXIT) IF BUFFER EMPTY
                                     ; BX = BASE ADDRESS OF BUFFER
        ;
        ;LOOP SENDING CHARACTERS TO OUTPUT DEVICE
        ;
        MOV     CL,AL                ;SAVE CHARACTER COUNT
        SUB     CH,CH                ;EXTEND CHARACTER COUNT TO 16 BITS
        MOV     SI,BX                ;SAVE BASE ADDRESS OF BUFFER
        CLD                          ;SELECT AUTOINCREMENTING
WRLLP:
        LODSB                        ;GET NEXT CHARACTER
        CALL    WRCHAR               ;SEND CHARACTER
        LOOP    WRLLP                ;CONTINUE UNTIL ALL CHARACTERS SENT
EXITWL:
        RET                          ;EXIT
```

```
;*******************************************************
;
; THE FOLLOWING SUBROUTINES ARE TYPICAL EXAMPLES FOR AN
; IBM PC RUNNING MS-DOS
;
;*******************************************************


;****************************************
;ROUTINE: WRCHAR
;PURPOSE: WRITE CHARACTER TO OUTPUT DEVICE
;ENTRY: REGISTER AL = CHARACTER
;EXIT:  NONE
;REGISTERS USED: AX,DL,F
;****************************************

WRCHAR:
;
;       SEND CHARACTER TO STANDARD OUTPUT DEVICE FROM REGISTER AL
;
        MOV     AH,DIRIO        ;DIRECT I/O FUNCTION
        MOV     DL,AL           ;CHARACTER IN REGISTER DL
        INT     21H             ;SEND CHARACTER TO OUTPUT DEVICE
        RET


;
;       SAMPLE EXECUTION:
;
RCBUF   EQU     0AH             ;MS-DOS READ KEYBOARD BUFFER FUNCTION

        ;MS-DOS READ KEYBOARD BUFFER FUNCTION USES
        ; THE FOLLOWING BUFFER FORMAT:
        ; BYTE 0: BUFFER LENGTH (MAXIMUM NUMBER OF CHARACTERS)
        ; BYTE 1: NUMBER OF CHARACTERS READ (LINE LENGTH)
        ; BYTES 2 ON: ACTUAL CHARACTERS


;CHARACTER EQUATES
CR      EQU     0DH             ;CARRIAGE RETURN FOR KEYBOARD
LF      EQU     0AH             ;LINE FEED FOR VIDEO DISPLAY
PROMPT  EQU     '?'             ;OPERATOR PROMPT = QUESTION MARK

SC8B:
        ;
        ;READ LINE FROM KEYBOARD
        ;
        MOV     AL,PROMPT       ;OUTPUT PROMPT (?)
        CALL    WRCHAR
        MOV     DX,OFFSET INBUFF ;POINT TO INPUT BUFFER
        MOV     AH,RCBUF        ;MS-DOS READ LINE FUNCTION
        INT     21H             ;READ LINE FROM KEYBOARD
        MOV     AL,LF           ;OUTPUT LINE FEED
        CALL    WRCHAR
        ;
        ;WRITE LINE ON VIDEO DISPLAY
```

```
;
MOV     BX,OFFSET INBUFF+1 ;POINT TO NUMBER OF CHARACTERS IN
                           ; BUFFER
MOV     AL,[BX]            ;GET LINE LENGTH
INC     BX                 ;POINT TO FIRST DATA BYTE
CALL    WRLINE             ;WRITE LINE
MOV     BX,OFFSET CRLF     ;OUTPUT CARRIAGE RETURN, LINE FEED
MOV     AL,2               ;LENGTH OF CRLF STRING
CALL    WRLINE             ;WRITE CRLF STRING
JMP     SC8B               ;REPEAT CLEAR, READ, WRITE SEQUENCE

;DATA SECTION
CRLF    DB      CR,LF              ;CARRIAGE RETURN, LINE FEED
LENBUF  EQU     10H                ;LENGTH OF INPUT BUFFER
INBUFF  DB      LENBUF             ;LENGTH OF INPUT BUFFER
        DB      LENBUF DUP(?)      ;DATA BUFFER

        END
```

8C CRC16 checking and generation (ICRC16, CRC16, GCRC16)

Generates a 16-bit cyclic redundancy check (CRC) based on the IBM Binary Synchronous Communications protocol (BSC or Bisync). Uses the polynomial $X^{16} + X^{15} + X^2 + 1$. Entry point ICRC16 initializes the CRC to 0 and the polynomial to its bit pattern. Entry point CRC16 combines the previous CRC with the one generated from the current data byte. Entry point GCRC16 returns the CRC.

Procedure Subroutine ICRC16 initializes the CRC to 0 and the polynomial to a 1 in each bit position corresponding to a power of X present in the formula. Subroutine CRC16 updates the CRC for a data byte. It shifts both the data and the CRC left eight times; after each shift, it exclusive-ORs the CRC with the polynomial if the exclusive-OR of the data bit and the CRC's most significant bit is 1. Subroutine CRC16 leaves the CRC in memory locations CRC (less significant byte) and CRC + 1 (more significant byte). Subroutine GCRC16 loads the CRC into register AX.

Entry conditions

1. For ICRC16: none

2. For CRC16: data byte in register AL, previous CRC in memory locations CRC (less significant byte) and CRC+1 (more significant byte), CRC polynomial in memory locations PLY (less significant byte) and PLY + 1 (more significant byte).

3. For GCRC16: CRC in memory locations CRC (less significant byte) and CRC + 1 (more significant byte).

Exit conditions

1. For ICRC16:
0 (initial CRC value) in memory locations CRC (less significant byte) and CRC + 1 (more significant byte)
CRC polynomial in memory locations PLY (less significant byte) and PLY + 1 (more significant byte)

2. For CRC16: CRC with current data byte included in memory locations CRC (less significant byte) and CRC + 1 (more significant byte)

3. For GCRC16: CRC in register AX

Examples

1. Generating a CRC.
   Call ICRC16 to initialize the polynomial and start the CRC at 0.
   Call CRC16 repeatedly to update the CRC for each data byte.
   Call GCRC16 to obtain the final CRC.
2. Checking a CRC.
   Call ICRC16 to initialize the polynomial and start the CRC at 0.
   Call CRC16 repeatedly to update the CRC for each data byte (including the stored CRC) for checking.
   Call GCRC16 to obtain the final CRC; it will be 0 if there were no errors.

Note that only ICRC16 depends on the particular CRC polynomial used. To change the polynomial, simply change the data ICRC16 loads into memory locations PLY (less significant byte) and PLY + 1 (more significant byte).

Reference

J. E. McNamara, *Technical Aspects of Data Communications*, 3rd ed., Digital Press, Digital Equipment Corp., Billerica, MA, 1989. This book contains explanations of CRC and communications protocols.

Registers used

1. By ICRC16: None
2. By CRC16: None
3. By GCRC16: AX

Execution time

1. For ICRC16: 40 cycles
2. For CRC16: 136 cycles overhead plus an average of 42 cycles per

data byte, assuming that the previous CRC and the polynomial must be exclusively-ORed in half of the iterations.

3. For GCRC16: 22 cycles

Program size

1. For ICRC16: 13 bytes
2. For CRC16: 48 bytes
3. For GCRC16: 4 bytes

Data memory required 4 bytes anywhere in RAM for the CRC (2 bytes starting at address CRC) and the polynomial (2 bytes starting at address PLY).

```
;       Title               Generate CRC-16
;       Name:               ICRC16, CRC16, GCRC16
;
;
;       Purpose:            Generate a 16 bit CRC based on IBM's Binary
;                           Synchronous Communications protocol. The CRC is
;                           based on the following polynomial:
;                             (^ indicates "to the power")
;                                 X^16 + X^15 + X^2 + 1
;
;                           To generate a CRC:
;                                1)  Call ICRC16 to initialize the CRC
;                                    polynomial and clear the CRC.
;                                2)  Call CRC16 for each data byte.
;                                3)  Call GCRC16 to obtain the CRC.
;                                    It should then be appended to the data,
;                                    high byte first.
;
;                           To check a CRC:
;                                1)  Call ICRC16 to initialize the CRC.
;                                2)  Call CRC16 for each data byte and
;                                    the 2 bytes of CRC previously generated.
;                                3)  Call GCRC16 to obtain the CRC. It will
;                                    be zero if no errors occurred.
;
;       Entry:              ICRC16 - None
;                           CRC16  - Register AL = Data byte
;                           GCRC16 - None
;
;       Exit:               ICRC16 - CRC, PLY initialized
;                           CRC16  - CRC updated
;                           GCRC16 - Register AX = CRC
;
```

```
;       Registers Used: ICRC16 - None
;                       CRC16  - None
;                       GCRC16 - AX
;
;       Time:           ICRC16 - 40 cycles
;                       CRC16 - 136 cycles overhead plus an average of
;                       42 cycles per data byte.  The loop timing
;                       assumes that half the iterations require
;                       EXCLUSIVE-ORing the CRC and the polynomial.
;                       GCRC16 - 22 cycles
;
;       Size:           Program 65 bytes
;                       Data    4 bytes
;


CRC16:
        ;
        ;SAVE ALL REGISTERS
        ;
        PUSHF                           ;SAVE ALL REGISTERS
        PUSH    AX
        PUSH    BX
        PUSH    CX
        PUSH    DX
        ;
        ;LOOP THROUGH EACH DATA BIT, GENERATING THE CRC
        ;
        MOV     CX,8                    ;8 BITS PER BYTE
        MOV     DX,[PLY]                ;GET POLYNOMIAL
        MOV     BX,[CRC]                ;GET CURRENT CRC VALUE
        MOV     AH,AL                   ;SAVE DATA
CRCLP:
        AND     AL,10000000B            ;GET BIT 7 OF DATA
        XOR     BH,AL                   ;EXCLUSIVE-OR BIT 7 WITH BIT 15 OF CRC
        SHL     BX,1                    ;SHIFT 16-BIT CRC LEFT
        JNC     CRCLP1                  ;BRANCH IF BIT 7 OF EXCLUSIVE-OR IS 0
        ;
        ;BIT 7 IS 1, SO EXCLUSIVE-OR CRC WITH POLYNOMIAL
        ;
        XOR     BX,DX                   ;EXCLUSIVE-OR CRC WITH POLYNOMIAL
        ;
        ;SHIFT DATA LEFT AND COUNT BITS
        ;
CRCLP1:
        SHL     AH,1                    ;SHIFT DATA LEFT
        MOV     AL,AH                   ;SAVE SHIFTED DATA
        LOOP    CRCLP                   ;JUMP IF NOT THROUGH 8 BITS
        MOV     [CRC],BX                ;SAVE UPDATED CRC
        ;
        ;RESTORE REGISTERS AND EXIT
        ;
        POP     DX                      ;RESTORE ALL REGISTERS
        POP     CX
        POP     BX
        POP     AX
```

```
        POPF
        RET

;*****************************************
;ROUTINE: ICRC16
;PURPOSE: INITIALIZE CRC AND PLY
;ENTRY: NONE
;EXIT:  CRC AND POLYNOMIAL INITIALIZED
;REGISTERS USED: NONE
;*****************************************

ICRC16:
        MOV     WORD PTR[CRC],0 ;INITIALIZE CRC TO 0
        MOV     WORD PTR[PLY],8005H  ;PLY = 8005H
                                ;8005 HEX REPRESENTS X^16+X^15+X^2+1
                                ;  THERE IS A 1 IS IN EACH BIT
                                ;  POSITION FOR WHICH A POWER APPEARS
                                ;  IN THE FORMULA (BITS 0, 2, AND 15)
        RET

;*****************************************
;ROUTINE: GCRC16
;PURPOSE: GET CRC VALUE
;ENTRY: NONE
;EXIT:  REGISTER AX = CRC VALUE
;REGISTERS USED: AX
;*****************************************

GCRC16:
        MOV     AX,[CRC]        ;AX = CRC
        RET

;DATA
CRC     DW      ?               ;CRC VALUE
PLY     DW      ?               ;POLYNOMIAL VALUE


;
;       SAMPLE EXECUTION:
;

        ;
        ;GENERATE CRC FOR THE NUMBER 1 AND CHECK IT
        ;
SC8C:
        CALL    ICRC16          ;INITIALIZE CRC, POLYNOMIAL
        MOV     AL,1            ;GENERATE CRC FOR 1
        CALL    CRC16
        CALL    GCRC16
        MOV     DX,AX           ;SAVE CRC IN REGISTER DX
        CALL    ICRC16          ;INITIALIZE AGAIN
        MOV     AL,1
        CALL    CRC16           ;CHECK CRC BY GENERATING IT FOR DATA
        MOV     AL,DH           ;AND STORED CRC ALSO - HIGH BYTE FIRST
        CALL    CRC16
        MOV     AL,DL           ;THEN LOW BYTE
```

```
        CALL    CRC16
        CALL    GCRC16              ;CRC SHOULD BE ZERO IN AX

        ;
        ;GENERATE CRC FOR THE SEQUENCE 0,1,2,...,255 AND CHECK IT
        ;
        CALL    ICRC16              ;INITIALIZE CRC, POLYNOMIAL
        SUB     AL,AL               ;START DATA BYTES AT 0
GENLP:
        CALL    CRC16               ;UPDATE CRC
        INC     AL                  ;ADD 1 TO PRODUCE NEXT DATA BYTE
        JNZ     GENLP               ;BRANCH IF NOT DONE

        CALL    GCRC16              ;GET RESULTING CRC
        MOV     DX,AX               ;AND SAVE IT IN DX
        ;
        ;CHECK CRC BY GENERATING IT AGAIN
        ;
        CALL    ICRC16              ;INITIALIZE CRC, POLYNOMIAL
        SUB     AL,AL               ;START DATA BYTES AT 0
CHKLP:
        CALL    CRC16               ;UPDATE CRC
        INC     AL                  ;ADD 1 TO PRODUCE NEXT DATA BYTE
        JNZ     CHKLP               ;BRANCH IF NOT DONE
        ;
        ;INCLUDE STORED CRC IN CHECK
        ;
        MOV     AL,DH               ;INCLUDE HIGH BYTE OF CRC
        CALL    CRC16
        MOV     AL,DL               ;INCLUDE LOW BYTE OF CRC
        CALL    CRC16

        CALL    GCRC16              ;GET RESULTING CRC
                                    ;IT SHOULD BE 0

        JMP     SC8C                ;REPEAT TEST

        END
```

8D I/O device table handler (IOHDLR)

Performs input and output in a device-independent manner using I/O control blocks and an I/O device table. The I/O device table is a linked list; each entry contains a link to the next entry, the device number, and starting addresses for routines that initialize the device, determine its input status, read data from it, determine its output status, and write data to it. An I/O control block is an array containing device number, operation number, device status, and the base address and length of the device's buffer. The user must pass IOHDLR the base address of an I/O control block and the data if only 1 byte is to be written. IOHDLR returns the status byte and the data (if only 1 byte is read).

This subroutine provides a device-independent way of handling I/O. The I/O device table must be constructed using subroutines INITDL, which creates an empty device list, and INSDL, which inserts a device at the head of the list.

An applications program performs I/O by obtaining or constructing an I/O control block and then calling IOHDLR. IOHDLR uses the I/O device table to transfer control to the I/O driver.

Procedure The program first initializes the status byte to 0, indicating no errors. It then searches the device table, trying to match the device number in the I/O control block. If it does not find a match, it exits with an error number in the status byte. If it finds a match, it checks for a valid operation and transfers control to the appropriate routine from the device table entry. That routine must then transfer control back to the original caller. If the operation is invalid (the operation number is too large or the starting address for the routine is 0), the program returns with an error number in the status byte.

Subroutine INITDL initializes the device list, setting the initial link to 0.

Subroutine INSDL inserts an entry at the head of the device list and sets its link field to the previous head of the list.

Entry conditions

1. IOHDLR:
Base address of I/O control block in register BX
Data byte (if the operation is to write one byte) in register AL

2. INITL: None

3. INSDL: Base address of a device table entry in register BX

Exit conditions

1. IOHDLR:
I/O control block status byte in register AL if an error is found; otherwise, the routine exits to the appropriate I/O driver.
Data byte in register AL if the operation is to read 1 byte.

2. INITL: Device list header (addresses DVLST and DVLST+1) cleared to indicate an empty list.

3. INSDL: Device table entry added to head of list.

Example

The example in the listing uses the following structure:

Input/output operations

Operation number	Operation
0	Initialize device
1	Determine input status
2	Read 1 byte from input device
3	Read *N* bytes (usually 1 line) from input device
4	Determine output status
5	Write 1 byte to output device
6	Write *N* bytes (usually 1 line) to output device

Input/output control block

Index	Contents
0	Device number
1	Operation number
2	Status
3	Unused byte (to align subsequent word-length parameters)
4	Low byte of base address of buffer
5	High byte of base address of buffer
6	Low byte of buffer length
7	High byte of buffer length

Device table entry

Index	Contents
0	Low byte of link field (base address of next element)
1	High byte of link field (base address of next element)
2	Device number
3	Unused byte (to align subsequent 16-bit parameters)
4	Low byte of starting address of device initialization routine
5	High byte of starting address of device initialization routine
6	Low byte of starting address of input status determination routine
7	High byte of starting address of input status determination routine
8	Low byte of starting address of input driver (read 1 byte only)
9	High byte of starting address of input driver (read 1 byte only)
10	Low byte of starting address of input driver (read *N* bytes or 1 line)
11	High byte of starting address of input driver (read *N* bytes or 1 line)
12	Low byte of starting address of output status determination routine
13	High byte of starting address of output status determination routine
14	Low byte of starting address of output driver (write 1 byte only)
15	High byte of starting address of output driver (write 1 byte only)
16	Low byte of starting address of output driver (write *N* bytes or 1 line)
17	High byte of starting address of output driver (write *N* bytes or 1 line)

If an operation is irrelevant or undefined (such as output status determination for a keyboard or input driver for a printer), the corresponding starting address in the device table is 0.

Status values

Value	Description
0	No errors
1	Bad device number (no such device)
2	Bad operation number (no such operation or invalid operation)
3	Input data available or output device ready
254	Buffer too small for use by MS-DOS function A (Read Console Buffer or Buffered Keyboard Input). This function requires 2 bytes for the buffer length and character count.

Registers used

1. IOHDLR: AX, BX, DX, F, SI

2. INITDL: None

3. INSDL: DI

Execution time

1. IOHDLR: 205 cycles overhead plus 59 cycles for each unsuccessful match of a device number

2. INITDL: 24 cycles

3. INSDL: 51 cycles

Program size

1. IOHDLR: 75 bytes

2. INITL: 7 bytes

3. INSDL: 11 bytes

Data memory required 5 bytes anywhere in RAM for the base address of the I/O control block (2 bytes starting at address IOCBA), the device list header (2 bytes starting at address DVLST), and temporary storage for data to be written without a buffer (1 byte at address BDATA).

```
;       Title           I/O Device Table Handler
;       Name:           IOHDLR
;
;       Purpose:        Perform I/O in a device independent manner.
;                       This can be done by accessing all devices
;                       in the same way using an I/O Control Block
;                       (IOCB) and a device table. The routines here
;                       allow the following operations:
;
;                       Operation number  Description
;                           0           Initialize Device
;                           1           Determine input status
;                           2           Read 1 byte
;                           3           Read N bytes
;                           4           Determine output status
;                           5           Write 1 byte
;                           6           Write N bytes
;
;                       Adding operations such as Open, Close, Delete,
;                       Rename,  and Append would allow for more complex
;                       devices such as floppy or hard disks.
;
;                       A IOCB is an array consisting of elements
;                       with the following form:
;
;                       IOCB + 0 = Device Number
;                       IOCB + 1 = Operation Number
;                       IOCB + 2 = Status
;                       IOCB + 3 = Unused byte (for alignment)
;                       IOCB + 4 = Low byte of buffer address
;                       IOCB + 5 = High byte of buffer address
;                       IOCB + 6 = Low byte of buffer length
;                       IOCB + 7 = High byte of buffer length
;
;                       The device table is implemented as a linked
;                       list. Two routines maintain the list: INITDL,
;                       which initializes it to empty, and INSDL,
;                       which inserts a device at its head.
;                       A device table entry has the following form:
;
;                       DVTBL + 0 = Low byte of link field
;                       DVTBL + 1 = High byte of link field
;                       DVTBL + 2 = Device Number
;                       DVTBL + 3 = Unused byte (for alignment)
;                       DVTBL + 4 = Low byte of device initialization
;                       DVTBL + 5 = High byte of device initialization
;                       DVTBL + 6 = Low byte of input status routine
;                       DVTBL + 7 = High byte of input status routine
;                       DVTBL + 8 = Low byte of input 1 byte routine
;                       DVTBL + 9 = High byte of input 1 byte routine
;                       DVTBL + 10= Low byte of input N bytes routine
;                       DVTBL + 11= High byte of input N bytes routine
;                       DVTBL + 12= Low byte of output status routine
;                       DVTBL + 13= High byte of output status routine
```

```
;                       DVTBL + 14= Low byte of output 1 byte routine
;                       DVTBL + 15= High byte of output 1 byte routine
;                       DVTBL + 16= Low byte of output N bytes routine
;                       DVTBL + 17= High byte of output N bytes routine
;
;       Entry:          Register BX = Base address of IOCB
;                       Register AL = For write 1 byte, contains the
;                                     data (no buffer is used).
;
;       Exit:           Register AL = Copy of the IOCB status byte
;                                     except contains the data for
;                                     read 1 byte (no buffer is used).
;                       Status byte of IOCB is 0 if the operation was
;                       completed successfully; otherwise, it contains
;                       the error number.
;
;                       Status value    Description
;                           0           No errors
;                           1           Bad device number
;                           2           Bad operation number
;                           3           Input data available or output
;                                       device ready
;                           254         Buffer too small for MS-DOS
;                                       function A (Read Console
;                                       Buffer or Buffered Keyboard
;                                       Input, part of INT 21H)
;
;       Registers Used: AX,BX,DX,F,SI
;
;       Time:           205 cycles overhead plus 59 cycles for each
;                       non-matching device in the table
;
;       Size:           Program 75 bytes
;                       Data     5 bytes
;

;IOCB AND DEVICE TABLE EQUATES
IOCBDN  EQU     0       ;IOCB DEVICE NUMBER
IOCBOP  EQU     1       ;IOCB OPERATION NUMBER
IOCBST  EQU     2       ;IOCB STATUS
IOCBBA  EQU     4       ;IOCB BUFFER BASE ADDRESS
IOCBBL  EQU     6       ;IOCB BUFFER LENGTH
DTLNK   EQU     0       ;DEVICE TABLE LINK FIELD
DTDN    EQU     2       ;DEVICE TABLE DEVICE NUMBER
DTSR    EQU     4       ;BEGINNING OF DEVICE TABLE SUBROUTINES
;OPERATION NUMBERS
NUMOP   EQU     7       ;NUMBER OF OPERATIONS
INIT    EQU     0       ;INITIALIZATION
ISTAT   EQU     1       ;INPUT STATUS
R1BYTE  EQU     2       ;READ 1 BYTE
RNBYTE  EQU     3       ;READ N BYTES
OSTAT   EQU     4       ;OUTPUT STATUS
W1BYTE  EQU     5       ;WRITE 1 BYTE
WNBYTE  EQU     6       ;WRITE N BYTES
;STATUS VALUES
NOERR   EQU     0       ;NO ERRORS
```

```
DEVERR  EQU     1       ;BAD DEVICE NUMBER
OPERR   EQU     2       ;BAD OPERATION NUMBER
DEVRDY  EQU     3       ;INPUT DATA AVAILABLE OR OUTPUT DEVICE READY
BUFERR  EQU     254     ;BUFFER TOO SMALL FOR MS-DOS READ CONSOLE BUFFER

IOHDLR:
        ;
        ;SAVE IOCB ADDRESS AND DATA (IF ANY)
        ;
        MOV     [IOCBA],BX      ;SAVE IOCB ADDRESS
        MOV     [BDATA],AL      ;SAVE DATA BYTE FOR WRITE 1 BYTE
        ;
        ;INITIALIZE STATUS BYTE TO INDICATE NO ERRORS
        ;
        MOV     BYTE PTR [BX+IOCBST],NOERR  ;SAVE NO ERRORS STATUS
                                ;  IN IOCB
        ;
        ;CHECK FOR VALID OPERATION NUMBER (WITHIN LIMIT)
        ;
        MOV     DL,[BX+IOCBOP]  ;GET OPERATION NUMBER FROM IOCB
        CMP     DL,NUMOP        ;IS OPERATION NUMBER WITHIN LIMIT?
        JAE     BADOP           ;JUMP IF OPERATION NUMBER TOO LARGE
        ;
        ;SEARCH DEVICE LIST FOR THIS DEVICE
        ;
        MOV     AL,[BX+IOCBDN]  ;GET IOCB DEVICE NUMBER
        MOV     BX,[DVLST]      ;GET LINK TO HEAD OF DEVICE LIST
        ;
        ;BX = POINTER TO DEVICE LIST
        ;DL = OPERATION NUMBER
        ;AL = REQUESTED DEVICE NUMBER
        ;
SRCHLP:
        ;CHECK IF AT END OF DEVICE LIST (LINK FIELD = 0000)
        ;
        TEST    BX,BX           ;TEST LINK FIELD
        JZ      BADDN           ;BRANCH IF NO MORE DEVICE ENTRIES
        ;
        ;CHECK IF CURRENT ENTRY MATCHES DEVICE IN IOCB
        ;
        CMP     AL,[BX+DTDN]    ;COMPARE DEVICE NUMBER, REQUESTED DEVICE
        JE      FOUND           ;BRANCH IF DEVICE FOUND
        ;
        ;DEVICE NOT FOUND, SO ADVANCE TO NEXT DEVICE
        ; TABLE ENTRY THROUGH LINK FIELD
        ; THAT IS, NEXT ENTRY = LINK FROM CURRENT ENTRY
        ;
        MOV     BX,[BX]         ;NEXT DEVICE = LINK FROM CURRENT DEVICE
        JMP     SRCHLP          ;CHECK NEXT ENTRY IN DEVICE TABLE
        ;
        ;FOUND DEVICE,  SO VECTOR TO APPROPRIATE ROUTINE IF ANY
        ;DL = OPERATION NUMBER IN IOCB
        ;
FOUND:
        ;GET ROUTINE ADDRESS (ZERO INDICATES INVALID OPERATION)
        SUB     DH,DH           ;EXTEND OPERATION NUMBER TO 16 BITS
```

```
        SHL     DX,1                ;MULTIPLY OPERATION NUMBER TIMES 2 TO
                                    ; INDEX INTO TABLE OF 16-BIT ADDRESSES
        MOV     SI,DX
        MOV     SI,DTSR[BX+SI]      ;GET SUBROUTINE ADDRESS FROM DEVICE
                                    ; TABLE
        TEST    SI,SI               ;TEST SUBROUTINE ADDRESS
        JZ      BADOP               ;JUMP IF OPERATION INVALID (ADDRESS = 0)
        MOV     AL,[BDATA]          ;AL = DATA BYTE FOR WRITE 1 BYTE
        MOV     BX,[IOCBA]          ;GET BASE ADDRESS OF IOCB
        JMP     [SI]                ;GOTO SUBROUTINE

BADDN:
        MOV     AL,DEVERR           ;ERROR CODE -- NO SUCH DEVICE
        JMP     EREXIT
BADOP:
        MOV     AL,OPERR            ;ERROR CODE -- NO SUCH OPERATION

EREXIT:
        MOV     BX,[IOCBA]          ;POINT TO IOCB
        MOV     [BX+IOCBST],AL      ;SET STATUS BYTE IN IOCB
        RET

;****************************************
;ROUTINE: INITDL
;PURPOSE: INITIALIZE DEVICE LIST TO EMPTY
;ENTRY: NONE
;EXIT:  DEVICE LIST SET TO NO ITEMS (ZERO LINK IN HEADER)
;REGISTERS USED: NONE
;****************************************

INITDL:
        ;INITIALIZE DEVICE LIST HEADER TO 0 TO INDICATE NO DEVICES
        MOV     WORD PTR [DVLST],0  ;HEADER = 0 (EMPTY LIST)
        RET


;****************************************
;ROUTINE: INSDL
;PURPOSE: INSERT DEVICE AT HEAD OF DEVICE LIST
;ENTRY: REGISTER BX = ADDRESS OF DEVICE TABLE ENTRY
;EXIT:  DEVICE INSERTED INTO DEVICE LIST
;REGISTERS USED: DI
;****************************************

INSDL:
        MOV     DI,[DVLST]          ;GET CURRENT HEAD OF DEVICE LIST
        MOV     [BX],DI             ;LINK NEW ENTRY TO CURRENT HEAD
        MOV     [DVLST],BX          ;LINK HEADER TO NEW ENTRY - IT IS NOW
                                    ; AT HEAD OF LIST
        RET

;
;DATA SECTION
IOCBA   DW      ?                   ;BASE ADDRESS OF IOCB
DVLST   DW      ?                   ;DEVICE LIST HEADER
BDATA   DB      ?                   ;DATA BYTE FOR WRITE 1 BYTE
```

```
;
;       SAMPLE EXECUTION:
;
;         This test routine sets up the MS-DOS console (CON) as
;       device 1 and the MS-DOS printer (PRN) as device 2.  The
;       routine then reads a line from the console and echoes
;       it to the console and the printer.
;
;
;CHARACTER EQUATES
CR      EQU     0DH                     ;CARRIAGE RETURN CHARACTER
LF      EQU     0AH                     ;LINE FEED CHARACTER

;MS-DOS EQUATES
CINP    EQU     1                       ;MS-DOS CONSOLE INPUT FUNCTION
COUTP   EQU     2                       ;MS-DOS CONSOLE OUTPUT FUNCTION
POUTP   EQU     5                       ;MS-DOS PRINTER OUTPUT FUNCTION
RCBUF   EQU     0AH                     ;MS-DOS READ CONSOLE BUFFER FUNCTION
CSTAT   EQU     0BH                     ;MS-DOS CONSOLE STATUS FUNCTION

SC8D:
        ;INITIALIZE DEVICE LIST
        CALL    INITDL                  ;CREATE EMPTY DEVICE LIST

        ;SET UP CONSOLE AS DEVICE 1 AND INITIALIZE IT
        MOV     BX,OFFSET CONDV ;POINT TO CONSOLE DEVICE ENTRY
        CALL    INSDL           ;ADD CONSOLE TO DEVICE LIST
        MOV     BX,OFFSET IOCB  ;INITIALIZE CONSOLE
        MOV     BYTE PTR [BX+IOCBOP],INIT       ;INITIALIZE OPERATION
        MOV     BYTE PTR [BX+IOCBDN],1          ;DEVICE NUMBER = 1
        CALL    IOHDLR

        ;SET UP PRINTER AS DEVICE 2 AND INITIALIZE IT
        MOV     BX,OFFSET PRTDV ;POINT TO PRINTER DEVICE ENTRY
        CALL    INSDL           ;ADD PRINTER TO DEVICE LIST
        MOV     BX,OFFSET IOCB  ;INITIALIZE PRINTER
        MOV     BYTE PTR [BX+IOCBOP],INIT       ;INITIALIZE OPERATION
        MOV     BYTE PTR [BX+IOCBDN],2          ;DEVICE NUMBER = 2
        CALL    IOHDLR

        ;
        ;LOOP READING LINES FROM CONSOLE, AND ECHOING THEM TO
        ; THE CONSOLE AND PRINTER UNTIL A BLANK LINE IS ENTERED
        ;
TSTLP:
        MOV     WORD PTR [IOCB+IOCBBA],OFFSET BUFFER
                                ;PLACE BUFFER ADDRESS IN IOCB
        MOV     BYTE PTR [IOCB+IOCBDN],1 ;DEVICE NUMBER = 1 (CONSOLE)
        MOV     BYTE PTR [IOCB+IOCBOP],RNBYTE ;OPERATION IS READ N BYTES
        MOV     WORD PTR [IOCB+IOCBBL],LENBUF ;SET BUFFER LENGTH TO LENBUF
        CALL    IOHDLR          ;READ LINE FROM CONSOLE
        ;
        ;SEND LINE FEED TO CONSOLE
        ;
        MOV     BYTE PTR [IOCB+IOCBOP],W1BYTE      ;OPERATION IS WRITE
                                ; 1 BYTE
```

```
        MOV     AL,LF                ;CHARACTER IS LINE FEED
        MOV     BX,OFFSET IOCB       ;GET BASE ADDRESS OF IOCB
        CALL    IOHDLR               ;WRITE 1 BYTE (LINE FEED)
        ;
        ;ECHO LINE TO DEVICES 1 AND 2
        ;
        MOV     AL,1                 ;ECHO LINE TO DEVICE 1
        CALL    ECHO
        MOV     AL,2                 ;ECHO LINE TO DEVICE 2
        CALL    ECHO
        ;
        ;STOP IF LINE LENGTH IS 0
        ;
        MOV     AX,[IOCB+IOCBBL]     ;GET LINE LENGTH
        TEST    AX,AX                ;TEST LINE LENGTH
        JNZ     TSTLP                ;JUMP IF LENGTH NOT ZERO

        JMP     SC8D                 ;AGAIN

ECHO:
        ;OUTPUT LINE
        MOV     [IOCB+IOCBDN],AL     ;SET DEVICE NUMBER IN IOCB
                                     ;NOTE THAT ECHO WILL SEND A LINE
                                     ; TO ANY DEVICE. THE DEVICE NUMBER
                                     ; IS IN REGISTER AL
        MOV     BYTE PTR [IOCB+IOCBOP],WNBYTE    ;SET OPERATION
                                     ; TO WRITE N BYTES
        MOV     BX,OFFSET IOCB       ;GET BASE ADDRESS OF IOCB
        CALL    IOHDLR               ;WRITE N BYTES

        ;OUTPUT CARRIAGE RETURN/LINE FEED
        MOV     BYTE PTR [IOCB+IOCBOP],W1BYTE    ;SET OPERATION
                                     ; TO WRITE 1 BYTE
        MOV     AL,CR                ;CHARACTER IS CARRIAGE RETURN
        MOV     BX,OFFSET IOCB       ;GET BASE ADDRESS OF IOCB
        CALL    IOHDLR               ;WRITE 1 BYTE
        MOV     AL,LF                ;CHARACTER IS LINE FEED
        MOV     BX,OFFSET IOCB       ;GET BASE ADDRESS OF IOCB
        CALL    IOHDLR               ;WRITE 1 BYTE
        RET

;
;       DATA SECTION
;
LENBUF  EQU     127                  ;I/O BUFFER LENGTH
BUFFER  DB      LENBUF DUP(?)        ;I/O BUFFER

;IOCB FOR PERFORMING IO
IOCB    DB      ?                    ;DEVICE NUMBER
        DB      ?                    ;OPERATION NUMBER
        DB      ?                    ;STATUS
        DB      ?                    ;UNUSED BYTE
        DW      ?                    ;BUFFER ADDRESS
        DW      ?                    ;BUFFER LENGTH

;DEVICE TABLE ENTRIES
```

```
CONDV   DW      0                   ;LINK FIELD
        DB      1                   ;DEVICE 1
        DB      ?                   ;UNUSED BYTE
        DW      CINIT               ;CONSOLE INITIALIZE
        DW      CISTAT              ;CONSOLE INPUT STATUS
        DW      CIN                 ;CONSOLE INPUT 1 BYTE
        DW      CINN                ;CONSOLE INPUT N BYTES
        DW      COSTAT              ;CONSOLE OUTPUT STATUS
        DW      COUT                ;CONSOLE OUTPUT 1 BYTE
        DW      COUTN               ;CONSOLE OUTPUT N BYTES

PRTDV   DW      0                   ;LINK FIELD
        DB      2                   ;DEVICE 2
        DB      ?                   ;UNUSED BYTE
        DW      PINIT               ;PRINTER INITIALIZE
        DW      0                   ;NO PRINTER INPUT STATUS
        DW      0                   ;NO PRINTER INPUT 1 BYTE
        DW      0                   ;NO PRINTER INPUT N BYTES
        DW      POSTAT              ;PRINTER OUTPUT STATUS
        DW      POUT                ;PRINTER OUTPUT 1 BYTE
        DW      POUTN               ;PRINTER OUTPUT N BYTES

;************************************
;CONSOLE I/O ROUTINES
;************************************

;CONSOLE INITIALIZE
CINIT:
        SUB     AL,AL               ;STATUS = NO ERRORS
        RET                         ;NO INITIALIZATION NECESSARY

;CONSOLE INPUT STATUS
CISTAT:
        PUSH    BX                  ;SAVE IOCB ADDRESS
        MOV     AH,CSTAT            ;MS-DOS CONSOLE STATUS FUNCTION
        INT     21H                 ;GET CONSOLE STATUS
        POP     BX                  ;RESTORE IOCB ADDRESS
        TEST    AL,AL               ;TEST CONSOLE STATUS
        JZ      CIS1                ;JUMP IF NO CHARACTER READY (AL = 0)
        MOV     AL,DEVRDY           ;INDICATE CHARACTER READY
CIS1:   MOV     BYTE PTR [BX+IOCBST],AL      ;STORE STATUS IN IOCB
        RET

;CONSOLE READ 1 BYTE
CIN:
        MOV     AL,CINP             ;MS-DOS CONSOLE INPUT FUNCTION
        INT     21H                 ;READ 1 BYTE FROM CONSOLE
        RET

;CONSOLE READ N BYTES
CINN:
        ;READ LINE USING MS-DOS READ CONSOLE BUFFER FUNCTION
        ;MS-DOS READ CONSOLE BUFFER FUNCTION USES
        ; THE FOLLOWING BUFFER FORMAT:
        ;  BYTE 0: BUFFER LENGTH (MAXIMUM NUMBER OF CHARACTERS)
```

```
        ;  BYTE 1: NUMBER OF CHARACTERS READ (LINE LENGTH)
        ;  BYTES 2 ON: ACTUAL CHARACTERS
        ;
        MOV     AL,[BX+IOCBBL]  ;GET BUFFER LENGTH (8 BITS, HIGH BYTE
                                ; ALWAYS 0 IN MS-DOS)
        SUB     AL,3            ;BUFFER MUST BE AT LEAST 3 CHARACTERS
                                ; TO ALLOW FOR MAXIMUM LENGTH AND LINE
                                ; LENGTH USED BY MS-DOS READ CONSOLE
                                ; BUFFER
        JAE     CINN1           ;JUMP IF BUFFER LARGE ENOUGH
        MOV     BYTE PTR [BX+IOCBST],BUFERR  ;SET ERROR STATUS - BUFFER
                                ; TOO SMALL - NO ROOM FOR DATA
CINN1:  INC     AL              ;ADD ONE BACK TO FIND AMOUNT OF ROOM
                                ; IN BUFFER FOR DATA (2 BYTES OVERHEAD)
        MOV     DI,[BX+IOCBBA]  ;GET BUFFER ADDRESS FROM IOCB
        PUSH    BX              ;SAVE IOCB ADDRESS
        PUSH    DI              ;SAVE BUFFER ADDRESS
        MOV     [DI],AL         ;SET MAXIMUM LENGTH IN BUFFER
        MOV     DX,DI
        MOV     AH,RCBUF        ;MS-DOS READ CONSOLE BUFFER FUNCTION
        INT     21H             ;READ BUFFER
        ;
        ;RETURN NUMBER OF CHARACTERS READ IN IOCB
        ;
        POP     DI              ;RESTORE BUFFER ADDRESS
        POP     BX              ;RESTORE IOCB ADDRESS
        MOV     AL,[DI+1]       ;GET NUMBER OF CHARACTERS READ
        MOV     [BX+IOCBBL],AL  ;SET BUFFER LENGTH IN IOCB
        MOV     BYTE PTR [BX+IOCBBL+1],0     ;UPPER BYTE OF LENGTH IS 0
        ;
        ;MOVE DATA TO START AT BASE ADDRESS OF BUFFER
        ;DROPPING OVERHEAD (BUFFER LENGTH, NUMBER OF CHARACTERS READ)
        ; RETURNED BY MS-DOS.  LINE LENGTH IS NOW IN IOCB
        ;
        TEST    AL,AL           ;TEST NUMBER OF CHARACTERS READ
        JZ      CINEND          ;EXIT IF NO CHARACTERS
        MOV     CL,AL           ;SAVE NUMBER OF CHARACTERS READ
        SUB     CH,CH           ;EXTEND NUMBER READ TO 16 BITS
        LEA     SI,[DI+2]       ;START SOURCE POINTER AT FIRST BYTE
                                ;  OF DATA (2 BYTES BEYOND BASE
                                ;  ADDRESS OF BUFFER)
        CLD                     ;SELECT AUTOINCREMENTING
   REP  MOVSB                   ;MOVE DATA DOWN IN MEMORY
        SUB     AL,AL           ;RETURN, NO ERRORS
CINEND: RET

;CONSOLE OUTPUT STATUS
COSTAT:
        MOV     AL,DEVRDY       ;STATUS - ALWAYS READY TO OUTPUT
        RET

;CONSOLE WRITE 1 BYTE
COUT:
        MOV     AH,COUTP        ;MS-DOS CONSOLE OUTPUT OPERATION
        MOV     DL,AL           ;DL = CHARACTER
        INT     21H             ;OUTPUT 1 BYTE
```

```
        SUB     AL,AL               ;STATUS = NO ERRORS
        RET


;CONSOLE WRITE N BYTES
COUTN:
        MOV     DI,OFFSET COUT  ;DI=ADDRESS OF OUTPUT CHARACTER ROUTINE
        CALL    OUTN            ;CALL OUTPUT N CHARACTERS
        SUB     AL,AL           ;STATUS = NO ERRORS
        RET

;***************************************
;PRINTER ROUTINES
;***************************************

;PRINTER INITIALIZE
PINIT:
        SUB     AL,AL           ;NOTHING TO DO, RETURN NO ERRORS
        RET

;PRINTER OUTPUT STATUS
POSTAT:
        MOV     AL,DEVRDY       ;STATUS = ALWAYS READY
        RET

;PRINTER OUTPUT 1 BYTE
POUT:
        MOV     AH,POUTP        ;MS-DOS PRINTER OUTPUT FUNCTION
        MOV     DL,AL           ;DL = CHARACTER
        INT     21H             ;OUTPUT TO PRINTER
        SUB     AL,AL           ;STATUS = NO ERRORS
        RET

;PRINTER OUTPUT N BYTES
POUTN:
        MOV     DI,OFFSET POUT  ;DI = ADDRESS OF OUTPUT ROUTINE
        CALL    OUTN            ;OUTPUT N CHARACTERS
        SUB     AL,AL           ;STATUS = NO ERRORS
        RET

;************************************************************
;ROUTINE: OUTN
;PURPOSE: OUTPUT N CHARACTERS
;ENTRY:   REGISTER DI = CHARACTER OUTPUT SUBROUTINE ADDRESS
;         REGISTER BX = BASE ADDRESS OF AN IOCB
;EXIT:    DATA OUTPUT
;REGISTERS USED: AL,CX,F,SI
;************************************************************
OUTN:
        ;
        ;GET NUMBER OF BYTES, EXIT IF LENGTH IS 0
        ; CX = NUMBER OF BYTES
        ;GET OUTPUT BUFFER ADDRESS FROM IOCB
        ; SI = BUFFER ADDRESS
        ;
        MOV     CX,[BX+IOCBBL]  ;GET BUFFER LENGTH FROM IOCB
```

```
        TEST    CX,CX           ;TEST BUFFER LENGTH
        JZ      EXOUTN          ;EXIT IF BUFFER EMPTY
        MOV     SI,[BX+IOCBBA]  ;GET BUFFER ADDRESS FROM IOCB
        CLD                     ;SELECT AUTOINCREMENTING
        ;
        ;SEND DATA FROM BUFFER TO OUTPUT DEVICE
        ;
OUTLP:
        LODSB                   ;GET DATA FROM BUFFER
        PUSH    SI              ;SAVE BUFFER POINTER, CHARACTER COUNT
        PUSH    CX
        CALL    DOSUB           ;OUTPUT CHARACTER
        POP     CX              ;RESTORE POINTER, COUNT
        POP     SI
        LOOP    OUTLP           ;CONTINUE UNTIL ALL CHARACTERS SENT
EXOUTN: RET

DOSUB:  JMP     [DI]            ;GOTO ROUTINE

        END
```

8E Initialize I/O ports (IPORTS)

Initializes a set of I/O ports from an array of port device addresses and data values. Examples are given of initializing the common 8086/8088 programmable I/O devices: 8250 Asynchronous Communications Element (ACE), 8251 Programmable Communication Interface (PCI), 8253 Programmable Interval Timer (PIT), and 8255 Programmable Peripheral Interface (PPI). Standard IBM PCs, for instance, use 8250, 8253, and 8255 devices.

This subroutine provides a generalized way to initialize I/O sections. The initialization may involve data ports, data direction registers that determine whether bits are inputs or outputs, control or command registers that determine the operating modes of programmable devices, counters (in timers and baud rate generators), priority registers, interrupt mask and vector registers, and other external registers or storage locations.

Tasks the user may perform with this routine include:

1. Assign bidirectional I/O lines as inputs or outputs.

2. Put initial values in output ports.

3. Enable or disable interrupts from peripheral chips.

4. Determine operating modes, such as whether inputs are latched, whether strobes are produced, how priorities are assigned, whether timers operate continuously or only on demand, and whether I/O is asynchronous, synchronous, or uses a block-oriented protocol.

5. Load starting values into timers and counters.

6. Select bit rates for communications.

7. Clear or reset devices that are not tied to the overall system reset line.

8. Initialize priority registers or assign initial priorities to interrupts or other operations.

9. Initialize vectors used to service interrupts, DMA requests, and other inputs.

Procedure For each port, the program obtains the number of bytes to be sent and the device address. It then sends the specified number of data values to the port. This approach does not depend on the number or type of devices in the I/O section. The user may add or delete devices or change the initialization by changing the array rather than the program.

Each array entry consists of the following:

1. Number of bytes to be sent to the port
2. Low byte of port address
3. High byte of port address
4. Data bytes in sequential order.

The array ends with a terminator that has 0 in its first byte.

Note that an entry may consist of an arbitrary number of bytes. The first byte contains the count, the second and third bytes the device address, and subsequent bytes the actual data values. The terminator need consist only of a single zero in the count.

Entry conditions

Base address of initialization array in register BX

Exit conditions

All data values sent to port addressess.

Example

Data: Number of ports to initialize = 3
Array elements are:
3 (number of bytes for port 1)
Low byte of port 1's address
High byte of port 1's address
First value for port 1
Second value for port 1
Third value for port 1
2 (number of bytes for port 2)
Low byte of port 2's address
High byte of port 2's address
First value for port 2
Second value for port 2

4 (number of bytes for port 3)
Low byte of port 3's address
High byte of port 3's address
First value for port 3
Second value for port 3
Third value for port 3
Fourth value for port 3
0 (terminator)

Result: Three values sent to port 1's device address
Two values sent to port 2's device address
Four values sent to port 3's device address

Registers used AL, CX, DX, F, SI

Execution time 20 cycles overhead plus $70 + 37 \times N$ cycles for each port entry, where N is the number of bytes sent. If, for example, there are 10 ports plus an average of 3 bytes sent per port, the execution time is

$$20 + 10 \times (70 + 37 \times 3) = 20 + 1810 = 1830 \text{ cycles}$$

Program size 22 bytes plus the size of the table (at least 3 bytes per port plus 1 byte for a terminator).

Data memory required None

```
;       Title           Initialize I/O Ports
;       Name:           IPORTS
;
;       Purpose:        Initialize I/O ports from an array of port
;                       addresses and values.
;
;       Entry:          Register BX = Base address of array
;
;                       The array consists of elements organized
;                       as follows: number of bytes to be sent to
;                       the port, port device address, data values
;                       for the port.  This sequence is repeated for
;                       any number of ports.  The array is terminated
;                       by an entry with 0 in the number of bytes.
;                          array+0 = Number of bytes for this port (N)
;                          array+1 = Low byte of port device address
;                          array+2 = High byte of port device address
```

```
;                          array+3 = First value for this port
;                                    .
;                                    .
;                          array+3+(N-1) = Last value for this port
;                                    .
;                                    .
;                                    .
;
;       Exit:           None
;
;       Registers Used: AL,CX,DX,F,SI
;
;       Time:           20 cycles overhead plus 70 + N X 37 cycles for
;                       each port, where N is the number of bytes sent.
;
;       Size:           Program 22 bytes
;


IPORTS:
        ;
        ;GET NUMBER OF DATA BYTES TO SEND TO CURRENT PORT
        ;EXIT IF NUMBER OF BYTES IS 0, INDICATING TERMINATOR
        ;
        MOV     CL,[BX]         ;GET NUMBER OF BYTES
        TEST    CL,CL           ;TEST FOR ZERO (TERMINATOR)
        JZ      EXIPOR          ;EXIT IF NUMBER OF BYTES = 0
        ;
        ;GET PORT ADDRESS AND POINTER TO FIRST DATA BYTE
        ;
        SUB     CH,CH           ;EXTEND NUMBER OF BYTES TO 16 BITS
        MOV     DX,[BX+1]       ;GET PORT DEVICE ADDRESS
        LEA     SI,[BX+3]       ;POINT TO FIRST DATA BYTE
        CLD                     ;SELECT AUTOINCREMENTING
        ;
        ;SEND DATA BYTES TO PORT ADDRESS
        ;
OUTLP:
        LODSB                   ;GET NEXT DATA BYTE
        OUT     DX,AL           ;OUTPUT DATA TO PORT
        LOOP    OUTLP           ;CONTINUE UNTIL ALL DATA BYTES
                                ; SENT TO CURRENT PORT
        JMP     IPORTS          ;PROCEED TO NEXT PORT ENTRY

EXIPOR: RET

;
;       SAMPLE EXECUTION:
;


;
;INITIALIZE
;  8253 PIT (PROGRAMMABLE INTERVAL TIMER)
;  8251 SERIAL INTERFACE (PROGRAMMABLE COMMUNICATION INTERFACE)
;  8255 PARALLEL INTERFACE (PROGRAMMABLE PERIPHERAL INTERFACE)
;  8250 SERIAL INTERFACE (ASYNCHRONOUS COMMUNICATIONS ELEMENT)
```

```
;
;
;ARBITRARY PORT ADDRESSES
;
;  8253 PIT ADDRESSES
;
PIT0    EQU     0F070H              ;8253 CHANNEL 0
PIT1    EQU     0F071H              ;8253 CHANNEL 1
PIT2    EQU     0F072H              ;8253 CHANNEL 2
PITMDE  EQU     0F073H              ;8253 MODE WORD
;
;  8251 PCI ADDRESSES
;
PCID    EQU     0F100H              ;8251 DATA PORT
PCIC    EQU     0F101H              ;8251 CONTROL/STATUS PORT
;
;  8255 PPI ADDRESSES
;
PPIPA   EQU     0F200H              ;8255 PORT A
PPIPB   EQU     0F201H              ;8255 PORT B
PPIPC   EQU     0F202H              ;8255 PORT C
PPIC    EQU     0F203H              ;8255 CONTROL PORT
;
;  8250 ACE ADDRESSES
;
ACERBR  EQU     0F400H              ;8250 RECEIVER BUFFER REGISTER
ACETHR  EQU     0F400H              ;8250 TRANSMITTER HOLDING REG
ACEIER  EQU     0F401H              ;8250 INTERRUPT ENABLE REGISTER
ACEIIR  EQU     0F402H              ;8250 INTERRUPT IDENTIFICATION
                                    ; REGISTER
ACELCR  EQU     0F403H              ;8250 LINE CONTROL REGISTER
ACEMCR  EQU     0F404H              ;8250 MODEM CONTROL REGISTER
ACELSR  EQU     0F405H              ;8250 LINE STATUS REGISTER
ACEMSR  EQU     0F406H              ;8250 MODEM STATUS REGISTER
ACESCR  EQU     0F407H              ;8250 SCRATCHPAD REGISTER
ACEDLL  EQU     0F400H              ;8250 DIVISOR LATCH (LSB)
ACEDLM  EQU     0F401H              ;8250 DIVISOR LATCH (MSB)


SC8E:
        MOV     BX,OFFSET PINIT     ;POINT TO INITIALIZATION ARRAY
        CALL    IPORTS              ;INITIALIZE PORTS
        MOV     DX,PCID             ;DUMMY READ TO BE SURE 8251 IS
        IN      AL,DX               ; IN CORRECT STATE
        MOV     DX,ACERBR           ;DUMMY READ TO BE SURE 8250 IS
        IN      AL,DX               ; IN CORRECT STATE - CLEAR STATUS
                                    ; AND POSSIBLE STRAY DATA
        JMP     SC8E                ;REPEAT TEST

;
;INITIALIZE 8253 PIT COUNTER 0
;
;

        ;
        ;  OPERATE COUNTER SO IT GENERATES A SQUARE WAVE, DECREMENTING
        ;   THE COUNTER ON THE NEGATIVE (FALLING) EDGE OF EACH
```

```
        ;   CLOCK PULSE.  THE PERIOD OF THE SQUARE WAVE IS THE
        ;   INITIAL VALUE LOADED INTO THE COUNTER.
        ;  MAKE COUNT BINARY, SET INITIAL VALUE TO 13 DECIMAL.
        ;  NOTE: 8253 RELOADS COUNTER WITH ORIGINAL COUNT AFTER EACH
        ;   SQUARE WAVE IS GENERATED.
        ;  NOTE: IF THE INITIAL VALUE IS ODD, THE PULSES ARE NOT REALLY
        ;   SQUARE.  THE OUTPUT FROM PIN 10 OF THE 8253 WILL BE HIGH
        ;   FOR (N+1)/2 COUNTS AND LOW FOR (N-1)/2 COUNTS, WHERE N IS
        ;   THE INITIAL VALUE.  IN THE PRESENT CASE, THE OUTPUT WILL
        ;   BE HIGH FOR 7 COUNTS AND LOW FOR 6 COUNTS.

        ;  THIS INITIALIZATION PRODUCES AN 8251 PCI CLOCK FOR 9600 BAUD
        ;   TRANSMISSION.
        ;  IT ASSUMES A 2 MHZ CLOCK INPUT TO PIN 9, SO A COUNT OF
        ;   2,000,000/153,600 = 13 WILL GENERATE A 153,600 (16 * 9600)
        ;   HZ SQUARE WAVE FOR PCI PINS 9 (TRANSMIT CLOCK) AND
        ;   25 (RECEIVE CLOCK).  PCI IS OPERATING IN DIVIDE BY
        ;   16 CLOCK MODE.
        ;
PINIT   DB      1                       ;OUTPUT ONE BYTE
        DW      PITMDE                  ;DESTINATION IS MODE REGISTER
        DB      00110110B               ;BIT 0 = 0 (BINARY COUNT)
                                        ;BITS 3..1 = 011 (MODE 3 - SQUARE
                                        ; WAVE RATE GENERATOR)
                                        ;BITS 5,4 = 11 (LOAD 2 BYTES TO
                                        ; COUNTER)
                                        ;BITS 7,6 = 00 (SELECT COUNTER 0)
        DB      2                       ;OUTPUT TWO BYTES
        DW      PIT0                    ;DESTINATION IS COUNTER 0
        DB      13                      ;LOW BYTE OF COUNTER
        DB      0                       ;HIGH BYTE OF COUNTER
;
;INITIALIZE 8251 FOR ASYNCHRONOUS SERIAL I/O.
;       RESET 8251 IN SOFTWARE BY SENDING IT 3 BYTES OF 0,
;         FOLLOWED BY 1 BYTE OF 40H (RESET COMMAND)
;       SET ASYNCHRONOUS MODE, 8-BIT CHARACTERS, NO PARITY,
;         2 STOP BITS, 16 TIMES CLOCK.
;       ENABLE TRANSMITTER AND RECEIVER, RESET ERROR
;         INDICATORS
        DB      6                       ;OUTPUT SIX BYTES
        DW      PCIC                    ;DESTINATION IS PCI CONTROL PORT
                                        ;ASYNCHRONOUS MODE INSTRUCTION
        DB      0                       ;RESET 8251 FOR SURE BY EXECUTING
        DB      0                       ; WORST-CASE INITIALIZATION SEQUENCE
        DB      0                       ; TO GUARANTEE COMMAND FORMAT
        DB      40H                     ; FOLLOWED BY A RESET COMMAND
        DB      11001110B               ;ASYNCHRONOUS MODE INSTRUCTION
                                        ;BITS 1,0 = 10 (16X BAUD RATE FACTOR)
                                        ;BITS 3,2 = 11 (8-BIT CHARACTERS)
                                        ;BIT 4 = 0 (PARITY DISABLED)
                                        ;BIT 5 = 0 (DON'T CARE)
                                        ;BITS 7,6 = 11 (2 STOP BITS)

                                        ;ASYNCHRONOUS COMMAND INSTRUCTION
        DB      00010111B               ;BIT 0 = 1 (TRANSMIT ENABLE)
                                        ;BIT 1 = 1 (DATA TERMINAL READY)
```

```
                                        ;BIT 2 = 1 (RECEIVE ENABLE)
                                        ;BIT 3 = 0 (NO BREAK CHARACTER)
                                        ;BIT 4 = 1 (ERROR RESET)
                                        ;BIT 5= 0 (NO REQUEST TO SEND)
                                        ;BIT 6 = 0 (NO RESET)
                                        ;BIT 7 = 0 (NOT HUNTING)
;
;INITIALIZE 8255 PPI (PARALLEL INTERFACE)
;
;         PORT A INPUT, PORT B OUTPUT, UPPER 4 BITS OF PORT
;         C OUTPUT, LOWER 4 BITS OF PORT C INPUT.  NO AUTOMATIC
;         HANDSHAKING SIGNALS (MODE 0 - BASIC I/O)
;
        DB      1                       ;OUTPUT 1 BYTE
        DW      PPIC                    ;DESTINATION IS PPI CONTROL PORT
        DB      10010001B               ;BIT 0 = 1 (LOWER PORT C INPUT)
                                        ;BIT 1 = 0 (PORT B OUTPUT)
                                        ;BIT 2 = 0 (PORT B MODE IS 0)
                                        ;BIT 3 = 0 (UPPER PORT C OUTPUT)
                                        ;BIT 4 = 1 (PORT A INPUT)
                                        ;BITS 6, 5 = 00 (PORT A MODE IS 0)
                                        ;BIT 7 = 1 (MODE SELECT COMMAND)

;
;INITIALIZE 8250 ACE (UART)
;
;         SELECT 8-BIT CHARACTERS, NO PARITY, 2 STOP BITS
;         CLOCK RATE = 1200 BAUD (REQUIRING A DIVISOR OF 96 IF THE
;         CLOCK IS DERIVED FROM A 1.8432 MHZ OSCILLATOR AS IN THE
;         IBM PC).
;         DISABLE ALL INTERRUPTS
;

        DB      1                       ;OUTPUT 1 BYTE
        DW      ACEIER                  ;DESTINATION IS INTERRUPT ENABLE
                                        ; REGISTER
        DB      0                       ;SET BIT 7 TO ACCESS DIVISOR LATCH
        DB      1                       ;OUTPUT 1 BYTE
        DW      ACELCR                  ;DESTINATION IS LINE CONTROL REGISTER
        DB      10000000B               ;SET BIT 7 TO ACCESS DIVISOR LATCH
        DB      1                       ;OUTPUT 1 BYTE
        DW      ACEDLM                  ;DESTINATION IS MSB OF DIVISOR LATCH
        DB      0                       ;HIGH BYTE OF DIVISOR = 0
        DB      1                       ;OUTPUT 1 BYTE
        DW      ACEDLL                  ;DESTINATION IS LSB OF DIVISOR LATCH
        DB      96                      ;LOW BYTE OF DIVISOR = 96
        DB      1                       ;OUTPUT 1 BYTE
        DW      ACELCR                  ;DESTINATION IS LINE CONTROL REGISTER
        DB      00000111                ;BITS 0,1 = 1 (8-BIT CHARACTERS)
                                        ;BIT 2 = 1 (2 STOP BITS)
                                        ;BIT 3 = 0 (DISABLE PARITY)
                                        ;BITS 4,5 = 0 (PARITY CONTROL-DON'T
                                        ;  CARE)
                                        ;BIT 6 = 0 (DISABLE BREAK)
                                        ;BIT 7 = 0 (ACCESS DATA REGISTER)
```

```
;       END OF PORT INITIALIZATION DATA
        DB      0                       ;TERMINATOR

        END
```

9 Interrupts

9A Unbuffered interrupt-driven I/O using an 8250 ACE (SINTIO)

Performs interrupt-driven input and output using an 8250 ACE (Asynchronous Communications Element or UART) and single-character input and output buffers. Consists of the following subroutines:

1. INCH reads a character from the input buffer.
2. INST determines whether the input buffer is empty.
3. OUTCH writes a character into the output buffer.
4. OUTST determines whether the output buffer is full.
5. INIT initializes the 8250 ACE, the software flags, and the interrupt system (vector and controller). The flags show when data is available for transfer between the main program and the interrupt service routines.
6. ACETST checks the operation of an 8250 ACE by putting it in the loopback mode and checking whether all characters can be sent and received back correctly.
7. IOSRVC (the interrupt service routine) identifies and services the interrupt. In response to the input interrupt, it reads a character from the 8250 ACE into the input buffer. In response to the output interrupt, it writes a character from the output buffer into the 8250 ACE.

Procedures

1. INCH waits for a character to become available, clears the Data Ready flag (RECDF), and loads the character into register AL.

2. INST sets the Carry flag from the Data Ready flag (RECDF).

3. OUTCH waits for the output buffer to empty, stores the character in the buffer, and sets the Character Available flag (TRNDF). If no output interrupt is expected (i.e. it has been cleared because it occurred when no data was available), OUTCH sends the data to the ACE immediately.

4. OUTST sets the Carry flag from the Character Available flag (TRNDF).

5. INIT initializes the 8250 ACE by placing values in its divisor latch and line control register, clears the software flags, sets up the interrupt vectors, and initializes the 8259 interrupt controller. See Subroutine 8E for more details about initializing an 8250 ACE.

One problem with I/O devices such as the 8250 ACE is that they operate at clock rates much lower than that of the CPU. A long wait time may be necessary between accesses to ensure a proper response. In non-pipelined processors, the delay caused by instruction fetch and decode is generally sufficient to avoid difficulties. However, in a pipelined processor like the 8086, instruction prefetch may make this delay very short. Furthermore, the traditional solution of placing NOPs after an access may not help since they may also be prefetched.

The easiest way to ensure sufficient wait time is to put a jump after each access. If this jump simply directs the processor to the next sequential instruction (i.e. JMP $+2), it works like a NOP. However, like any jump, it clears out the pipeline, thus forcing a substantial delay between accesses. Furthermore, JMP itself is a slow-executing instruction. We have put a JMP $+2 instruction after each 8250 access in the subroutines.

6. ACETST puts the 8250 ACE in its loopback mode. It then attempts to send and receive back all possible characters (00–FF). If a character is received incorrectly, ACETST returns immediately with the Carry set and the character's value in AL. If all characters are received correctly, it returns with the Carry cleared.

7. IOSRVC examines the ACE's interrupt identification register to determine whether the interrupt is from the transmitter (bits 0–2 = 010). If not, it assumes the interrupt is from the receiver. It then reads the data from the 8250 ACE, saves it in memory, and sets the Data

Ready flag (RECDF). The lack of buffering causes the loss of unread data at this point.

If the output interrupt occurred, the program determines whether data is available. If it is, the program sends it to the 8250 ACE and clears the Character Available flag (TRNDF). If not, the program simply clears the output interrupt (in the 8259 interrupt controller). Note that reading the interrupt identification register in an 8250 ACE is sufficient by itself to clear a transmitter interrupt. Thus clearing the 8259 interrupt removes all traces of the transmitter interrupt from the system, allowing the recognition of later receiver or transmitter interrupts on the same line.

Most 8086 interrupt systems have a controller that responds to interrupt acknowledgements from the CPU and contains prioritization, vectoring, and other management logic. The example in the listing uses the popular 8259 Programmable Interrupt Controller (PIC). The 8259 PIC latches interrupt requests from peripheral chips, blocks subsequent requests from the same and lower priority level, and generates source identification to vector the 8086. The service routine must send the 8259 PIC an End-of-Interrupt (EOI) command before concluding to unblock subsequent requests.

Note that when the 8259 is in its usual 'edge detect' mode, it recognizes only transitions on the interrupt lines. Thus, an interrupt from a peripheral chip can cause only a single processor interrupt, no matter how long it remains active. Jigour has described the 8259 device in detail in 'Using the 8259A Programmable Interrupt Controller,' Intel Application Note AP-59, Intel Corporation, Santa Clara, CA, 1979.

The special problem with the output interrupt is that it may occur when no data is available. It cannot be ignored or it will assert itself indefinitely, creating an endless loop. The solution is simply to clear the 8259 PIC's interrupt by sending it an EOI command. Remember that reading the 8250's interrupt identification register clears the transmitter interrupt automatically if it is active.

But now a new problem arises when output data becomes available. That is, since the interrupt has been cleared, it obviously cannot inform the system that the 8250 ACE is ready to transmit. The solution is a flag that is cleared if the output interrupt has occurred without being serviced. We call this flag Output Interrupt Expected (OIE).

The initialization routine clears OIE (since the 8250 ACE surely starts out ready to transmit). The output service routine clears it when an output interrupt occurs that cannot be serviced (no data is available) and sets it after sending data to the 8250 (in case it might have been cleared). Now the output routine OUTCH can check OIE to determine whether the output interrupt has already occurred (0 indicates it has, FF hex that it has not). If no output interrupt is expected, OUTCH simply sends the data immediately.

Unserviceable interrupts occur only with output devices, since input devices always have data ready to transfer when they request service. Thus, output devices cause more initialization and sequencing problems in interrupt-driven systems than do input devices.

Entry conditions

1. INCH: none
2. INST: none
3. OUTCH: character to transmit in register AL
4. OUTST: none
5. INIT: none
6. ACETST: none

Exit conditions

1. INCH: character in register AL
2. INST: Carry = 0 if input buffer is empty, 1 if it is full
3. OUTCH: none
4. OUTST: Carry = 0 if output buffer is empty, 1 if it is full
5. INIT: none
6. ACETST: Carry = 0 and register AL = 0 if loopback test succeeds for all characters, Carry = 1 and register AL contains value for which test failed otherwise

---

Registers used

1. INCH: AL, F
2. INST: AL, F
3. OUTCH: AL, DX, F

4. OUTST: F

5. INIT: AL, BX, DX

6. ACETST: AL, BL, DX, F

Execution time

1. INCH: 96 cycles if a character is available

2. INST: 20 cycles

3. OUTCH: 149 cycles if the output buffer is empty and an output interrupt is expected, 88 additional cycles to send the data to the ACE if no output interrupt is expected.

4. OUTST: 39 cycles

5. INIT: 447 cycles

6. ACETST: Depends on 8250's baud rate and number of bits per character, since a complete test requires the sending and receiving of 256 characters. For 11-bit characters at 1200 baud, a complete test takes about 2.35 s.

7. IOSRVC: 223 cycles to service an input interrupt if a character is ready, 169 cycles to service an output interrupt if no data is available, 275 cycles to service an output interrupt if the output buffer is full.

Note: The execution times for IOSRVC do not include the 8086's interrupt response time (51 cycles).

Program size 281 bytes, not including the loopback test (47 bytes).

Data memory required 5 bytes anywhere in RAM for the received data (address RECDAT), receive data flag (address RECDF), transmit data (address TRNDAT), transmit data flag (address TRNDF), and output interrupt expected flag (address OIE).

```
;       Title           Simple interrupt input and output using an 8250
;                       ACE and single character buffers.
;       Name:           SINTIO
;

;       Purpose:        This program includes 5 subroutines that
;                       perform interrupt driven input and output using
```

```
;                    an 8250 UART.  It also contains an I/O
;                    interrupt service routine and a loopback test
;                    routine for the 8250 device.
;
;                    INCH
;                      Read a character.
;                    INST
;                      Determine input status (whether input
;                      buffer is empty).
;                     OUTCH
;                      Write a character.
;                    OUTST
;                      Determine output status (whether output
;                      buffer is full).
;                    INIT
;                      Initialize UART and interrupt system
;                    ACETST
;                      Test 8250 ACE operation
;                    IOSRVC
;                      Respond to 8250 ACE I/O interrupts
;
;
;       Entry:       INCH
;                      No parameters.
;                    INST
;                      No parameters.
;                    OUTCH
;                      Register AL = character to transmit
;                    OUTST
;                      No parameters.
;                    INIT
;                      No parameters.
;                    ACETST
;                      No parameters
;
;       Exit:        INCH
;                      Register AL = character received
;                    INST
;                      Carry = 0 if input buffer is empty,
;                      1 if character is available.
;                    OUTCH
;                      No parameters
;                    OUTST
;                      Carry = 0 if output buffer is empty,
;                      1 if it is full.
;                    INIT
;                      No parameters.
;                    ACETST
;                      Carry = 0 and register AL = 0 if 8250 ACE
;                      passes loopback test, Carry = 1 and register
;                      AL contains value for which test failed
;                      otherwise.
;
;       Registers Used: INCH
;                      AL,F
;                    INST
```

```
;                               AL,F
;                             OUTCH
;                               AL,DX,F
;                             OUTST
;                               F
;                             INIT
;                               AL,BX,DX
;                             ACETST
;                               AL,BL,DX,F
;
;       Time:                 INCH
;                               96 cycles if a character is available
;                             INST
;                               20 cycles
;                             OUTCH
;                               149 cycles if output buffer is empty and
;                               output interrupt is expected
;                             OUTST
;                               39 cycles
;                             INIT
;                               447 cycles
;                             ACETST
;                               Depends on 8250's baud rate and number of
;                               bits per character, since a complete test
;                               requires the 8250 to send and receive 256
;                               characters
;                             IOSRVC
;                               223 cycles to service an input interrupt if
;                               a character is ready, 275 cycles to service
;                               an output interrupt if the output buffer is
;                               full, 169 cycles to service an output
;                               interrupt if no data is available. These times
;                               do not include the 8086's interrupt response
;                               time (51 cycles).
;
;       Size:                 Program   328 bytes
;                             Data      5 bytes
;


;
;ESTABLISH SEGMENT ADDRESS FOR USE IN INTERRUPT VECTORS
;
CSEG        EQU       0F81H               ;ARBITRARY BASE ADDRESS OF CODE
                                          ; SEGMENT - USUALLY ESTABLISHED
                                          ; IN A SEGMENT STATEMENT NOT
                                          ; SHOWN HERE
;
;8250 ACE (UART) EQUATES
; 8250 IS PROGRAMMED FOR
;   1200 BAUD ASSUMING A 1.8432 MHZ OSCILLATOR INPUT (AS ON IBM PC)
;   8-BIT CHARACTERS
;   2 STOP BITS
;   NO PARITY
;ARBITRARY 8250 ACE PORT ADDRESSES (TAKEN FROM IBM PC)
;
ACEBASE     EQU       3F8H                ;ACE BASE ADDRESS
```

```
ACERBR  EQU     3F8H            ;ACE RECEIVER BUFFER REGISTER
ACETHR  EQU     3F8H            ;ACE TRANSMITTER HOLDING REGISTER
ACEIER  EQU     3F9H            ;ACE INTERRUPT ENABLE REGISTER
ACEIIR  EQU     3FAH            ;ACE INTERRUPT IDENTIFICATION REGISTER
ACELCR  EQU     3FBH            ;ACE LINE CONTROL REGISTER
ACEMCR  EQU     3FCH            ;ACE MODEM CONTROL REGISTER
ACELSR  EQU     3FDH            ;ACE LINE STATUS REGISTER
ACEMSR  EQU     3FEH            ;ACE MODEM STATUS REGISTER
ACESCR  EQU     3FFH            ;ACE SCRATCHPAD REGISTER
ACEDLL  EQU     3F8H            ;ACE DIVISOR LATCH (LSB)
ACEDLM  EQU     3F9H            ;ACE DIVISOR LATCH (MSB)

;INTERRUPT VECTOR
ASYNIV  EQU     0030H           ;ASYNCHRONOUS I/O INTERRUPT VECTOR

;8250 LINE CONTROL INSTRUCTION
LCMODE  EQU     00000111B       ;BITS 1,0 = 11 (8 BIT WORD LENGTH)
                                ;BIT 2 = 1 (2 STOP BITS)
                                ;BIT 3 = 0 (PARITY DISABLED)
                                ;BITS 5,4 = 00 (DON'T CARE)
                                ;BIT 6 = 0 (DISABLE BREAK)
                                ;BITS 7 = 0 (POINT TO DATA REGISTER)
;8250 MODEM CONTROL INSTRUCTION
MCMODE  EQU     00000011B       ;BIT 0 = 1 (SET DATA TERMINAL READY)
                                ;BIT 1 = 1 (SET REQUEST TO SEND)
                                ;BITS 3,2 = 00 (DON'T CARE)
                                ;BIT 4 = 0 (DISABLE INTERNAL LOOPBACK)
                                ;BITS 7,6,5 = 000 (DON'T CARE)

;8250 INTERRUPT ENABLE INSTRUCTION
INTCMD  EQU     00000011B       ;BIT 0 = 1 (ENABLE RECEIVE DATA
                                ; INTERRUPT)
                                ;BIT 1 = 1 (ENABLE TRANSMITTER EMPTY
                                ; INTERRUPT)
                                ;BIT 2 = 0 (DISABLE LINE STATUS
                                ; INTERRUPT)
                                ;BIT 3 = 0 (DISABLE MODEM STATUS
                                ; INTERRUPT)
                                ;BITS 4-7 = 0 (DON'T CARE)

;8250 DIVISOR LATCH ACCESS INSTRUCTION
DLADDR  EQU     10000000B       ;BIT 7 = 1 (POINT TO DIVISOR LATCH)

;8250 DIVISOR LATCH VALUE (96 FOR 1200 BAUD ASSUMING A 1.8432 MHZ
;  OSCILLATOR INPUT
DIVLS   EQU     96              ;LESS SIGNIFICANT BYTE OF DIVISOR
                                ;OUTPUT FREQUENCY EQUALS THE INPUT
                                ; FREQUENCY/(BAUD DIVISOR X 16)
                                ; = 1.8432 MHZ/(96 X 16) = 1200 BAUD
DIVMS   EQU     0               ;MORE SIGNIFICANT BYTE OF DIVISOR

;8259 PROGRAMMABLE INTERRUPT CONTROLLER (PIC) EQUATES
; 8259 PIC IS PROGRAMMED FOR
;  SINGLE DEVICE (RATHER THAN MULTIPLE 8259'S)
;  FULLY NESTED MODE
;  ALL INTERRUPTS ENABLED
```

```
;  INTERRUPT LEVELS 8-15
;ARBITRARY 8259 PIC PORT ADDRESSES
PIC0    EQU     20H             ;PIC PORT 1
PIC1    EQU     21H             ;PIC PORT 2

;8259 INITIALIZATION COMMAND BYTES ICW1, ICW2, AND ICW4 (NO ICW3
;  NEEDED IN SINGLE 8259 SYSTEMS)
ICW1    EQU     00010011B       ;BIT 0 = 1 (ICW4 NEEDED IN 8086 SYSTEMS)
                                ;BIT 1 = 1 (SINGLE 8259)
                                ;BIT 2 = 0 (NOT USED WITH 8086/8088)
                                ;BIT 3 = 0 (EDGE DETECT)
                                ;BIT 4 = 1 (FIXED)
                                ;BITS 5,6,7 = 000 (NOT USED IN 8086/88)
ICW2    EQU     00001000B       ;BITS 7-3 = 00001 (5 MSB'S OF SOURCE
                                ;  IDENTIFICATION CODE)
                                ;BITS 2-0 = 000 (NOT USED)
ICW4    EQU     00001001B       ;BIT 0 = 1 (8086/88 SYSTEM)
                                ;BIT 1= 0 (NO AUTOMATIC END OF
                                ;  INTERRUPT)
                                ;BIT 2 = 0 (DON'T CARE)
                                ;BIT 3 = 1 (BUFFERED DATA BUS)
                                ;BIT 4 = 0 (NO CASCADING)
                                ;BITS 7-5 = 000 (NOT USED)
;8259 OPERATING COMMAND BYTE
EOI     EQU     00100000B       ;END OF INTERRUPT COMMAND BYTE

;
;       READ A CHARACTER FROM INPUT BUFFER
;
INCH:
        CALL    INST            ;GET INPUT STATUS
        JNC     INCH            ;WAIT IF NO CHARACTER AVAILABLE
        PUSHF                   ;SAVE CURRENT INTERRUPT STATUS
        CLI                     ;DISABLE INTERRUPTS WHILE CHANGING
                                ;  SOFTWARE FLAG
        MOV     BYTE PTR [RECDF],0 ;INDICATE INPUT BUFFER EMPTY
        MOV     AL,[RECDAT]     ;GET CHARACTER FROM INPUT BUFFER
        POPF                    ;RESTORE PREVIOUS INTERRUPT STATUS
        RET

;
;       DETERMINE INPUT STATUS (CARRY = 1 IF DATA AVAILABLE, 0 IF NOT)
;
INST:
        MOV     AL,[RECDF]      ;GET DATA READY FLAG
        SHR     AL,1            ;SET CARRY FROM DATA READY FLAG
                                ; CARRY = 1 IF CHARACTER AVAILABLE
        RET

;
;     WRITE A CHARACTER INTO OUTPUT BUFFER
;     SEND IT ON TO ACE IF NO OUTPUT INTERRUPT EXPECTED
;
OUTCH:

;WAIT FOR OUTPUT BUFFER TO EMPTY, STORE NEXT CHARACTER
```

```
WAITOC:
        CALL     OUTST                ;GET OUTPUT STATUS
        JC       WAITOC               ;WAIT IF OUTPUT BUFFER FULL
        PUSHF                         ;SAVE CURRENT INTERRUPT STATUS
        CLI                           ;DISABLE INTERRUPTS WHILE WORKING
                                      ; WITH SOFTWARE FLAGS
        MOV      [TRNDAT],AL          ;STORE CHARACTER IN INPUT BUFFER
        MOV      BYTE PTR [TRNDF],0FFH     ;INDICATE INPUT BUFFER FULL
        MOV      AL,[OIE]             ;TEST OUTPUT INTERRUPT EXPECTED FLAG
        TEST     AL,AL
        JNZ      EXITOC               ;BRANCH IF OUTPUT INTERRUPT EXPECTED
        CALL     OUTDAT               ;OTHERWISE, SEND CHARACTER TO ACE NOW
EXITOC: POPF                          ;RESTORE PREVIOUS INTERRUPT STATUS
        RET

;
;    DETERMINE OUTPUT STATUS (CARRY = 1 IF OUTPUT BUFFER FULL)
;
OUTST:
        PUSH     AX                   ;SAVE REGISTER AX
        MOV      AL,[TRNDF]           ;GET TRANSMIT FLAG
        SHR      AL,1                 ;SET CARRY FROM TRANSMIT FLAG
        POP      AX                   ;RESTORE REGISTER AX
        RET                           ;CARRY = 1 IF BUFFER FULL, 0 IF NOT

;
;INITIALIZE INTERRUPT SYSTEM AND 8250 ACE
;
INIT:
        ;
        ;DISABLE INTERRUPTS DURING INITIALIZATION BUT SAVE
        ;  PREVIOUS VALUE OF INTERRUPT FLAG
        ;
        PUSHF                         ;SAVE CURRENT INTERRUPT STATUS
        CLI                           ;DISABLE INTERRUPTS DURING
                                      ; INITIALIZATION
        ;
        ;INITIALIZE 8250 ACE (UART)
        ;
        MOV      DX,ACEIER            ;POINT TO INTERRUPT ENABLE REGISTER
        SUB      AL,AL                ;RESET INTERRUPT ENABLES
        OUT      DX,AL
        JMP      $+2                  ;DELAY BETWEEN 8250 OPERATIONS
        MOV      DX,ACELCR            ;POINT TO LINE CONTROL REGISTER
        MOV      AL,DLADDR            ;ADDRESS DIVISOR LATCH
        OUT      DX,AL
        JMP      $+2                  ;DELAY BETWEEN 8250 OPERATIONS
        MOV      DX,ACEDLM            ;POINT TO DIVISOR LATCH - MSB
        MOV      AL,DIVMS             ;SET MSB OF DIVISOR
        OUT      DX,AL
        JMP      $+2                  ;DELAY BETWEEN 8250 OPERATIONS
        MOV      DX,ACEDLL            ;POINT TO DIVISOR LATCH - LSB
        MOV      AL,DIVLS             ;SET LSB OF DIVISOR
        OUT      DX,AL
        JMP      $+2                  ;DELAY BETWEEN 8250 OPERATIONS
        MOV      DX,ACELCR            ;POINT TO LINE CONTROL REGISTER
```

```
        MOV     AL,LCMODE       ;SET ACE FOR 8-BIT WORDS, 2 STOP
                                ; BITS, NO PARITY
        OUT     DX,AL
        JMP     $+2             ;DELAY BETWEEN 8250 OPERATIONS
        MOV     DX,ACEMSR       ;POINT TO MODEM STATUS REGISTER
        IN      AL,DX           ;READ TO CLEAR POSSIBLE OLD INTERRUPT
        JMP     $+2             ;DELAY BETWEEN 8250 OPERATIONS
        MOV     DX,ACELSR       ;POINT TO LINE STATUS REGISTER
        IN      AL,DX           ;CLEAR ERROR INDICATORS, CHECK FOR DATA
        JMP     $+2             ;DELAY BETWEEN 8250 OPERATIONS
        SHR     AL,1            ;CHECK IF DATA READY
        JNC     SETINT          ;JUMP IF NO DATA
        MOV     DX,ACERBR       ;POINT TO RECEIVER BUFFER REGISTER
        IN      AL,DX           ;READ BUFFER TO EMPTY IT FOR SURE
        JMP     $+2             ;DELAY BETWEEN 8250 OPERATIONS
SETINT:
        MOV     DX,ACEIER       ;POINT TO INTERRUPT ENABLE REGISTER
        MOV     AL,INTCMD       ;ENABLE RECEIVE, TRANSMIT INTERRUPTS
        OUT     DX,AL
        JMP     $+2             ;DELAY BETWEEN 8250 OPERATIONS
        MOV     DX,ACEMCR       ;POINT TO MODEM CONTROL REGISTER
        MOV     AL,MCMODE       ;MODEM CONTROL COMMAND
        OUT     DX,AL
        JMP     $+2             ;DELAY BETWEEN 8250 OPERATIONS
        ;
        ;INITIALIZE SOFTWARE FLAGS
        ;
        SUB     AL,AL
        MOV     [RECDF],AL      ;NO INPUT DATA AVAILABLE
        MOV     [TRNDF],AL      ;OUTPUT BUFFER EMPTY
        MOV     [OIE],AL        ;INDICATE NO OUTPUT INTERRUPT NEEDED
                                ; 8250 READY TO TRANSMIT INITIALLY
        ;
        ;INITIALIZE INTERRUPT VECTOR
        ;
        PUSH    DS              ;SAVE CURRENT DATA SEGMENT
        SUB     AX,AX           ;ACCESS INTERRUPT VECTOR IN SEGMENT
                                ; 0
        MOV     DS,AX
        MOV     AX,OFFSET IOSRVC   ;GET OFFSET FOR SERVICE ROUTINE
        MOV     BX,ASYNIV       ;GET INTERRUPT VECTOR LOCATION
        MOV     [BX],AX         ;LOAD OFFSET INTO INTERRUPT VECTOR
        MOV     AX,CSEG         ;GET CODE SEGMENT NUMBER
        MOV     [BX+2],AX       ;LOAD CODE SEGMENT NUMBER INTO
                                ; INTERRUPT VECTOR
        POP     DS              ;RESTORE CURRENT DATA SEGMENT
        ;
        ;INITIALIZE 8259 INTERRUPT CONTROLLER
        ;
        ;IF THE 8259 WAS PREVIOUSLY INITIALIZED AND YOU WANT TO ENABLE
        ; AN ADDITIONAL INTERRUPT, EXECUTE THE FOLLOWING CODE (SHOWN
        ; ENABLING INTERRUPT 4)
        ;
        MOV     DX,PIC1         ;GET CURRENT INTERRUPT MASKS
        IN      AL,PIC1
        AND     AL,11101111B    ;ENABLE INTERRUPT 4 ALSO
```

```
        OUT     PIC1,AL
        POPF                    ;RESTORE PREVIOUS INTERRUPT STATUS
        RET
        ;
        ;TO INITIALIZE THE 8259 AND ENABLE ALL INTERRUPTS, EXECUTE
        ; THE FOLLOWING CODE
        ;
        MOV     DX,PIC0         ;SEND FIRST COMMAND BYTE TO PIC PORT 0
        MOV     AL,ICW1
        OUT     DX,AL
        MOV     DX,PIC1         ;SEND SECOND COMMAND BYTE TO PIC PORT 1
        MOV     AL,ICW2
        OUT     DX,AL
        MOV     AL,ICW4         ;SEND FINAL COMMAND BYTE TO PIC PORT 1
        OUT     DX,AL
        POPF                    ;RESTORE PREVIOUS INTERRUPT STATUS
        RET

;
;ASYNCHRONOUS I/O INTERRUPT HANDLER
;
IOSRVC:
        PUSH    AX              ;SAVE REGISTERS
        PUSH    DX
        MOV     DX,ACEIIR       ;POINT TO INTERRUPT ID REGISTER
        IN      AL,DX           ;READ CURRENT INTERRUPT STATUS
        JMP     $+2             ;DELAY BETWEEN 8250 OPERATIONS
        CMP     AL,00000010B    ;CHECK IF TRANSMITTER EMPTY INTERRUPT
        JZ      TXINTR          ;JUMP IF TRANSMITTER INTERRUPT
                                ;NOTE THAT IF THE TRANSMITTER INTERRUPT
                                ; IS ACTIVE, READING THE INTERRUPT
                                ; IDENTIFICATION REGISTER WILL CLEAR IT
;
;INPUT (READ) INTERRUPT HANDLER
;
RCINTR:
        ;
        ;READ LINE STATUS TO CLEAR POSSIBLE ERROR FLAGS
        ;
        MOV     DX,ACELSR       ;POINT TO LINE STATUS REGISTER
        IN      AL,DX           ;READ TO CLEAR ERROR FLAGS
        JMP     $+2             ;DELAY BETWEEN 8250 OPERATIONS
        ;
        ;READ DATA AND SAVE IT IN INPUT BUFFER
        ;INDICATE INPUT DATA AVAILABLE
        ;
        MOV     DX,ACERBR       ;POINT TO RECEIVER BUFFER REGISTER
        IN      AL,DX
        JMP     $+2             ;DELAY BETWEEN 8250 OPERATIONS
        MOV     [RECDAT],AL     ;SAVE DATA IN INPUT BUFFER
        MOV     BYTE PTR [RECDF],0FFH  ;INDICATE INPUT DATA AVAILABLE
        JMP     IOEXIT          ;JUMP TO END OF SERVICE ROUTINE
;
;OUTPUT (WRITE) INTERRUPT HANDLER
;
TXINTR:
```

```
        MOV     AL,[TRNDF]          ;TEST DATA AVAILABLE FLAG
        TEST    AL,AL
        JZ      NODATA              ;JUMP IF NO DATA TO TRANSMIT
        CALL    OUTDAT              ;SEND DATA TO 8250 ACE
        JMP     IOEXIT              ;JUMP TO END OF SERVICE ROUTINE
;
;IF AN OUTPUT INTERRUPT OCCURS WHEN NO DATA IS AVAILABLE,
; WE MUST CLEAR IT (IN THE 8259) TO AVOID AN ENDLESS LOOP.  LATER,
; WHEN A CHARACTER BECOMES AVAILABLE, WE CALL THE OUTPUT ROUTINE
; OUTDAT TO SEND THE DATA WITHOUT WAITING FOR AN INTERRUPT.
; THE OUTPUT ROUTINE MUST ALSO SET THE OUTPUT INTERRUPT EXPECTED
; FLAG AFTERWARDS. THIS PROCEDURE OVERCOMES THE PROBLEM OF AN
; UNSERVICED OUTPUT INTERRUPT ASSERTING ITSELF REPEATEDLY,
; WHILE STILL ENSURING THAT OUTPUT INTERRUPTS ARE RECOGNIZED.
;THE PROBLEM IS THAT AN OUTPUT DEVICE MAY REQUEST SERVICE BEFORE
; THE COMPUTER HAS ANYTHING TO SEND (UNLIKE AN INPUT DEVICE THAT
; HAS DATA WHEN IT REQUESTS SERVICE).
;NOTE THAT THE 8250 TRANSMITTER INTERRUPT IS CLEARED AUTOMATICALLY
; BY READING THE INTERRUPT IDENTIFICATION REGISTER, SO ONLY THE
; 8259 LEVEL MUST BE HANDLED IN THIS WAY.
;
NODATA:
        MOV     BYTE PTR [OIE],0    ;DO NOT EXPECT AN INTERRUPT
IOEXIT:
        MOV     DX,PICO             ;CLEAR 8259 INTERRUPT
        MOV     AL,EOI
        OUT     DX,AL
        POP     DX                  ;RESTORE REGISTERS
        POP     AX
        IRET

;*************************************
;ROUTINE: OUTDAT
;PURPOSE: SEND A CHARACTER TO THE UART
;ENTRY: TRNDAT = CHARACTER TO SEND
;EXIT:  NONE
;REGISTERS USED: AL,DX
;**************************************

OUTDAT:
        MOV     DX,ACETHR           ;POINT TO TX HOLDING REGISTER
        MOV     AL,[TRNDAT]         ;GET DATA FROM OUTPUT BUFFER
        OUT     DX,AL               ;SEND DATA TO 8250 ACE
        JMP     $+2                 ;DELAY BETWEEN 8250 OPERATIONS
        MOV     BYTE PTR [TRNDF],0 ;INDICATE OUTPUT BUFFER EMPTY
        MOV     BYTE PTR [OIE],0FFH     ;INDICATE OUTPUT INTERRUPT
                                    ;  EXPECTED - OIE = FF HEX
        RET

;
;TEST 8250 ASYNCHRONOUS COMMUNICATIONS ELEMENT (ACE) BY PUTTING IT
;  IN THE LOOPBACK MODE AND SENDING AND RECEIVING ALL POSSIBLE
;  CHARACTERS (00 THROUGH FF)

ACETST:
        ;
```

```
        ;PUT 8250 ACE IN LOOPBACK MODE
        ;
        MOV     DX,ACEMCR           ;POINT TO MODEM CONTROL REGISTER
        IN      AL,DX               ;GET CURRENT VALUE
        JMP     $+2                 ;DELAY BETWEEN 8250 OPERATIONS
        OR      AL,00010000B        ;ENABLE LOOPBACK MODE
        OUT     DX,AL
        JMP     $+2                 ;DELAY BETWEEN 8250 OPERATIONS
        ;
        ;TEST 8250 BY SENDING AND RECEIVING VALUES 00 THROUGH FF
        ;EXIT IMMEDIATELY WITH CARRY SET IF ERROR
        ;CLEAR CARRY IF TEST SUCCEEDS FOR ALL VALUES
        ;
        SUB     BL,BL               ;START TEST BYTE AT ZERO
TSTCHR:
        MOV     AL,BL               ;GET CHARACTER
        CALL    OUTCH               ;SEND CHARACTER TO 8250 ACE
WTRET:
        CALL    INST                ;WAIT FOR CHARACTER TO RETURN
        JNC     WTRET
        CALL    INCH                ;GET RETURNED CHARACTER
        CMP     AL,BL               ;COMPARE CHARACTER SENT TO ONE
                                    ; RETURNED
        STC                         ;INDICATE POSSIBLE ERROR
        JNE     EXTEST              ;EXIT WITH CARRY SET IF ERROR
                                    ; NOTE: CHARACTER THAT CAUSED ERROR
                                    ; IS IN BL
        INC     BL                  ;PROCEED TO NEXT CHARACTER
        JNZ     TSTCHR              ;CONTINUE UNTIL ALL CHARACTERS TESTED
        CLC                         ;INDICATE NO ERRORS (NOTE BL = 0 HERE)
        ;
        ;DISABLE LOOPBACK MODE AND EXIT
        ;
EXTEST:
        PUSHF                       ;SAVE FLAGS (PARTICULARLY CARRY)
        MOV     DX,ACEMCR           ;POINT TO MODEM CONTROL REGISTER
        IN      AL,DX               ;GET CURRENT VALUE
        JMP     $+2                 ;DELAY BETWEEN 8250 OPERATIONS
        AND     AL,11101111B        ;DISABLE LOOPBACK MODE
        OUT     DX,AL
        JMP     $+2                 ;DELAY BETWEEN 8250 OPERATIONS
        MOV     AL,BL               ;GET CHARACTER THAT CAUSED ERROR
                                    ; OR 0 IF TEST SUCCEEDED
        POPF                        ;RESTORE FLAGS (PARTICULARLY CARRY)
        RET                         ;EXIT (C=0 IF TEST SUCCEEDED, 1 IF NOT)

;
;DATA SECTION
;
RECDAT  DB      ?                   ;RECEIVE DATA
RECDF   DB      ?                   ;RECEIVE DATA FLAG
                                    ;  (0 = NO DATA, FF = DATA AVAILABLE)
TRNDAT  DB      ?                   ;TRANSMIT DATA
TRNDF   DB      ?                   ;TRANSMIT DATA FLAG
                                    ;  (0 = BUFFER EMPTY, FF = BUFFER FULL)
OIE     DB      ?                   ;OUTPUT INTERRUPT EXPECTED
```

```
                                        ; (0 = NO INTERRUPT EXPECTED,
                                        ; FF = INTERRUPT EXPECTED)
;
;       SAMPLE EXECUTION:
;
;CHARACTER EQUATES
ESCAPE  EQU     1BH                     ;ASCII ESCAPE CHARACTER
TESTCH  EQU     'A'                     ;TEST CHARACTER = A

SC9A:
        CALL    INIT                    ;INITIALIZE 8250 ACE, INTERRUPT SYSTEM
        STI                             ;ENABLE CPU INTERRUPTS
        ;
        ;SIMPLE EXAMPLE - READ AND ECHO CHARACTERS
        ; UNTIL AN ESC IS RECEIVED
        ;
LOOP:
        CALL    INCH                    ;READ CHARACTER
        PUSH    AX                      ;SAVE CHARACTER
        CALL    OUTCH                   ;ECHO CHARACTER
        POP     AX                      ;RESTORE CHARACTER
        CMP     AL,ESCAPE               ;IS CHARACTER AN ESCAPE?
        JNE     LOOP                    ;STAY IN LOOP IF NOT
        ;
        ;AN ASYNCHRONOUS EXAMPLE
        ; OUTPUT "A" TO CONSOLE CONTINUOUSLY BUT ALSO LOOK AT
        ; INPUT SIDE, READING AND ECHOING ANY INPUT CHARACTERS.
        ;
ASYNLP:
        ;
        ;OUTPUT AN "A" IF OUTPUT IS NOT BUSY
        ;
        CALL    OUTST                   ;IS OUTPUT BUSY?
        JC      ASYNLP                  ;JUMP IF IT IS
        MOV     AL,TESTCH
        CALL    OUTCH                   ;OUTPUT TEST CHARACTER
        ;
        ;CHECK INPUT PORT
        ;ECHO CHARACTER IF ONE IS AVAILABLE
        ;EXIT ON ESCAPE CHARACTER
        ;
        CALL    INST                    ;IS INPUT DATA AVAILABLE?
        JNC     ASYNLP                  ;JUMP IF NOT (SEND ANOTHER "A")
        CALL    INCH                    ;GET CHARACTER
        CMP     AL,ESCAPE               ;IS IT AN ESCAPE?
        JE      DONE                    ;BRANCH IF IT IS
        CALL    OUTCH                   ;ELSE ECHO CHARACTER
        JMP     ASYNLP                  ;AND CONTINUE

DONE:
        JMP     SC9A                    ;REPEAT TEST

        END
```

9B Unbuffered interrupt-driven I/O using an 8255 PPI (PINTIO)

Performs interrupt-driven input and output using an 8255 PPI and single-character input and output buffers. Consists of the following subroutines:

1. INCH reads a character from the input buffer.
2. INST determines whether the input buffer is empty.
3. OUTCH writes a character into the output buffer.
4. OUTST determines whether the output buffer is full.
5. INIT initializes the 8255 PPI, the interrupt vectors, and the software flags. The flags indicate whether data is available for transfer between the main program and the interrupt service routines.
6. IOSRVC (the actual interrupt service routine) determines which interrupt occurred and provides the proper service. In response to the input interrupt, it reads a character from the 8255 PPI into the input buffer. In response to the output interrupt, it writes a character from the output buffer into the 8255 PPI.

Procedure

1. INCH waits for a character to become available, clears the Data Ready flag (RECDF), and loads the character into register AL.
2. INST sets the Carry flag from the Data Ready flag (RECDF).
3. OUTCH waits for the output buffer to empty, places the character from register AL in the buffer, and sets the character available flag (TRNDF). If an unserviced output interrupt has occurred (i.e. the output device has requested service when no data was available), OUTCH sends the data to the 8255 PPI immediately.
4. OUTST sets Carry from the Character Available flag (TRNDF).
5. INIT clears the software flags, sets up the interrupt vectors, initializes the 8259 interrupt controller, and initializes the 8255 PPI by loading its control register and interrupt enable flip-flops. See Subroutine 8E for more details about initializing 8255 PPIs.
6. IOSRVC examines the 8255 PPI's status and control signals to determine which interrupt occurred. If an input interrupt occurred, it reads the data from the 8255 PPI, saves it in memory, and sets the Data

Ready flag (RECDF). The lack of buffering causes the loss of unread data at this point.

If an output interrupt occurred, IOSRVC determines whether output data is available. If not, it simply clears the output interrupt in the 8259 controller and disables it in the 8255 PPI. If data is available, IOSRVC sends it to the 8255 PPI and clears the Character Available flag (TRNDF).

Most 8086 interrupt systems have a controller that responds to interrupt acknowledgements from the CPU and contains priority, vectoring, and other management logic. The example in the listing uses the popular 8259 Programmable Interrupt Controller (PIC). The 8259 PIC latches interrupt requests from peripheral chips, blocks subsequent requests from the same and lower priority level, and generates source identification to vector the 8086. The service routine must send the 8259 PIC an End-of-Interrupt (EOI) command before concluding to unblock subsequent requests.

Note that when the 8259 is in its usual 'edge detect' mode, it recognizes only transitions on the interrupt lines. Thus, an interrupt from a peripheral chip can cause only a single processor interrupt, no matter how long it remains active. Jigour has described the 8259 device in detail in 'Using the 8259A Programmable Interrupt Controller,' Intel Application Note AP-59, Intel Corporation, Santa Clara, CA, 1979.

The special problem with the output interrupt is that it may occur when no data is available. It cannot be ignored or it will assert itself indefinitely, creating an endless loop. Part of the solution is simply to clear the 8259 PIC interrupt by sending the device an EOI command.

However, this still leaves the 8255 interrupt active, thus blocking input interrupts since they are tied to the same 8259 input. The program must therefore also disable the PPI's output interrupt. This would not be necessary if the two 8255 interrupt outputs were tied to different 8259 inputs. The output interrupt could then remain active without affecting the system. As noted earlier, it would not be recognized again in the 8259's edge detect mode.

But now a new problem arises when output data becomes available. That is, since the interrupt has been cleared in the 8259 and disabled in the 8255, it obviously cannot inform the system that the 8255 PPI is ready to transmit. The solution is a flag that indicates (with a 0 value) that the output interrupt has occurred without being serviced. We call this flag Output Interrupt Expected (OIE).

The initialization routine clears OIE and disables the PPI's output interrupt (since the output device starts out ready for data). The output service routine does the same thing when an output interrupt occurs that cannot be serviced (no data is available). It also sets OIE and re-enables the PPI's output interrupt after sending data to the 8255 PPI (to allow for a possible non-interrupt-driven entry). Now the output routine OUTCH can check OIE to determine whether the output interrupt has already occurred (0 indicates it has, FF hex that it has not). If no output interrupt is expected, OUTCH simply sends the data immediately.

Unserviceable interrupts occur only with output devices, since input devices always have data ready to transfer when they request service. Thus, output devices cause more initialization and sequencing problems in interrupt-driven systems than do input devices.

Entry conditions

1. INCH : none
2. INST: none
3. OUTCH: character to transmit in register AL
4. OUTST: none
5. INIT: none

Exit conditions

1. INCH: character in register AL
2. INST: Carry = 0 if input buffer is empty, 1 if it is full.
3. OUTCH: none
4. OUTST: Carry = 0 if output buffer is empty, 1 if it is full.
5. INIT: none

Registers used

1. INCH: AL, F
2. INST: AL, F
3. OUTCH: AL, DX, F
4. OUTST: AL, F
5. INIT: AL, BX, DX

Execution time

1. INCH: 96 cycles if a character is available
2. INST: 20 cycles
3. OUTCH: 149 cycles if the output buffer is not full and an output interrupt is expected; 91 additional cycles to send the data to the 8255 PPI if no output interrupt is expected.
4. OUTST: 20 cycles
5. INIT: 221 cycles
6. IOSRVC: 159 cycles to service an input interrupt, 172 cycles to service an output interrupt if no data is available, 235 cycles to service an output interrupt if the output buffer is full. These times do not include the 8086's interrupt response time (51 cycles).

Program size 206 bytes

Data memory required 5 bytes anywhere in RAM for the received data (address RECDAT), receive data flag (address RECDF), transmit data (address TRNDAT), transmit data flag (address TRNDF), and output interrupt expected flag (address OIE).

```
;       Title           Simple interrupt input and output using an 8255
;                       PPI and single character buffers
;       Name:           PINTIO
;

;       Purpose:        This program consists of 5 subroutines that
;                       perform interrupt driven input and output using
;                       an 8255 PPI. It also includes an I/O interrupt
;                       service routine.
;
;                       INCH
;                         Read a character.
;                       INST
;                         Determine input status (whether input
;                         buffer is empty).
;                       OUTCH
;                         Write a character.
;                       OUTST
;                         Determine output status (whether output
;                         buffer is full).
;                       INIT
;                         Initialize 8255 PPI and interrupt system.
;                       IOSRVC
```

```
;                       Respond to 8255 PPI I/O interrupts
;
;       Entry:          INCH
;                         No parameters.
;                       INST
;                         No parameters.
;                       OUTCH
;                         Register AL = character to transmit
;                       OUTST
;                         No parameters.
;                       INIT
;                         No parameters.
;
;       Exit:           INCH
;                         Register AL = character.
;                       INST
;                         Carry = 0 if input buffer is empty,
;                         1 if character is available.
;                       OUTCH
;                         No parameters
;                       OUTST
;                         Carry = 0 if output buffer is
;                         empty, 1 if it is full.
;                       INIT
;                         No parameters.
;
;       Registers Used: INCH
;                         AL,F
;                       INST
;                         AL,F
;                       OUTCH
;                         AL,F
;                       OUTST
;                         AL,F
;                       INIT
;                         AL,BX,DX
;
;       Time:           INCH
;                         96 cycles if a character is available
;                       INST
;                         20 cycles
;                       OUTCH
;                         149 cycles if output buffer is not full and
;                         output interrupt is expected
;                       OUTST
;                         20 cycles
;                       INIT
;                         221 cycles
;                       IOSRVC
;                         159 cycles to service an input interrupt,
;                         235 cycles to service an output interrupt
;                         if the output buffer is full, 172 cycles
;                         to service an output interrupt if no data
;                         is available.
;
;       Size:           Program 206 bytes
```

```
;                       Data 5 bytes
;

;
;ESTABLISH SEGMENT ADDRESS FOR USE IN INTERRUPT VECTORS
;
CSEG    EQU     0F81H           ;ARBITRARY BASE ADDRESS OF CODE SEGMENT
                                ;USUALLY ESTABLISHED IN A SEGMENT
                                ; STATEMENT NOT SHOWN HERE
;
;INTERRUPT VECTOR
;
PRLLIV  EQU     003CH           ;PARALLEL I/O INTERRUPT VECTOR
;
;8255 PPI EQUATES
; 8255 PPI IS PROGRAMMED FOR
;  BOTH PORTS IN MODE 1 (STROBED INPUT AND OUTPUT)
;  PORT A INPUT
;  PORT B OUTPUT
;  PORT C HANDSHAKE SIGNALS
;ARBITRARY 8255 PPI PORT ADDRESSES
;
PPIA    EQU     0FF00H          ;PORT A DATA
PPIB    EQU     0FF01H          ;PORT B DATA
PPIC    EQU     0FF02H          ;PORT C DATA
PPICTRL EQU     0FF03H          ;CONTROL PORT
;
;8255 PPI CONTROL BYTES
;
OPMODE  EQU     10110100B       ;CONTROL BYTE TO OPERATE BOTH PORTS IN
                                ; MODE 1, PORT A INPUT, PORT B OUTPUT
PAIE    EQU     00001001B       ;ENABLE A INTERRUPT - SET BIT 4 OF C
PAID    EQU     00001000B       ;DISABLE A INTERRUPT - CLEAR BIT 4 OF C
PBIE    EQU     00000101B       ;ENABLE B INTERRUPT - SET BIT 2 OF C
PBID    EQU     00000100B       ;DISABLE B INTERRUPT - CLEAR BIT 2 OF C
;
;8259 PROGRAMMABLE INTERRUPT CONTROLLER (PIC) EQUATES
; 8259 PIC IS PROGRAMMED FOR
;  SINGLE DEVICE (RATHER THAN MULTIPLE 8259'S)
;  FULLY NESTED MODE
;  ALL INTERRUPTS ENABLED
;  INTERRUPT LEVELS 8-15
;ARBITRARY 8259 PIC PORT ADDRESSES
;
PIC0    EQU     20H             ;PIC PORT 1
PIC1    EQU     21H             ;PIC PORT 2

;8259 INITIALIZATION COMMAND BYTES ICW1, ICW2, AND ICW4 (NO ICW3
;  NEEDED IN SINGLE 8259 SYSTEMS)
ICW1    EQU     00010011B       ;BIT 0 = 1 (ICW4 NEEDED IN 8086 SYSTEMS)
                                ;BIT 1 = 1 (SINGLE 8259)
                                ;BIT 2 = 0 (NOT USED WITH 8086/8088)
                                ;BIT 3 = 0 (EDGE DETECT)
                                ;BIT 4 = 1 (FIXED)
                                ;BITS 5,6,7 = 000 (NOT USED IN 8086/88)
ICW2    EQU     00001000B       ;BITS 7-3 = 00001 (5 MSB'S OF SOURCE
```

```
                                        ; IDENTIFICATION CODE)
                                        ;BITS 2-0 = 000 (NOT USED)
ICW4    EQU     00001001B               ;BIT 0 = 1 (8086/88 SYSTEM)
                                        ;BIT 1 = 0 (NO AUTOMATIC END OF
                                        ;  INTERRUPT)
                                        ;BIT 2 = 0 (DON'T CARE)
                                        ;BIT 3 = 1 (BUFFERED DATA BUS)
                                        ;BIT 4 = 0 (NO CASCADING)
                                        ;BITS 7-5 = 000 (NOT USED)
IMASK   EQU     00111100B               ;MASK OUT LEVELS 2 THROUGH 5

;8259 OPERATING COMMAND BYTE
EOI     EQU     00100000B               ;END OF INTERRUPT COMMAND BYTE

;
;READ A CHARACTER FROM INPUT BUFFER
;
INCH:
        CALL    INST                    ;GET INPUT STATUS
        JNC     INCH                    ;WAIT IF NO CHARACTER AVAILABLE
        PUSHF                           ;SAVE CURRENT INTERRUPT STATUS
        CLI                             ;DISABLE INTERRUPTS WHILE CHANGING
                                        ; SOFTWARE FLAG
        MOV     BYTE PTR [RECDF],0          ;INDICATE INPUT BUFFER EMPTY
        MOV     AL,[RECDAT]             ;GET CHARACTER FROM INPUT BUFFER
        POPF                            ;RESTORE PREVIOUS INTERRUPT STATUS
        RET

;
;DETERMINE INPUT STATUS (CARRY = 1 IF DATA AVAILABLE, 0 IF NOT)
;
INST:
        MOV     AL,[RECDF]              ;GET DATA READY FLAG
        SHR     AL,1                    ;SET CARRY FROM DATA READY FLAG
                                        ; CARRY = 1 IF CHARACTER AVAILABLE
        RET

;
;WRITE A CHARACTER INTO OUTPUT BUFFER
;
OUTCH:
        PUSH    AX                      ;SAVE CHARACTER TO WRITE
        ;
        ;WAIT FOR OUTPUT BUFFER TO EMPTY, STORE NEXT CHARACTER
WAITOC:
        CALL    OUTST                   ;GET OUTPUT STATUS
        JC      WAITOC                  ;WAIT IF OUTPUT BUFFER FULL
        POP     AX                      ;RESTORE CHARACTER TO WRITE
        PUSHF                           ;SAVE CURRENT INTERRUPT STATUS
        CLI                             ;DISABLE INTERRUPTS WHILE WORKING WITH
                                        ; SOFTWARE FLAGS
        MOV     [TRNDAT],AL             ;STORE CHARACTER IN OUTPUT BUFFER
        MOV     BYTE PTR [TRNDF],0FFH   ;INDICATE OUTPUT BUFFER FULL
        MOV     AL,[OIE]
        TEST    AL,AL                   ;TEST OUTPUT INTERRUPT EXPECTED FLAG
        JNZ     EXITOT                  ;EXIT IF OUTPUT INTERRUPT EXPECTED
```

```
        CALL    OUTDAT          ;SEND CHARACTER IMMEDIATELY IF
                                ; NO OUTPUT INTERRUPT EXPECTED
EXITOT:
        POPF                    ;RESTORE PREVIOUS INTERRUPT STATUS
        RET


;
;DETERMINE OUTPUT STATUS (CARRY = 1 IF OUTPUT BUFFER FULL)
;
OUTST:
        MOV     AL,[TRNDF]      ;GET TRANSMIT FLAG
        SHR     AL,1            ;SET CARRY FROM TRANSMIT FLAG
        RET                     ;CARRY = 1 IF BUFFER FULL


;
;INITIALIZE INTERRUPT SYSTEM AND 8255 PPI
;
INIT:
        ;
        ;DISABLE INTERRUPTS DURING INITIALIZATION BUT SAVE
        ;  PREVIOUS STATE OF INTERRUPT FLAG
        ;
        PUSHF                   ;SAVE CURRENT INTERRUPT FLAG
        CLI                     ;DISABLE INTERRUPTS DURING
                                ; INITIALIZATION
        ;
        ;INITIALIZE SOFTWARE FLAGS
        ;
        SUB     AL,AL
        MOV     [RECDF],AL      ;NO INPUT DATA AVAILABLE
        MOV     [TRNDF],AL      ;OUTPUT BUFFER EMPTY
        MOV     [OIE],AL        ;INDICATE NO OUTPUT INTERRUPT NEEDED
                                ; 8255 READY INITIALLY
        ;
        ;INITIALIZE INTERRUPT VECTOR
        ;
        PUSH    DS              ;SAVE CURRENT DATA SEGMENT
        SUB     AX,AX           ;ACCESS INTERRUPT VECTOR IN SEGMENT
                                ;  0
        MOV     DS,AX
        MOV     AX,OFFSET IOSRVC   ;GET OFFSET FOR SERVICE ROUTINE
        MOV     BX,PRLLIV       ;GET INTERRUPT VECTOR LOCATION
        MOV     [BX],AX         ;LOAD OFFSET INTO INTERRUPT VECTOR
        MOV     AX,CSEG         ;GET CODE SEGMENT NUMBER
        MOV     [BX+2],AX       ;LOAD CODE SEGMENT NUMBER INTO
                                ; INTERRUPT VECTOR
        POP     DS              ;RESTORE CURRENT DATA SEGMENT
        ;
        ;INITIALIZE 8259 INTERRUPT CONTROLLER
        ;
        MOV     DX,PIC0         ;SEND FIRST COMMAND BYTE TO PIC PORT 0
        MOV     AL,ICW1
        OUT     DX,AL
        MOV     DX,PIC1         ;SEND SECOND COMMAND BYTE TO PIC PORT 1
```

```
        MOV     AL,ICW2
        OUT     DX,AL
        MOV     AL,ICW4         ;SEND FINAL COMMAND BYTE TO PIC PORT 1
        OUT     DX,AL
        MOV     AL,IMASK        ;MASK INTERRUPT LEVELS 2 THROUGH 5
        OUT     DX,AL
        ;
        ;INITIALIZE 8255 PPI
        ;
        MOV     AL,OPMODE       ;BOTH PORTS IN STROBED I/O MODE (1)
        MOV     DX,PPICTRL      ;  PORT A INPUT, PORT B OUTPUT
        OUT     DX,AL
        ;
        ;ENABLE 8255 PPI INPUT INTERRUPT, DISABLE OUTPUT INTERRUPT
        ;
        MOV     AL,PAIE         ;ENABLE PORT A (INPUT) INTERRUPT
        OUT     DX,AL
        MOV     AL,PBID         ;DISABLE PORT B (OUTPUT) INTERRUPT
        OUT     DX,AL           ; (SINCE PPI SURELY STARTS OUT READY
                                ;  READY TO TRANSMIT)
        POPF                    ;RESTORE FLAGS (REENABLES INTERRUPTS
                                ; IF THEY WERE ENABLED WHEN INIT WAS
                                ; CALLED)
        RET

;
;PARALLEL I/O INTERRUPT HANDLER
;
IOSRVC:
        ;
        ;IDENTIFY INTERRUPT SOURCE BY EXAMINING STATUS/CONTROL PORT
        ; (8255 PORT C)
        ;
        PUSH    AX              ;SAVE REGISTERS
        PUSH    DX
        MOV     DX,PPIC         ;POINT TO STATUS/CONTROL PORT
        IN      AL,DX           ;READ STATUS/CONTROL PORT
        TEST    AL,00000001B    ;BIT 0 = 1 IF WRITE INTERRUPT
        JNZ     WRHDLR          ;JUMP IF WRITE INTERRUPT
        TEST    AL,00001000B    ;BIT 3 = 1 IF READ INTERRUPT
        JZ      IOEXIT          ;EXIT IF NEITHER ONE OCCURRED
                                ;THIS TEST PROTECTS AGAINST FALSE
                                ; INTERRUPTS
;
;INPUT (READ) INTERRUPT HANDLER
;
RDHDLR:
        ;
        ;READ DATA AND SAVE IT IN INPUT BUFFER
        ;INDICATE INPUT DATA AVAILABLE
        ;
        MOV     DX,PPIA         ;READ DATA FROM 8255 PPI PORT A
        IN      AL,DX
        MOV     [RECDAT],AL     ;SAVE DATA IN INPUT BUFFER
        MOV     BYTE PTR [RECDF],0FFH   ;INDICATE CHARACTER AVAILABLE
        JMP     IOEXIT          ;EXIT INTERRUPT SERVICE ROUTINE
```

```
;
;OUTPUT (WRITE) INTERRUPT HANDLER
;
WRHDLR:
        ;
        ;CHECK IF DATA IS AVAILABLE
        ;IF SO, SEND IT TO 8255 PPI
        ;
        MOV     AL,[TRNDF]          ;TEST DATA AVAILABLE FLAG
        TEST    AL,AL
        JZ      NODATA              ;JUMP IF NO DATA TO TRANSMIT
        CALL    OUTDAT              ;SEND DATA TO 8255 PPI
        JMP     IOEXIT              ;EXIT INTERRUPT SERVICE ROUTINE
;
;IF AN OUTPUT INTERRUPT OCCURS WHEN NO DATA IS AVAILABLE,
; WE MUST CLEAR IT (IN THE 8259) TO AVOID AN ENDLESS LOOP.  FURTHERMORE,
; WE MUST DISABLE IT (IN THE 8255) TO UNBLOCK INPUT INTERRUPTS.
; LATER, WHEN A CHARACTER BECOMES AVAILABLE, WE NEED TO KNOW THAT AN
; OUTPUT INTERRUPT HAS OCCURRED WITHOUT BEING SERVICED.  THE KEY
; TO DOING THIS IS THE OUTPUT INTERRUPT EXPECTED FLAG OIE.  THIS FLAG IS
; CLEARED WHEN AN OUTPUT INTERRUPT HAS OCCURRED BUT HAS NOT BEEN
; SERVICED.  IT IS ALSO CLEARED INITIALLY SINCE THE 8255 PPI STARTS
; OUT READY.  OIE IS SET WHENEVER DATA IS ACTUALLY SENT TO THE PPI.
; THUS THE OUTPUT ROUTINE OUTCH CAN CHECK OIE TO DETERMINE WHETHER
; TO SEND THE DATA IMMEDIATELY OR WAIT FOR AN OUTPUT INTERRUPT.
;THE PROBLEM IS THAT AN OUTPUT DEVICE MAY REQUEST SERVICE BEFORE
; THE COMPUTER HAS ANYTHING TO SEND (UNLIKE AN INPUT DEVICE THAT
; HAS DATA WHEN IT REQUESTS SERVICE).  THE OIE FLAG SOLVES THE
; PROBLEM OF AN UNSERVICED OUTPUT INTERRUPT ASSERTING ITSELF
; REPEATEDLY, WHILE STILL ENSURING THE RECOGNITION OF OUTPUT
; INTERRUPTS.
;
NODATA:
        MOV     BYTE PTR [OIE],0    ;DO NOT EXPECT AN INTERRUPT
        MOV     DX,PPICTRL          ;DISABLE 8255 PPI OUTPUT INTERRUPT
        MOV     AL,PBID
        OUT     DX,AL
IOEXIT:
        MOV     DX,PICO             ;CLEAR 8259 INTERRUPT
        MOV     AL,EOI
        OUT     DX,AL
        POP     DX                  ;RESTORE REGISTERS
        POP     AX
        IRET

;*************************************
;ROUTINE: OUTDAT
;PURPOSE: SEND CHARACTER TO 8255 PPI
;ENTRY: TRNDAT = CHARACTER TO SEND
;EXIT:  NONE
;REGISTERS USED: AL,DX
;**************************************

OUTDAT:
        MOV     DX,PPIB
        MOV     AL,[TRNDAT]         ;GET DATA FROM OUTPUT BUFFER
```

```
        OUT     DX,AL               ;SEND DATA TO 8255 PPI
        MOV     BYTE PTR [TRNDF],0 ;INDICATE OUTPUT BUFFER EMPTY
        MOV     BYTE PTR [OIE],0FFH ;INDICATE OUTPUT INTERRUPT EXPECTED
                                    ;  OIE = FF HEX
        MOV     DX,PPICTRL          ;ENABLE 8255 PPI OUTPUT INTERRUPT
        MOV     AL,PBIE             ; (IN CASE IT WAS DISABLED EARLIER)
        OUT     DX,AL
        RET

;DATA SECTION
RECDAT  DB      ?                   ;RECEIVE DATA
RECDF   DB      ?                   ;RECEIVE DATA FLAG (0 = NO DATA,
                                    ;  FF = DATA)
TRNDAT  DB      ?                   ;TRANSMIT DATA
TRNDF   DB      ?                   ;TRANSMIT DATA FLAG
                                    ;  (0 = BUFFER EMPTY, FF = BUFFER FULL)
OIE     DB      ?                   ;OUTPUT INTERRUPT EXPECTED
                                    ; ( 0 = INTERRUPT OCCURRED WITHOUT
                                    ;  BEING SERVICED, FF = INTERRUPT
                                    ;  SERVICED)
;
;       SAMPLE EXECUTION:
;
;CHARACTER EQUATES
;
ESCAPE  EQU     1BH                 ;ASCII ESCAPE CHARACTER
TESTCH  EQU     'A'                 ;TEST CHARACTER = A

SC9B:
        CALL    INIT                ;INITIALIZE 8255 PPI, INTERRUPT SYSTEM
        STI                         ;ENABLE INTERRUPTS
        ;
        ;SIMPLE EXAMPLE - READ AND ECHO CHARACTERS
        ; UNTIL AN ESC IS RECEIVED
        ;
LOOP:
        CALL    INCH                ;READ CHARACTER
        PUSH    AX                  ;SAVE CHARACTER
        CALL    OUTCH               ;ECHO CHARACTER
        POP     AX                  ;RESTORE CHARACTER
        CMP     AL,ESCAPE           ;IS CHARACTER AN ESCAPE?
        JNE     LOOP                ;STAY IN LOOP IF NOT
        ;
        ;AN ASYNCHRONOUS EXAMPLE
        ; OUTPUT "A" TO CONSOLE CONTINUOUSLY BUT ALSO LOOK AT
        ; INPUT SIDE, READING AND ECHOING INPUT CHARACTERS.
        ;
ASYNLP:
        ;OUTPUT AN "A" IF OUTPUT IS NOT BUSY
        CALL    OUTST               ;IS OUTPUT BUSY?
        JC      ASYNLP              ;BRANCH (WAIT) IF IT IS
        MOV     AL,TESTCH
        CALL    OUTCH               ;OUTPUT TEST CHARACTER
        ;
        ;CHECK INPUT PORT
```

```
        ;ECHO CHARACTER IF ONE IS AVAILABLE
        ;EXIT ON ESCAPE CHARACTER
        ;
        CALL    INST            ;IS INPUT DATA AVAILABLE?
        JNC     ASYNLP          ;BRANCH IF NOT (SEND ANOTHER "A")
        CALL    INCH            ;GET CHARACTER
        CMP     AL,ESCAPE       ;IS IT AN ESCAPE?
        JE      DONE            ;BRANCH IF IT IS
        CALL    OUTCH           ;ELSE ECHO CHARACTER
        JMP     ASYNLP          ;AND CONTINUE

DONE:
        JMP     SC9B            ;REPEAT TEST

        END
```

9C Buffered interrupt-driven I/O using an 8250 ACE (SINTB)

Performs interrupt-driven input and output using an 8250 ACE (Asynchronous Communications Element or UART) and multiple-character buffers. Consists of the following subroutines:

1. INCH reads a character from the input buffer.

2. INST determines whether the input buffer is empty.

3. OUTCH writes a character into the output buffer.

4. OUTST determines whether the output buffer is full.

5. INIT initializes the 8250 ACE, the buffers, and the interrupt system (vector and controller).

6. IOSRVC (the interrupt service routine) identifies and services the interrupt. In response to the input interrupt, it reads a character from the 8250 ACE into the input buffer. In response to the output interrupt, it writes a character from the output buffer into the 8250 ACE.

Procedure

1. INCH waits for a character to become available, gets the character from the head of the input buffer, moves the head of the buffer up one position, and decreases the input buffer counter by 1.

2. INST clears Carry if the input buffer counter is 0 and sets it otherwise.

3. OUTCH waits until there is space in the output buffer (i.e. until the output buffer is not full), stores the character at the tail of the buffer, moves the tail up one position, and increases the output buffer counter by 1.

4. OUTST sets Carry if the output buffer counter is equal to the buffer's length (i.e. if the output buffer is full) and clears Carry otherwise.

5. INIT first initializes the 8250 ACE by placing values in its divisor latch and line control register. Next it clears the buffer counters and sets all buffer pointers to the buffers' base addresses. It then sets up the interrupt vector and initializes the 8259 interrupt controller. See Subroutine 8E for more details about initializing 8250 ACEs. INIT also clears the output interrupt expected flag, indicating that the ACE is initially ready to transmit data, although it cannot cause an output interrupt.

6. IOSRVC examines the ACE's interrupt identification vector to determine whether the interrupt is from the transmitter (bits 0–2 = 010). If not, it assumes the interrupt is from the receiver. It then reads the data from the 8250 ACE and checks whether the input buffer is full. If it is, IOSRVC simply discards the character. If not, IOSRVC adds 1 to the input buffer counter, stores the character at the tail of the input buffer, and moves the tail of the buffer up one position.

If the output interrupt occurred, IOSRVC determines whether data is available. If it is, IOSRVC takes the character from the head of the output buffer and sends it to the 8250 ACE. It then moves the head up one position and subtracts 1 from the output buffer counter. If data is not available, the program simply clears the output interrupt (in the 8259 interrupt controller). Note that reading the interrupt identification register in an 8250 ACE is sufficient by itself to clear a transmitter interrupt. Thus clearing the 8259 interrupt removes all traces of the transmitter interrupt from the system, allowing the recognition of later receiver or transmitter interrupts on the same line.

The new problem with multiple-character buffers is the management of queues. The main program must read the data in the order in which the input interrupt service routine receives it. Similarly, the output interrupt service routine must send the data in the order in which the main program stores it. Thus we have the following requirements for handling input:

1. The main program must know whether the input buffer is empty.

2. If the input buffer is not empty, the main program must know where the oldest character is (i.e. the one that was received first).

3. The input interrupt service routine must know whether the input buffer is full.

4. If the input buffer is not full, the input interrupt service routine must know where the next empty place is (i.e. where it should store the new character).

The output interrupt service routine and the main program have similar requirements for the output buffer, although the roles of sender and receiver are reversed.

We meet requirements 1 and 3 by maintaining a counter ICNT. INIT initializes ICNT to 0, the interrupt service routine adds 1 to it whenever it receives a character (assuming the buffer is not full), and the main program subtracts 1 from it whenever it removes a character from the buffer. Thus the main program can determine whether the input buffer is empty by checking if ICNT is 0. Similarly, the interrupt service routine can determine whether the input buffer is full by checking if ICNT is equal to the size of the buffer.

We meet requirements 2 and 4 by maintaining two pointers, IHEAD and ITAIL, defined as follows:

1. ITAIL is the address of the next empty location in the input buffer.
2. IHEAD is the address of the oldest character in the input buffer.

INIT initializes IHEAD and ITAIL to the base address of the input buffer. Whenever the interrupt service routine receives a character, it puts it in the buffer at ITAIL and moves ITAIL up one position (assuming that the buffer is not full). Whenever the main program reads a character, it removes it from the buffer at IHEAD and moves IHEAD up one position. Thus IHEAD 'chases' ITAIL across the buffer with the service routine entering characters at one end (the tail) while the main program removes them from the other end (the head).

The occupied part of the buffer thus could start and end anywhere. If either IHEAD or ITAIL reaches the physical end of the buffer, we simply set it back to the base address. Thus we allow wraparound on the buffer; i.e. the occupied part of the buffer could start near the end (say, at byte #195 of a 200-byte buffer) and continue back past the beginning (say, to byte #10). Then IHEAD would be BASE+194, ITAIL would be BASE+9, and the buffer would contain 15 characters occupying addresses BASE+194 through BASE+199 and BASE through BASE+8.

Entry conditions

1. INCH: none
2. INST: none
3. OUTCH: character to transmit in register AL.
4. OUTST: none
5. INIT: none

Exit conditions

1. INCH: character in register AL.
2. INST: Carry = 0 if input buffer is empty, 1 if a character is available
3. OUTCH: none
4. OUTST: Carry = 0 if output buffer is not full, 1 if it is full
5. INIT: none

Registers used

1. INCH: AL, BX, F
2. INST: AL, F
3. OUTCH: AL, BX, DX, F
4. OUTST: F
5. INIT: AL, BX, DX

Execution time

1. INCH: approximately 180 cycles if a character is available
2. INST: 27 cycles
3. OUTCH: approximately 210 cycles if the output buffer is not full and an output interrupt is expected. Approximately an additional 149 cycles if no output interrupt is expected.
4. OUTST: 51 cycles
5. INIT: 515 cycles
6. IOSRVC: 322 cycles to service an input interrupt if a character is ready and the input buffer is not full, 342 cycles to service an output interrupt if the output buffer is not empty, 187 cycles to service an output interrupt if the buffer is empty. These times do not include the 8086's interrupt response time (51 cycles).

Program size 374 bytes

Data memory required 11 bytes anywhere in RAM for the heads and tails of the input and output buffers (2 bytes starting at addresses IHEAD, ITAIL, OHEAD, and OTAIL, respectively), the number of characters in the buffers (2 bytes at addresses ICNT and OCNT), and the output interrupt expected flag (address OIE). This does not include the actual input and output buffers. The input buffer starts at address IBUF and its size is IBSZ; the output buffer starts at address OBUF and its size is OBSZ.

```
;       Title           Simple interrupt input and output using an 8250
;                       ACE and multiple character buffers.
;       Name:           SINTB
;
;
;       Purpose:        This program includes 5 subroutines that
;                       perform interrupt driven input and output using
;                       an 8250 UART.  It also contains an I/O
;                       interrupt service routine and a loopback test
;                       routine for the 8250 device.
;
;                       INCH
;                         Read a character.
;                       INST
;                         Determine input status (whether input
;                         buffer is empty).
;                       OUTCH
;                         Write a character.
;                       OUTST
;                         Determine output status (whether output
;                         buffer is full).
;                       INIT
;                         Initialize UART and interrupt system
;                       IOSRVC
;                         Respond to 8250 ACE I/O interrupts
;
;
;       Entry:          INCH
;                         No parameters.
;                       INST
;                         No parameters.
;                       OUTCH
;                         Register AL = character to transmit
;                       OUTST
;                         No parameters.
;                       INIT
;                         No parameters.
;
;       Exit:           INCH
;                         Register AL = character received
;                       INST
;                         Carry = 0 if input buffer is empty,
;                         1 if character is available.
;                       OUTCH
```

```
;                       No parameters
;                     OUTST
;                       Carry = 0 if output buffer is empty,
;                       1 if it is full.
;                     INIT
;                       No parameters.
;
;       Registers Used: INCH
;                       AL,BX,F
;                     INST
;                       AL,F
;                     OUTCH
;                       AL,BX,DX,F
;                     OUTST
;                       F
;                     INIT
;                       AL,BX,DX
;
;       Time:         INCH
;                       180 cycles if a character is available
;                     INST
;                       27 cycles
;                     OUTCH
;                       210 cycles if output buffer is empty and
;                       output interrupt is expected
;                     OUTST
;                       51 cycles
;                     INIT
;                       515 cycles
;                     IOSRVC
;                       322 cycles to service an input interrupt if
;                       a character is ready and the input buffer
;                       is not full, 342 cycles to service an output
;                       interrupt if the output buffer is not empty,
;                       187 cycles to service an output interrupt if
;                       the output buffer is empty.  These times
;                       do not include the 8086's interrupt response
;                       time (51 cycles).
;
;       Size:         Program  374 bytes
;                     Data     11 bytes
;


;
;ESTABLISH SEGMENT ADDRESS FOR USE IN INTERRUPT VECTORS
;
CSEG      EQU      0F81H              ;ARBITRARY BASE ADDRESS OF CODE
                                      ; SEGMENT - USUALLY ESTABLISHED
                                      ; IN A SEGMENT STATEMENT NOT
                                      ; SHOWN HERE
;
;8250 ACE (UART) EQUATES
; 8250 IS PROGRAMMED FOR
;  1200 BAUD ASSUMING A 1.8432 MHZ OSCILLATOR INPUT (AS ON IBM PC)
;  8-BIT CHARACTERS
;  2 STOP BITS
```

```
;  NO PARITY
;ARBITRARY 8250 ACE PORT ADDRESSES (TAKEN FROM IBM PC)
;
ACEBASE EQU     3F8H            ;ACE BASE ADDRESS
ACERBR  EQU     3F8H            ;ACE RECEIVER BUFFER REGISTER
ACETHR  EQU     3F8H            ;ACE TRANSMITTER HOLDING REGISTER
ACEIER  EQU     3F9H            ;ACE INTERRUPT ENABLE REGISTER
ACEIIR  EQU     3FAH            ;ACE INTERRUPT IDENTIFICATION REGISTER
ACELCR  EQU     3FBH            ;ACE LINE CONTROL REGISTER
ACEMCR  EQU     3FCH            ;ACE MODEM CONTROL REGISTER
ACELSR  EQU     3FDH            ;ACE LINE STATUS REGISTER
ACEMSR  EQU     3FEH            ;ACE MODEM STATUS REGISTER
ACESCR  EQU     3FFH            ;ACE SCRATCHPAD REGISTER
ACEDLL  EQU     3F8H            ;ACE DIVISOR LATCH (LSB)
ACEDLM  EQU     3F9H            ;ACE DIVISOR LATCH (MSB)

;INTERRUPT VECTOR
ASYNIV  EQU     0030H           ;ASYNCHRONOUS I/O INTERRUPT VECTOR

;8250 LINE CONTROL INSTRUCTION
LCMODE  EQU     00000111B       ;BITS 1,0 = 11 (8 BIT WORD LENGTH)
                                ;BIT 2 = 1 (2 STOP BITS)
                                ;BIT 3 = 0 (PARITY DISABLED)
                                ;BITS 5,4 = 00 (DON'T CARE)
                                ;BIT 6 = 0 (DISABLE BREAK)
                                ;BITS 7 = 0 (POINT TO DATA REGISTER)
;8250 MODEM CONTROL INSTRUCTION
MCMODE  EQU     00000011B       ;BIT 0 = 1 (SET DATA TERMINAL READY)
                                ;BIT 1 = 1 (SET REQUEST TO SEND)
                                ;BITS 3,2 = 00 (DON'T CARE)
                                ;BIT 4 = 0 (DISABLE INTERNAL LOOPBACK)
                                ;BITS 7,6,5 = 000 (DON'T CARE)

;8250 INTERRUPT ENABLE INSTRUCTION
INTCMD  EQU     00000011B       ;BIT 0 = 1 (ENABLE RECEIVE DATA
                                ; INTERRUPT)
                                ;BIT 1 = 1 (ENABLE TRANSMITTER EMPTY
                                ; INTERRUPT)
                                ;BIT 2 = 0 (DISABLE LINE STATUS
                                ; INTERRUPT)
                                ;BIT 3 = 0 (DISABLE MODEM STATUS
                                ; INTERRUPT)
                                ;BITS 4-7 = 0 (DON'T CARE)

;8250 DIVISOR LATCH ACCESS INSTRUCTION
DLADDR  EQU     10000000B       ;BIT 7 = 1 (POINT TO DIVISOR LATCH)

;8250 DIVISOR LATCH VALUE (96 FOR 1200 BAUD ASSUMING A 1.8432 MHZ
;  OSCILLATOR INPUT
DIVLS   EQU     96              ;LESS SIGNIFICANT BYTE OF DIVISOR
                                ;OUTPUT FREQUENCY EQUALS THE INPUT
                                ; FREQUENCY/(BAUD DIVISOR X 16)
                                ; = 1.8432 MHZ/(96 X 16) = 1200 BAUD
DIVMS   EQU     0               ;MORE SIGNIFICANT BYTE OF DIVISOR

;8259 PROGRAMMABLE INTERRUPT CONTROLLER (PIC) EQUATES
```

```
; 8259 PIC IS PROGRAMMED FOR
;  SINGLE DEVICE (RATHER THAN MULTIPLE 8259'S)
;  FULLY NESTED MODE
;  ALL INTERRUPTS ENABLED
;  INTERRUPT LEVELS 8-15
;ARBITRARY 8259 PIC PORT ADDRESSES
PIC0    EQU     20H             ;PIC PORT 1
PIC1    EQU     21H             ;PIC PORT 2

;8259 INITIALIZATION COMMAND BYTES ICW1, ICW2, AND ICW4 (NO ICW3
;  NEEDED IN SINGLE 8259 SYSTEMS)
ICW1    EQU     00010011B       ;BIT 0 = 1 (ICW4 NEEDED IN 8086 SYSTEMS)
                                ;BIT 1 = 1 (SINGLE 8259)
                                ;BIT 2 = 0 (NOT USED WITH 8086/8088)
                                ;BIT 3 = 0 (EDGE DETECT)
                                ;BIT 4 = 1 (FIXED)
                                ;BITS 5,6,7 = 000 (NOT USED IN 8086/88)
ICW2    EQU     00001000B       ;BITS 7-3 = 00001 (5 MSB'S OF SOURCE
                                ;  IDENTIFICATION CODE)
                                ;BITS 2-0 = 000 (NOT USED)
ICW4    EQU     00001001B       ;BIT 0 = 1 (8086/88 SYSTEM)
                                ;BIT 1 = 0 (NO AUTOMATIC END OF
                                ;  INTERRUPT)
                                ;BIT 2 = 0 (DON'T CARE)
                                ;BIT 3 = 1 (BUFFERED DATA BUS)
                                ;BIT 4 = 0 (NO CASCADING)
                                ;BITS 7-5 = 000 (NOT USED)
;8259 OPERATING COMMAND BYTE
EOI     EQU     00100000B       ;END OF INTERRUPT COMMAND BYTE

;       READ A CHARACTER FROM INPUT BUFFER
;
INCH:
        CALL    INST            ;GET INPUT STATUS
        JNC     INCH            ;WAIT IF NO CHARACTER AVAILABLE
        PUSHF                   ;SAVE CURRENT INTERRUPT STATUS
        CLI                     ;DISABLE INTERRUPTS WHILE CHANGING
                                ;  SOFTWARE FLAG
        DEC     BYTE PTR [ICNT] ;REDUCE INPUT BUFFER COUNT BY 1
        MOV     BX,[IHEAD]      ;GET CHARACTER FROM HEAD OF INPUT BUFFER
        MOV     AL,[BX]
        CALL    INCIPTR         ;MOVE HEAD POINTER UP 1 WITH WRAPAROUND
        MOV     [IHEAD],BX
        POPF                    ;RESTORE PREVIOUS INTERRUPT STATUS
        RET

;
;       DETERMINE INPUT STATUS (CARRY = 1 IF DATA AVAILABLE, 0 IF NOT)
;
INST:
        MOV     AL,[ICNT]       ;TEST INPUT BUFFER COUNT
        TEST    AL,AL           ;NOTE THAT TEST ALWAYS CLEARS CARRY
        JZ      EXINST          ;BRANCH (EXIT) IF BUFFER EMPTY
        STC                     ;SET CARRY TO INDICATE DATA AVAILABLE
EXINST:
        RET
```

```
;
;	WRITE A CHARACTER INTO OUTPUT BUFFER
;	SEND IT ON TO ACE IF NO OUTPUT INTERRUPT EXPECTED
;
OUTCH:

;WAIT UNTIL OUTPUT BUFFER NOT FULL, THEN STORE NEXT CHARACTER
WAITOC:
	CALL	OUTST		;GET OUTPUT STATUS
	JC	WAITOC		;WAIT IF OUTPUT BUFFER FULL
	PUSHF			;SAVE CURRENT INTERRUPT STATUS
	CLI			;DISABLE INTERRUPTS WHILE WORKING
				;  WITH SOFTWARE FLAGS
	INC	BYTE PTR [OCNT]	;INCREASE OUTPUT BUFFER COUNT BY 1
	MOV	BX,[OTAIL]	;POINT AT NEXT EMPTY BYTE IN BUFFER
	MOV	[BX],AL		;STORE CHARACTER AT TAIL OF BUFFER
	CALL	INCOPTR		;MOVE TAIL POINTER UP 1 WITH WRAPAROUND
	MOV	[OTAIL],BX
	MOV	AL,[OIE]	;TEST OUTPUT INTERRUPT EXPECTED FLAG
	TEST	AL,AL
	JNZ	EXITOC		;BRANCH IF OUTPUT INTERRUPT EXPECTED
	CALL	OUTDAT		;OTHERWISE, SEND CHARACTER TO ACE NOW
EXITOC: POPF			;RESTORE PREVIOUS INTERRUPT STATUS
	RET

;
;	DETERMINE OUTPUT STATUS (CARRY = 1 IF OUTPUT BUFFER FULL)
;
OUTST:
	PUSH	AX		;SAVE REGISTER AX
	MOV	AL,SZOBUF-1	;GET OUTPUT BUFFER SIZE MINUS 1
	CMP	AL,[OCNT]	;IS OUTPUT BUFFER FULL?
	POP	AX		;RESTORE REGISTER AX
	RET			;CARRY = 1 IF BUFFER FULL, 0 IF NOT

;
;INITIALIZE INTERRUPT SYSTEM AND 8250 ACE
;
INIT:
	;
	;DISABLE INTERRUPTS DURING INITIALIZATION BUT SAVE
	;  PREVIOUS STATE OF INTERRUPT FLAG
	;
	PUSHF			;SAVE CURRENT INTERRUPT FLAG
	CLI			;DISABLE INTERRUPTS DURING
				; INITIALIZATION
	;
	;INITIALIZE 8250 ACE (UART)
	;
	MOV	DX,ACEIER	;POINT TO INTERRUPT ENABLE REGISTER
	SUB	AL,AL		;RESET INTERRUPT ENABLES
	OUT	DX,AL
	JMP	$+2		;DELAY BETWEEN 8250 OPERATIONS
	MOV	DX,ACELCR	;POINT TO LINE CONTROL REGISTER
	MOV	AL,DLADDR	;ADDRESS DIVISOR LATCH
	OUT	DX,AL
```

```
        JMP     $+2             ;DELAY BETWEEN 8250 OPERATIONS
        MOV     DX,ACEDLM       ;POINT TO DIVISOR LATCH - MSB
        MOV     AL,DIVMS        ;SET MSB OF DIVISOR
        OUT     DX,AL
        JMP     $+2             ;DELAY BETWEEN 8250 OPERATIONS
        MOV     DX,ACEDLL       ;POINT TO DIVISOR LATCH - LSB
        MOV     AL,DIVLS        ;SET LSB OF DIVISOR
        OUT     DX,AL
        JMP     $+2             ;DELAY BETWEEN 8250 OPERATIONS
        MOV     DX,ACELCR       ;POINT TO LINE CONTROL REGISTER
        MOV     AL,LCMODE       ;SET ACE FOR 8-BIT WORDS, 2 STOP
                                ; BITS, NO PARITY
        OUT     DX,AL
        JMP     $+2             ;DELAY BETWEEN 8250 OPERATIONS
        MOV     DX,ACEMSR       ;POINT TO MODEM STATUS REGISTER
        IN      AL,DX           ;READ TO CLEAR POSSIBLE OLD INTERRUPT
        JMP     $+2             ;DELAY BETWEEN 8250 OPERATIONS
        MOV     DX,ACELSR       ;POINT TO LINE STATUS REGISTER
        IN      AL,DX           ;CLEAR ERROR INDICATORS, CHECK FOR DATA
        JMP     $+2             ;DELAY BETWEEN 8250 OPERATIONS
        SHR     AL,1            ;CHECK IF DATA READY
        JNC     SETINT          ;JUMP IF NO DATA
        MOV     DX,ACERBR       ;POINT TO RECEIVER BUFFER REGISTER
        IN      AL,DX           ;READ BUFFER TO EMPTY IT FOR SURE
        JMP     $+2             ;DELAY BETWEEN 8250 OPERATIONS
SETINT:
        MOV     DX,ACEIER       ;POINT TO INTERRUPT ENABLE REGISTER
        MOV     AL,INTCMD       ;ENABLE RECEIVE, TRANSMIT INTERRUPTS
        OUT     DX,AL
        JMP     $+2             ;DELAY BETWEEN 8250 OPERATIONS
        MOV     DX,ACEMCR       ;POINT TO MODEM CONTROL REGISTER
        MOV     AL,MCMODE       ;MODEM CONTROL COMMAND
        OUT     DX,AL
        JMP     $+2             ;DELAY BETWEEN 8250 OPERATIONS
        ;
        ;INITIALIZE BUFFER POINTERS AND COUNTERS
        ;INDICATE NO OUTPUT INTERRUPT EXPECTED
        ;
        SUB     AL,AL
        MOV     [ICNT],AL       ;INPUT BUFFER EMPTY
        MOV     [OCNT],AL       ;OUTPUT BUFFER EMPTY
        MOV     [OIE],AL        ;INDICATE NO OUTPUT INTERRUPT NEEDED
                                ; 8250 READY TO TRANSMIT INITIALLY
        MOV     BX,OFFSET IBUF  ;MAKE INPUT HEAD AND TAIL POINTERS
        MOV     [IHEAD],BX      ; POINT TO BASE ADDRESS OF INPUT
        MOV     [ITAIL],BX      ; BUFFER
        MOV     BX,OFFSET OBUF  ;MAKE OUTPUT HEAD AND TAIL POINTERS
        MOV     [OHEAD],BX      ; POINT TO BASE ADDRESS OF OUTPUT
        MOV     [OTAIL],BX
        ;
        ;INITIALIZE INTERRUPT VECTOR
        ;
        PUSH    DS              ;SAVE CURRENT DATA SEGMENT
        SUB     AX,AX           ;ACCESS INTERRUPT VECTOR IN SEGMENT
                                ; 0
        MOV     DS,AX
```

```
        MOV     AX,OFFSET IOSRVC    ;GET OFFSET FOR SERVICE ROUTINE
        MOV     BX,ASYNIV           ;GET INTERRUPT VECTOR LOCATION
        MOV     [BX],AX             ;LOAD OFFSET INTO INTERRUPT VECTOR
        MOV     AX,CSEG             ;GET CODE SEGMENT NUMBER
        MOV     [BX+2],AX           ;LOAD CODE SEGMENT NUMBER INTO
                                    ; INTERRUPT VECTOR
        POP     DS                  ;RESTORE CURRENT DATA SEGMENT
        ;
        ;INITIALIZE 8259 INTERRUPT CONTROLLER
        ;
        ;IF THE 8259 WAS PREVIOUSLY INITIALIZED AND YOU WANT TO ENABLE
        ; AN ADDITIONAL INTERRUPT, EXECUTE THE FOLLOWING CODE (SHOWN
        ; ENABLING INTERRUPT 4)
        ;
        MOV     DX,PIC1             ;GET CURRENT INTERRUPT MASKS
        IN      AL,PIC1
        AND     AL,11101111B        ;ENABLE INTERRUPT 4 ALSO
        OUT     PIC1,AL
        POPF                        ;RESTORE PREVIOUS INTERRUPT STATUS
        RET
        ;
        ;TO INITIALIZE THE 8259 AND ENABLE ALL INTERRUPTS, EXECUTE
        ; THE FOLLOWING CODE
        ;
        MOV     DX,PIC0             ;SEND FIRST COMMAND BYTE TO PIC PORT 0
        MOV     AL,ICW1
        OUT     DX,AL
        MOV     DX,PIC1             ;SEND SECOND COMMAND BYTE TO PIC PORT 1
        MOV     AL,ICW2
        OUT     DX,AL
        MOV     AL,ICW4             ;SEND FINAL COMMAND BYTE TO PIC PORT 1
        OUT     DX,AL
        POPF                        ;RESTORE PREVIOUS INTERRUPT STATUS
        RET

;
;ASYNCHRONOUS I/O INTERRUPT HANDLER
;
IOSRVC:
        PUSH    AX                  ;SAVE REGISTERS
        PUSH    BX
        PUSH    DX
        MOV     DX,ACEIIR           ;POINT TO INTERRUPT ID REGISTER
        IN      AL,DX               ;READ CURRENT INTERRUPT STATUS
        JMP     $+2                 ;DELAY BETWEEN 8250 OPERATIONS
        CMP     AL,00000010B        ;CHECK IF TRANSMITTER EMPTY INTERRUPT
        JZ      TXINTR              ;JUMP IF TRANSMITTER INTERRUPT
                                    ;NOTE THAT IF THE TRANSMITTER INTERRUPT
                                    ; IS ACTIVE, READING THE INTERRUPT
                                    ; IDENTIFICATION REGISTER WILL CLEAR IT

;
;INPUT (READ) INTERRUPT HANDLER
;
RCINTR:
        ;
        ;READ LINE STATUS TO CLEAR POSSIBLE ERROR FLAGS
```

```
        ;
        MOV     DX,ACELSR         ;POINT TO LINE STATUS REGISTER
        IN      AL,DX             ;READ TO CLEAR ERROR FLAGS
        JMP     $+2               ;DELAY BETWEEN 8250 OPERATIONS
        ;
        ;READ DATA AND SAVE IT IN INPUT BUFFER IF THERE IS ROOM
        ;IF NOT, EXIT, DISCARDING CHARACTER
        ;
        MOV     DX,ACERBR         ;POINT TO RECEIVER BUFFER REGISTER
        IN      AL,DX
        JMP     $+2               ;DELAY BETWEEN 8250 OPERATIONS
        MOV     BL,[ICNT]         ;GET INPUT BUFFER COUNT
        CMP     BL,SZIBUF         ;CHECK IF INPUT BUFFER IS FULL
        JAE     IOEXIT            ;JUMP (EXIT) IF INPUT BUFFER IS FULL
        ;
        ;INPUT BUFFER NOT FULL, SO STORE CHARACTER AT TAIL
        ;INCREMENT TAIL POINTER AND BUFFER COUNT
        ;
        INC     BYTE PTR[ICNT]    ;INCREMENT INPUT BUFFER COUNT
        MOV     BX,[ITAIL]        ;STORE CHARACTER AT TAIL OF INPUT BUFFER
        MOV     [BX],AL
        CALL    INCIPTR           ;INCREMENT TAIL POINTER WITH WRAPAROUND
        MOV     [ITAIL],BX
        JMP     IOEXIT            ;JUMP TO END OF SERVICE ROUTINE

;
;OUTPUT (WRITE) INTERRUPT HANDLER
;
TXINTR:
        MOV     AL,[OCNT]         ;TEST OUTPUT BUFFER COUNT
        TEST    AL,AL
        JZ      NODATA            ;JUMP IF NO DATA TO TRANSMIT
        CALL    OUTDAT            ;SEND DATA TO 8250 ACE
        JMP     IOEXIT            ;JUMP TO END OF SERVICE ROUTINE
;
;IF AN OUTPUT INTERRUPT OCCURS WHEN NO DATA IS AVAILABLE,
; WE MUST CLEAR IT (IN THE 8259) TO AVOID AN ENDLESS LOOP.  LATER,
; WHEN A CHARACTER BECOMES AVAILABLE, WE CALL THE OUTPUT ROUTINE
; OUTDAT TO SEND THE DATA WITHOUT WAITING FOR AN INTERRUPT.
; THE OUTPUT ROUTINE MUST ALSO SET THE OUTPUT INTERRUPT EXPECTED
; FLAG AFTERWARDS. THIS PROCEDURE OVERCOMES THE PROBLEM OF AN
; UNSERVICED OUTPUT INTERRUPT ASSERTING ITSELF REPEATEDLY,
; WHILE STILL ENSURING THAT OUTPUT INTERRUPTS ARE RECOGNIZED.
;THE PROBLEM IS THAT AN OUTPUT DEVICE MAY REQUEST SERVICE BEFORE
; THE COMPUTER HAS ANYTHING TO SEND (UNLIKE AN INPUT DEVICE THAT
; HAS DATA WHEN IT REQUESTS SERVICE).
;NOTE THAT THE 8250 TRANSMITTER INTERRUPT IS CLEARED AUTOMATICALLY
; BY READING THE INTERRUPT IDENTIFICATION REGISTER, SO ONLY THE
; 8259 LEVEL MUST BE HANDLED IN THIS WAY.
;
NODATA:
        MOV     BYTE PTR [OIE],0   ;DO NOT EXPECT AN INTERRUPT
IOEXIT:
        MOV     DX,PICO           ;CLEAR 8259 INTERRUPT
        MOV     AL,EOI
        OUT     DX,AL
```

```
        POP     DX                  ;RESTORE REGISTERS
        POP     BX
        POP     AX
        IRET

;****************************************
;ROUTINE: OUTDAT
;PURPOSE: SEND A CHARACTER TO 8250 ACE FROM THE OUTPUT BUFFER
;ENTRY: OHEAD CONTAINS THE ADDRESS OF THE CHARACTER TO SEND
;EXIT:  NONE
;REGISTERS USED: AL,BX,DX,F
;****************************************

OUTDAT:
        MOV     BX,[OHEAD]          ;GET DATA FROM HEAD OF OUTPUT BUFFER
        MOV     AL,[BX]
        MOV     DX,ACETHR           ;POINT TO TX HOLDING REGISTER
        OUT     DX,AL               ;SEND DATA TO 8250 ACE
        JMP     $+2                 ;DELAY BETWEEN 8250 OPERATIONS
        CALL    INCOPTR             ;INCREMENT HEAD POINTER WITH WRAPAROUND
        MOV     [OHEAD],BX          ;SAVE HEAD POINTER
        DEC     BYTE PTR [OCNT]     ;DECREMENT OUTPUT BUFFER COUNT
        MOV     BYTE PTR [OIE],OFFH     ;INDICATE OUTPUT INTERRUPT
                                    ;  EXPECTED - OIE = FF HEX
        RET

;****************************************
;ROUTINE: INCIPTR
;PURPOSE: INCREMENT INPUT BUFFER POINTER WITH WRAPAROUND
;ENTRY: BX = POINTER
;EXIT:  BX = POINTER INCREMENTED WITH WRAPAROUND
;REGISTERS USED: BX,F
;****************************************

INCIPTR:
        INC     BX                  ;INCREMENT POINTER BY 1
        CMP     BX,EIBUF            ;COMPARE POINTER, END OF BUFFER
        JNE     RETINC              ;BRANCH IF NOT EQUAL
        MOV     BX,OFFSET IBUF      ;IF EQUAL, SET POINTER BACK TO BASE
                                    ; ADDRESS OF BUFFER
RETINC:
        RET

;****************************************
;ROUTINE: INCOPTR
;PURPOSE: INCREMENT OUTPUT BUFFER POINTER WITH WRAPAROUND
;ENTRY: BX = POINTER
;EXIT:  BX = POINTER INCREMENTED WITH WRAPAROUND
;REGISTERS USED: BX,F
;****************************************

INCOPTR:
        INC     BX                  ;INCREMENT POINTER BY 1
        CMP     BX,EOBUF            ;COMPARE POINTER, END OF BUFFER
        JNE     RETONC              ;BRANCH IF NOT EQUAL
```

```
        MOV     BX,OFFSET OBUF  ;IF EQUAL, SET POINTER BACK TO BASE
                                ; ADDRESS OF BUFFER
RETONC:
        RET


;
;DATA SECTION
;
IHEAD   DW      ?               ;POINTER TO OLDEST CHARACTER IN INPUT
                                ; BUFFER (NEXT CHARACTER TO READ)
ITAIL   DW      ?               ;POINTER TO NEWEST CHARACTER IN INPUT
                                ; BUFFER (LATEST CHARACTER RECEIVED)
ICNT    DB      ?               ;NUMBER OF CHARACTERS IN INPUT BUFFER
OHEAD   DW      ?               ;POINTER TO OLDEST CHARACTER IN OUTPUT
                                ; BUFFER (NEXT CHARACTER TO SEND)
OTAIL   DW      ?               ;POINTER TO NEWEST CHARACTER IN OUTPUT
                                ; BUFFER (LATEST CHARACTER WRITTEN)
OCNT    DB      ?               ;NUMBER OF CHARACTERS IN OUTPUT BUFFER
SZIBUF  EQU     10              ;SIZE OF INPUT BUFFER
IBUF    DW      SZIBUF DUP(?)   ;INPUT BUFFER
EIBUF   EQU     OFFSET IBUF+SZIBUF ;END OF INPUT BUFFER
SZOBUF  EQU     10              ;SIZE OF OUTPUT BUFFER
OBUF    DW      SZOBUF DUP(?)   ;OUTPUT BUFFER
EOBUF   EQU     OFFSET OBUF+SZOBUF ;END OF OUTPUT BUFFER
OIE     DB      ?               ;OUTPUT INTERRUPT EXPECTED
                                ; (0 = NO INTERRUPT EXPECTED,
                                ; FF = INTERRUPT EXPECTED)

;
;       SAMPLE EXECUTION:
;
;CHARACTER EQUATES
ESCAPE  EQU     1BH             ;ASCII ESCAPE CHARACTER
TESTCH  EQU     'A'             ;TEST CHARACTER = A

SC9C:
        CALL    INIT            ;INITIALIZE 8251 PCI, INTERRUPT SYSTEM
        STI                     ;ENABLE CPU INTERRUPTS
        ;
        ;SIMPLE EXAMPLE - READ AND ECHO CHARACTERS
        ; UNTIL AN ESC IS RECEIVED
        ;
LOOP:
        CALL    INCH            ;READ CHARACTER
        PUSH    AX              ;SAVE CHARACTER
        CALL    OUTCH           ;ECHO CHARACTER
        POP     AX              ;RESTORE CHARACTER
        CMP     AL,ESCAPE       ;IS CHARACTER AN ESCAPE?
        JNE     LOOP            ;STAY IN LOOP IF NOT
        ;
        ;AN ASYNCHRONOUS EXAMPLE
        ; OUTPUT "A" TO CONSOLE CONTINUOUSLY BUT ALSO LOOK AT
        ; INPUT SIDE, READING AND ECHOING ANY INPUT CHARACTERS.
        ;
ASYNLP:
```

```
        ;
        ;OUTPUT AN "A" IF OUTPUT IS NOT BUSY
        ;
        CALL    OUTST           ;IS OUTPUT BUSY?
        JC      ASYNLP          ;JUMP IF IT IS
        MOV     AL,TESTCH
        CALL    OUTCH           ;OUTPUT TEST CHARACTER
        ;
        ;CHECK INPUT PORT
        ;ECHO CHARACTER IF ONE IS AVAILABLE
        ;EXIT ON ESCAPE CHARACTER
        ;
        CALL    INST            ;IS INPUT DATA AVAILABLE?
        JNC     ASYNLP          ;JUMP IF NOT (SEND ANOTHER "A")
        CALL    INCH            ;GET CHARACTER
        CMP     AL,ESCAPE       ;IS IT AN ESCAPE?
        JE      DONE            ;BRANCH IF IT IS
        CALL    OUTCH           ;ELSE ECHO CHARACTER
        JMP     ASYNLP          ;AND CONTINUE

DONE:
        JMP     SC9C            ;REPEAT TEST

        END
```

9D Real-time clock and calendar (CLOCK)

Maintains a time-of-day 24-hour clock and a calendar based on a real-time clock interrupt generated from an 8253 Programmable Interval Timer (PIT). Consists of the following subroutines:

1. CLOCK returns the base address of the clock variables.

2. ICLK initializes the interrupt system, timer chip, and clock variables.

3. CLKINT updates the clock after each interrupt (assumed to be spaced one tick apart).

Procedure

1. CLOCK loads the base address of the clock variables into register BX. The variables are stored in the following order: ticks, seconds, minutes, hours, days, months, less significant byte of year, and more significant byte of year.

2. ICLK initializes the interrupt vector and controller, the 8253 PTM, and the clock variables. The arbitrary starting time is 00:00.00 (12 a.m.) 1 January 1980. A real application would obviously require outside intervention to load or change the clock.

3. CLKINT decrements the remaining tick count by 1 and updates the other clock variables if necessary. Of course, seconds and minutes are always less than 60 and hours are always less than 24. The day of the month must be less than or equal to the last day for the current month; an array of the last days of each month begins at address LASTDY.

If the month is February, the program checks if the current year is a leap year. This involves determining whether the two least significant bits of memory location YEAR are both 0s. If the current year is a leap year, February has 29 days instead of the usual 28.

If the new month number exceeds 12 (December), a carry to the year number is necessary. The program must reinitialize the variables properly when carries occur; i.e. TICK to DTICK; seconds, minutes, and hours to 0; day and month to 1 (meaning the first day and January, respectively).

Entry conditions

1. CLOCK: none
2. ICLK: none
3. CLKINT: none

Exit conditions

1. CLOCK: base address of clock variables in register BX
2. ICLK: none
3. CLKINT: none

Examples

These examples assume that the tick rate is DTICK Hz (less than 256 Hz – typical values would be 60 Hz or 100 Hz) and that the clock and calendar are saved in memory locations

TICK	number of ticks remaining before a carry occurs, counted down from DTICK
SEC	seconds (0 to 59)
MIN	minutes (0 to 59)
HOUR	hour of day (0 to 23)
DAY	day of month (1 to 28, 29, 30, or 31, depending on month)
MONTH	month of year (1 through 12 for January through December)
YEAR and YEAR+1	current year

1. Starting values are 7 March 1987, 11:59.59 p.m. and 1 tick left. That is:

(TICK) = 1
(SEC) = 59
(MIN) = 59
(HOUR) = 23
(DAY) = 07
(MONTH) = 03
(YEAR and YEAR+1) = 1987

Result (after the tick): 8 March 1987, 12:00.00 a.m. and DTICK ticks. That is:

(TICK) = DTICK
(SEC) = 0
(MIN) = 0
(HOUR) = 0
(DAY) = 08
(MONTH) = 03
(YEAR and YEAR+1) = 1987

2. Starting values are 31 December 1987, 11:59.59 p.m. and 1 tick left. That is:

(TICK) = 1
(SEC) = 59
(MIN) = 59
(HOUR) = 23
(DAY) = 31
(MONTH) = 12
(YEAR and YEAR+1) = 1987

Result (after the tick): 1 January 1988, 12:00.00 a.m. and DTICK ticks. That is:

(TICK) = DTICK
(SEC) = 0
(MIN) = 0
(HOUR) = 0
(DAY) = 1
(MONTH) = 1
(YEAR and YEAR+1) = 1988

Registers used

1. CLOCK: BX

2. ICLK: AX, BX, DX

3. CLKINT: none

Execution time

1. CLOCK: 12 cycles

2. ICLK: 269 cycles

3. CLKINT: 157 cycles if only TICK must be decremented, 518 cycles maximum if changing to a new year. These include the 8086's interrupt response time (51 cycles).

Program size 230 bytes

Data memory required 8 bytes anywhere in RAM for the clock variables (starting at address CLKVAR)

```
;       Title               Real time clock and calendar
;       Name:               CLOCK
;
;
;       Purpose:            This program maintains a time of day 24 hour
;                           clock and a calendar based on a real time clock
;                           interrupt from an 8253 programmable timer.
;
;                           CLOCK
;                             Returns base address of clock variables
;                           ICLK
;                             Initializes 8253 timer and clock interrupt
;
;       Entry:              CLOCK
;                             None
;                           ICLK
;                             None
;
;       Exit:               CLOCK
;                             Register BX = Base address of time variables
;                           ICLK
;                             None
;
;       Registers Used: CLOCK
;                             BX
;                           ICLK
;                             AX,BX,DX
;
;       Time:               CLOCK
;                             12 cycles
;                           ICLK
;                             269 cycles
;                           CLKINT
;                             If decrementing tick only, 157 cycles
;                             Maximum if changing to a new year, 518
;                             cycles
;                             These include the 8086's interrupt response
;                             time (51 cycles).
;
;       Size:               Program    230 bytes
;                           Data       8 bytes
```

```
;
;
;ESTABLISH SEGMENT ADDRESS FOR USE IN INTERRUPT VECTOR
;
CSEG     EQU     0F81H             ;ARBITRARY BASE ADDRESS OF CODE SEGMENT
                                   ;USUALLY ESTABLISHED IN A SEGMENT
                                   ; DIRECTIVE NOT SHOWN HERE
;
;MONTH EQUATES
;
JAN      EQU     1                 ;JANUARY
FEB      EQU     2                 ;FEBRUARY
DEC      EQU     12                ;DECEMBER
;
;INTERRUPT VECTOR
;
CLKIV    EQU     0020H             ;REAL-TIME CLOCK INTERRUPT VECTOR
;
;8253 PROGRAMMABLE INTERVAL TIMER (PIT)
;
;INITIALIZE COUNTER 0 OF 8253 PIT AS 100 HZ SQUARE WAVE
; GENERATOR FOR USE IN TIME-OF-DAY CLOCK.
;SQUARE WAVE IS GENERATED FROM PIN 10 OF THE 8253, WHICH IS
; CONNECTED TO PIN 21 OF AN 8259 PROGRAMMABLE INTERRUPT
; CONTROLLER (PIC)
;THE CLOCK INTERRUPT IS THUS TIED TO INTERRUPT VECTOR
;WE ASSUME A 4.77 MHZ CLOCK (STANDARD IBM PC VALUE) INTO PIN 18
; OF THE 8253, SO THAT A COUNTER VALUE OF 4,770,000/100 = 47,700
; IS NEEDED TO GENERATE A 100 HZ SQUARE WAVE

;ARBITRARY PORT ADDRESSES FOR 8253 PIT
:
PIT0       EQU   40H               ;8253 COUNTER 0
PIT1       EQU   41H               ;8253 COUNTER 1
PIT2       EQU   42H               ;8253 COUNTER 2
PITMDE     EQU   43H               ;8253 CONTROL WORD REGISTER

;8253 PIT MODE BYTE, COUNTER VALUE
PITCTRL    EQU   00110110B         ;BIT 0 = 0 (BINARY MODE)
                                   ;BITS 3..1 = 011 (MODE 3 - SQUARE WAVE
                                   ; GENERATOR)
                                   ;BITS 5,4 = 11 (LOAD 2 BYTES TO COUNTER)
                                   ;BITS 7,6 = 00 (PROGRAM COUNTER 0)
PITCNT     EQU   47700             ;COUNTER VALUE = 47700

;
;DEFAULT TICK VALUE (100 HZ REAL-TIME CLOCK)
;
DTICK      EQU   100               ;DEFAULT TICK VALUE

;
;8259 PROGRAMMABLE INTERRUPT CONTROLLER (PIC) EQUATES
; 8259 PIC IS PROGRAMMED FOR
;  SINGLE DEVICE (RATHER THAN MULTIPLE 8259'S)
;  FULLY NESTED MODE
;  ALL INTERRUPTS ENABLED
```

```
;  INTERRUPT LEVELS 8-15
;ARBITRARY 8259 PIC PORT ADDRESSES
PIC0    EQU     20H                 ;PIC PORT 1
PIC1    EQU     21H                 ;PIC PORT 2

;8259 INITIALIZATION COMMAND BYTES ICW1, ICW2, AND ICW4 (NO ICW3
;  NEEDED IN SINGLE 8259 SYSTEMS)
ICW1    EQU     00010011B           ;BIT 0 = 1 (ICW4 NEEDED IN 8086 SYSTEMS)
                                    ;BIT 1 = 1 (SINGLE 8259)
                                    ;BIT 2 = 0 (NOT USED WITH 8086/8088)
                                    ;BIT 3 = 0 (EDGE DETECT)
                                    ;BIT 4 = 1 (FIXED)
                                    ;BITS 5,6,7 = 000 (NOT USED IN 8086/88)
ICW2    EQU     00001000B           ;BITS 7-3 = 00001 (5 MSB'S OF SOURCE
                                    ;  IDENTIFICATION CODE)
                                    ;BITS 2-0 = 000 (NOT USED)
ICW4    EQU     00001001B           ;BIT 0 = 1 (8086/88 SYSTEM)
                                    ;BIT 1 = 0 (NO AUTOMATIC END OF
                                    ;  INTERRUPT)
                                    ;BIT 2 = 0 (DON'T CARE)
                                    ;BIT 3 = 1 (BUFFERED DATA BUS)
                                    ;BIT 4 = 0 (NO CASCADING)
                                    ;BITS 7-5 = 000 (NOT USED)
;8259 OPERATING COMMAND BYTE
EOI     EQU     00100000B           ;END OF INTERRUPT COMMAND BYTE

;
;RETURN BASE ADDRESS OF CLOCK VARIABLES
;
CLOCK:
        MOV     BX,CLKVAR           ;GET BASE ADDRESS OF CLOCK VARIABLES
        RET

;
;INITIALIZE 8253 PIT COUNTER AS A CLOCK INTERRUPT
;
ICLK:
        PUSHF                       ;SAVE CURRENT INTERRUPT FLAG
        CLI                         ;DISABLE INTERRUPTS DURING
                                    ; INITIALIZATION
        ;
        ;INITIALIZE INTERRUPT VECTOR
        ;
        PUSH    DS                  ;SAVE CURRENT DATA SEGMENT
        SUB     AX,AX               ;ACCESS INTERRUPT VECTOR IN SEGMENT
                                    ; 0
        MOV     DS,AX
        MOV     AX,OFFSET CLKINT ;GET OFFSET FOR SERVICE ROUTINE
        MOV     BX,CLKIV            ;GET INTERRUPT VECTOR LOCATION
        MOV     [BX],AX             ;LOAD OFFSET INTO INTERRUPT VECTOR
        MOV     AX,CSEG             ;GET CODE SEGMENT NUMBER
        MOV     [BX+2],AX           ;LOAD CODE SEGMENT NUMBER INTO
                                    ; INTERRUPT VECTOR
        POP     DS                  ;RESTORE CURRENT DATA SEGMENT
        ;
        ;INITIALIZE 8259 INTERRUPT CONTROLLER
```

```
        ;
        MOV     DX,PICO          ;SEND FIRST COMMAND BYTE TO PIC PORT 0
        MOV     AL,ICW1
        OUT     DX,AL
        MOV     DX,PIC1          ;SEND SECOND COMMAND BYTE TO PIC PORT 1
        MOV     AL,ICW2
        OUT     DX,AL
        MOV     AL,ICW4          ;SEND FINAL COMMAND BYTE TO PIC PORT 1
        OUT     DX,AL
        ;
        ;INITIALIZE 8253 PROGRAMMABLE INTERVAL TIMER
        ;
        MOV     DX,PITMDE        ;OUTPUT CONTROL BYTE
        MOV     AL,PITCTRL
        OUT     DX,AL
        MOV     DX,PITO
        MOV     AX,PITCNT        ;OUTPUT INITIAL COUNT IN 2 BYTES
        OUT     DX,AL
        MOV     AL,AH
        OUT     DX,AL
        ;
        ;INITIALIZE CLOCK VARIABLES TO ARBITRARY VALUE
        ;JANUARY 1, 1980 00:00.00 (12 A.M.)
        ;A REAL CLOCK WOULD NEED OUTSIDE INTERVENTION
        ; TO SET OR CHANGE VALUES
        ;
        MOV     BYTE PTR [TICK],DTICK      ;INITIALIZE TICKS
        SUB     AX,AX
        MOV     BYTE PTR [SEC],AL  ;SECOND = 0
        MOV     BYTE PTR [MIN],AL  ;MINUTE = 0
        MOV     BYTE PTR [HOUR],AL ;HOUR = 0
        INC     AX                 ;AX = 1
        MOV     BYTE PTR [DAY],AL  ;DAY = 1 (FIRST)
        MOV     BYTE PTR [MONTH],AL  ;MONTH (JANUARY)
        MOV     AX,1980            ;YEAR = 1980
        MOV     WORD PTR [YEAR],AX
        POPF                       ;RESTORE PREVIOUS INTERRUPT FLAG
        RET


:
;REAL-TIME CLOCK INTERRUPT HANDLER
;
CLKINT:
        ;
        ;SUBTRACT 1 FROM TICK COUNT, CARRY IF IT REACHES ZERO
        ;
        PUSH    AX                 ;SAVE REGISTERS
        PUSH    BX
        PUSH    DX
        DEC     BYTE PTR [TICK] ;SUBTRACT 1 FROM TICK COUNT
        JNZ     EXITCL             ;JUMP IF TICK COUNT NOT ZERO
        MOV     BYTE PTR [TICK],DTICK   ;SET TICK COUNT BACK TO DEFAULT
        ;
        ;ADD 1 TO SECONDS, CARRY IF IT REACHES 60
        ;
```

```
        INC     BYTE PTR [SEC]  ;INCREMENT TO NEXT SECOND
        MOV     AL,[SEC]        ;SECONDS = 60?
        CMP     AL,60
        JB      EXITCL          ;EXIT IF BELOW 60 SECONDS
        MOV     [SEC],0         ;ELSE SECONDS = 0
        ;
        ;ADD 1 TO MINUTES, CARRY IF IT REACHES 60
        ;
        INC     BYTE PTR [MIN]  ;INCREMENT TO NEXT MINUTE
        MOV     AL,[MIN]        ;MINUTES = 60?
        CMP     AL,60
        JB      EXITCL          ;EXIT IF BELOW 60 MINUTES
        MOV     [MIN],0         ;ELSE MINUTES = 0
        ;
        ;ADD 1 TO HOURS, CARRY IF IT REACHES 24
        ;
        INC     BYTE PTR [HOUR] ;INCREMENT TO NEXT HOUR
        MOV     AL,[HOUR]       ;HOURS = 24?
        CMP     AL,24
        JB      EXITCL          ;EXIT IF BELOW 24 HOURS
        MOV     [HOUR],0        ;ELSE HOURS = 0
        ;
        ;ADD 1 TO DAY, CARRY IF IT REACHES END OF MONTH
        ;
        MOV     AL,[DAY]        ;GET DAY
        INC     BYTE PTR [DAY]  ;INCREMENT TO NEXT DAY
        SUB     BH,BH           ;MAKE MONTH INTO 16-BIT INDEX
        MOV     BL,[MONTH]
        CMP     AL,[BX+OFFSET LASTDY-1] ;IS CURRENT DAY END OF MONTH?
        JB      EXITCL          ;EXIT IF NOT AT END OF MONTH
        ;
        ;DETERMINE IF THIS IS END OF FEBRUARY IN A LEAP
        ; YEAR (YEAR DIVISIBLE BY 4)
        ;
        XCHG    AL,BL           ;GET MONTH
        CMP     AL,FEB          ;IS THIS FEBRUARY?
        JNE     INCMTH          ;JUMP IF NOT, INCREMENT MONTH
        MOV     AX,[YEAR]       ;IS IT A LEAP YEAR?
        AND     AL,00000011B
        JNZ     INCMTH          ;JUMP IF NOT
        ;
        ;FEBRUARY OF A LEAP YEAR HAS 29 DAYS, NOT 28 DAYS
        ;
        CMP     BL,29
        JB      EXITCL          ;EXIT IF NOT 1ST OF MARCH
        ;
        ;ADD 1 TO MONTH, CARRY IF IT REACHES 13
        ;
INCMTH:
        MOV     BYTE PTR [DAY],1   ;DAY = 1
        MOV     AL,[MONTH]      ;GET OLD MONTH
        INC     BYTE PTR [MONTH]   ;INCREMENT MONTH
        CMP     AL,DEC          ;WAS OLD MONTH DECEMBER?
        JB      EXITCL          ;EXIT IF NOT
        MOV     BYTE PTR [MONTH],JAN ;ELSE CHANGE MONTH TO JANUARY
        INC     WORD PTR [YEAR]    ;AND INCREMENT YEAR
```

```
EXITCL:
        MOV     DX,PICO             ;CLEAR 8259 INTERRUPT
        MOV     AL,EOI
        OUT     DX,AL
        POP     DX                  ;RESTORE REGISTERS
        POP     BX
        POP     AX
        IRET

;ARRAY OF LAST DAYS OF EACH MONTH
LASTDY  DB      31                  ;JANUARY
        DB      28                  ;FEBRUARY (EXCEPT LEAP YEARS)
        DB      31                  ;MARCH
        DB      31                  ;MAY
        DB      30                  ;JUNE
        DB      31                  ;JULY
        DB      31                  ;AUGUST
        DB      30                  ;SEPTEMBER
        DB      31                  ;OCTOBER
        DB      30                  ;NOVEMBER
        DB      31                  ;DECEMBER

;CLOCK VARIABLES
TICK    DB      ?                   ;TICKS LEFT IN CURRENT SECOND
CLKVAR  EQU     OFFSET TICK
SEC     DB      ?                   ;SECONDS
MIN     DB      ?                   ;MINUTES
HOUR    DB      ?                   ;HOURS
DAY     DB      ?                   ;DAY (1 TO NUMBER OF DAYS IN A MONTH)
MONTH   DB      ?                   ;MONTH 1=JANUARY .. 12=DECEMBER
YEAR    DW      ?                   ;YEAR

;
;       SAMPLE EXECUTION
;

;CLOCK VARIABLE INDEXES
TCKIDX  EQU     0                   ;INDEX TO TICK
SECIDX  EQU     1                   ;INDEX TO SECOND
MINIDX  EQU     2                   ;INDEX TO MINUTE
HRIDX   EQU     3                   ;INDEX TO HOUR
DAYIDX  EQU     4                   ;INDEX TO DAY
MTHIDX  EQU     5                   ;INDEX TO MONTH
YRIDX   EQU     6                   ;INDEX TO YEAR

SC9D:
        CALL    ICLK                ;INITIALIZE CLOCK

        ;INITIALIZE CLOCK TO 2/7/87 14:00:00 (2 PM, FEB. 7, 1987)
        CALL    CLOCK               ;BX = ADDRESS OF CLOCK VARIABLES
        SUB     AL,AL
        MOV     [BX+SECIDX],AL  ;SECONDS = 0
        MOV     [BX+MINIDX],AL  ;MINUTES = 0
        MOV     BYTE PTR [BX+HRIDX],14  ;HOUR = 14 (2 PM)
        MOV     BYTE PTR [BX+DAYIDX],7  ;DAY = 7
        MOV     BYTE PTR [BX+MTHIDX],FEB ;MONTH = FEBRUARY (2)
```

```
        MOV     WORD PTR [BX+YRIDX],1986    ;YEAR = 1986
        ;
        ;WAIT FOR CLOCK TO BE 2/7/87 14:01:20 (2:01.20 PM, FEB. 7, 1987)
        ;
        ;NOTE: MUST BE CAREFUL TO EXIT IF CLOCK IS ACCIDENTALLY
        ; SET AHEAD.  IF WE CHECK ONLY FOR EQUALITY, WE MIGHT NEVER
        ; FIND IT.  THUS WE HAVE >= IN TESTS BELOW, NOT JUST =.
        ;
        ;WAIT FOR YEAR >= TARGET YEAR
        CALL    CLOCK               ;BX = BASE ADDRESS OF CLOCK VARIABLES
        MOV     AX,TYEAR            ;AX = YEAR TO WAIT FOR
WAITYR:
        ;COMPARE CURRENT YEAR AND TARGET YEAR
        CMP     AX,[BX+YRIDX]
        JB      WAITYR              ;BRANCH IF YEAR NOT >= TARGET YEAR
        ;
        ;WAIT FOR REST OF TIME UNITS TO BE GREATER THAN OR EQUAL
        ;  TO TARGET VALUES
        ;
WTTIM:
        MOV     AL,NTUNIT           ;GET NUMBER OF UNITS TO TEST (TICKS
                                    ; NOT INCLUDED)
        SUB     AH,AH               ;EXTEND NUMBER OF UNITS TO 16 BITS
        MOV     SI,AX               ;SAVE INDEX OF LAST TIME UNIT
        MOV     DI,OFFSET TARGET    ;POINT TO LAST TARGET UNIT
        ADD     DI,AX
        ;
        ;CHECK UNITS CONSECUTIVELY, MOVING FROM LONGEST TO SHORTEST
        ;
WTUNIT:
        MOV     AL,[BX+SI]          ;GET TIME UNIT
        CMP     AL,[DI]             ;COMPARE IT TO TARGET UNIT
        JL      WTUNIT              ;WAIT UNTIL TARGET MET OR EXCEEDED
        DEC     DI                  ;POINT TO NEXT TARGET UNIT
        DEC     SI                  ;POINT TO NEXT TIME UNIT
        JNZ     WTUNIT              ;LOOP UNTIL ALL TARGETS MET
        JMP     SC9D                ;THEN REPEAT TEST

;
;TARGET TIME - 2/7/87, 14:01:20 (2:01.20 PM, FEB. 7, 1987)
;
TYEAR   DW      1987                ;TARGET YEAR
NTUNIT  DB      5                   ;NUMBER OF TIME UNITS IN COMPARISON
TARGET  DB      0,20,1,14,7,2       ;TARGET TIME (SEC,MIN,HR,DAY,MONTH)
                                    ;STARTS WITH TICKS (ALWAYS ZERO)

        END
```

A 8086 instruction set summary

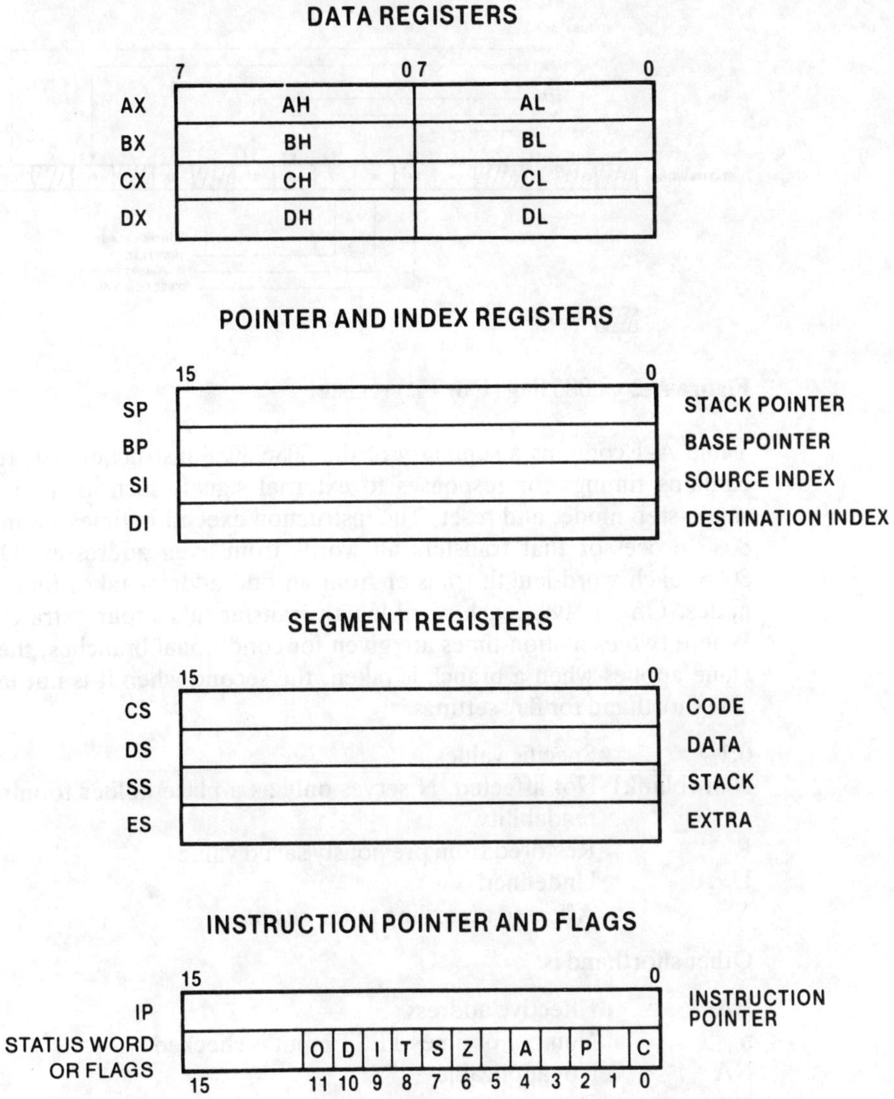

Figure A-1 8086 register structure

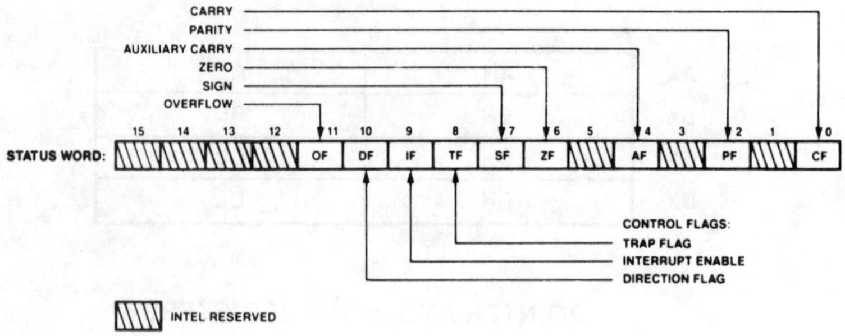

Figure A-2 8086 flag (F or FL) register

Table A-1 contains a summary of the 8086/8088 instruction set. It also contains timings for responses to external signals such as interrupts, single-step mode, and reset. The instruction execution times assume an 8086 processor that transfers all words from even addresses. On an 8086, each word-length transfer from an odd address takes four extra cycles. On an 8088, each word-length transfer takes four extra cycles. Where two execution times are given for conditional branches, the first value applies when a branch is taken, the second when it is not taken. The shorthand for flag settings is:

0,1	Specific values
N or (blank)	Not affected, N serves only as a place holder to improve readability
R	Restored from previously saved value
U	Undefined
X	Affected according to the result

Other shorthand is:

EA	Effective address
n	Number of times TEST input is checked
NA	Not applicable
rep	Repetition

Table A-2 shows how many extra clock cycles are needed to calculate the effective address in the various addressing modes.

Table A-1 8086/8088 instruction set summary*

Mnemonic	Description	Clock Cycles	Number of bytes	Flags O	D	I	T	S	Z	A	P	C
AAA	ASCII adjust for addition	4	1	U	N	N	N	U	U	X	U	X
AAD	ASCII adjust for division	60	2	U	N	N	N	X	X	U	X	U
AAM	ASCII adjust for multiplication	83	1	U	N	N	N	X	X	U	X	U
AAS	ASCII adjust for subtraction	4	1	U	N	N	N	U	U	X	U	X
ADC	Add with carry			X	N	N	N	X	X	X	X	X
	Immediate to accumulator	4	2-3									
	Immediate to memory	17+EA	3-6									
	Immediate to register	4	3-4									
	Memory to register	9+EA	2-4									
	Register to memory	16+EA	2-4									
	Register to register	3	2									
ADD	Add			X	N	N	N	X	X	X	X	X
	Immediate to accumulator	4	2-3									
	Immediate to memory	17+EA	3-6									
	Immediate to register	4	3-4									
	Memory to register	9+EA	2-4									
	Register to memory	16+EA	2-4									
	Register to register	3	2									
AND	Logical AND			0	N	N	N	X	X	U	X	0
	Immediate with accumulator	4	2-3									
	Immediate with memory	17+EA	3-6									
	Immediate with register	4	3-4									
	Memory with register	9+EA	2-4									
	Register with memory	16+EA	2-4									
	Register with register	3	2									
CALL	Jump to subroutine											
	Intersegment direct	28	5									
	Intersegment indirect	37+EA	2-4									
	Intrasegment direct	19	3									
	Intrasegment register indirect	16	2									
	Intrasegment memory indirect	21+EA	2-4									
CBW	Convert (extend) byte to word	2	1									
CLC	Clear carry	2	1	N	N	N	N	N	N	N	N	0
CLD	Clear direction flag (set autoincrementing)	2	1	N	0	N	N	N	N	N	N	N
CLI	Clear interrupt enable flag (disable interrupts)	2	1	N	N	0	N	N	N	N	N	N
CMC	Complement carry	2	1	N	N	N	N	N	N	N	N	X
CMP	Compare			X	N	N	N	X	X	X	X	X
	Immediate to accumulator	4	2-3									
	Immediate to memory	17+EA	3-6									
	Immediate to register	4	3-4									
	Memory to register	9+EA	2-4									
	Register to memory	16+EA	2-4									
	Register to register	3	2									
CMPS/	Compare string		1	X	N	N	N	X	X	X	X	X
CMPSB	Compare byte string											
CMPSW	Compare word string											
	Not repeated	22										
	Repeated	9+22/rep										
CWD	Convert (extend) word to	5	1									

	double word			
DAA	Decimal adjust for addition	4	1	U N N N X X X X X
DAS	Decimal adjust for subtraction	4	1	U N N N X X X X X
DEC	Decrement by 1			X N N N X X X X N
	8-bit register	3	2	
	Memory	15+EA	2-4	
	16-bit register	2	1	
DIV	Unsigned divide			U N N N U U U U U
	8-bit memory	(86-96)+EA	2-4	
	8-bit register	80-90	2	
	16-bit memory	(150-168)+EA	2-4	
	16-bit register	144-162	2	
ESC	Escape (coprocessor instruction)			
	Memory	8+EA	2-4	
	Register	2	2	
HLT	Halt	2	1	
IDIV	Integer divide			U N N N U U U U U
	8-bit memory	(107-118)+EA	2-4	
	8-bit register	101-112	2	
	16-bit memory	(171-190)+EA	2-4	
	16-bit register	165-184	2	
IMUL	Integer multiply			X N N N U U U U X
	8-bit memory	(86-104)+EA	2-4	
	8-bit register	80-98	2	
	16-bit memory	(134-160)+EA	2-4	
	16-bit register	128-154	2	
IN	Input			
	Fixed port address	10	2	
	Variable port address	8	1	
INC	Increment by 1			X N N N X X X X N
	8-bit register	3	2	
	Memory	15+EA	2-4	
	16-bit register	2	1	
INT	Software interrupt (trap)			N N 0 0 N N N N N
	Type not 3	51	2	
	Type 3	52	1	
INTO	Interrupt if overflow		2	N N 0 0 N N N N N
	Interrupt not taken	4		
	Interrupt taken	53		
INTR	External maskable interrupt	61	NA	N N 0 0 N N N N N
IRET	Return from interrupt	24	1	R R R R R R R R R
JA	Jump if above	16/4	2	
JAE	Jump if above or equal	16/4	2	
JB	Jump if below	16/4	2	
JBE	Jump if below or equal	16/4	2	
JC	Jump if carry	16/4	2	
JCXZ	Jump if CX is zero	16/4	2	
JE	Jump if equal	16/4	2	
JG	Jump if greater	16/4	2	
JGE	Jump if greater or equal	16/4	2	
JL	Jump if less	16/4	2	
JLE	Jump if less or equal	16/4	2	
JMP	Jump			
	Intersegment direct	15	5	
	Intersegment indirect	24+EA	2-4	
	Intrasegment direct	15	3	

	Intrasegment direct short	15	2	
	Intrasegment memory indirect	18+EA	2-4	
	Intrasegment register indirect	11	2	
JNA	Jump if not above	16/4	2	
JNAE	Jump if not above or equal	16/4	2	
JNB	Jump if not below	16/4	2	
JNBE	Jump if not below or equal	16/4	2	
JNC	Jump if not carry	16/4	2	
JNE	Jump if not equal	16/4	2	
JNG	Jump if not greater	16/4	2	
JNGE	Jump if not greater or equal	16/4	2	
JNL	Jump if not less	16/4	2	
JNLE	Jump if not less or equal	16/4	2	
JNO	Jump if no overflow	16/4	2	
JNP	Jump if parity odd	16/4	2	
JNS	Jump if not sign	16/4	2	
JNZ	Jump if not zero	16/4	2	
JO	Jump if overflow	16/4	2	
JP	Jump if parity even	16/4	2	
JPE	Jump if parity even	16/4	2	
JPO	Jump if parity odd	16/4	2	
JS	Jump if sign	16/4	2	
JZ	Jump if zero	16/4	2	
LAHF	Load AH from flags	4	1	
LDS	Load pointer using DS	16+EA	2-4	
LEA	Load effective address	2+EA	2-4	
LES	Load pointer using ES	16+EA	2-4	
LOCK	Lock bus	2	1	
LODS/	Load string		1	
LODSB/	Load byte string			
LODSW	Load word string			
	Not repeated	12		
	Repeated	9+13/rep		
LOOP	Loop	17/5	2	
LOOPE	Loop if equal	18/6	2	
LOOPNE	Loop if not equal	19/5	2	
LOOPNZ	Loop if not zero	19/5	2	
LOOPZ	Loop if zero	18/6	2	
MOV	Move			
	Accumulator to memory	10	3	
	Immediate to memory	10+EA	3-6	
	Immediate to register	4	2-3	
	Memory to accumulator	10	3	
	Memory to register	8+EA	2-4	
	Memory to segment register	8+EA	2-4	
	Register to memory	9+EA	2-4	
	Register to register	2	2	
	Register to segment register	2	2	
	Segment register to memory	9+EA	2-4	
	Segment register to register	2	2	
MOVS/	Move string		1	
MOVSB/	Move byte string			
MOVSW	Move word string			
	Not repeated	18		
	Repeated	9+17/rep		
MUL	Unsigned multiply			X N N N U U U U X

	8-bit memory	(76-83)+EA	2-4	
	8-bit register	70-77	2	
	16-bit memory	(124-139)+EA	2-4	
	16-bit register	118-133	2	
NEG	Negate			X N N N X X X X X
	Memory	16+EA	2-4	
	Register	3	2	
NMI	External nonmaskable interrupt	50	NA	N N 0 0 N N N N N
NOP	No operation	3	1	
NOT	Logical NOT			
	Memory	16+EA	2-4	
	Register	3	2	
OR	Logical OR			0 N N N X X U X 0
	Immediate with accumulator	4	2-3	
	Immediate with memory	17+EA	3-6	
	Immediate with register	4	3-4	
	Memory with register	9+EA	2-4	
	Register with memory	16+EA	2-4	
	Register with register	3	2	
OUT	Output			
	Fixed port address	10	2	
	Variable port address	8	1	
POP	Load word from stack			
	Memory	17+EA	2-4	
	Register	8	1	
POPF	Load flags from stack	8	1	R R R R R R R R R
PUSH	Store word on stack			
	Memory	16+EA	2-4	
	Register	11	1	
	Segment register	10	1	
PUSHF	Store flags on stack	10	1	
RCL	Rotate left through carry			X N N N N N N N X
	Memory with single-shift	15+EA	2-4	
	Memory with variable-shift	20+EA+4/bit	2-4	
	Register with single-shift	2	2	
	Register with variable-shift	8+4/bit	2	
RCR	Rotate right through carry			X N N N N N N N X
	Memory with single-shift	15+EA	2-4	
	Memory with variable-shift	20+EA+4/bit	2-4	
	Register with single-shift	2	2	
	Register with variable-shift	8+4/bit	2	
REP	Repeat string operation	2	1	
REPE	Repeat string operation while equal	2	1	
REPNE	Repeat string operation while not equal	2	1	
REPNZ	Repeat string operation while not zero	2	1	
REPZ	Repeat string operation while zero	2	1	
RESET	External Reset signal (starting at least 50 microseconds after power-up)	10	NA	N N 0 0 N N N N N
RET	Return from subroutine			
	Intersegment	18	1	
	Intersegment with constant	17	3	
	Intrasegment	8	1	

	Intrasegment with constant	12	3	
ROL	Rotate left			X N N N N N N N X
	Memory with single-shift	15+EA	2-4	
	Memory with variable-shift	20+EA+4/bit	2-4	
	Register with single-shift	2	2	
	Register with variable-shift	8+4/bit	2	
ROR	Rotate right			X N N N N N N N X
	Memory with single-shift	15+EA	2-4	
	Memory with variable-shift	20+EA+4/bit	2-4	
	Register with single-shift	2	2	
	Register with variable-shift	8+4/bit	2	
SAHF	Store AH into flags	4	1	N N N N R R R R R
SAL/	Shift arithmetic left			X N N N N N N N X
SHL	Shift logical left			
	Memory with single-shift	15+EA	2-4	
	Memory with variable-shift	20+EA+4/bit	2-4	
	Register with single-shift	2	2	
	Register with variable-shift	8+4/bit	2	
SAR	Shift arithmetic right			X N N N X X U X X
	Memory with single-shift	15+EA	2-4	
	Memory with variable-shift	20+EA+4/bit	2-4	
	Register with single-shift	2	2	
	Register with variable-shift	8+4/bit	2	
SBB	Subtract with borrow			X N N N X X X X X
	Immediate from accumulator	4	2-3	
	Immediate from memory	17+EA	3-6	
	Immediate from register	4	3-4	
	Memory from register	9+EA	2-4	
	Register from memory	16+EA	2-4	
	Register from register	3	2	
SCAS/	Scan string		1	X N N N X X X X X
SCASB/	Scan byte string			
SCASW	Scan word string			
	Not repeated	15		
	Repeated	9+15/rep		
SEGMENT	Segment override prefix	2	1	
SHR	Shift logical right			X N N N N N N N X
	Memory with single-shift	15+EA	2-4	
	Memory with variable-shift	20+EA+4/bit	2-4	
	Register with single-shift	2	2	
	Register with variable-shift	8+4/bit	2	
Single	Step (Trap flag interrupt)	50	NA	N N 0 0 N N N N N
STC	Set carry	2	1	N N N N N N N N 1
STD	Set direction flag (set autodecrementing)	2	1	N 1 N N N N N N N
STI	Set interrupt enable flag (enable interrupts)	2	1	N N 1 N N N N N N
STOS/	Store string		1	
STOSB/	Store byte string			
STOSW	Store word string			
	Not repeated	11		
	Repeated	9+10/rep		
SUB	Subtract			X N N N X X X X X
	Immediate from accumulator	4	2-3	
	Immediate from memory	17+EA	3-6	
	Immediate from register	4	3-4	

	Memory from register	9+EA	2-4	
	Register from memory	16+EA	2-4	
	Register from register	3	2	
TEST	Bit test (non-destructive logical AND)			O N N N X X U X O
	Immediate with accumulator	4	2-3	
	Immediate with memory	17+EA	3-6	
	Immediate with register	4	3-4	
	Memory with register	9+EA	2-4	
	Register with register	3	2	
WAIT	Wait while TEST input high	3+5n	1	
	(n is the number of times input is checked)			
XCHG	Exchange			
	Register with accumulator	3	1	
	Register with memory	17+EA	2-4	
	Register with register	4	2	
XLAT	Translate (table lookup)	11	1	
XOR	Logical exclusive OR			O N N N X X U X O
	Immediate with accumulator	4	2-3	
	Immediate with memory	17+EA	3-6	
	Immediate with register	4	3-4	
	Memory with register	9+EA	2-4	
	Register with memory	16+EA	2-4	
	Register with register	3	2	

Table A-2 Execution times for addressing modes

Addressing mode	Number of clock cycles
Based indexed	
[BP+DI] or [BX+SI]	7
[BP+SI] or [BX+DI]	8
Based indexed relative	
DISP[BP+DI] or DISP[BX+SI]	11
DISP[BP+SI] or DISP[BX+DI]	12
Direct	6
Register indirect	5
Register relative	9

B Programming reference for the 8255 PPI*

PIN CONFIGURATION

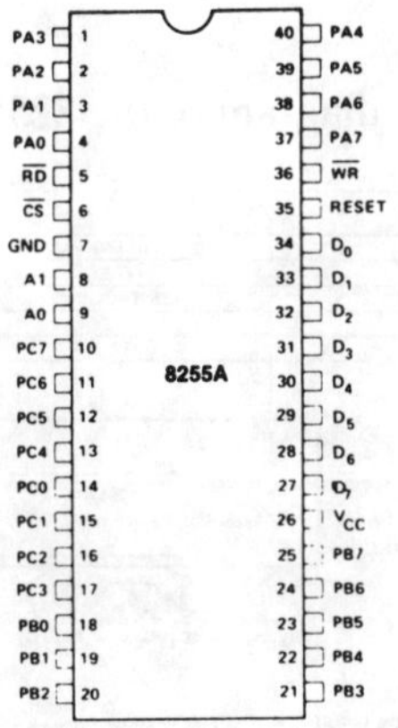

PIN NAMES

D_7-D_0	DATA BUS (BI DIRECTIONAL)
RESET	RESET INPUT
$\overline{CS}$	CHIP SELECT
RD	READ INPUT
WR	WRITE INPUT
A0, A1	PORT ADDRESS
PA7-PA0	PORT A (BIT)
PB7-PB0	PORT B (BIT)
PC7-PC0	PORT C (BIT)
V_{CC}	+5 VOLTS
GND	0 VOLTS

Figure B-1 8255 pin assignments

*Reprinted by permission of Intel Corporation, copyright 1985

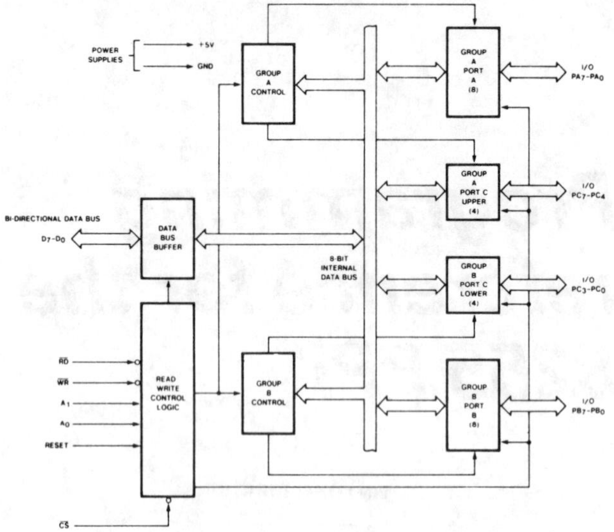

Figure B-2 Block diagram of the 8255 Programmable Peripheral Interface (PPI)

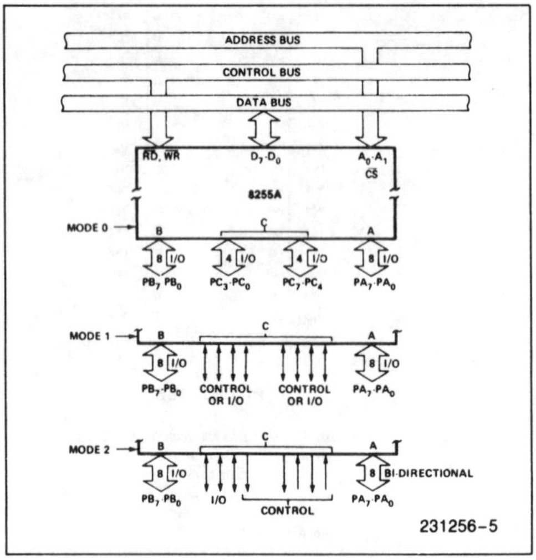

Figure B-3 8255 mode definitions and bus interface

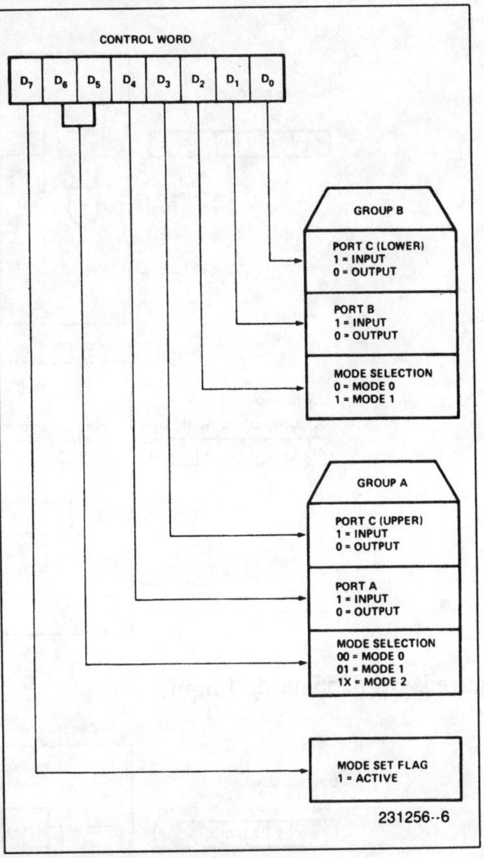

Figure B-4 8255 mode definition format

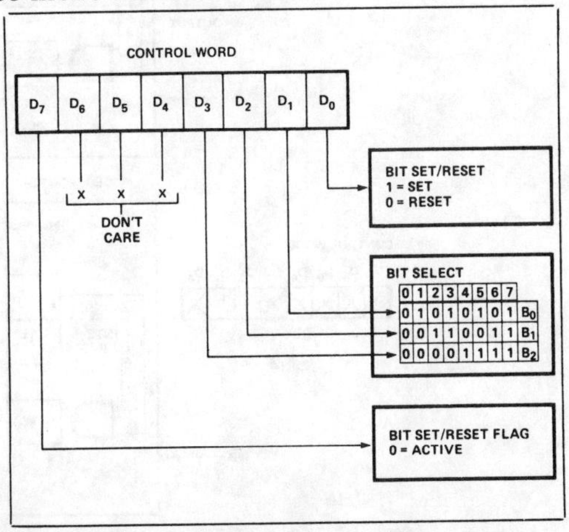

Figure B-5 8255 bit set/reset format

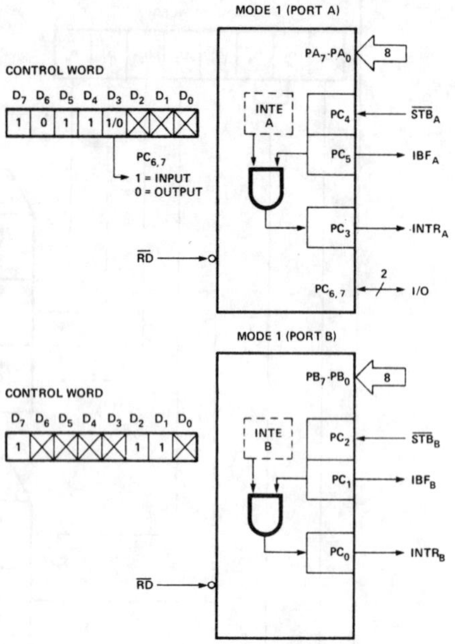

Figure B-6 8255 mode 1 input

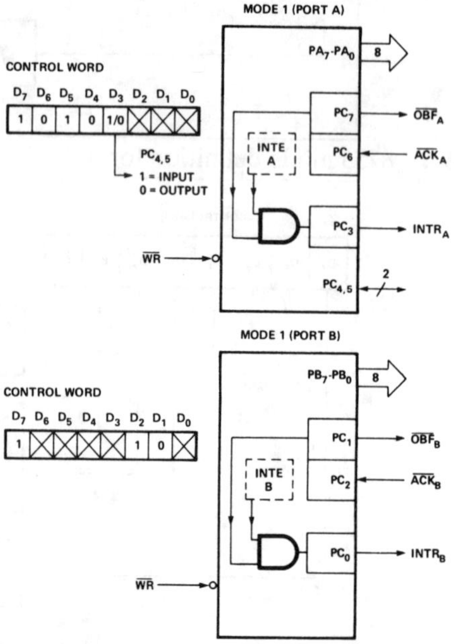

Figure B-7 8255 mode 1 output

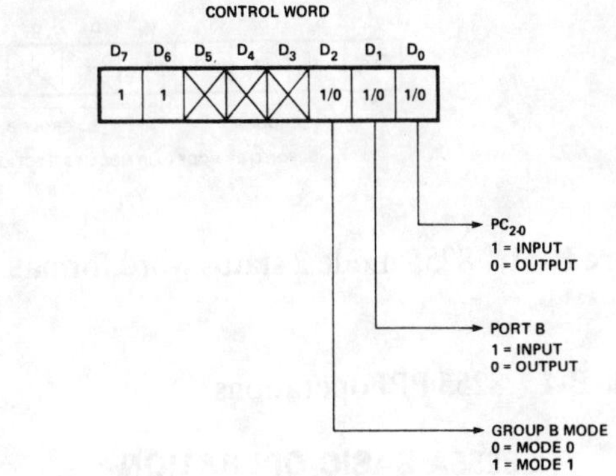

Figure B-8 8255 mode 2 control word

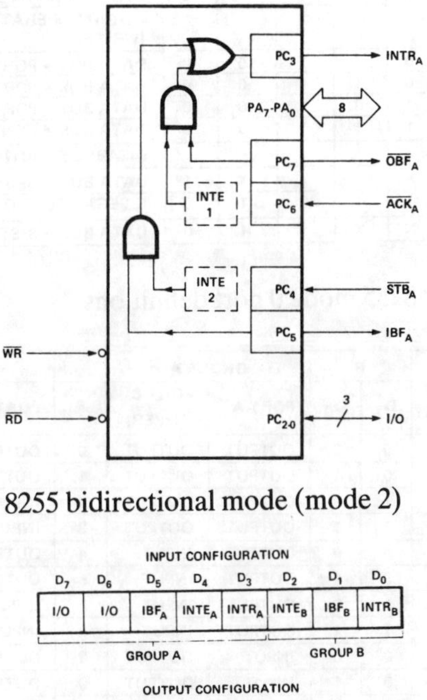

Figure B-9 8255 bidirectional mode (mode 2)

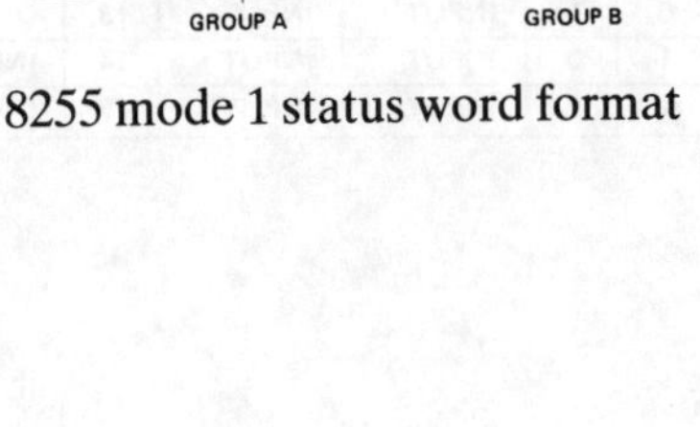

Figure B-10 8255 mode 1 status word format

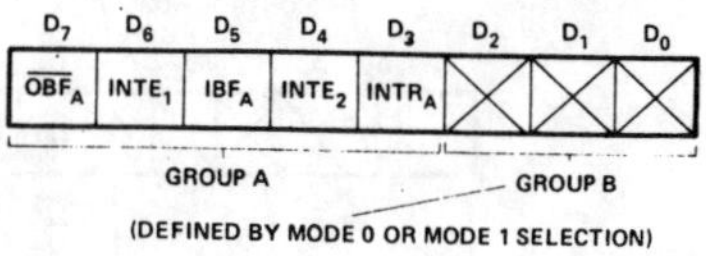

Figure B-11 8255 mode 2 status word format

Table B-1 8255 PPI operations

8255A BASIC OPERATION

A_1	A_0	$\overline{RD}$	$\overline{WR}$	$\overline{CS}$	INPUT OPERATION (READ)
0	0	0	1	0	PORT A ⇒ DATA BUS
0	1	0	1	0	PORT B ⇒ DATA BUS
1	0	0	1	0	PORT C ⇒ DATA BUS
					OUTPUT OPERATION (WRITE)
0	0	1	0	0	DATA BUS ⇒ PORT A
0	1	1	0	0	DATA BUS ⇒ PORT B
1	0	1	0	0	DATA BUS ⇒ PORT C
1	1	1	0	0	DATA BUS ⇒ CONTROL
					DISABLE FUNCTION
X	X	X	X	1	DATA BUS ⇒ 3-STATE
1	1	0	1	0	ILLEGAL CONDITION
X	X	1	1	0	DATA BUS ⇒ 3-STATE

Table B-2 8255 mode 0 port definitions

A		B		GROUP A			GROUP B	
D_4	D_3	D_1	D_0	PORT A	PORT C (UPPER)	#	PORT B	PORT C (LOWER)
0	0	0	0	OUTPUT	OUTPUT	0	OUTPUT	OUTPUT
0	0	0	1	OUTPUT	OUTPUT	1	OUTPUT	INPUT
0	0	1	0	OUTPUT	OUTPUT	2	INPUT	OUTPUT
0	0	1	1	OUTPUT	OUTPUT	3	INPUT	INPUT
0	1	0	0	OUTPUT	INPUT	4	OUTPUT	OUTPUT
0	1	0	1	OUTPUT	INPUT	5	OUTPUT	INPUT
0	1	1	0	OUTPUT	INPUT	6	INPUT	OUTPUT
0	1	1	1	OUTPUT	INPUT	7	INPUT	INPUT
1	0	0	0	INPUT	OUTPUT	8	OUTPUT	OUTPUT
1	0	0	1	INPUT	OUTPUT	9	OUTPUT	INPUT
1	0	1	0	INPUT	OUTPUT	10	INPUT	OUTPUT
1	0	1	1	INPUT	OUTPUT	11	INPUT	INPUT
1	1	0	0	INPUT	INPUT	12	OUTPUT	OUTPUT
1	1	0	1	INPUT	INPUT	13	OUTPUT	INPUT
1	1	1	0	INPUT	INPUT	14	INPUT	OUTPUT
1	1	1	1	INPUT	INPUT	15	INPUT	INPUT

Table B-3 Summary of 8255 operating modes

	MODE 0		MODE 1		MODE 2
	IN	OUT	IN	OUT	GROUP A ONLY
PA_0	IN	OUT	IN	OUT	↔
PA_1	IN	OUT	IN	OUT	↔
PA_2	IN	OUT	IN	OUT	↔
PA_3	IN	OUT	IN	OUT	↔
PA_4	IN	OUT	IN	OUT	↔
PA_5	IN	OUT	IN	OUT	↔
PA_6	IN	OUT	IN	OUT	↔
PA_7	IN	OUT	IN	OUT	↔
PB_0	IN	OUT	IN	OUT	— (MODE 0 OR MODE 1 ONLY)
PB_1	IN	OUT	IN	OUT	—
PB_2	IN	OUT	IN	OUT	—
PB_3	IN	OUT	IN	OUT	—
PB_4	IN	OUT	IN	OUT	—
PB_5	IN	OUT	IN	OUT	—
PB_6	IN	OUT	IN	OUT	—
PB_7	IN	OUT	IN	OUT	—
PC_0	IN	OUT	$INTR_B$	$INTR_B$	I/O
PC_1	IN	OUT	IBF_B	$\overline{OBF}_B$	I/O
PC_2	IN	OUT	$\overline{STB}_B$	$\overline{ACK}_B$	I/O
PC_3	IN	OUT	$INTR_A$	$INTR_A$	$INTR_A$
PC_4	IN	OUT	$\overline{STB}_A$	I/O	$\overline{STB}_A$
PC_5	IN	OUT	IBF_A	I/O	IBF_A
PC_6	IN	OUT	I/O	$\overline{ACK}_A$	$\overline{ACK}_A$
PC_7	IN	OUT	I/O	$\overline{OBF}_A$	$\overline{OBF}_A$

C ASCII character set

LSD	MSD	0 000	1 001	2 010	3 011	4 100	5 101	6 110	7 111
0	0000	NUL	DLE	SP	0	@	P	`	p
1	0001	SOH	DC1	!	1	A	Q	a	q
2	0010	STX	DC2	"	2	B	R	b	r
3	0011	ETX	DC3	#	3	C	S	c	s
4	0100	EOT	DC4	$	4	D	T	d	t
5	0101	ENQ	NAK	%	5	E	U	e	u
6	0110	ACK	SYN	&	6	F	V	f	v
7	0111	BEL	ETB	'	7	G	W	g	w
8	1000	BS	CAN	(	8	H	X	h	x
9	1001	HT	EM	)	9	I	Y	i	y
A	1010	LF	SUB	*	:	J	Z	j	z
B	1011	VT	ESC	+	;	K	[	k	}
C	1100	FF	FS	,	<	L	\	l	¦
D	1101	CR	GS	−	=	M	]	m	{
E	1110	SO	RS	.	>	N	^	n	~
F	1111	SI	US	/	?	O	_	o	DEL

Note On most computers, one can enter a non-printing ASCII character (i.e. those below 20 hex) by pressing the CONTROL (CTRL) key and the key corresponding to the character 40 hex higher. For example, one can enter an ETX (03) character by pressing CTRL and C (43 hex). See Table 8-1 for the equivalences.

D 8087 instruction set summary*

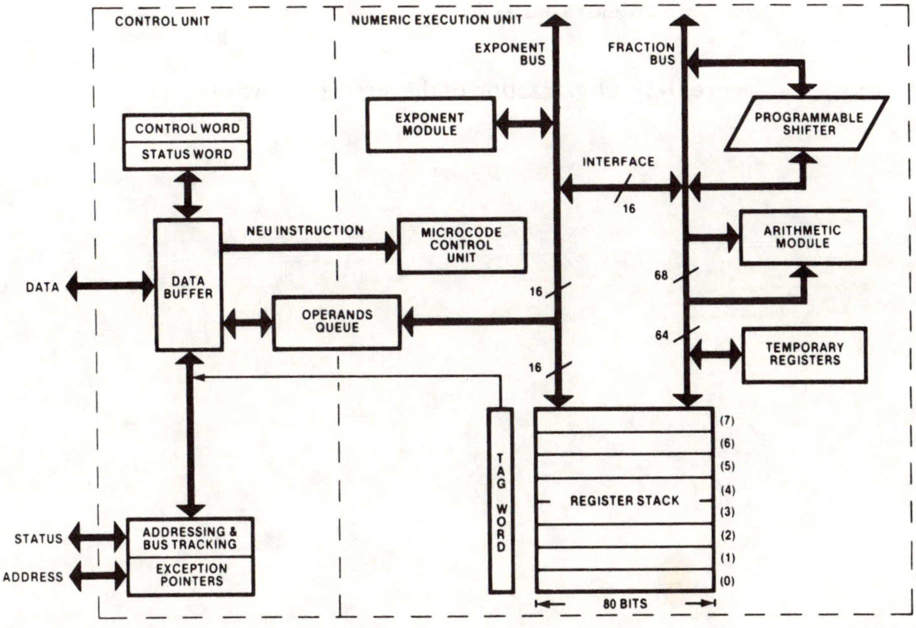

Figure D-1 8086/8087 internal organization

*Reprinted by permission of Intel Corporation, copyright 1985.

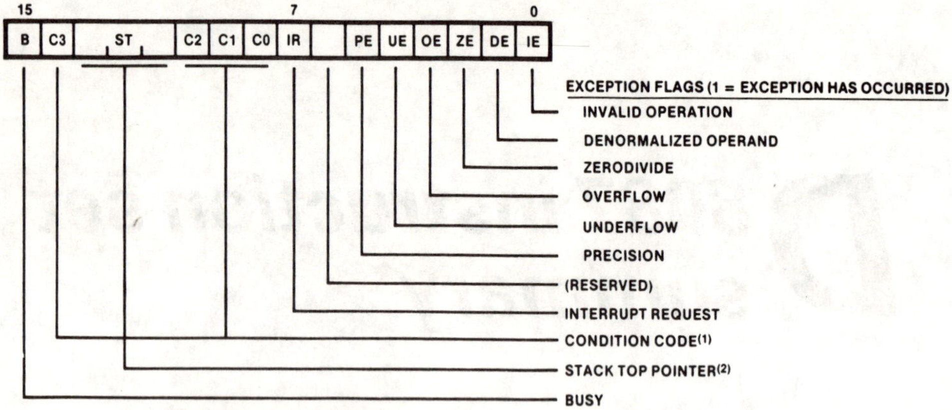

(1) See descriptions of compare, test, examine and remainder instructions in section S.7 for condition code interpretation.

(2) ST values:
000 = register 0 is stack top
001 = register 1 is stack top
•
•
•
111 = register 7 is stack top

Figure D-2 Organization of the 8087 status word

Table D-1 8087 instruction set codes, memory requirements, and execution times*

Data Transfer	Encoding (byte 1)	Encoding (byte 2)	Optional 8,16 Bit Displacement	Clock Count Range: 32 Bit Real	32 Bit Integer	64 Bit Real	16 Bit Integer
FLD = LOAD	MF			00	01	10	11
Integer/Real Memory to ST(0)	ESCAPE MF 1	MOD 0 0 0 R/M	DISP	38–56 + EA	52–60 + EA	40–60 + EA	46–54 + EA
Long Integer Memory to ST(0)	ESCAPE 1 1 1	MOD 1 0 1 R/M	DISP	60–68 + EA			
Temporary Real Memory to ST(0)	ESCAPE 0 1 1	MOD 1 0 1 R/M	DISP	53–65 + EA			
BCD Memory to ST(0)	ESCAPE 1 1 1	MOD 1 0 0 R/M	DISP	290–310 + EA			
ST(i) to ST(0)	ESCAPE 0 0 1	1 1 0 0 0 ST(i)		17–22			
FST = STORE							
ST(0) to Integer/Real Memory	ESCAPE MF 1	MOD 0 1 0 R/M	DISP	84–90 + EA	82–92 + EA	96–104 + EA	80–90 + EA
ST(0) to ST(i)	ESCAPE 1 0 1	1 1 0 1 0 ST(i)		15–22			
FSTP = STORE AND POP							
ST(0) to Integer/Real Memory	ESCAPE MF 1	MOD 0 1 1 R/M	DISP	86–92 + EA	84–94 + EA	98–106 + EA	82–92 + EA
ST(0) to Long Integer Memory	ESCAPE 1 1 1	MOD 1 1 1 R/M	DISP	94–105 + EA			
ST(0) to Temporary Real Memory	ESCAPE 0 1 1	MOD 1 1 1 R/M	DISP	52–58 + EA			
ST(0) to BCD Memory	ESCAPE 1 1 1	MOD 1 1 0 R/M	DISP	520–540 + EA			
ST(0) to ST(i)	ESCAPE 1 0 1	1 1 0 1 1 ST(i)		17–24			
FXCH = Exchange ST(i) and ST(0)	ESCAPE 0 0 1	1 1 0 0 1 ST(i)		10–15			
Comparison							
FCOM = Compare							
Integer/Real Memory to ST(0)	ESCAPE MF 0	MOD 0 1 0 R/M	DISP	60–70 + EA	78–91 + EA	65–75 + EA	72–86 + EA
ST(i) to ST (0)	ESCAPE 0 0 0	1 1 0 1 0 ST(i)		40–50			
FCOMP = Compare and Pop							
Integer/Real Memory to ST(0)	ESCAPE MF 0	MOD 0 1 1 R/M	DISP	63–73 + EA	80–93 + EA	67–77 + EA	74–88 + EA
ST(i) to ST(0)	ESCAPE 0 0 0	1 1 0 1 1 ST(i)		45–52			
FCOMPP = Compare ST(1) to ST(0) and Pop Twice	ESCAPE 1 1 0	1 1 0 1 1 0 0 1		45–55			
FTST = Test ST(0)	ESCAPE 0 0 1	1 1 1 0 0 1 0 0		38–48			
FXAM = Examine ST(0)	ESCAPE 0 0 1	1 1 1 0 0 1 0 1		12–23			

			Optional 8,16 Bit Displacement	Clock Count Range: 32 Bit Real	32 Bit Integer	64 Bit Real	16 Bit Integer
Constants		MF		00	01	10	11
FLDZ = LOAD + 0.0 into ST(0)	ESCAPE 0 0 1	1 1 1 0 1 1 1 0		11–17			
FLD1 = LOAD + 1.0 into ST(0)	ESCAPE 0 0 1	1 1 1 0 1 0 0 0		15–21			
FLDPI = LOAD π into ST(0)	ESCAPE 0 0 1	1 1 1 0 1 0 1 1		16–22			
FLDL2T = LOAD $\log_2 10$ into ST(0)	ESCAPE 0 0 1	1 1 1 0 1 0 0 1		16–22			
FLDL2E = LOAD $\log_2 e$ into ST(0)	ESCAPE 0 0 1	1 1 1 0 1 0 1 0		15–21			
FLDLG2 = LOAD $\log_{10} 2$ into ST(0)	ESCAPE 0 0 1	1 1 1 0 1 1 0 0		18–24			
FLDLN2 = LOAD $\log_e 2$ into ST(0)	ESCAPE 0 0 1	1 1 1 0 1 1 0 1		17–23			
Arithmetic							
FADD = Addition							
Integer/Real Memory with ST(0)	ESCAPE MF 0	MOD 0 0 0 R/M	DISP	90–120 + EA	108–143 + EA	95–125 + EA	102–137 + EA
ST(i) and ST(0)	ESCAPE d P 0	1 1 0 0 0 ST(i)		70–100 (Note 1)			
FSUB = Subtraction							
Integer/Real Memory with ST(0)	ESCAPE MF 0	MOD 1 0 R R/M	DISP	90–120 + EA	108–143 + EA	95–125 + EA	102–137 + EA
ST(i) and ST(0)	ESCAPE d P 0	1 1 1 0 R R/M		70–100 (Note 1)			
FMUL = Multiplication							
Integer/Real Memory with ST(0)	ESCAPE MF 0	MOD 0 0 1 R/M	DISP	110–125 + EA	130–144 + EA	112–168 + EA	124–138 + EA
ST(i) and ST(0)	ESCAPE d P 0	1 1 0 0 1 R/M		90–145 (Note 1)			
FDIV = Division							
Integer/Real Memory with ST(0)	ESCAPE MF 0	MOD 1 1 R R/M	DISP	215–225 + EA	230–243 + EA	220–230 + EA	224–238 + EA
ST(i) and ST(0)	ESCAPE d P 0	1 1 1 1 R R/M		193–203 (Note 1)			
FSQRT = Square Root of ST(0)	ESCAPE 0 0 1	1 1 1 1 1 0 1 0		180–186			
FSCALE = Scale ST(0) by ST(1)	ESCAPE 0 0 1	1 1 1 1 1 1 0 1		32–38			
FPREM = Partial Remainder of ST(0) ÷ ST(1)	ESCAPE 0 0 1	1 1 1 1 1 0 0 0		15–190			
FRNDINT = Round ST(0) to Integer	ESCAPE 0 0 1	1 1 1 1 1 1 0 0		16–50			

NOTE:
1. If P = 1 then add 5 clocks.

			Optional 8,16 Bit Displacement	Clock Count Range
FXTRACT = Extract Components of St(0)	ESCAPE 0 0 1	1 1 1 1 0 1 0 0		27–55
FABS = Absolute Value of ST(0)	ESCAPE 0 0 1	1 1 1 0 0 0 0 1		10–17
FCHS = Change Sign of ST(0)	ESCAPE 0 0 1	1 1 1 0 0 0 0 0		10–17
Transcendental				
FPTAN = Partial Tangent of ST(0)	ESCAPE 0 0 1	1 1 1 1 0 0 1 0		30–540
FPATAN = Partial Arctangent of ST(0) – ST(1)	ESCAPE 0 0 1	1 1 1 1 0 0 1 1		250–800
F2XM1 = $2^{ST(0)} - 1$	ESCAPE 0 0 1	1 1 1 1 0 0 0 0		310–630
FYL2X = ST(1) · Log_2 |ST(0)|	ESCAPE 0 0 1	1 1 1 1 0 0 0 1		900–1100
FYL2XP1 = ST(1) · Log_2 [ST(0) + 1]	ESCAPE 0 0 1	1 1 1 1 1 0 0 1		700–1000
Processor Control				
FINIT = Initialize 8087	ESCAPE 0 1 1	1 1 1 0 0 0 1 1		2–8
FENI = Enable Interrupts	ESCAPE 0 1 1	1 1 1 0 0 0 0 0		2–8
FDISI = Disable Interrupts	ESCAPE 0 1 1	1 1 1 0 0 0 0 1		2–8
FLDCW = Load Control Word	ESCAPE 0 0 1	MOD 1 0 1 R/M	DISP	7–14 + EA
FSTCW = Store Control Word	ESCAPE 0 0 1	MOD 1 1 1 R/M	DISP	12–18 + EA
FSTSW = Store Status Word	ESCAPE 1 0 1	MOD 1 1 1 R/M	DISP	12–18 + EA
FCLEX = Clear Exceptions	ESCAPE 0 1 1	1 1 1 0 0 0 1 0		2–8
FSTENV = Store Environment	ESCAPE 0 0 1	MOD 1 1 0 R/M	DISP	40–50 + EA
FLDENV = Load Environment	ESCAPE 0 0 1	MOD 1 0 0 R/M	DISP	35–45 + EA
FSAVE = Save State	ESCAPE 1 0 1	MOD 1 1 0 R/M	DISP	197 – 207 + EA
FRSTOR = Restore State	ESCAPE 1 0 1	MOD 1 0 0 R/M	DISP	197 – 207 + EA
FINCSTP = Increment Stack Pointer	ESCAPE 0 0 1	1 1 1 1 0 1 1 1		6–12
FDECSTP = Decrement Stack Pointer	ESCAPE 0 0 1	1 1 1 1 0 1 1 0		6–12

			Clock Count Range
FFREE = Free ST(i)	ESCAPE 1 0 1	1 1 0 0 0 ST(i)	9-16
FNOP = No Operation	ESCAPE 0 0 1	1 1 0 1 0 0 0 0	10-16
FWAIT = CPU Wait for 8087	1 0 0 1 1 0 1 1		3+5n*

*n = number of times CPU examines TEST line before 8087 lowers BUSY.

NOTES:

1. if mod=00 then DISP=0*, disp-low and disp-high are absent
   if mod=01 then DISP=disp-low sign-extended to 16-bits, disp-high is absent
   if mod=10 then DISP=disp-high; disp-low
   if mod=11 then r/m is treated as an ST(i) field
2. if r/m=000 then EA=(BX) + (SI) +DISP
   if r/m=001 then EA=(BX) + (DI) +DISP
   if r/m=010 then EA=(BP) + (SI) +DISP
   if r/m=011 then EA=(BP) + (DI) +DISP
   if r/m=100 then EA=(SI) + DISP
   if r/m=101 then EA=(DI) + DISP
   if r/m=110 then EA=(BP) + DISP
   if r/m=111 then EA=(BX) + DISP

   except if mod=000 and r/m=110 then EA =disp-high: disp-low.
3. MF= Memory Format
   00—32-bit Real
   01—32-bit Integer
   10—64-bit Real
   11—16-bit Integer
4. ST(0)= Current stack top
   ST(i) i^{th} register below stack top
5. d= Destination
   0—Destination is ST(0)
   1—Destination is ST(i)
6. P= Pop
   0—No pop
   1—Pop ST(0)
7. R= Reverse: When d=1 reverse the sense of R
   0—Destination (op) Source
   1—Source (op) Destination
8. For **FSQRT**: $-0 \le ST(0) \le +\infty$
   For **FSCALE**: $-2^{15} \le ST(1) < +2^{15}$ and ST(1) integer
   For **F2XM1**: $0 \le ST(0) \le 2^{-1}$
   For **FYL2X**: $0 < ST(0) < \infty$
   $-\infty < ST(1) < +\infty$
   For **FYL2XP1**: $0 \le |ST(0)| < (2-\sqrt{2})/2$
   $-\infty < ST(1) < \infty$
   For **FPTAN**: $0 \le ST(0) \le \pi/4$
   For **FPATAN**: $0 \le ST(0) < ST(1) < +\infty$